Introduction to Operating Systems and Networks

Ruth A. Watson

Kent State University

PEARSON

Prentice
Hall

Pearson Education, Inc.,
Upper Saddle River, New Jersey, 07458

Library of Congress Cataloging-in-Publication Data

Watson, Ruth,
   Introduction to operating systems and networks / by Ruth Watson.—1st ed.
     p. cm.
   Includes bibliographical references and index.
   ISBN 0-13-111894-3
   1. Operating systems (Computers)   2. Local area networks (Computer networks)   I. Title.

   QA76.76.O63W3915 2003
   005.4'469—dc21

                           2003040560

Vp/Publisher: Natalie E. Anderson
Executive Acquisitions Editor: Jodi Mcpherson
Senior Project Managers (Editorial): Eileen Clark and Thomas Park
Assistant Editor: Melissa Edwards
Editorial Assistants: Jodi Bolognese and Jasmine Slowik
Senior Media Project Manager: Cathi Profitko
Senior Marketing Manager: Sharon K. Turkovich
Marketing Assistant: Danielle Torio
Manager, Production: Gail Steier de Acevedo
Project Manager (Production): Audri Anna Bazlen
Permissions Supervisor: Suzanne Grappi
Associate Director, Manufacturing: Vincent Scelta
Manufacturing Buyer: Natacha St. Hill Moore
Manufacturing Coordinator: Indira Gutierrez
Design Manager: Maria Lange
Art Director: Pat Smythe
Interior Design: Dorothy Bungert
Cover Design: Marjory Dressler
Cover Illustration/Photo: Marjory Dressler
Composition/Full-Service Project Management: Preparè
Cover Printer: Phoenix
Printer/Binder: Quebecor World-Dubuque

Microsoft® and Windows® are registered trademarks of the Microsoft Corporation in the U.S.A. and other countries. Screen shots and icons reprinted with permission from the Microsoft Corporation. This book is not sponsored or endorsed by or affiliated with the Microsoft Corporation.

Pearson Education LTD.
Pearson Education Singapore, Pte. Ltd
Pearson Education, Canada, Ltd
Pearson Education–Japan
Pearson Education Australia PTY, Limited
Pearson Education North Asia Ltd
Pearson Educación de Mexico, S.A. de C.V.
Pearson Education Malaysia, Pte. Ltd

10 9 8 7 6 5 4 3 2 1

ISBN 0-13-111894-3

To my husband, Bill, who never fails to find new ways to show me he loves me.

Brief Contents

Contents

Preface

About This Edition

This book is intended to provide a foundation for students who wish to enter into the field of Information Technology (IT). The first half provides a hands-on introduction to the Microsoft Windows 2000/XP desktop operating systems and is intended to demystify many aspects of using a personal computer as well as foster improved efficiency. The second half introduces local area networks, keeping in mind that not all students plan to become a network administrator. However, anyone working in IT will no doubt be in a networked environment and should have a basic understanding of a local area network.

FOR THE INSTRUCTOR

Instructor Resources

Instructor's Resource CD-ROM   The **Instructor's Resource CD-ROM** that is available with *Introduction to Operating Systems and Networks* contains:

- Instructor's Manual in Word and PDF
- Solutions to all questions and exercises from the book and Web site
- PowerPoint lectures with PresMan software
- A Windows-based test manager and the associated test bank in Word format with over 1,500 new questions

Tools for Online Learning

www.prenhall.com/   This text is accompanied by a companion Web site at www.prenhall.com/watson This Web site is designed to bring you and your students a richer, more interactive Web experience.

Features of this new site include the ability for you to customize your homepage with real-time news headlines, current events, exercises, an interactive study guide, and downloadable supplements.

FOR THE STUDENT

Welcome to *Introduction to Operating Systems and Networks*! As you read through the chapters, you should follow along with any demonstrations. As with any learning activity, you will learn more by doing. Additional activities are found at the end of every chapter. Many of the activities are designed to promote a more proactive approach to learning. The field of IT is a rapidly evolving one and anyone who enters it should expect to continue learning.

Activities such as looking up new technology terms will not only allow you to begin building an impressive technology vocabulary to amaze and astound your friends, they will also enable you to determine what online resources are available and which are better. Once you are working in IT, you will come to rely on them as you encounter new experiences with technology. Please read on, and enjoy!

Acknowledgments

We are grateful for the assistance from the following reviewers of this edition: Debby Carter, Doug Cross, Julendia C. Gaillard, Vik Pant, and Sydney Shewchuk.

Author Notes

I enjoyed every minute I worked on this project but the final product is not the work of a single person. Many contributed in various ways. I would like to thank my colleagues who supplied the initial encouragement: Irene Edge, Ken Vinciquerra and Will Ward. Larry Jones was an ever helpful resource with his ability to remember details from the past. Albert Ingram, who showed me the way, always deserves thanks. This book was also strengthened by the comments of external reviewers. Lastly, I especially appreciate the patience and professionalism of everyone at Prentice Hall who worked on this project.

Introduction to Operating Systems

OBJECTIVES

After reading this chapter, you will be able to:

- Explain what an operating system does
- List the three main components of any operating system
- Differentiate between using the left and right mouse buttons
- Explain the role of the Start button
- Explain the role of the Quick Launch Toolbar
- Demonstrate how to create shortcuts in the Quick Launch Toolbar
- Explain the role of the Taskbar
- Demonstrate how to use Task Manager to terminate a process

INTRODUCTION

Although it is perhaps the most commonly used operating system, Microsoft Windows certainly isn't the only operating system. To determine which operating system is the best choice and why you might choose one over another, it might help to first determine what the operating system does.

The operating system (OS) is an example of a computer program. Programs are simply lines of code and code is another way of saying written instructions. Operating system programmers write code that will respond to the user in specific ways. For instance, when you click on an object such as the Start button or right click on the desktop there is usually some response. The response isn't magic; the programmers wrote code to respond in a specific way to your actions. The objects being clicked on are graphical representations of individual parts of the whole operating system.

Most operating systems are comprised of three main components: the kernel, the file system, and the shell, or user interface. The Microsoft Windows desktop is an example of a GUI shell. GUI (pronounced "gooey") stands for "graphical user interface." Each of these three components is discussed throughout this book but, briefly, the kernel is the core of the operating system. The file system keeps track of directories and files. And the user interface, or shell, is what we interact with either by entering a command at a prompt or by using some sort of a pointing device, such as a mouse. The hardware components that make up a computer cannot operate without an operating system.

There are actually two parts to a computer: the hardware and the software. Software can either be system software or application software. It is the software that manipulates the hardware. It is the role of the operating system, the most important system software, to act like a middleman for the user and the hardware. The operating system interprets what we want the computer or the application programs to do and gives the appropriate instructions to the hardware to carry out our wishes.

Perhaps the primary reason for selecting a specific operating system depends on what applications you plan to use. Different operating systems are better designed for certain tasks than others. Some Computer Aided Design (CAD)-intensive users might argue that UNIX is the better operating system for them. Graphics designers involved in marketing or publishing are often found using the Macintosh operating system.

GENERAL WINDOWS DEVELOPMENT OVERVIEW

Microsoft Windows has been around since the early 1980s but wasn't commonly used until the early 1990s, when Microsoft released version 3.0 which was quickly followed by version 3.1. Currently, Microsoft has a whole family of Windows operating systems. One side of the family grew out of DOS. DOS stands for "Disk Operating System." Windows Me, Windows 95/98, Windows 3.1/3.11 and all previous versions of Windows come from this side of the family. They are considered backwards-compatible with DOS. In essence, they included all the things that DOS could do and then new components or features were built on top of DOS.

In the early to mid-1990s, the Microsoft operating system programmers came up with another side of the Microsoft family. They named it Windows NT. The code was not backwards-compatible with DOS; they started completely from scratch. They did this because they wanted the operating system to be more stable and more secure. Windows 2000 Professional, Windows 2000 Server, and Windows XP are from this side of the family.

Originally, Microsoft marketed the DOS side of their family for home users and the NT side for business. At this point, Microsoft is moving away from the DOS side of the family and future operating systems will be based on NT code but there will be different versions for different types of users. For example, for home use there is the Windows XP Home edition and another for the office, called Windows XP Professional.

No matter which operating system you choose, they all pretty much do the same fundamental thing. An operating system acts as an interface between the computer and the user. It interprets what we want the computer to do by transforming our input commands into a language that the computer understands. At its most basic level, a computer really only understands the electronic state of on or off. Binary math, a Base 2 numbering system, represents the state of on and off by using 1s and 0s. Since it would be a bit tedious for humans to speak in a native computer language, an operating system comes in quite handy, especially an object-oriented operating system that allows you to point and click. Think of it— everything you see on the computer desktop is "clickable." They are all objects that, when you click on them, produce varying results.

Figure 1.1

Depending on what you want to do, sometimes you click on an object with the left mouse button and sometimes you click with the right mouse button.

What is the difference? For the most part, with the default mouse configuration in Windows you click with the left button when you want to select something. You click with the right mouse button when you want a context-sensitive menu to pop up with options pertaining to the object you've clicked on. Figure 1.1 is a context-sensitive menu you might see if you right click the desktop.

NOTES Right click on the desktop and see what your options are in the context-sensitive menu. Then right click the My Network Places icon. Then right click the My Computer icon. Everything you click on should have a few different options in the context-sensitive menu that pops up. This is also true if you right click in applications such as Microsoft Word. In fact, in Microsoft Word, right clicking on different parts of the document will also give different options in the context sensitive-menu.

The menu options change because the application is programmed to offer choices that will better assist you based on what a typical user might be trying to do at any given point in time. The options that you have available when you right click the desktop all pertain to customizing or manipulating the objects on your desktop. The Active Desktop option makes your desktop act like a Web page. You can also arrange your icons, refresh the screen, paste shortcuts to the desktop, create a new folder or other object, and configure the properties of your desktop. Chapter 5 deals with customizing your desktop.

Of course, before the days of the mouse, most computer users worked in DOS using a command line interface (see Figure 1.2) as opposed to a graphical user interface.

Figure 1.2

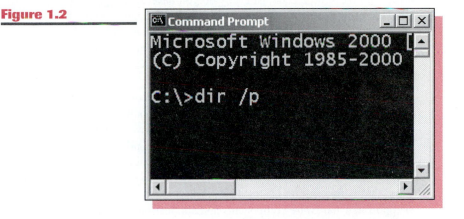

With DOS you have to know the exact alphanumeric keyboard command to do anything. In the example shown, the screen would be filled with a listing of the files and directories in the current directory (C:). The command DIR has several switches that can be used with it. A switch allows you to add a parameter to the initial command to modify the outcome. The /p switch shown in the example would fill the screen with the listing and then pause so you can read the directory listing a screen at a time rather than have it all fly by too quickly.

As computer usage became more popular over time, the number of files we wanted to store increased and organization became extremely important. So the early computer developers had to devise a way to logically divide a disk up and allow you to organize files. That means they also had to come up with a good way to reference a file.

Why did they call it a "C:" drive? Well, it did have to be named something. And in the beginning, most early personal computers didn't have a hard drive; they only had floppy drives. In many cases, they had two. That explains why the first hard drive on a computer is called the C: drive; A: and B: were already taken for names for the floppy drives.

So disk drives are named using letters of the alphabet. We create folders on these disk drives to help us organize our files on a disk. You wouldn't want to put all of your files in one folder. It would be too difficult to keep track of them and find them when you need them. It also makes it more difficult for the file system to keep track of them.

In the early days of personal computing (early 1980s), DOS was an improvement over speaking 1s and 0s but a lot of people still found it tedious. DOS wasn't the only personal computer operating system at the time; Macintoshes had a completely different operating system, for instance.

Other operating systems include AS400, OS/2, UNIX, Linux, Novell Netware, Banyan Vines, VMS, and many others. Some are for personal computers (PCs), some for mainframes, some for supercomputers, and others for local area networks. In addition, some operating systems are written by students in classes.

Linux is an example of an open source operating system. You can download it from the Internet for free with the source code. Not only do you have the programs necessary to install the operating system on your computer, you also can see and edit the actual code of the operating system. You can even add to the source code and upload it back to the Internet. Linux is unusual in that aspect; most companies would not want you to see their source code. Linux wasn't created by one company, however. It was originally developed by Linus Torvalds while he was a college student and then, over time, many people all over the world added source code.

Why would you want to add to the source code of an operating system? Say you download Linux and install it on your computer. You might want to be able to print documents while using your new operating system. But Linux was written by people all over the world and they may not have the same printer that you do. In order to print, you need to install a printer driver. A printer driver is a file that you install on your computer that tells your operating system how to communicate with your printer. If no other Linux user has the same printer as you, there's no reason for anyone except you to write a driver for it. And that is how Linux has evolved. Programmers all over the world offer additional pieces of code to support new hardware components and applications to run on Linux.

OVERVIEW OF THE MICROSOFT WINDOWS DESKTOP

The desktop is the entire window that fills your computer screen and its contents, including the Start button, the Quick Launch Toolbar, the colors of your desktop, the icons on the desktop and the fonts used for them, any images you might use for the background, the Taskbar, and the System Tray. Figure 1.3 is an example of the Windows XP Professional desktop. Figure 1.3 shows the desktop and the Taskbar with the Start button, Quick Launch Toolbar, minimized applications, an additional toolbar, and the System Tray with the clock.

Start Menu

In most cases, you launch (start) an application by clicking on the Start button and then finding the application. Rather than using the mouse you can also use the keyboard, however. Locate the "flying windows" keys on your keyboard. They are usually to the right and left of the space bar. Pressing one of the flying windows keys is the same as clicking on Start with the mouse.

Program applications such as Microsoft Word or CorelDraw will be under the Programs option on the menu in Windows 2000 Professional and the All Programs option in Windows XP Professional.

The My Recent Documents option in Figure 1.4 shows the last several files (of all types) opened by you when using the computer. Microsoft Windows 2000 Professional and XP Professional both keep track of individual users. The files you see listed in Documents in Windows 2000 Professional or My Recent Documents in Windows XP Professional will be any files accessed on a specific computer when using the same account, or username. There are also folders to store graphics and music for individual users. In Windows 2000 Professional, the My Pictures folder is found in My Documents. In Windows XP Professional, both the My Pictures and My Music folders are found in My Documents and links to them are included in the Start Menu for easy access.

You can get to the Control Panel or configure a printer under the Start > Settings option in Windows 2000 Professional or Start > Control Panel in Windows XP Professional.

The Search option can help you find files and folders and is explained in Chapter 2. The Run option will run any program that you type in.

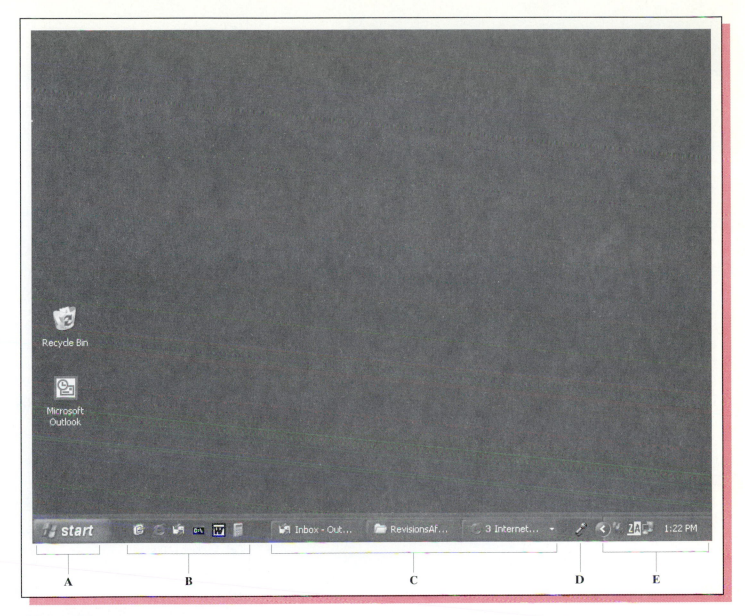

Figure 1.3

A—Start Menu
B—Quick Launch Toolbar
C—Minimized Applications
D—Additional Toolbar
E—System Tray

CHECK IT OUT

1. Click Start > Run and then type in CMD
2. What happened?

   Cmd.exe is the name of the executable file you just ran. It displays the command prompt window and is found in the WINNT\system32 folder on a Windows 2000 computer and in Windows\system32 in Windows XP. You can also access it by clicking Start > Programs or All Programs > Accessories > Command Prompt. It is part of the Windows operating system. The programmers who wrote the Windows operating system wrote the code for the cmd.exe program.

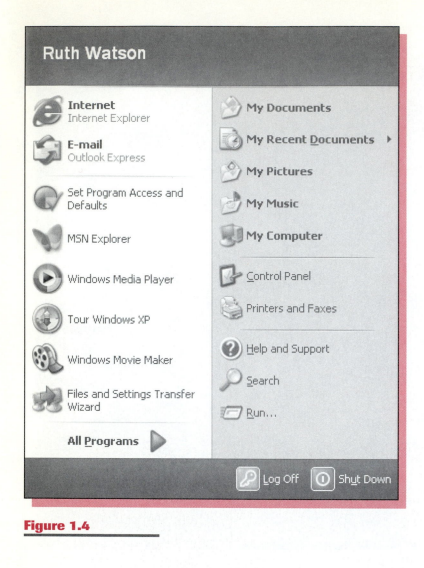

Figure 1.4

Figure 1.5

Figure 1.6

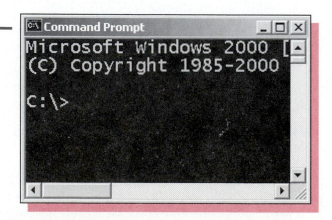

In Windows 2000 Professional, the Help option in the Start menu is exactly what you'd think it is. You can use help to look up terms and concepts relating to the Windows operating system (see Figure 1.7).

Figure 1.7

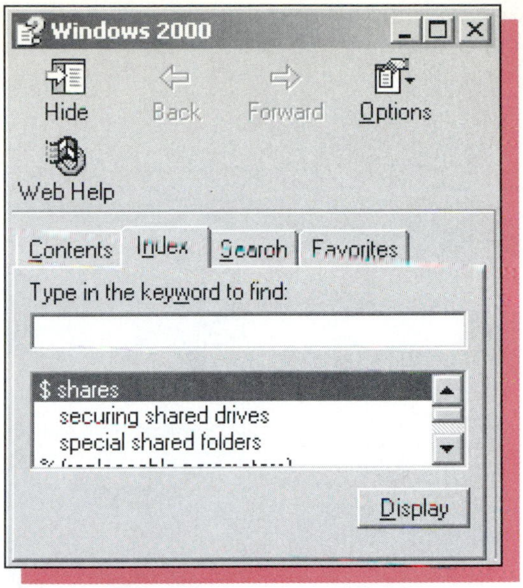

The Contents tab offers you more of a Table of Contents-type view. The Index tab allows you to search by keyword and it also has an alphabetized list of items. The Search tab scans through all of the text in the help documents and will often offer a less focused result than Index. The favorites tab allows you to bookmark a Help document once you have found it.

In Windows XP Professional, the Help and Support Center has similar features and allows you to search using the index, bookmark favorites, and keep a history of the Help documents you have viewed (see Figure 1.8).

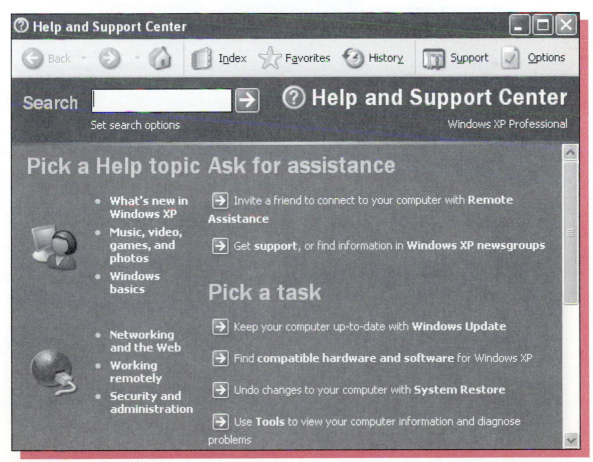

Figure 1.8

The two arrows shown at the bottom of the menu in Figure 1.9 is called a chevron. The chevron is telling you that there are actually more programs available on your PC but you are only being shown the last few programs that you used. To see the entire list, either click on the chevron or wait a few seconds and the list will expand.

Figure 1.9

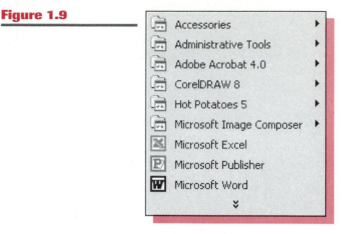

The arrows to the right of menu options are telling you that yet another menu will pop out to the right if you select that option (see Figure 1.9).

Any time a menu option has an ellipsis (…) after it, this indicates that if you select this option you will see yet another window of options. The Start > Run option is an example. If you select it, you will see the window shown in Figure 1.10.

Figure 1.10

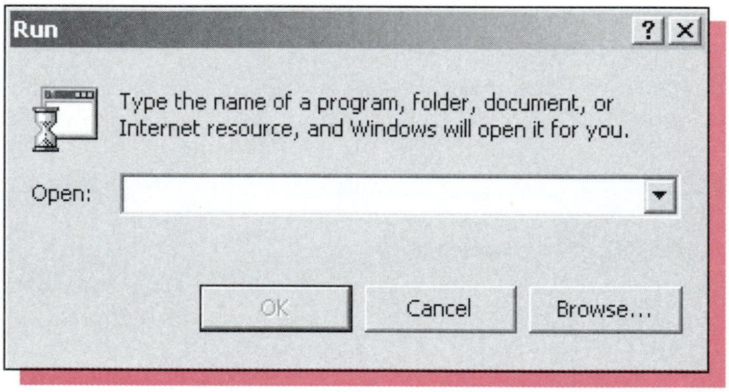

Whenever you open a window (e.g., My Computer or Microsoft Word), you'll have three control buttons in the upper right hand corner (see Figure 1.11).

The "minus sign" button will minimize the window. The middle button will restore the window. And the X button will close the window.

You can also close the window up by double clicking the computer icon in the upper left hand corner. A third method is to click on File and then Close. This window is also showing a vertical (up and down) scroll bar. You can resize the window by resting your mouse pointer on any one of the edges or corners, holding down the left mouse button, and dragging the corner of the window.

Quick Launch Toolbar

A quicker way to launch a program is to click on its icon in the Quick Launch Toolbar. As shown in Figure 1.12, the Quick Launch Toolbar is directly to the right of the Start button and has shortcuts to programs that you use most often. If the Quick Launch Toolbar is not currently showing on the Taskbar, right click anywhere on the Taskbar and select Toolbars > Quick Launch.

The leftmost icon in the Quick Launch Toolbar shown is the Show Desktop icon in Windows 2000 Professional (see Figure 1.12). The Show Desktop icon in Windows XP Professional is the leftmost icon in Figure 1.13. Clicking the Show Desktop icon will minimize all of your open applications at once and

Figure 1.11

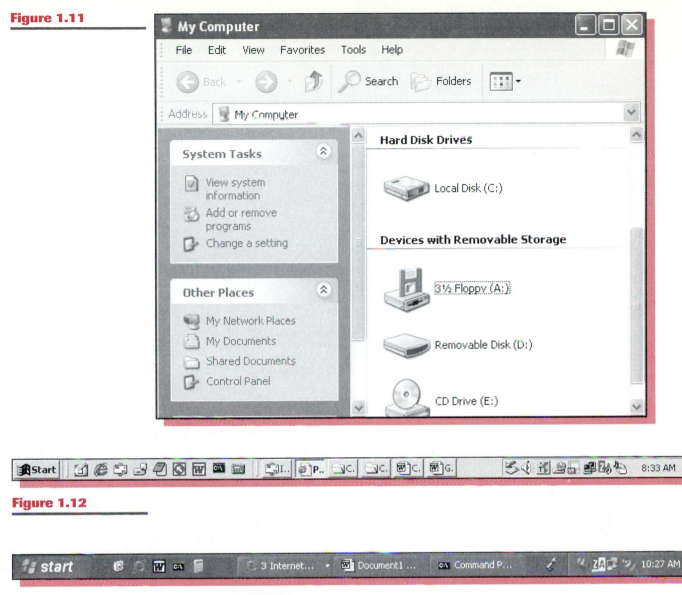

Figure 1.12

Figure 1.13

display the desktop. Windows XP Professional groups the minimized applications to better organize them. In Figure 1.13, there are three different Internet Explorer windows open but when minimized they are grouped together to save space on the Taskbar. You can individually select one to restore it by clicking on the group and selecting the appropriate window. You are also given the option to close all of the minimized, grouped applications at once.

NOTES   Open Microsoft Word, then open Microsoft Excel, or Paint, etc. Then click the Show Desktop icon in the Quick Launch Toolbar. The open applications will become minimized on the Taskbar. Clicking the Show Desktop icon again will restore all of the open applications or you can restore them individually by clicking on the appropriate button on the taskbar.

Some applications put an icon in the Quick Launch Toolbar automatically when they're installed but you can add your own. Right click anywhere on the Quick Launch Toolbar where there isn't an icon. You might need to expand the toolbar by grabbing the divider bar to the right of it and dragging it further to the right. In Figure 1.12, the divider bar referenced looks like a raised, vertical line. In Figure 1.13, the divider bar is a dotted, vertical line. Both divider bars are immediately to the right of the calculator icon. The divider bars separate the toolbars on the Taskbar. In Windows XP Professional, the toolbars on the Taskbar are locked by default and the divider bar does not show. To unlock the toolbars, right click on the Taskbar and choose Unlock Toolbars. To lock them again, right click and choose Lock the Taskbar (Figure 1.14).

Figure 1.14

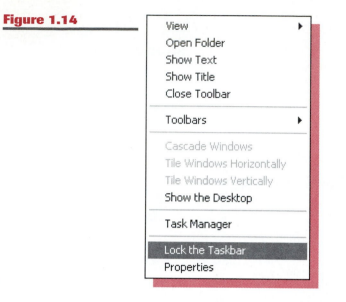

CHECK IT OUT   When you right click on the Quick Launch Toolbar you'll get a context menu with an option to Open in Windows 2000 Professional and Open Folder in Windows XP Professional. It's actually just a special folder on your computer with shortcuts to applications in it. When you select Open or Open Folder, the Quick Launch window opens showing you the shortcuts to programs that already exist.

You're going to create another shortcut in the Quick Launch folder. To do so,

1. Right click anywhere in the Quick Launch Folder window.

2. From the context menu select New > Shortcut.

3. In the Create Shortcut wizard, click the Browse button and browse for the application. This is the tough part. You need to know where it is. For example, let's do a shortcut for the calculator. In Windows 2000 Professional it is in the WINNT\System32 folder and in Windows XP Professional it is found in the Windows\System32 folder.

4. After you find calc.exe, click on it to select it, click OK and then Next.

5. You can enter a name for your shortcut. A default name is suggested. Overwrite the default by typing Calculator.

6. Click Finish and then close the Quick Launch window.

7. You should have a new icon in the Quick Launch toolbar.

You could also make a shortcut on your desktop to an application. Right click anywhere on your desktop where there isn't currently an icon and then follow Steps 2–7 above.

If you want a shortcut to the floppy disk, just type in A: instead of browsing for a file.

Where is the Quick Launch folder on your computer? One way to find it is to backtrack. Right click on the Quick Launch Toolbar and choose Open or Open Folder from the context menu. In the Address bar you can see the path to the folder (see Figure 1.15).

Taskbar

The Taskbar lets you move between applications without having to open and close them. Instead, you minimize them by clicking on the minus sign in the upper right corner of the window and they shrink down to the Taskbar. When you want to work with them again, just click the icon on the Taskbar once

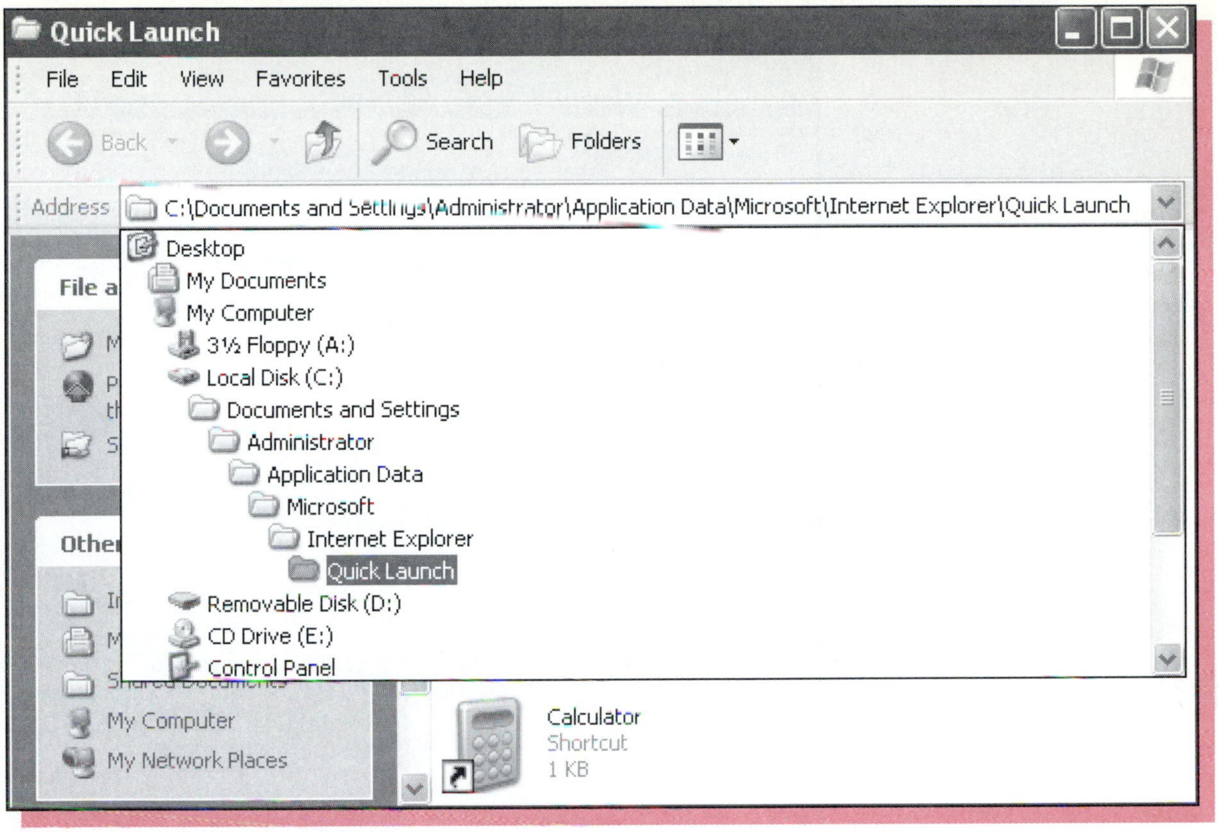

Figure 1.15

and the window expands. The Taskbar can also have additional toolbars on it to make it easier to access other resources. To see which toolbars are available, right click on the Taskbar and choose Toolbars.

NOTES Open several windows and then minimize them using the Show Desktop icon. Then click on a minimized application on the Taskbar to work on it again. Another way of toggling between the applications is to use the ALT+ TAB keys on the keyboard. Hold down the ALT key on the keyboard and then tap the TAB key. A window will pop up with an icon for each open window. As you press the tab key the focus switches between the icons (see Figure 1.16). When you release the ALT key, you will switch to the window of the last icon to have the focus.

Figure 1.16

If you right click on the Taskbar and choose Properties, you will be able to make some configuration changes (see Figure 1.17). For instance, some people prefer the Taskbar to always show, whereas others want it to hide when they aren't using it.

Figure 1.17

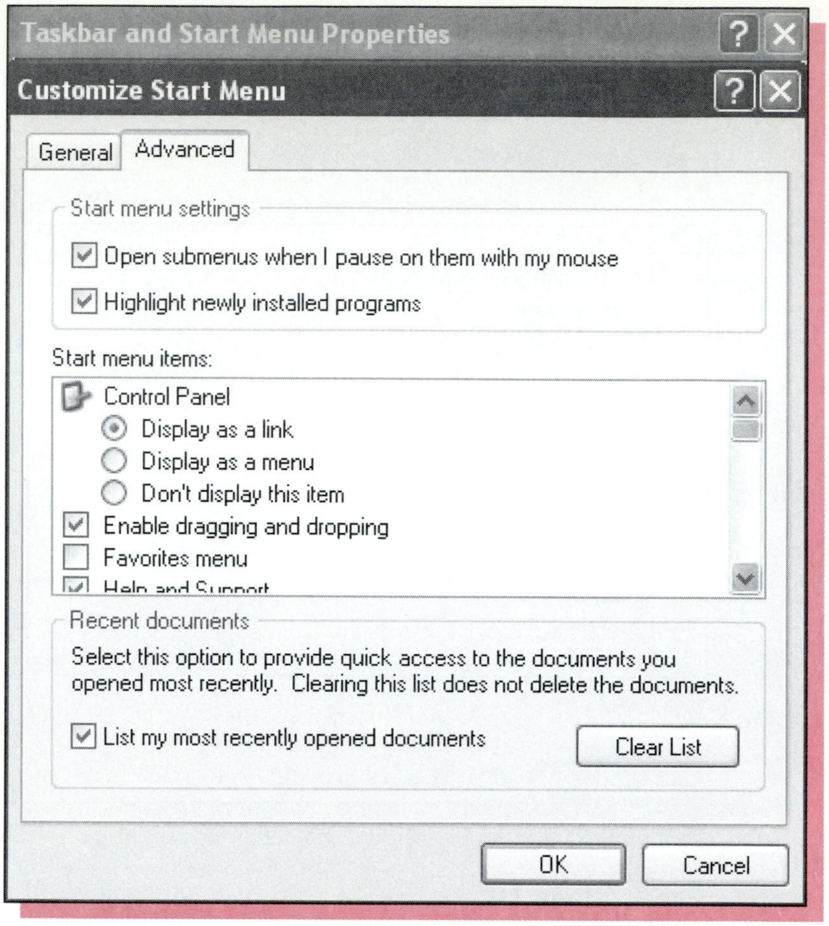

CHECK IT OUT

1. What options are listed under the Advanced tab? In Windows 2000 Professional, there are only two tabs: General and Advanced. To get to the Advanced tab in Windows XP Professional, choose the Start Menu tab, Customize, and then Advanced.

2. Can you find where to clear the documents listed in the Taskbar and Start Menu properties window?

System Tray

The System Tray displays an icon for the clock and other applications. These applications are loaded when your computer is turned on ("boots") and differ from computer to computer depending on what applications are installed. For instance, you might have an icon for your antivirus software, an icon for your volume (sound), etc. If you place your mouse pointer on top of any of the icons (without clicking), the name of the application will pop up.

You can change the time or date on the clock by double clicking on the clock (see Figure 1.18). If you want to change the time, highlight the part of the time that you want to change and either use the up/down arrows to the right or just enter the number manually. Click OK when you're done to set the date/time. The time will automatically adjust for Daylight Saving Time.

Task Manager

Sometimes an application freezes up and you need to terminate the process without having to reboot. You can get to the Windows Task Manager a few different ways. One method is to do a CTRL+ALT+DEL. Another is to right click on the Taskbar and choose Task Manager. If you want to terminate an application, select the application in the Applications tab (see Figure 1.19) and click the End Task button at the bottom of the window. While you're there, what options do you see under the

Figure 1.18

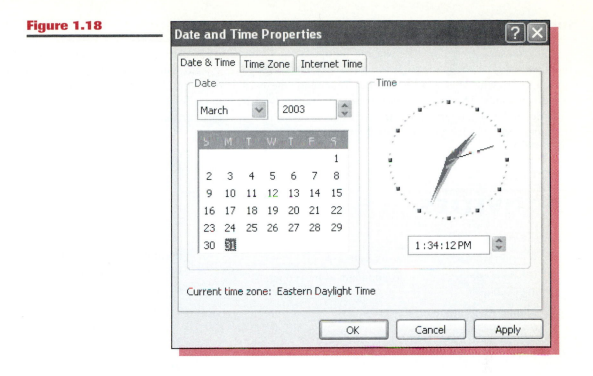

Processes and Performance tabs? You won't want to make any changes here now but you should see that there is still a lot to learn about what the operating system does. The Processes window is showing all of the executable programs currently running and the Performance tab gives an overview of how the computer is performing. Windows XP Professional also has a Networking tab that allows you to monitor the network traffic to your computer.

Figure 1.19

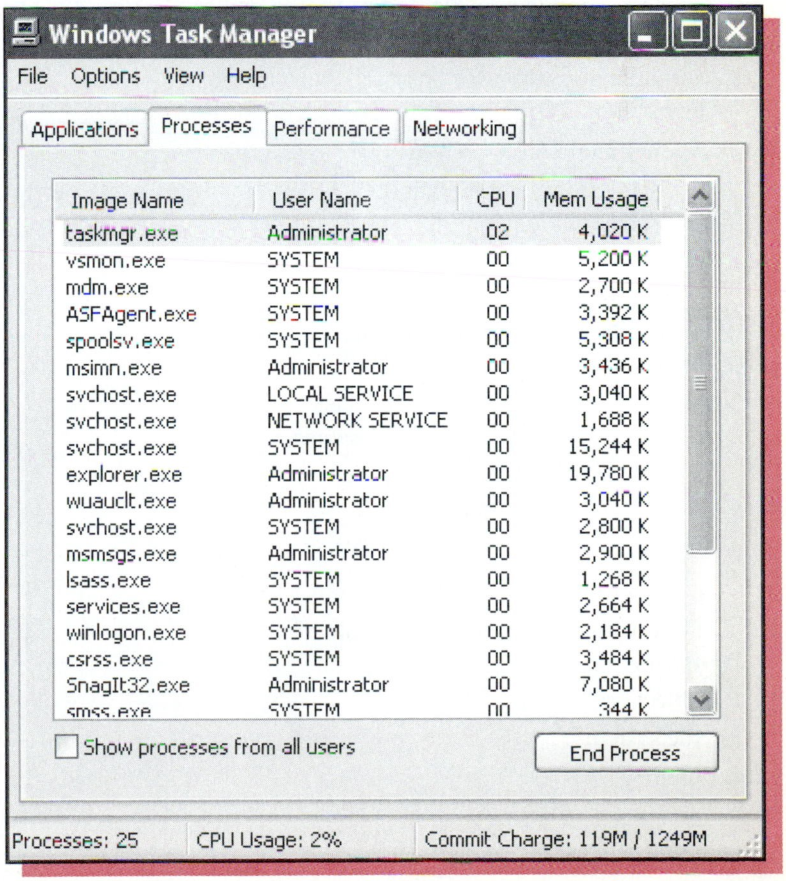

Summary

It's important to remember that without an operating system computers are just really big paperweights. The operating system interprets what you want to do into a language the hardware understands. There are many different operating systems available, and which operating system you decide to use is usually dependent on what you want to do. Once you have made your selection, learning as much as you can about the operating system will help you to be more productive. No matter which one you choose, however, all operating systems have three main components: the file system, the kernel, and a user interface, or shell.

ACTIVITIES

Review Questions

1. Why do we need an operating system?
2. What are the three main components of most operating systems?
3. What does GUI mean?
4. What is a desktop?
5. What is a Quick Launch toolbar?

Hands-on

1. Using the Internet, find five different operating systems not named in this chapter. Give a brief description of each.
2. Using www.webopedia.com or another online technical dictionary, explain the difference between a mainframe, a minicomputer, and a supercomputer.
3. Using www.webopedia.com or another online technical dictionary, explain what an open source operating system is.
4. Using the Internet, find at least two application programs that would be used on a Macintosh computer.
5. Using Windows Help, define what a shortcut is.

Important Terms

Using www.webopedia.com or another online technical dictionary, define:

binary math	GUI	shell
code	kernel	source code
DOS	object oriented	
file system	operating system	

Multiple Choice Questions

1. **The operating system is an example of a computer _____.**
   a. object
   b. file system
   c. program
   d. desktop

2. **Most operating systems are comprised of three main components: the _____, the file system and the shell.**
   a. desktop
   b. kernel
   c. user interface
   d. code

3. **The _____ keeps track of directories and files.**
   a. kernel
   b. file system
   c. shell
   d. user interface

4. **Most often, you click with the _____ button when you want to select something.**
   a. middle
   b. left
   c. right
   d. all of the above

5. **Before the days of Windows, users interfaced with the operating system through a _____ interface.**
   a. graphical
   b. object oriented
   c. command utility
   d. command line

6. **The _____ is often used as part of a path.**
   a. comma
   b. forward slash
   c. backslash
   d. semicolon

7. **The _____ is often used in a switch.**
   a. comma
   b. forward slash
   c. backslash
   d. semicolon

8. The _____ is the entire window that fills your computer screen and its contents.

    a. System Tray

    b. Taskbar

    c. Desktop

    d. Quick Launch Toolbar

9. A quicker way to launch a program is to click on it in the _____.

    a. System Tray

    b. Taskbar

    c. Desktop

    d. Quick Launch Toolbar

10. The _____ lets you move between applications without having to open and close them all the time.

    a. System Tray

    b. Taskbar

    c. Desktop

    d. Quick Launch Toolbar

11. You will find the clock and icons for certain applications in the _____.

    a. System Tray

    b. Taskbar

    c. Desktop

    d. Quick Launch Toolbar

2 Windows File and Environment Management

OBJECTIVES

After reading this chapter, you will be able to:

- Demonstrate how to navigate directories structures using Windows
- Demonstrate how to create a directory structure using Windows
- Explain the role of special folders
- Explain why files are different sizes
- Explain what a file attribute is
- Explain why a disk is formatted
- Copy and move files
- Explain what a file version is
- Explain the difference between Save and Save As
- Demonstrate how to search for files and folders
- Explain file types and file associations

INTRODUCTION

To successfully and confidently navigate around your computer, you need to understand the file structure of the operating system and be able to organize your files and folders. Although you have the ability to create your own folders where files would be stored, there are also special folders that are automatically created when the operating system is installed. These special folders have specific roles, and understanding what they are can make working with computers a little easier. In addition, understanding the file size, file type, and file attributes is also important.

ORGANIZATION

There is a difference between a file system and file management. Although there are many different file systems, they all perform the same basic functions. A file system, one of the three main components of any operating system, allows you to create and manage folders and files. FAT, FAT32, and NTFS are examples of file systems. The file system keeps track of where you store your folders and files so you can easily retrieve them and also determines the security options you have available to secure your files. File systems are discussed further in Chapter 7—Introduction to Networks.

Folders, also known by an older term, directories, allow us to organize our files so we can more easily find them. There are some special folders that help us to do that more efficiently.

My Documents

The My Documents folder is the default location into which most applications want to store your data files. In Windows 95/98, the My Documents folder that is automatically created when the operating system is installed is the same for everyone. Access to the My Documents folder is conveniently located on the Desktop so you can get to it quickly. But there is a problem if more than one person is using the computer. They will be using the same My Documents folder. That folder is actually found in c:\windows\desktop\My Documents if your operating system is installed on the C: drive.

The string c:\windows\desktop\My Documents is referred to as a path. It is the path you would take to get to the folder My Documents. If you were in Windows 95/98, you could open My Computer and go to the C: drive, then the Windows folder, then to the Desktop folder and then to the My Documents folder. A path has specific syntax that includes the drive letter, the colon, and the backslashes. Syntax isn't a computer term. In school, when you learned how to properly form a sentence you were learning the proper syntax of spelling and grammar and word order. The operating system would not understand your own version of a path; you must follow the rules of spelling and grammar and order(syntax) that the computer requires.

Windows 2000 Professional and Windows XP Professional resolve the problem of different users accessing the same My Documents folder by keeping track of who you are and actually having a different directory structure for each person who uses the computer. That is all transparent to the user, however.

Windows 2000 Professional and Windows XP Professional also place the My Documents folder for easy access. But the folder itself is actually in c:\Documents and Settings*your logon name*\My Documents. *Your logon name* refers to a folder that stores folders, such as My Documents, files, and other information that pertains to the login (username) you use to access the computer. You'll also see other folders in the Documents and Settings folder for other users who access the same computer.

NOTES   **Open My Computer and navigate to the Documents and Settings*your login name* folder. What other folders do you see? These folders store information related to your login account such as your desktop settings, your folders and files, and the options you see in the Start Menu.**

Desktop

The Desktop folder holds everything that you see on your desktop. Assuming that Windows is installed on the C: drive, if you navigate to c:\Documents and Settings*your login name*\desktop, what do you see?

Now that you are there, click on the little down arrow of the dropdown list in the address bar. In the directory structure that you see in the dropdown list, you should see the path that you just took expanded in the list but you should also see an icon for the desktop at the very top. Select it. What do you see now? You should see the very same thing. The desktop icon at the top of the list is just another shortcut pointing to the same place (c:\Documents and Settings*your login name*\desktop) even though you don't see the entire path as well.

Figure 2.1

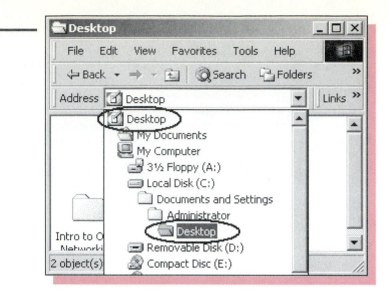

Recycle Bin

The Recycle Bin is actually pretty handy. Almost every file that you delete goes into the Recycle Bin. The Recycle Bin is configured automatically to be able to store files that equal 10% of the size of your hard disk. Files deleted from floppy disks and Zip disks do not go to the Recycle Bin.

Right click on the Recycle Bin icon and choose Properties to view the dialogue box in Figure 2.2. If you have more than one hard disk in your computer, you could have a different Recycle Bin for each disk by clicking the radio button (Configure Drives Independently) at the top of the dialogue box shown here.

Figure 2.2

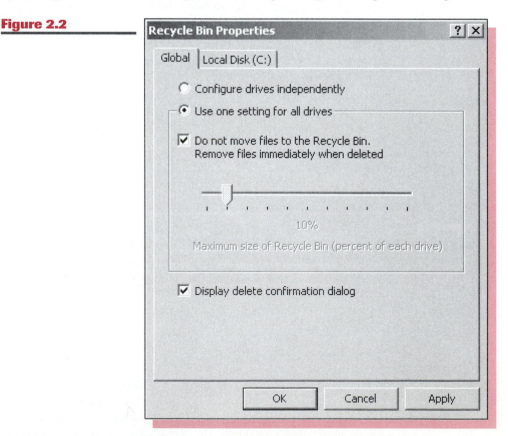

You can also change the percentage of each disk used for the Recycle Bin. In addition, you can tell it to skip the Recycle Bin altogether and actually get rid of a file when you delete it by selecting the check box that says "Do not move files to the Recycle Bin."

The Recycle Bin can be thought of as a second chance. If you accidentally delete a file, you can still get it back by opening the Recycle Bin, right clicking on the file, and choosing Restore. If hard disk space is at a premium on your computer, you can also empty the Recycle Bin once you've made sure you really don't need anything in it. To delete a file without sending it to the Recycle Bin, hold down the SHIFT key on the keyboard when you delete the file. A message box will ask to confirm the file deletion and then delete the file without sending it to the Recycle Bin.

How do you know if there are files in the Recycle Bin? The icon changes.

CHECK IT OUT

Minimize everything by clicking on the Show Desktop icon in the Quick Launch Toolbar. Then:

1. Right click anywhere on your desktop where there isn't currently an icon.

2. From the context menu, choose New > Text Document.

3. Accept the default name NEW TEXT DOCUMENT by pressing the ENTER key on the keyboard.

4. The new document should still be selected (highlighted) so next press the DELETE key on the keyboard or right click on the file and choose DELETE from the context menu.

5. You'll get a confirm deletion message. Click YES.

6. Look carefully at the Recycle Bin icon.

7. Right click the Recycle Bin and choose EMPTY.

8. Look again at the Recycle Bin icon.

9. Do you notice a difference?

Figure 2.3 is showing a full Recycle Bin and Figure 2.4 is showing an empty Recycle Bin.

Figure 2.3   **Figure 2.4**

Briefcase

The Briefcase was originally designed for users who also have a notebook computer and often work on the same files in two different places. If you put the file in the Briefcase and then connect your PC directly to your notebook via a cable, the two different versions of the file would be synchronized.

If you don't have a Briefcase on your desktop, you can right click the desktop and choose New > Briefcase. This would also work with removable drives, like Zip drives. The difference is you are connecting the Zip drive first to one machine and then the other rather than using a direct cable. Microsoft put a Briefcase on the desktop in earlier versions of the Windows operating system but found it wasn't as popular as was first imagined. Windows 2000 Professional and Windows XP Professional do not have the Briefcase icon on their desktop by default.

Another option for synchronizing files is to work with them offline. This option is primarily for users in a networked environment who are accessing files in shares over the network but want to take them somewhere else and work with them or want to continue working with them even if a connection with the network is lost.

My Network Places

My Network Places keeps track of the computers around you in a networked environment. You can also use My Network Places to create shortcuts to folders on remote computers that you have permission to read from and/or write to. The computer you work on is considered the local computer and any other computer you access is remote. For instance, if you have an instructor who wants you to send your files to a folder on a server at school, you can create a shortcut here so that you can just drop files into it and they're actually placed on the remote computer. This task is accomplished by using FTP (File Transfer Protocol) which is discussed in more detail later in the book.

If you use Microsoft FrontPage to compose Web pages on a remote server, you will see the shortcuts to the remote folders here as well.

To set up a shortcut to an FTP folder, click Add a Network Place and then type in the address of the FTP server you have been given permission to access. When you click on the shortcut to the folder in My Network Places, it will prompt you for a username and password, if appropriate.

Figure 2.5

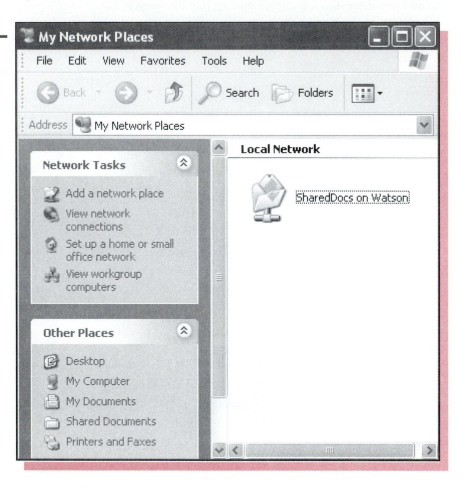

Send To

If you right click on a file or folder, one of the options in the context menu that you will have is Send To. This option allows you to quickly copy a file to a floppy disk, Zip disk, etc.

Figure 2.6

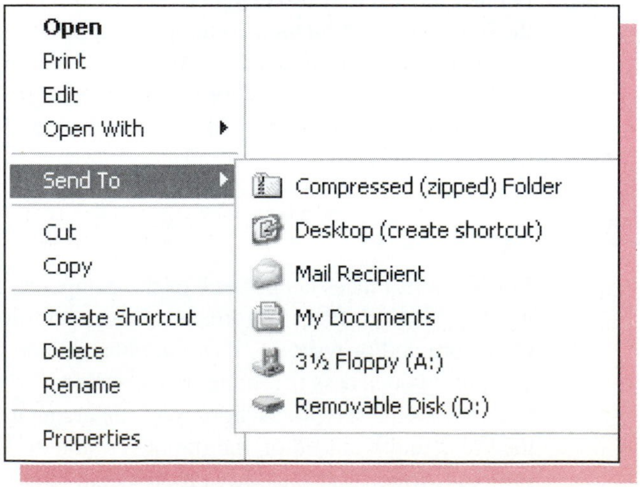

NOTES   Minimize everything again using the Show Desktop icon and create another text file. Right click the text file. What are your Send To options?

You can add options to the Send To menu because it is actually just a folder on your computer with shortcuts in it. In Windows 2000, the send to folder is stored where your desktop and My Documents folders are. Navigate to c:\Documents and Settings*your login name*\Sendto. If you want to add another place to send files to easily, create a shortcut to the folder here.

Send To is a hidden folder by default. To view it, you must first tell the operating system that you want to see hidden folders and files. The steps to do so are covered later in this chapter.

Start Menu

The Start menu is a folder as well. You should find it under c:\Documents and Settings\all users. However, you don't have to look there; you can also work directly in the menu. Click on Start > Programs or All Programs, and point your mouse to the Programs menu that lists all of your applications. Then right click. What options do you see in the context menu? You should see an option to reorder the list of applications (sort by name). Often, applications aren't listed alphabetically, making them harder to find. Reordering them alphabetically makes it a lot easier to find them.

Figure 2.7

```
Open
Run as...
Pin to Start menu

Send To              ▶

Cut
Copy

Create Shortcut
Delete
Rename

Sort by Name
Properties
```

Quick Launch

The Quick Launch Toolbar was discussed in Chapter 1. It is another folder on your computer in which you can place shortcuts. The Quick Launch Toolbar is directly to the right of the Start menu button. Click one time on any of the icons to launch the associated application. You can also reorder the icons. Point to one of the icons in the Quick Launch Toolbar, hold down the left mouse button and drag the icon to a new position. An I-beam marker displays to indicate the potential new position. Release the mouse button when you have the icon where you want it. To delete an icon in the Quick Launch toolbar, right click on it and choose Delete from the context menu. This will not delete the application from the computer. It only removes the shortcut from the Quick Launch Toolbar.

Figure 2.8

Designing Your Own Directory Structure

Organizing the files and folders on a computer is very much like using a filing cabinet. Just as we place paper files into folders and then put the folders into drawers, we also place computer files into folders and then move the folders onto disks. The trick is to be able to design a structure for storing your files and folders so you can easily find your files when needed.

In addition to the special folders you already have, it's up to you to design the directory structure of your computer. You will create the folders and files and decide which folder to place the files in. In a Windows environment, you can use either My Computer or Windows Explorer. Both options allow you to do the same thing but the interface is slightly different; you just want to choose the one that you're most comfortable with. Most applications, such as Microsoft Word, will also allow you to create folders when you are saving the file. You may find that is the easiest way.

Some folders are created automatically when software is installed. For instance, when Microsoft Windows is installed as the operating system on your computer, it automatically creates a folder called My Documents for you to place your files in. That's nice, but once you start getting a lot of files, having them all in one folder makes it difficult to find them. So you might keep My Documents, but put more folders inside of it that make sense for what you do.

Figure 2.9

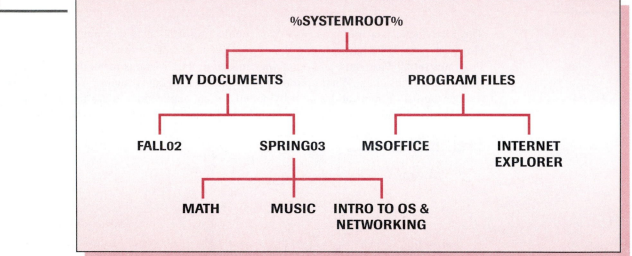

In the example file structure in Figure 2.9, there are two folders in the root of C:—My Documents and Program Files. Both of these folders are created automatically when the operating system is installed but, depending on the version of the operating system, they may be in different places. The root is the topmost directory within a directory structure.

Within Program Files are two additional folders. These were installed when Microsoft Office and Internet Explorer (IE) were installed. Applications such as Office and IE by default want to be installed in Program Files but that is not required. For instance, some people have more than one hard drive and prefer to install their applications on one drive and store their data files on another.

The My Documents folder shown in Figure 2.9 has two folders also: Fall02 and Spring03. That would make sense if you need to organize things in terms of semesters. These are folders that you would have to create; they would not be created automatically. Within the Spring03 folder are three additional folders that you would need to create. These folders would represent individual classes in the Spring 03 semester. Those folders would hold files related to the respective classes.

Many operating system file structures are hierarchical and use terminology similar to trees: thus the root of a structure is simply the topmost directory. The root of your floppy disk is A: and the root of your hard disk is C:. You can create additional directories inside this root. These directories are referred to as either subdirectories or folders: the terms are synonymous. In DOS, folders and subfolders are called directories and subdirectories. Windows refers to them now as folders in an attempt to make it easier to understand by using the analogy of a filing cabinet.

NAVIGATION

There are several different ways to navigate, or move around inside, the directory structure on your computer. The method you use may be determined by your comfort level or the task at hand. Believe it or not, there are still some things that you can only do using a command prompt and knowing how to find your way around in the command prompt will help. You'll see how to navigate using DOS commands in Chapter 3.

Using My Computer

The My Computer icon on your desktop (see Figure 2.10) lets you do everything you could do in DOS and more, but instead of having to remember all of the DOS commands, you can simply point and click.

Figure 2.10

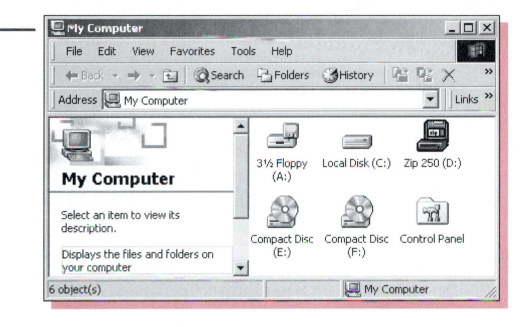

You can also customize how you're viewing the contents of folders. Click View on the menu bar and you'll see that you have 4 options to view the contents: large icons, small icons, list, and details. Check each one out to see which you prefer. In addition to listing the files, the details view has columns detailing certain attributes about the files, including their name, size, type, and the date they were last modified.

If you click on a column heading, such as the Modified column, the files will be reordered by the date they were modified. If you click on the Name column, the files will be alphabetized by name. Clicking on the Type column groups them by type of file. There are other options for columns to display. To see what the options are, right click on one of the columns and choose More. Figure 2.11 is an example of a list of additional columns that could be displayed.

Figure 2.11

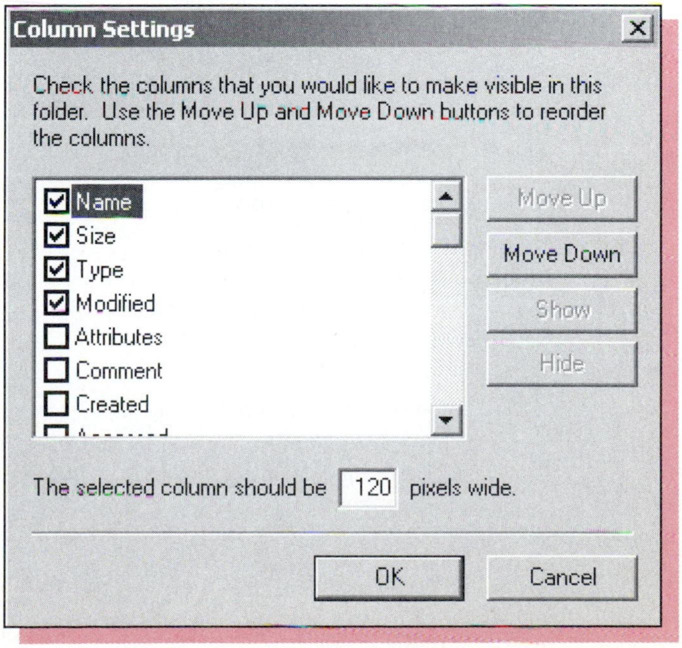

If you need to get to your floppy drive, hard drive(s), CD-ROM drives or removable drives (e.g., Zip drives), My Computer is one place where you could start.

NOTES   **Practice navigating. Double click the C: drive. What do you see? Now choose the folder called My Documents. In Windows 2000 Professional, My Documents is found on the desktop. In Windows XP Professional, it is in the Start menu. You can right click on My Documents in Windows XP Professional and place a shortcut to it on the desktop if you prefer.**

To navigate to a folder, click on it in My Computer or My Documents. But how do you get back to where you were? In the same way that you navigate through Web pages in a Web browser, you should see Back and Forward buttons as in Figure 2.12. To go back up one directory from My Documents, you could click the Back button to get back to the root of C: or you could click the Up button to go up one directory at a time.

Notice that the Back and Forward buttons have little dropdown arrows on them. If you click on the down arrow, you'll see that it is keeping a history of where you've been and you can quickly go back to it by selecting it from the dropdown list. Web browsers usually have that feature as well.

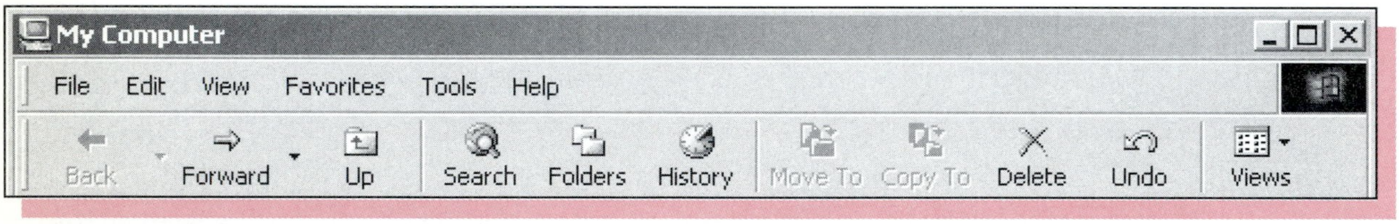

Figure 2.12

In addition to the Back, Forward, and Up buttons, there are several others. The next section of buttons deals with finding your files a little differently. The Search button is actually similar to the Search option from the Start menu and you use it to help you find files. The Folders button opens another window on the left of the screen and is the same thing you'll see when you launch Windows Explorer. The History button lets you search for the Web sites you have visited on certain days.

In Windows 2000 Professional, the next section of buttons deals with moving, copying, and deleting files. And, of course, the Undo button undoes the last thing you did that you didn't want to do. The Views button gives you the four options mentioned earlier (large icons, small icons, list, and details).

Figure 2.13

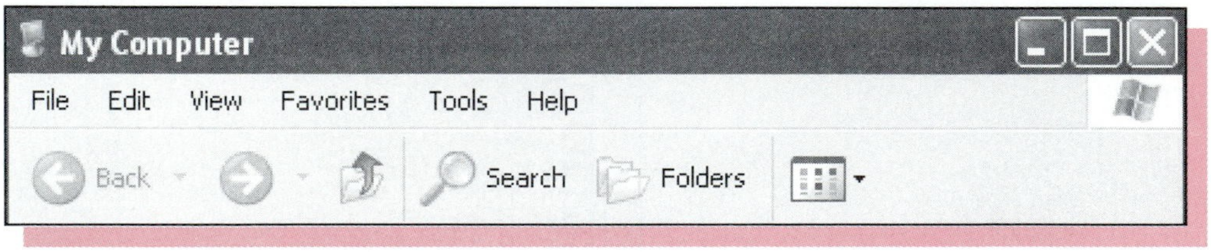

Windows XP Professional has a simplified toolbar to help navigate but the important buttons are still there to navigate back, forward, and up one directory.

If you would prefer to single click on a file rather than double clicking to open the file or folder, you can configure that setting by going to Tools > Folder Options. At the bottom of the window you should see Click Items as Follows.

Once you customize the way you view your files and folders, you can force that setting to take effect for every folder you view. Again, click on Tools > Folder Options, then select the View tab. You can click the Like Current Folder button to set all of your other folders with the same settings.

Figure 2.14

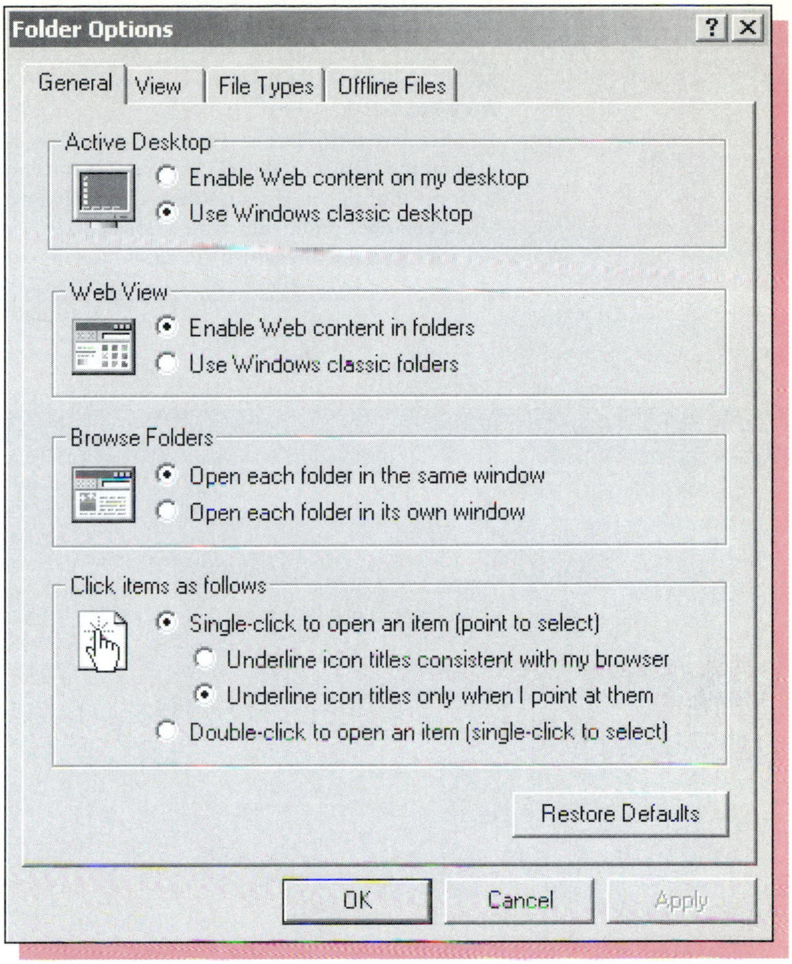

Using Windows Explorer

Windows Explorer and Internet Explorer are not the same thing. Internet Explorer is a Web browser that allows you to navigate the Internet. Windows Explorer is a tool that lets you more easily navigate the files and folders on your computer.

Figure 2.15

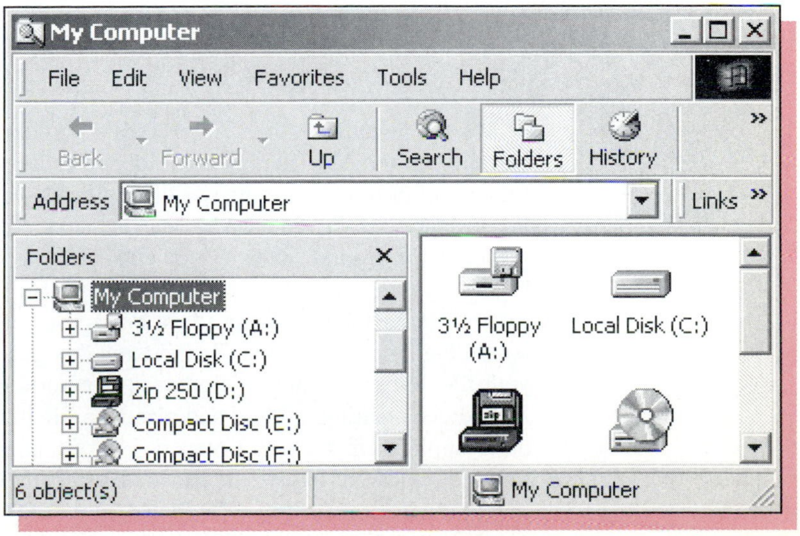

NOTES   Click Start > Programs or All Programs > Accessories > Windows Explorer. This is similar to opening My Computer except the Folders button is selected. The folder structure of your computer is listed in the left window.

There are plus signs next to each folder. You can either click the folder name or click the plus sign to expand the view. Practice clicking first on the name of the folder in the left pane (e.g., My Computer) and then the plus sign next to it. What is the difference between the two? Does something different happen when you click on the file name versus clicking on the plus sign? The plus sign expands the contents in the left pane and the minus sign collapses the contents.

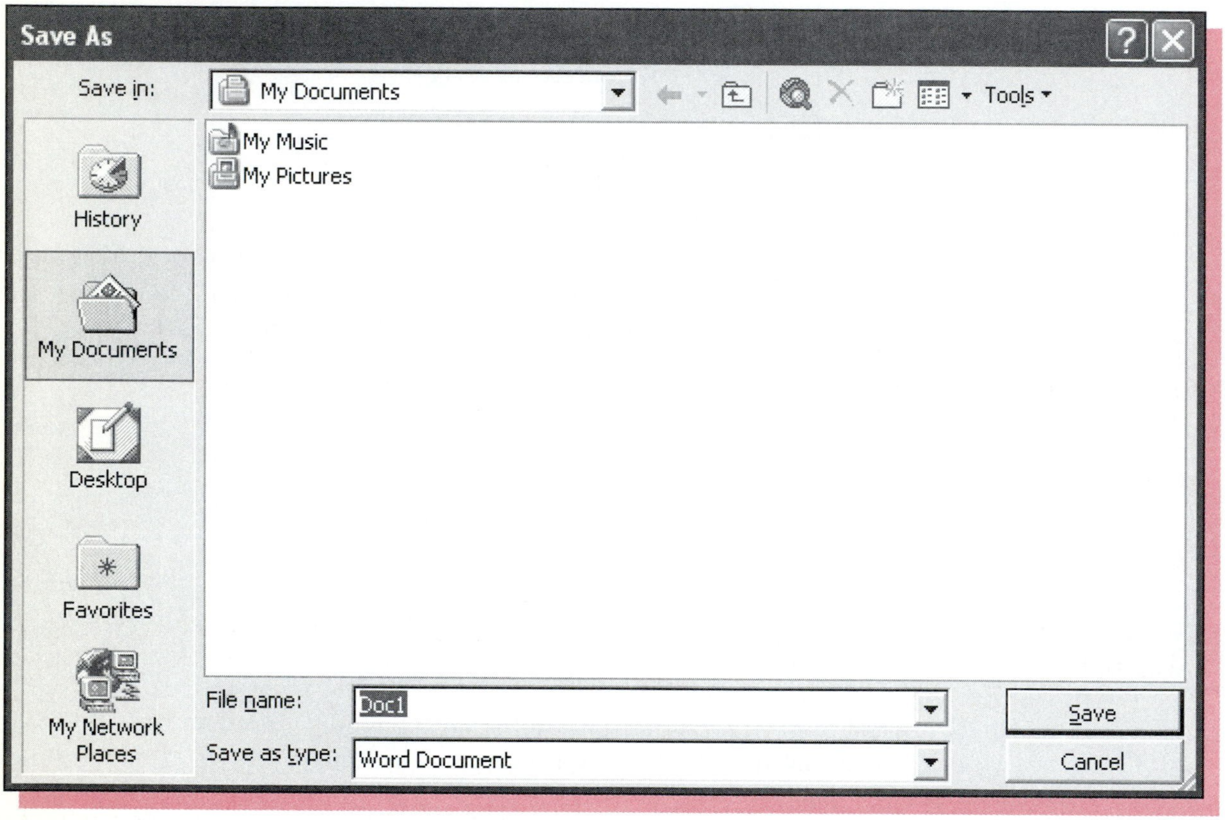

Figure 2.16

Most applications allow you to create a folder when you are saving the file. In Figure 2.16, you are currently in the My Documents folder. You can save the file in the My Documents folder or create a folder within it and save the file there. Or you could navigate to another folder several different ways. For instance, notice the dropdown arrow next to the words "My Documents" where it says "Save in." If you click the dropdown arrow, you will see a list of the directory structure on your computer as shown in Figure 2.17.

Also notice the left side of the graphic. You could quickly navigate to the desktop by clicking the button on the left and save the file there but that generally isn't recommended as the primary place to save your files simply because it clutters up your desktop.

Practice creating a folder and placing a file in it using an application. Open Microsoft Word or some other application such as Notepad or WordPad and type a few words. Then click File > Save. What folder does it want to save the file in? By default, it should suggest the My Documents folder. Instead of saving it there, create a new folder called Word Docs. Then save the file in it.

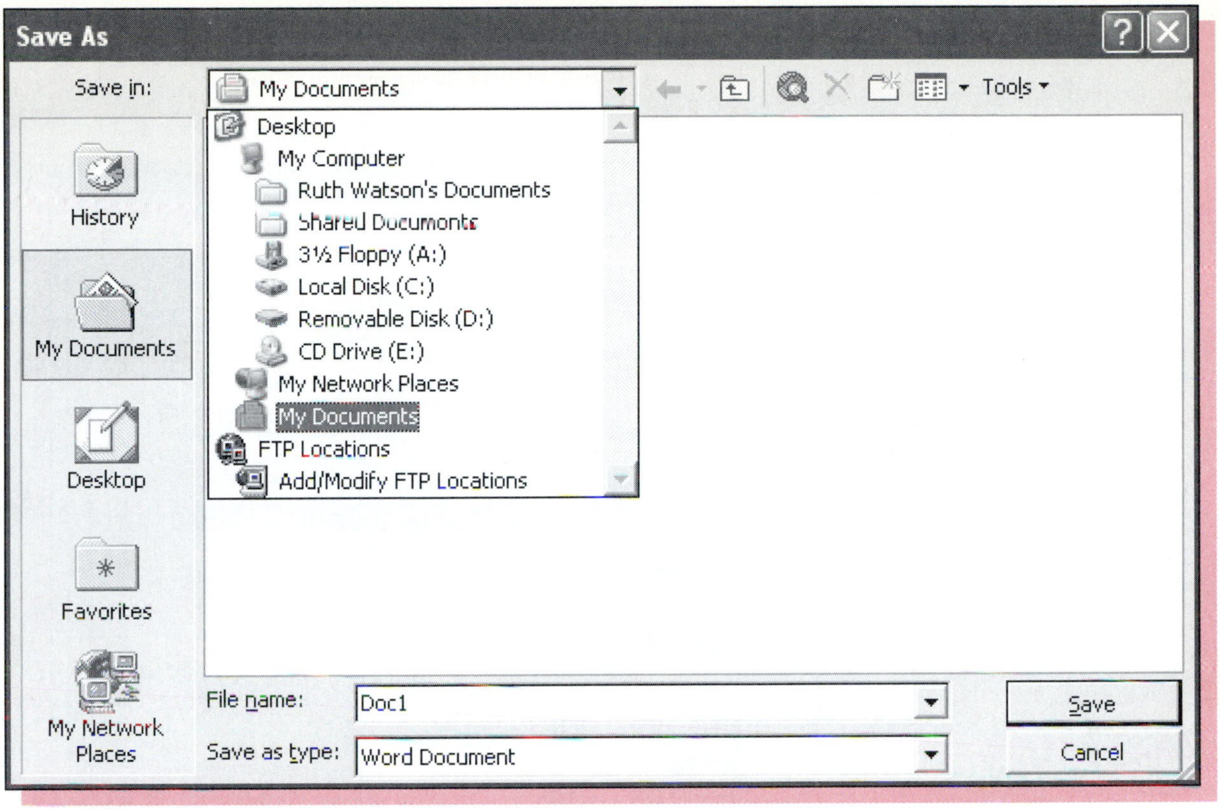

Figure 2.17

FILES

Data are pieces of information. Files are a collection of data. There are many different kinds of files, including text files and executable files, or programs. Every time we open an application such as Microsoft Word or Excel and create a document of some type, that document is a file that may or may not fit on a floppy disk. How many files can a floppy disk hold? How big are files? Why are some files bigger than others? Why would you have to format a floppy disk? Why do they call it a floppy disk?

Shown in Figure 2.18 is a folder named "Intro to OS & Networking" with 2 folders and a file inside of it. The file, named "THIS IS A FILE," is a Microsoft Word document. Not only does the

Figure 2.18

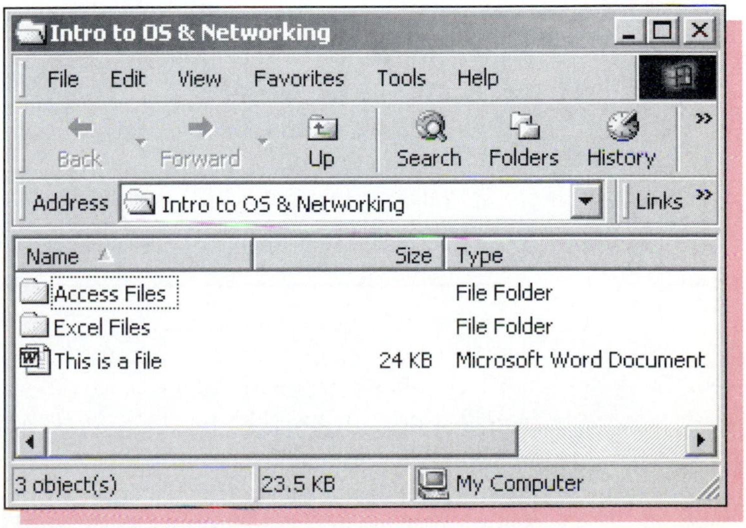

Explorer window tell you that under the column heading "Type," but you can also tell by the icon used to represent the file. The W on top of what looks like a piece of paper is trying to tell you it's a Word document.

Figure 2.19

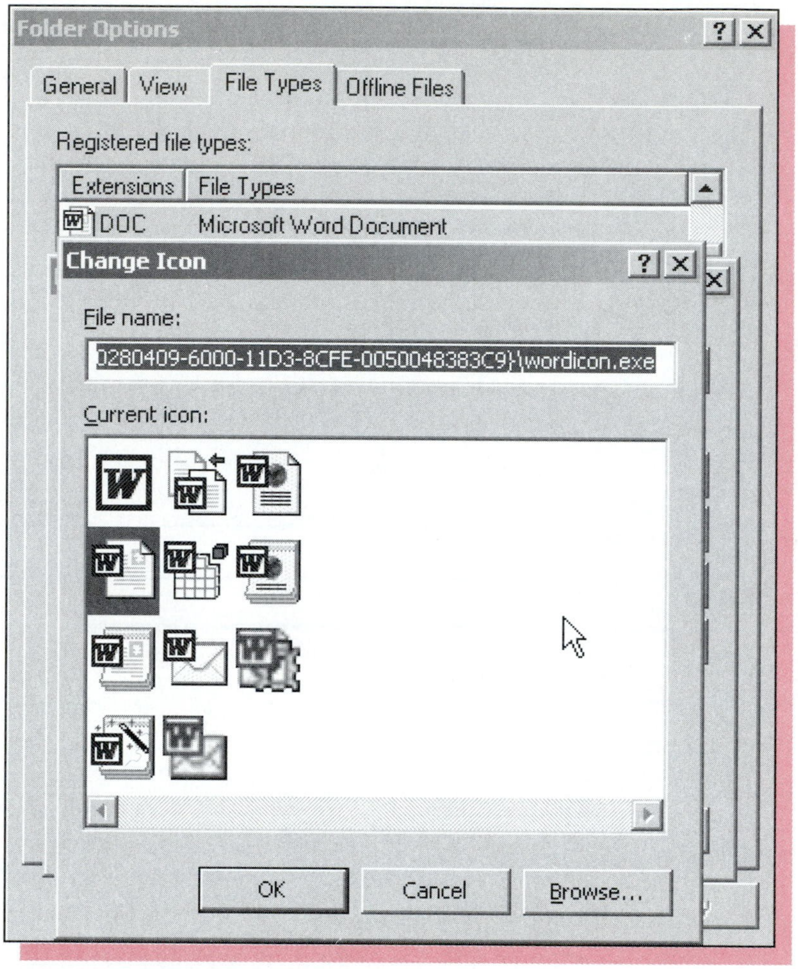

CHECK IT OUT

The icons that represent a specific application, such as the W icon for Word, can be changed.

1. Open My Computer by double clicking the My Computer icon on the desktop.
2. Click on Tools > Folder Options.
3. Go to the File Types tab.
4. Click one time on the DOC file type to select it.
5. Click the Advanced button.
6. Click the Change Icon button.
7. Select the icon you want to use and click Ok.

File Size

Different files are different sizes. Sometimes that is simply due to the length of the file contents and sometimes it's due to the type of file you are saving. For instance, a Microsoft Word file has more overhead with it than a simple text file created with Notepad. Microsoft Word inserts additional markup information into the file so it knows how the text is formatted, etc.

The document shown in Figure 2.18 is actually rather small at 24 kilobytes. A kilobyte is roughly 1000 bytes. A byte is 8 bits. A bit represents a 1 or a 0 which in turn represents the electronic state of on or off that a computer understands.

Figure 2.20

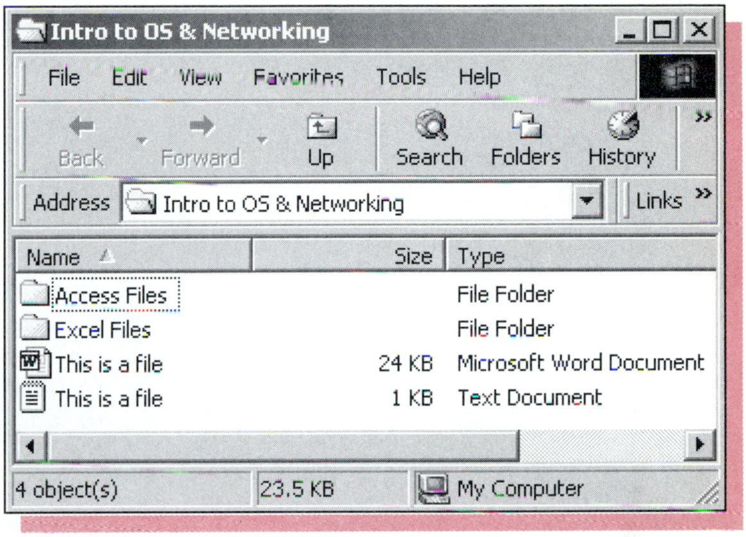

NOTES

Create two documents using the same text. Create one using Microsoft Word and save it as THIS IS A FILE.DOC. Create another using Notepad and save it as THIS IS A FILE.TXT. In this example, there are two different kinds of files: a Microsoft Word document and a text file created with Notepad. Microsoft Word automatically puts the .doc extension on every document and Notepad automatically uses the .txt extension.

Both files have the same words in them. Both files have the same name but their file extensions are different. The document created with Notepad is only 1 KB versus the 24 KB file created with Microsoft Word.

Now try it again. Use Microsoft Paint to create a file and type the same text in it. How large is the file when you save it?

In Figure 2.20 the file size of the Microsoft Word document is shown as 24 KB. In the Command prompt, that same file would be shown as approximately 24,000 because it is referencing it in terms of bytes. So 24 kilobytes is equal to approximately 24,000 bytes. If a floppy disk holds 1.44 megabytes (MB) that means it holds 1440 kilobytes, which in turn would be approximately 1,440,000 bytes. That means there is plenty of room on the floppy disk to hold a small file of 24 KB or 24,000 bytes.

File Attributes

Files have different attributes, or characteristics, associated with them. Examples of these attributes are Read Only, Hidden, and Archive. If you right click on a file and choose Properties you can see check boxes to make a file Read Only or Hidden. In the My Computer window when you are viewing your files, one of the available columns is Attributes. If a file is flagged with an "A" attribute, you will see it there. If the Attributes column is not displayed in My Computer, right click on any of the available columns and choose Attributes from the context menu.

The Read Only attribute might be used in an environment where multiple people must access the same file but you don't want them to accidentally alter the file. This attribute will display a warning if someone tries to change the contents of the file. The Archive attribute is in reference to backing up files. For instance, if a file is flagged with the A attribute for "archive" that means the file needs to be backed up.

Figure 2.21

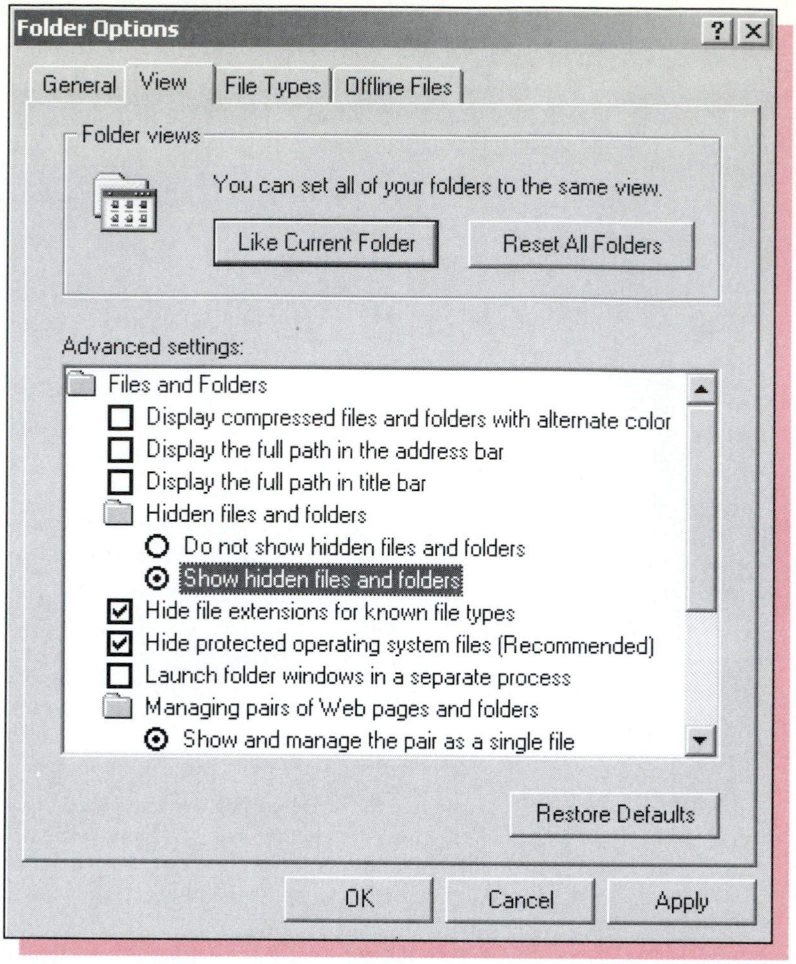

Figure 2.21

The Hidden attribute is important. Many of the system files on your computer are hidden. Microsoft does this on purpose so that you won't accidentally delete a file that is needed to run the computer. Actually, there is a difference between hidden files and system files. While most system files are hidden, not all hidden files are system files.

If you ever want to view hidden files, open My Computer. Click on Tools > Folder Options. Click on the View tab. Here you can tell it to show hidden files and folders. These are the files and folders that are hidden but are not system files. You can also uncheck the Hide file extensions for known file types so you can see what the real name of the file is.

The last thing you might uncheck is Hide protected operating system files. Again, these are files used by your operating system and are very important. As you can see, Microsoft does not recommend that you do that. Neither do I.

Removable Disks

If you try to save a file to a floppy disk and there isn't enough room, you will get an error message telling you that. If you can't fit a file(s) on a floppy disk, you do have other options. You can compress the files using a tool such as Winzip, or you can use a different kind of removable disk such as a Zip disk. Currently, Zip disks can hold either 100 MB or 250 MB depending on the Zip drive. If the Zip drive is designed to handle 100 MB disks, it can only read 100 MB disks. However, if it is designed to handle 250 MB disks, it can read both 100 MB disks and 250 MB disks. Writeable and rewriteable CD-ROM drives are becoming more popular as they become more affordable. Currently, a CD (compact disc) can hold 700 MB.

You need to take care of a floppy disk. Floppy disks shouldn't be exposed to extreme temperatures or magnets, you shouldn't put a floppy disk on top of a monitor, and you shouldn't physically abuse it by dropping it or banging it against something.

Floppy disks are called floppy disks because they did used to be floppy. They also used to be larger. Currently a floppy disk is 3.5″ wide but used to be 5.25″ wide several years ago. Inside the hard plastic shell of the floppy disk is a mylar-coated disk sometimes called a cookie. That's where the data is actually written. When you insert the floppy disk into the computer, it pulls the metal cover over to one side to expose the cookie. Take a peek: carefully pull the metal cover to one side and check out the cookie. The metal cover is just there to protect the cookie when the disk is not in the computer. The metal cover can get bent and stuck inside the floppy drive, so be careful not to use a disk if the metal cover looks bent. If you should ever come across a floppy disk with a bent metal cover, you can pull the metal cover off completely, copy the contents of the disk to another disk, and then throw the old disk out.

Sometimes you might want to "write protect" your floppy disk so that files cannot be written to it or data on the disk cannot be overwritten or erased. You would still be able to read the files, however. To write protect the floppy, turn it over and look at the back. You should see a little lever on the bottom right hand corner. Flip it down so you can see through. The floppy is now write protected and can't be written to: you'll get an error message if you try. You can, however, still read from the floppy. Why would you want to write protect a floppy disk? Think in terms of viruses. If your floppy can't be written to, a virus can't be written to it.

As previously mentioned, a floppy disk can hold 1.44 megabytes (MB) when it is formatted. A label on the disk might say it can hold 2 MB if it is unformatted. Of course, you can't actually save anything on it until it is formatted. Formatting a disk prepares it for use. When you format a disk, the computer tells the disk what kind of operating system it's using so that the two are compatible. The disk has to be able to keep track of all the files you place on it. A little table, an index, to do that is created when the disk is formatted. That's why there is no longer 2 MB on the floppy after it is formatted; some of it is used by the file system to keep track of the files. On a floppy disk, the table is called the File Allocation Table (FAT).

As it happens, when you save a file to a disk the file isn't saved in one chunk. It's actually broken up into pieces and spread over the disk wherever the pieces will fit. The table or index keeps track of where all the pieces are so you can get them back when you try to access the file.

Many floppies come preformatted now, but they weren't always. So you don't usually need to format a new floppy but sometimes you may want to format a floppy just to clean it up and get rid of any old files on it and to reset the index table.

Figure 2.22

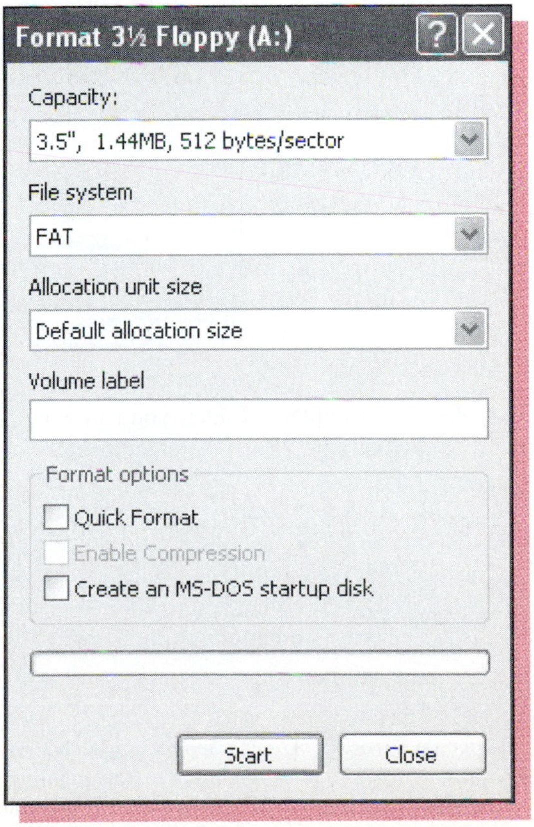

To format the floppy, open up My Computer and right click on the floppy drive (A:).

Choose Format from the context menu.

Warning   this will remove all files from your floppy disk!

Click Start and wait for your disk to be formatted.

Once done, you can close the window.

The Quick Format option is much quicker but doesn't actually delete the files from the floppy. It simply breaks all the pointers in the table or index to the files on the floppy so it looks like they aren't there anymore. If the disk has never been formatted, you may get an error message telling you that a quick format is not an option; in that case, you must do a full format.

Creating and Maintaining Files and Folders

Effectively managing files and folders does not only means creating them: you should also be able to reorganize your drives by copying and moving them. When you copy files and folders that means that you now have more than one instance of the file or folder. Not only is the file or folder still where it was originally, but you're making a duplicate of it and placing it somewhere else. We often do this if we want to take a copy of a file onto a removable disk such as a floppy or a Zip disk or to make a backup copy of a file—an extra copy "just in case."

Moving a file or folder is not the same as copying it. If you move ("Cut"), you still only have one instance of the file or folder. Think of it this way: if you make a copy of your house key, you now have two keys. If you move your house key from one side of a table to the other side, you still only have one key.

First, think about where you want to create the folder. The default place to store files is in the My Documents folder. That is usually a good place to develop the directory structure that makes the most sense for what you do.

Figure 2.23

In the My Documents folder, you can either right click and select New > Folder from the context menu or click on File > New > Folder from the menu.

You'll get an icon called "New Folder" that looks like a manila folder. The name of the folder is highlighted. It's waiting for you to type a new name and then confirm the new name by pressing the Enter key. Call this one "Fall Classes."

The fact that it is highlighted means that you don't have to try to erase what is there first (New Folder). Simply start typing and it will automatically overwrite the current text with whatever you enter. This is true anytime something is highlighted.

NOTES   Open up a word processing application such as Word, Notepad, or WordPad. Type in the sentence: "This is a sentence." Then highlight the text by pointing your mouse at one end of the sentence, holding down the mouse key and painting across with your mouse to highlight the text.

Then type in this sentence: "I just overwrote the text." What happened? Even if it had been a graphic instead of text, you would have overwritten it. Anytime something is selected (highlighted) you are telling the computer that the next time you do something, you want the results to take place here.

Copying and Moving

Now back to creating folders. Create a second folder in My Documents and name it "Spring Classes." Open up the Fall Classes folder and create a text file in it called "SCHEDULE." One way to create a text file is by right clicking in the Fall Classes folder and selecting New > text document from the list. A document is created with the default name of NEW TEXT DOCUMENT but it is highlighted, waiting for you to enter the real name of the file.

Figure 2.24

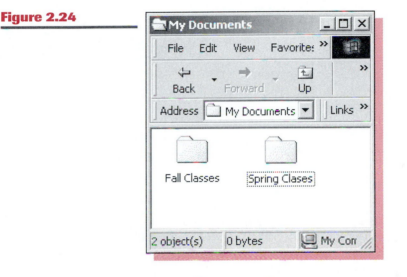

If you need to rename a folder or file because of a typo or a change of mind, you can right click on the file or folder and choose Rename from the context menu.

In the My Documents window, you have several navigation options. Perhaps the quickest way to get back up one level is to either click the Back button or the Up button shown here. After creating the SCHEDULE file in the Fall Classes folder, go back up one level to the My Documents folder.

Now confirm that the file is only in the Fall Classes folder by checking the contents of the Spring Classes folder. Not there? Good. Now move it there from the Fall Classes folder. Go back to the Fall Classes folder, right click on the file and choose Cut. Using Cut is the same as moving. In previous Windows versions the option was called "move," but apparently that was too confusing and Microsoft now uses the word "cut."

Go to the Spring Classes folder, right click, and Paste. By the way, anytime you right click in a folder, you also get the option to Arrange Icons. Try it. What are the options? So where is the file called "Schedule" now? Is it in both folders or only one? Why?

Now let's copy the file from the Spring Classes folder to the Fall Classes folder. Right click on the file, choose Copy, and then navigate to the Fall Classes folder and Paste. Or, you could click on Edit, Paste from the menu bar or the Paste button in My Computer. Where is the Schedule file now? You should have one copy each in both the Fall Classes and Spring Classes folders.

Version Control

What happens to the copy of the file in the Fall Classes folder if you make changes to the file in the Spring Classes folder?

NOTES   **Go to the Spring Classes folder and right click on the file. Choose Open. Notepad should open to a blank document. Type in: "This is new text." Click File on the menu bar and Save. Then click File and Exit to close Notepad.**

Now check the Schedule file in the Fall Classes folder by opening it. Is it still an exact copy of the other file? How could you update it so they're both the same again?

Copy the file in the Spring Classes folder and then paste it in the Fall Classes folder. What happens when you try?

Figure 2.25

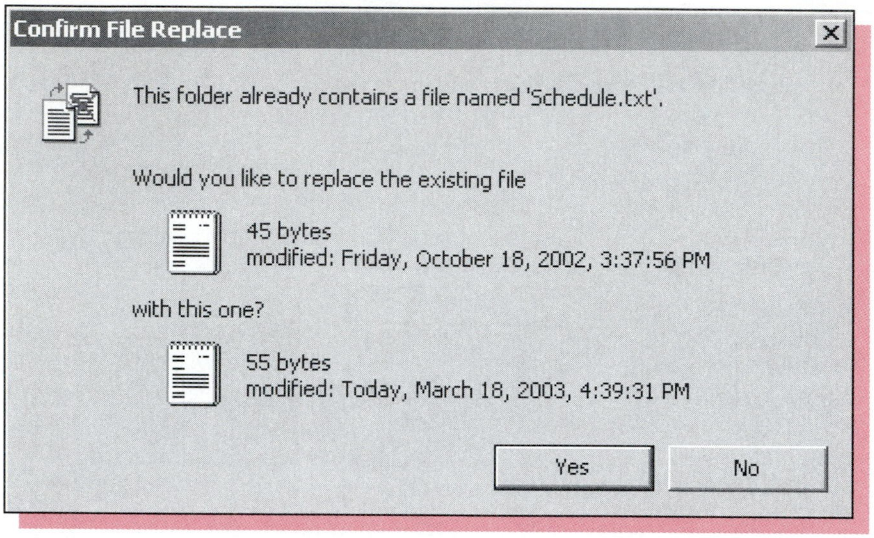

Confirm File Replace

This folder already contains a file named 'Schedule.txt'.

Would you like to replace the existing file

45 bytes
modified: Friday, October 18, 2002, 3:37:56 PM

with this one?

55 bytes
modified: Today, March 18, 2003, 4:39:31 PM

[Yes]   [No]

In the example shown, which file is more current? How can you tell? The most current file will have the most current date and time stamp.

It is important to note that if you copy a file then you have a duplicate of the file but the two files are not connected in anyway. They are separate files. If you make changes to one copy, the other copy isn't automatically updated. Each copy of the file is referred to as a different version of the file. Keeping track of file versions is important.

Another way to create a file is to open the application first. Let's use Notepad. Click on Start > Programs or All Programs > Accessories > Notepad. Type in this sentence: "This is another file." Click on File and Save. Where does it want to save it? Navigate to the Spring Classes folder and save it there. What if you also want to save another copy somewhere else right now? What is the easiest way? Click on File > Save. What happens? Where is the file saved? Try this one more time except this time, click on File > Save As—instead of Save. What is the difference? The very first time you save a file, the Save and Save As menu options both bring you to the Save As window. Once you have named your file and chosen the folder to save it in, however, your results will be different. Each successive time you choose Save after the file is initially named, it simply updates the file with any additional content you have added and doesn't ask for any information from you, such as where to save it or what to name it. You would choose the Save As option only if you plan to name it something different or save it somewhere else.

What if you want to move an entire folder with all of the files inside? Create a new folder in My Documents called "Classes." Now drag the Fall Classes folder onto the Classes folder and drop it. Check that it is in the Classes folder.

Now change your mind. Click the Undo button on the toolbar. The folder should go back to the My Documents folder where it was. This time, move both folders into the Classes folder at the same time. There is always more than one way to do something. One way to do this is to click one time on the Fall Classes folder, hold down the Ctrl key and click one time on the Spring Classes folder. Both should now be highlighted. Point to the highlighted area and drag and drop into the Classes folder.

Another way is to change to the List or Details view so you can see the files a little more easily. Holding the Ctrl key works for selecting noncontiguous (nonadjacent) files. If the files are contiguous (adjacent), you can click one time on the first file in the range you want, hold down the Shift key, and then click one time on the last file in the range to highlight them all at once.

What are some other ways to cut, copy, and paste? Click on Edit on the menu bar. Do you notice the shortcut keys to the right of them? For every mouse click you make there is usually a keyboard shortcut that you can use instead. The keyboard shortcut for Copy is Ctrl+C, Cut is Ctrl+X, and Paste is Ctrl+V.

Searching For Files and Folders

OK, it happens to the best of us. No matter how great the directory structure we create for ourselves to keep track of our files, every now and then we lose track of a file or folder. How can we easily find files or folders, even if we don't remember what we named them?

Figure 2.26

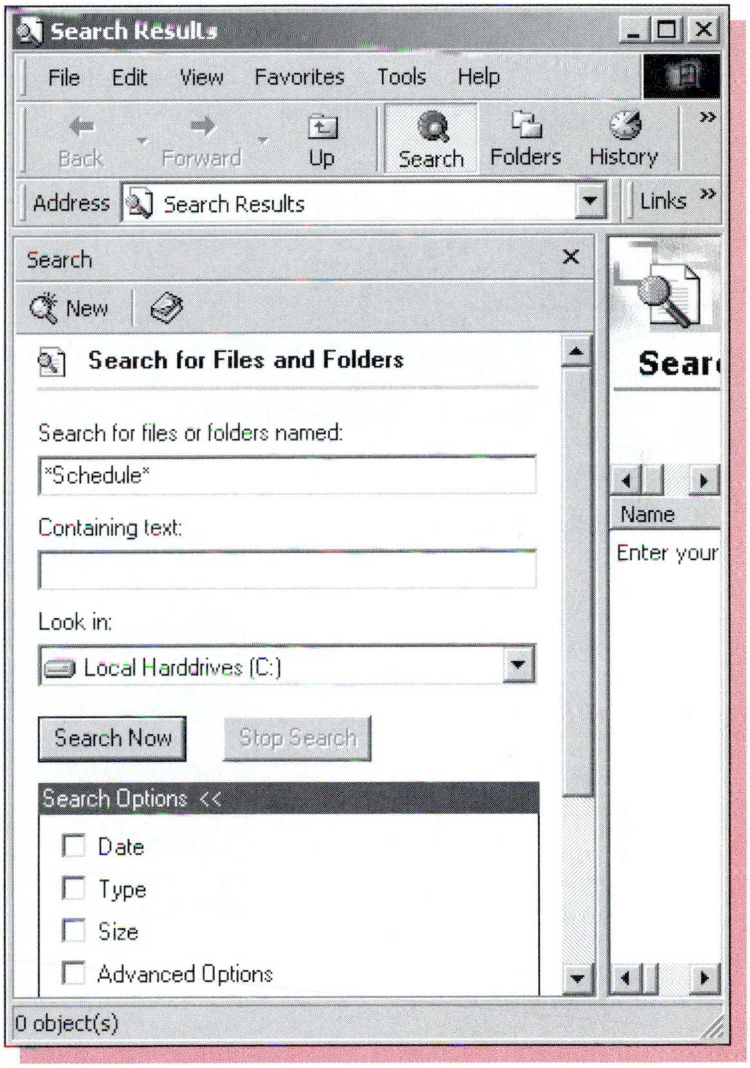

Click on Start > Search > For Files or Folders or click on Search in the My Computer window. What is the difference if you do it one way versus the other? Notice what is says in the Look in path where the search will take place. By default, the first method will perform a search on the local hard drives unless you manually change the path to narrow the search. The second method focuses the search on the folder you are viewing when you click the Search button.

If you can remember part of the filename, you can use wild cards to fill in the blanks. The asterisk is used as a wildcard to replace an infinite number of characters. The question mark is used as a wildcard to replace a single character. For instance, if I had named a file MY SCHEDULE OF CLASSES, an asterisk before and after the word SCHEDULE would find it.

NOTES   Rename the file SCHEDULE in the Fall Classes folder to MY SCHEDULE OF CLASSES. Do a search using *SCHEDULE* with the wildcards. What happened? Now try the search again without the leading wildcard, SCHEDULE*, to see the difference. What happened? Why?

As you can see from Figure 2.26, you can also search files containing specific text if you can't remember the name but do recall some of the contents.

In addition you have the search options. Searching by date is a handy feature if something bad happens to your computer. You can search for anything created or modified since the last time it was working correctly to help troubleshoot the problem.

For instance, if you notice that your computer started acting funny today you might do a search on all files modified or created in the last one day. Sometimes it's because files were modified, sometimes it's a virus, and sometimes it doesn't have anything to do with what you did that day. It's just one step in the overall troubleshooting process that you might take.

In the Search Results window on the right, you will see a listing of all files that match your search criteria. Sometimes it's easier to scan through the list if they are alphabetized or sorted by date. Click one time on the titles of each column to see it resort. What are the names of the column titles? What happens if you right click on one of them?

You should see columns for the name of the file or folder, the folder it is in, the type of file, and when it was modified. To reorder the list based on one of the columns, click once on the column heading.

File Types and Associations

If you navigate to the My Documents folder and see the icon for a Word document that you want to open, all you need to do is click on the file and the computer automatically knows to launch Microsoft Word. How does it know that? How does the computer determine correctly which files are associated with the application that created them?

Figure 2.27

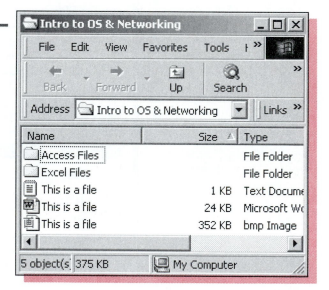

You may not see it in My Computer but in addition to whatever you name a file that you create with Microsoft Word, the filename is followed by an extension. For instance, the file "THIS IS A FILE" created with Microsoft Word is actually called "THIS IS A FILE.DOC."

Right click in the My Documents folder. The options listed to create new files are dependent upon the software applications installed on the computer you are sitting at.

You no doubt have the option to create a new text document, so create one and call it: THIS IS A FILE without typing a dot or anything after it.

Next create a Microsoft Word document with the same name, THIS IS A FILE, and use a third application, such as Microsoft Paint, to create a third document with the same name.

Why does the computer let you create three different files in the same folder with the same name? Why didn't it just overwrite the first file with the second when you tried to save it with the same name?

The answer is because they don't really have the same name. Not completely, that is. The full name of the first file shown in the preceding example is THIS IS A FILE.DOC, the second is THIS IS A FILE.TXT, and the third is THIS IS A FILE.BMP. The file name includes the file extension.

Although the current view settings are not configured to show the file extensions in the example above, it is telling you the type of file to the right of the filename, and the icons are also representative. In contrast, Figure 2.28 is an example showing the filename with the file extensions.

Figure 2.28

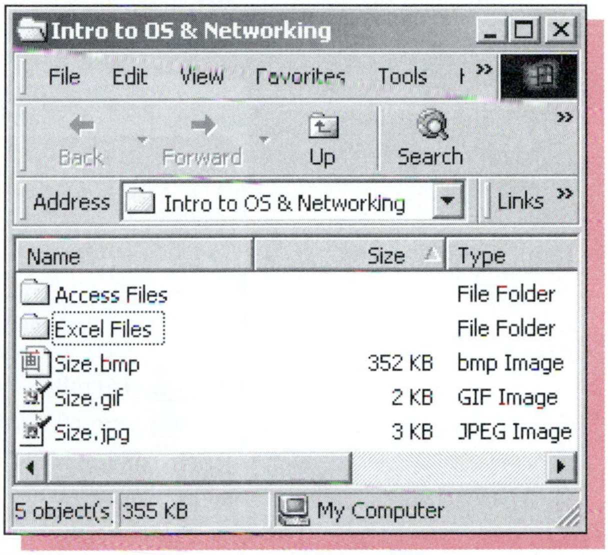

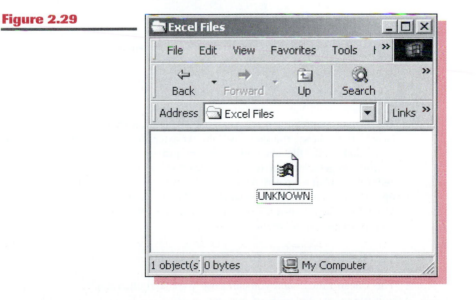

When you install applications such as Microsoft Word or Corel PhotoPaint, the applications register themselves with your operating system. They tell the operating system what file types belong to them. This information is stored in the registry. Think of the registry as a database that your operating system uses to keep track of applications and other information regarding how your computer is configured. When an application is installed, an entry is made in the registry listing what file extensions the application uses and ensuring that the application is associated with those file extensions.

To see what file types are associated with different applications, open My Computer > Tools > Folder Options > File Types. You can change what application should be used to open a file. Typically you won't want to but in some rare cases it is necessary.

Figure 2.29

If your Windows operating system encounters a file and doesn't know what application is associated with it, it uses a default icon such as the "flying windows" icon in Windows 2000 Professional. If you try to open the file by clicking on it in Windows 2000 Professional, the operating system will present a window to you listing all of the applications currently on your computer. In Windows XP Professional, it first asks if Windows should go online to look for the program that created it but also gives the option to select the program from a list. It wants you to choose which application you think will open the file. This usually happens when someone gives you a file on disk or e-mails it to you. On your computer you must have the same application program that they used to create the file or one that recognizes the file type.

Figure 2.30

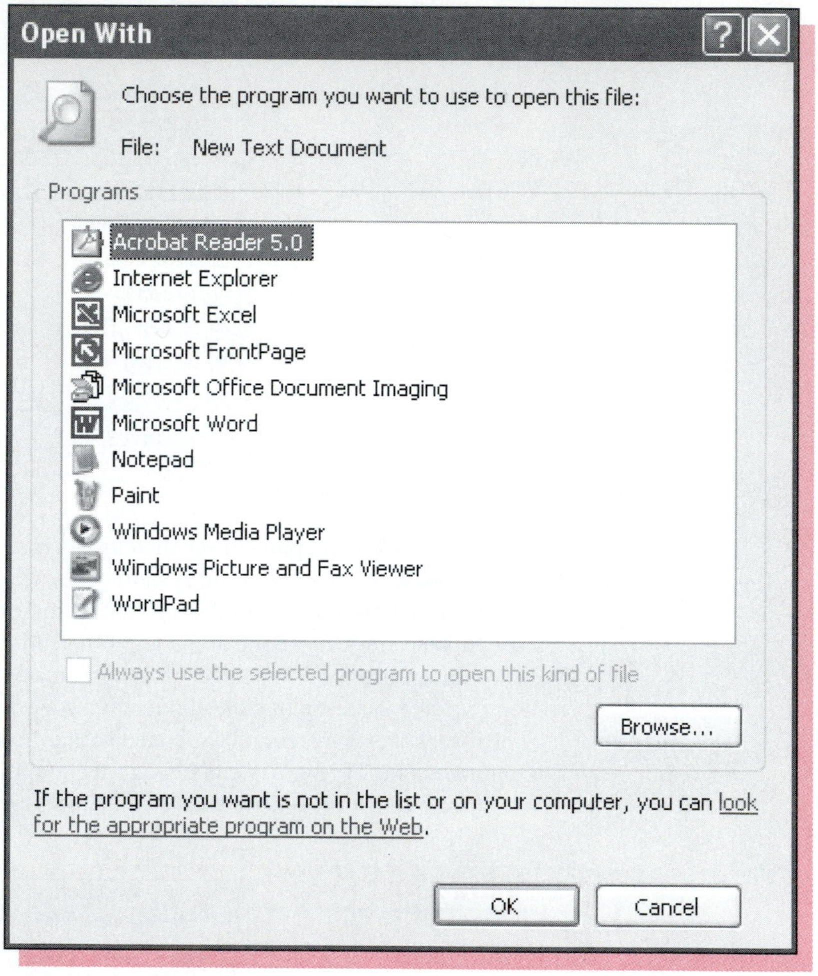

NOTES

First change your View settings to show file extensions (My Computer > Tools > Folder Options > View > and uncheck Hide file extensions for known types). Right click in the My Documents folder and create a NEW TEXT DOCUMENT. You should see the TXT extension. Then rename the file and leave off the extension (right click on the file, choose Rename and just get rid of the .TXT part).

You will get a message telling you that if you change a file extension, the file may become unusable. Tell it YES. What happens? What icon is used to represent the file? What happens if you click on the file to open it? A default icon is used whenever the operating system does not know what application is associated with a file or when the file type is unknown. Because the file extension has been deleted, there is nothing to indicate what the file type is.

This doesn't mean that you can't use Word and other applications to open types of files other than the default file associated with an application. But your best option would be to open Word first and then use Word to open the file. For example, your extensionless file isn't registered with Word but is really just a text file that Word can open. Double clicking the file won't launch Word and open it but you would still be able to open Word first and then open the file.

What file options does Word recognize automatically?

NOTES

Open Word. Click File, Save As, and check the list of file types.

Some file types are universal and can be recognized by most current applications. For instance, RTF (rich text format): this file type can be recognized by both Macintosh and Windows computers. In addition, most word processing applications can use it. However, the RTF format is not as prone to viruses as some other word processing documents are.

If you create a picture using Microsoft Paint, what icon is used to let you know it is a Paint file? What file extension is used?

Now let's go back to the message telling you that if you change a file extension, the file may become unusable. Under what conditions do you think that might happen?

Let's say you rename the Paint file you just created and give it a .doc extension. The operating system knows it is supposed to use Microsoft Word to open .doc files. What icon is used to represent the file after you change the name? What happens when you try to open the Paint image with the .doc extension?

So what are some of the common file types?

FILE TYPE	FILE EXTENSION
Microsoft Publisher	.pub
Microsoft Word	.doc, .dot
Microsoft Excel	.xls
Microsoft Access	.mdb
Microsoft PowerPoint	.ppt
Web page	.htm, .html, .asp, .aspx
Adobe Acrobat	.pdf
Sound File	.au, .wav, .snd, .mid
Movie File	.mpg, .avi
Graphics	.gif, .png, .jpg, .tif, .psp

Note: This list is not comprehensive

Earlier we renamed a Paint file with a .doc extension. The operating system then thought it was a Microsoft Word document but Microsoft Word was unable to open it. Well, that's not entirely true, it did open it; it simply didn't know what to do with it.

Since a graphics application such as Paint will allow you to save the file in different formats and can read different formats such as gif, jpg, and bmp, does that mean you could simply rename a gif file with a jpg extension and it will still work?

The answer is "not really." Some of it has to do with the compression algorithm used when the file was created. Gif files have their own way of saving a file and the information about the file (e.g., amount of colors it can display) and other file types such as jpg do it differently. So you might be able to open the file after changing the extension, but changing a gif into a jpg isn't going to allow it to display millions of colors. The different file types have a great deal to do with the size of the file as well.

To view all of the file extensions recognized on your computer, in My Computer or Windows Explorer, click Tools > Folder Options > File Types (see Figure 2.31).

NOTES

Using Paint, draw a simple circle and save the same file three different times as three different file types: bmp, gif, and jpg. Notice the difference in size.

Generally speaking, a bmp file really doesn't have much compression and the files are always fairly large. The most commonly used graphic file types in Web pages are gif and jpg. The png file type is supposed to eventually replace the gif file type due to legal issues. The main difference between a gif/png file and a jpg file is the number of colors it can display. So a gif/png file type would be appropriate for a simple graphic that you might draw yourself using Paint, whereas the jpg file type is more appropriate for a picture with millions of colors that you scan in.

Figure 2.31

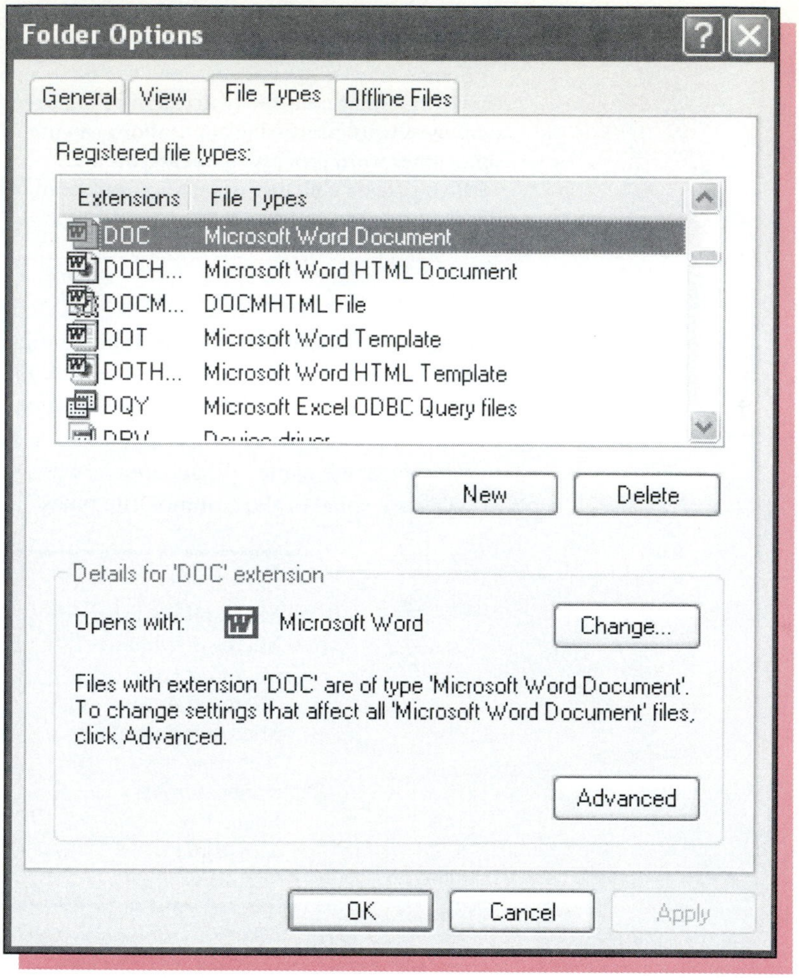

Summary

One of the biggest hurdles that new computer users face is navigating successfully. In addition to the directories created on the computer when the operating system is installed, you will also create your own to store your data files. Understanding where the folders are, how to navigate between them, and their function is difficult at first but is an important step when learning about an operating system.

Directories, now more commonly called folders, are similar to the manila folders you would use in a filing cabinet. You place your documents (files) into the folders in some order that makes sense to you. How you organize your files and folders on your computer will determine how easy it will be for you to find them when you want them. In addition, understanding the roles of special folders can allow you to take shortcuts.

ACTIVITIES

Review Questions

1. The first time you save a file, what is the difference between Save and Save As? For any subsequent time you save a file, what is the difference between Save and Save As?

2. What would you do to find a file that you knew was created eight days ago but you didn't know what it was called or where it was saved?

3. What does .RTF stand for? Why is it best to save a file as an RTF file if you plan to share it with someone?

4. Which is the correct answer if you wish to keep the most current version of the file (see Figure 2.32)?

5. How does the operating system know which applications are associated with specific file extensions?

Hands-on

1. To determine how much space you have on the hard disk, open My Computer and right click on the C:. Choose Properties from the context menu. How large is the C drive? How much space is free? How much space is used?

Figure 2.32

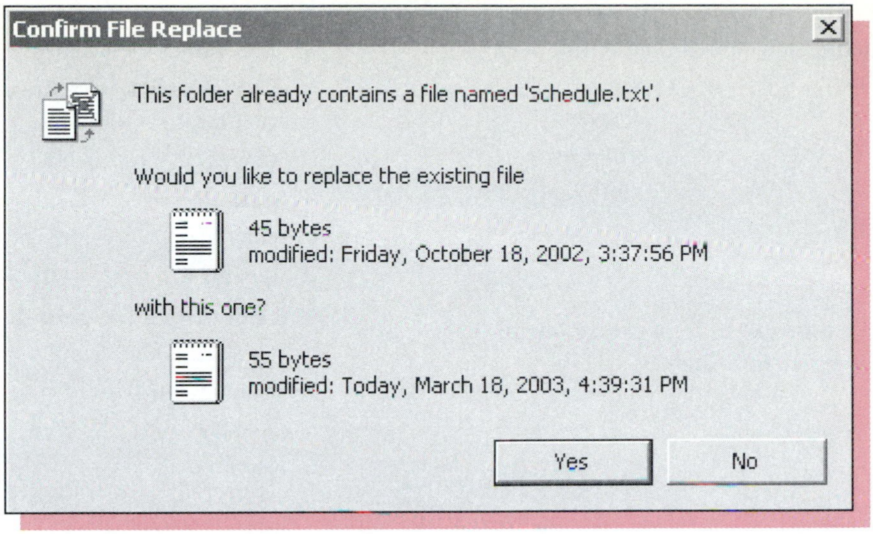

2. Using the Internet, list three typical file extensions for graphic files not shown as examples in the module.

3. Draw a directory structure that you might create for the classes you are taking this semester.

4. Create a file and save it to the hard drive, delete it, and then explain the steps you need to take to restore it from the Recycle Bin.

5. Explain why you might see Figure 2.33 and what it is expecting you to do.

Figure 2.33

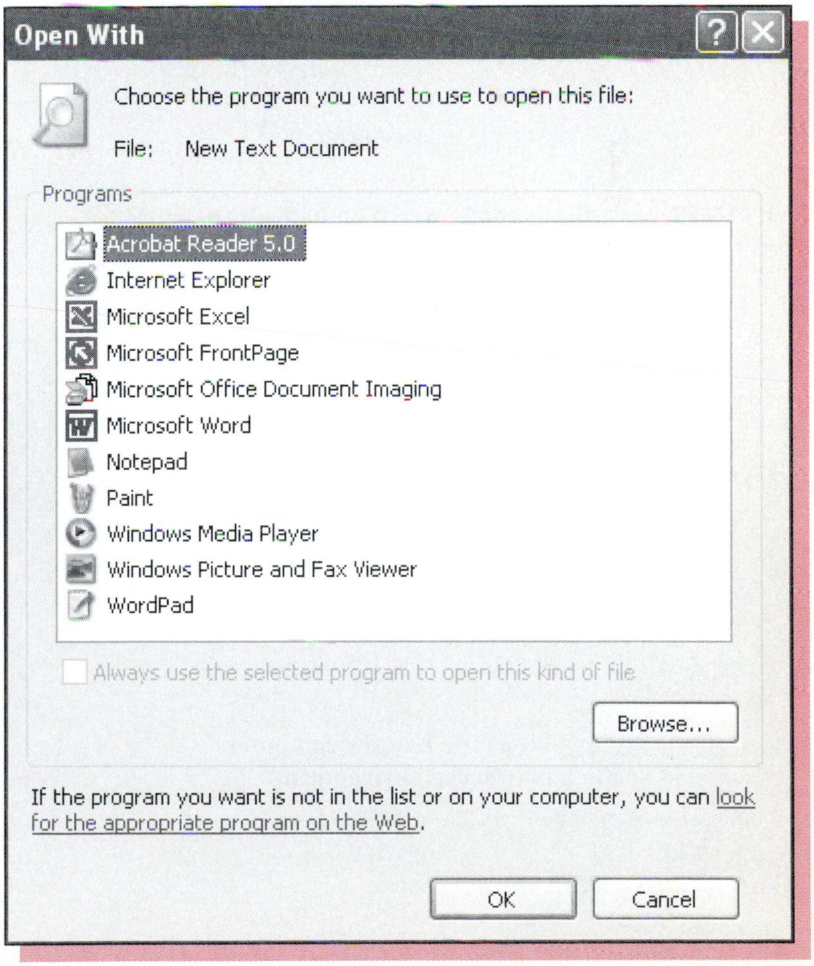

Important Terms

Using www.webopedia.com or another online technical dictionary, define:

bit	gif	kilobyte
bmp	gigabyte	megabyte
byte	hierarchical	registry
directory	jpg	

Multiple Choice Questions

1. _____ allow(s) us to organize our files so we can more easily find them.
   a. Navigation
   b. Folders
   c. Desktop
   d. None of the above

2. The _____ folder is the default place that most applications want to store your data files in.
   a. Start menu
   b. Recycle Bin
   c. Program Files
   d. My Documents

3. _____ is referred to as a path using the proper syntax.
   a. c;windows/desktop
   b. c:>
   c. c:\windows\desktop\My Documents
   d. c:/winnt/system32

4. The Recycle Bin is configured automatically to be able to store files equal to _____ of the size of your hard disk.
   a. 1 percent
   b. 5 percent
   c. 10 percent
   d. 15 percent

5. The _____ was really designed for users who also have a notebook computer and often work in files in two different places.
   a. Briefcase
   b. Suitcase
   c. Desktop
   d. Start menu

6. _____ keeps track of the computers around you in a networked environment.
   a. My Computers
   b. FTP
   c. Add Network Place
   d. My Network Places

7. If you right click on a file or folder, one of the context menu options is _____.
   a. remote
   b. send to
   c. copy to
   d. rename to

8. You can drop a file onto the start button to add it to the _____.
   a. Quick Launch Toolbar
   b. Taskbar
   c. Start menu
   d. Recycle Bin

9. Many operating system directory structures are _____.
   a. discrete
   b. disparate
   c. virtual
   d. hierarchical

10. The _____ of a directory structure is the topmost directory on the disk.
    a. root
    b. tree
    c. subdirectory
    d. base

11. If you prefer to _____ on a file versus _____, you can configure that setting by going into Tools, Folder Options.
    a. single click/double click
    b. double click/single click
    c. both of the above
    d. none of the above

12. _____ Explorer is a Web browser that allows you to more easily navigate the Internet.
    a. Windows
    b. Netscape
    c. Internet
    d. Microsoft

13. _____ Explorer is a tool that lets you more easily navigate the files and folders on your computer.
    a. Windows
    b. Netscape
    c. Internet
    d. Microsoft

14. **A floppy disk can hold _____ when it is formatted.**
    a. 2.0 MB
    b. 1.44 KB
    c. 1.44 MB
    d. 2.0 KB

15. **Examples of file _____ are read only, hidden, and archive.**
    a. types
    b. sizes
    c. attributes
    d. formats

16. **If you _____ a file you now have more than one instance of it; if you _____ a file, you only have one instance of the file.**
    a. borrow/delete
    b. move/copy
    c. copy/move
    d. none of the above

17. **Each copy of the file is referred to as a different _____ of the file.**
    a. attribute
    b. element

    c. version
    d. facet

18. **The _____ wildcard is used to replace an infinite number of characters.**
    a. !
    b. ?
    c. *
    d. &

19. **The _____ wildcard is used to replace a single character.**
    a. !
    b. ?
    c. *
    d. &

20. **To select noncontiguous files, hold down the _____ key when selecting the files.**
    a. Alt
    b. Ctrl
    c. Shift
    d. Space Bar

OBJECTIVES

After reading this chapter, you will be able to:

- Explain what DOS is
- Explain what GUI is
- Explain what a pipe is
- Demonstrate how to create a directory structure using DOS commands
- Demonstrate how to navigate a directory structure using DOS commands
- Demonstrate how to use the DOS edit program
- Explain what the 8.3 naming convention is
- Differentiate between copying and moving files
- Demonstrate how to use wildcard characters
- Demonstrate how to redirect output using DOS commands
- Demonstrate how to customize the command window interface
- Demonstrate how to write a batch file

INTRODUCTION

Although a graphical user interface is now the most common way to interact with the operating system on a computer, a fundamental knowledge of DOS commands remains important. A basic knowledge of DOS commands and the proper syntax of paths and switches will provide a solid foundation no matter which area of Information Technology you choose for a career. Often, this one area of knowledge will separate an average computer user from a true master. To really unleash the power of an operating system—or perhaps, more importantly, to control it—you still need to understand how to use command line statements. Even with Windows operating systems, DOS is still the underlying foundation and some of the more powerful utilities can only be done at a command line.

WHAT DOS IS

DOS stands for "Disk Operating System" and has been around since the very early 1980s. Like Microsoft Windows, DOS is also an operating system and has a user interface, or shell. Unlike the graphical user interface (GUI) used to interact with Windows, you interact with DOS via a prompt and the commands you enter. The command line is a user interface, but not a very friendly one. Shells, or more friendly user interfaces, are designed to make it easier for you to interact with the computer by acting like an interpreter. Microsoft's DOS is also known as MS-DOS but other companies had their own versions and examples are PC-DOS and DR-DOS.

The first version of MS-DOS was released in 1981. Over time, Microsoft released upgrades and new versions. Usually operating system upgrades are released to address buggy code, security issues, and other problems. New operating system releases are usually intended to address more major issues or implement enhanced features such as the ability to address a hard drive or a 3.5″ wide floppy drive instead of the older 5.25″-wide disk drives. It is easy to tell the difference between an upgrade and a whole new version based on the name. If the name of an operating system changes from DOS version (v.) 1.0 to DOS v. 1.25, it is an upgrade. If it changes from DOS v. 1.25 to DOS v. 2.0, it is usually a new operating system release. When the numbers to the left of the dot change, it is a new version. When the numbers to the right of the dot change, it is usually an upgrade. A new version may also address buggy code and security issues, but should introduce new features as well. The last separate release of MS-DOS was version 6.22 in 1994. Newer versions of DOS are still released and are shipped as an underlying foundation to the Windows operating system. You can enter DOS commands using the Command prompt or by writing batch files, which are discussed later in this chapter.

If you want to open a document in Windows, you click the document icon with your mouse. The GUI takes care of telling the operating system what you really want to do—edit the file. With DOS, there is no graphical user interface but there is still an interface and you key in the commands yourself. So, you are interacting more directly with the operating system and you have to learn the language that DOS understands.

Figure 3.1

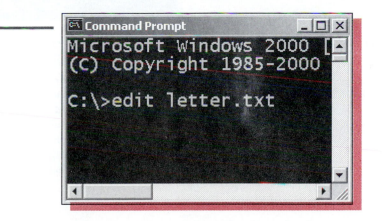

DOS isn't the only operating system that allows you to enter commands at a prompt. Novell Netware, UNIX, Linux, VAX/VMS and many others all had their start at the command line.

The reason for that was simple. In the early stages of computers, the rest of the hardware such as the video card, processor, and memory didn't support a graphical user interface. As technology advanced, our methods of interacting with the operating system did also.

As technology continues to advance, what methods of interaction do you expect to see in the future? Think about voice recognition software, for instance. Although several companies have such software on the market today, the technology is still in its infancy. However, as computer processor speeds and other components continue to improve, voice recognition software will be able to reliably replace the keyboard and mouse.

Don't get your hopes up too high, however. It has been 20 years since DOS appeared and DOS still has its uses. If or when the day of voice recognition software comes, no doubt tech support staff will still need to know how to use a command line utility and understand the syntax of a command line statement.

Understanding the Syntax

The word "syntax" is simply referring to the rules you follow to create sentences that are understandable to those around you. To interact with the operating system using command line statements, you have to learn the rules of another language. DOS has one way of doing things and its own set of rules; UNIX and Linux use different commands and have their own rules to follow and so on with other operating systems.

As old as DOS seems, it has also progressed over time and the available commands have changed. To find out what the current commands are that you can use, open up a DOS or Command Prompt window which emulates the DOS environment while in Windows. In Windows 2000 Professional and Windows XP Professional, it is found under Start > Programs > Accessories and is called "Command Prompt." You can also click Start > Run and then type in CMD. This is known as the command interpreter and is the DOS shell, or user interface. Its job is to take any commands you enter and pass them off to the operating system to execute. If you accidentally make a typo when you enter the command, you aren't given much assistance in the Command Prompt window but you should see an error message.

Once there, type in Help and press the Enter key. You should see a list of commands and a brief description of each scroll by. No doubt it scrolled by too quickly for you to read them all. You have two options: either use the scroll bar on the right side of the window to see all of the commands or start learning some DOS commands.

Figure 3.2

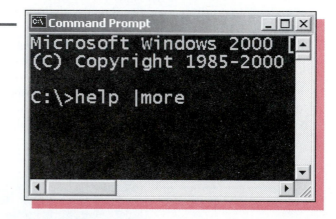

> **NOTES** This time enter the command Help|more. The straight line in front of the word *more* is called a pipe. It is often found near the Enter key on the keyboard and you'll have to hold down the Shift key to use it. When used with *more*, the pipe command filters the default output to make it easier to read. Rather than scrolling by too quickly, you will now see one screen at a time and it will pause until you tell it to move on. To scroll to the next screen, press the spacebar. Pressing the Enter key will scroll one line at a time. Pressing the spacebar will scroll one screen at a time, comparable to a page of information rather than one line of information.

In Chapter 1—Introduction to Operating Systems, you learned how to see a directory listing of files and subdirectories. Keying in dir /p will show you a listing and pause to show one screenful at a time. You should also see additional information such as the date and time the file was created or modified and also the names of subdirectories. In contrast, dir /w lists the contents without that additional information and also spreads the list horizontally across the screen versus listing them vertically one line at a time. Switches also can be combined. For instance, you can use both switches with the command DIR to further customize the output (DIR /P/W).

Let's take a closer look at some of the commands you see when you type Help. What do you suppose the Assoc command is for?

> **NOTES** Type in Assoc and see what happens. Look familiar? In Chapter 2—Windows File and Environment Management, you learned that files are associated with applications. The operating system knows that any file ending with a .doc extension, for instance, is a Word document. It knows that because when an application is installed, it registers its file associations with the operating system.

Also in Chapter 2, you learned that files have attributes such as system, read only, or hidden. What happens when you type in Attrib? You should see a listing of files with such attributes. To learn more about a command, type in the command followed by /?.

Figure 3.3

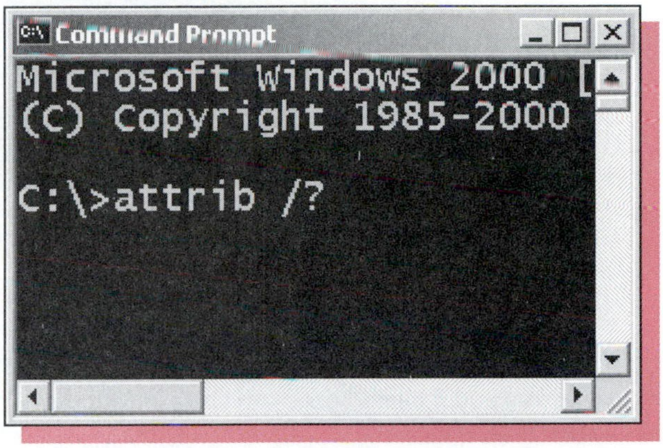

That shows you the correct syntax to use and also gives a brief description of the command. Many of the commands have switches (e.g., /) and other parameters (e.g., +, −) that can be appended to customize the command.

To change file attributes using DOS, you use either the plus sign to turn an attribute on or the minus sign to turn it off. For example, to make a file named LETTERS.TXT hidden the syntax of the command is Attrib +h LETTERS.TXT.

We'll continue to learn more of these commands throughout this chapter. For now, let's move on to navigating in DOS and creating file structures.

Navigation Using DOS

Before the advent of GUI, users navigated through the file structures and accessed folders using DOS commands at a prompt.

Figure 3.4

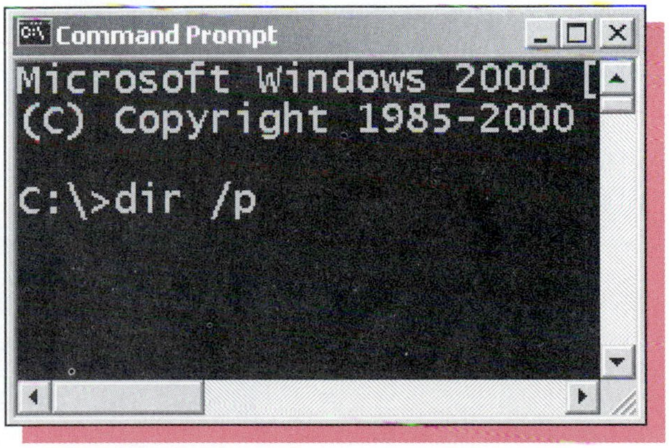

The prompt, in this case C:\>, is giving you a reference point. It's telling you which folder or directory on the computer you're in currently. In the days of DOS, folders were called directories. Any directory below another directory (a folder within a folder) was called a subdirectory.

NOTES   Click on Start, Programs, Accessories, Command Prompt. Type in dir /p (dir, space, forward slash, p) to see what happens. A Command Prompt window emulating the DOS environment will appear.

Figure 3.5

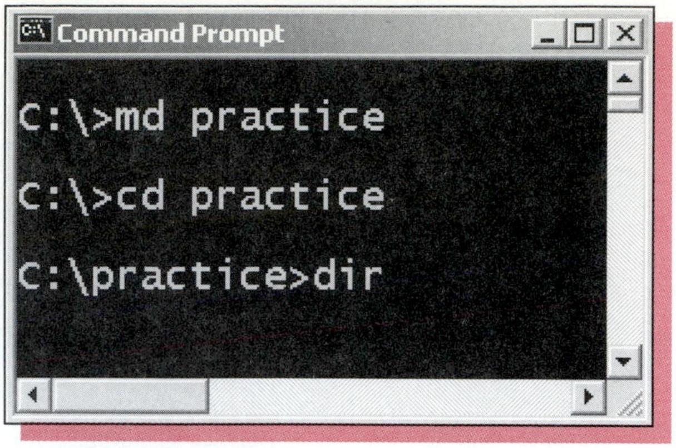

To create a new directory, type md (for Make Directory), a space and then the name of a directory (e.g., practice). The earlier versions of DOS were limited to 8 characters (with no spaces) to the left of the dot and 3 characters (with no spaces) to the right of the dot, so long file and directory names weren't really an option then.

Once you've made your directory, type dir /p again to see if it's there. Then you'll need to change to that directory. The command to change directories is cd followed by the name of the directory. So, if you called your directory "practice," the command is cd practice.

The DOS window remembers what you've typed in so you can save a few keystrokes. After entering a couple of commands, use the Up arrow on the keyboard to recall previous commands without having to type them again.

If you type the DOS command dir you'll see there's nothing really in the practice directory yet. The prompt, C:\practice>, is giving you a reference of where you are. To go back up one directory level at a time, you used cd .. (cd dot dot).

That's the change directory command with 2 dots after it. In the world of computers, two dots signifies "up one directory." One dot signifies the current directory.

If you were several directories deep (e.g., C:\documents and settings\administrator\desktop) but wanted to quickly go back to the root of the drive (C:), you could use the change directory command with a backslash (e.g., cd \). Although DOS will recognize the command if you do not enter a space between the cd and the backslash (\), it is technically correct to enter the space. However, if you ever use Linux or another variation of UNIX, the space is required.

Figure 3.6

There aren't many options for customizing your environment when using the Command prompt, but you can change the prompt itself.

NOTES   Change to your practice directory (cd practice). Type PROMPT My New Prompt.
The PROMPT pg will set it back to normal.
The PROMPT /? command will tell you all the switches you can use.

Some examples include:

$G > (greater-than sign)

$L < (less-than sign)

$N Current drive

$P Current drive and path

$Q = (equal sign)

That explains why PROMPT pg would give us the prompt C:\practice> .
$p is the current drive, C:, and the rest of the path, \practice, while $g gives us the greater than sign.
What are some more DOS commands? Type Help and they'll scroll by.

Designing Your Own Directory Structure

The commands to make a directory are very simple. Visualizing how you want to create the directory structure can be tricky. Let's say you want to create the following directory structure.

Figure 3.7

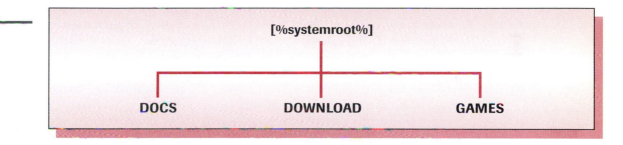

The word "%systemroot%" in the example shown is referencing the root of the directory. It is not unusual to have a computer's hard disk partitioned into smaller sections with different operating systems on each. Depending on the computer you are using for this class, the root of your directory might be C:, F:, G:, etc. and, of course, the root of a floppy drive would be A:.

In your DOS command window, check the prompt to learn more about what partition you are on and the path of the directory where you currently are. If your prompt isn't indicating that you are at the root, or topmost level, key in cd \ (cd, space, backslash). That will bring you quickly to the root of a drive no matter how deep into the directory structure you are.

Next, you want to create three folders. In this particular example, all three of the subdirectories you want to make are directly off the root. So you only need to enter three commands. First, type in md docs and then press the enter key. Then repeat the steps to create the download subdirectory and the games subdirectory. DOS is not case sensitive so it doesn't matter if you use uppercase or lowercase. UNIX and Linux are case sensitive which means Games and games would be two different directories.

To see if you were successful, enter the dir /p command and check the directory listing for your new subdirectories.

Figure 3.8

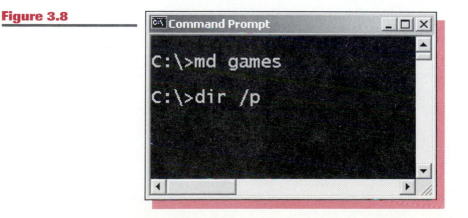

Figure 3.9

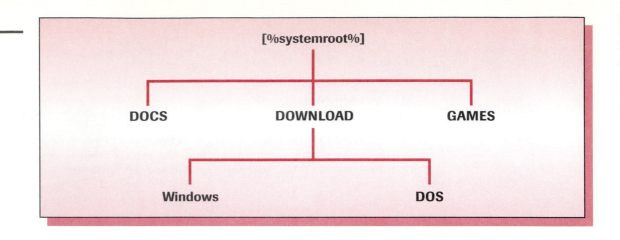

All of that should seem simple enough. It starts to get tricky when the directory structure gets a bit more complicated.

This example is similar to the previous example but has two additional subdirectories to create. But where would you create them? In the previous example, your prompt indicated you were in the root of the partition. That is exactly where you should be to create the docs, download, and games subdirectories. However, the windows and subdirectories are contained within the download subdirectory. To create them successfully, you must first change your location before you enter the md commands. To change your directory path or location, enter the command cd for Change Directory followed by the name of the directory you want to switch to.

Notice that your prompt will change to reflect your current path. At this point, you create the additional subdirectories, windows and dos.

Figure 3.10

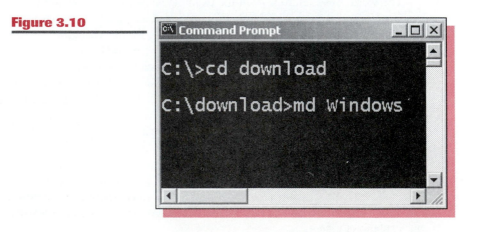

So you have created five new subdirectories. What is the full path to the new dos subdirectory you created? If your root directory is C:, the answer is C:\download\dos. To create the five new subdirectories, you entered a total of 6 commands:

md docs

md download

md games

cd download

md windows

md dos

Could you have created the same directory structure using only four commands? Let's test the theory with another example.

Figure 3.11

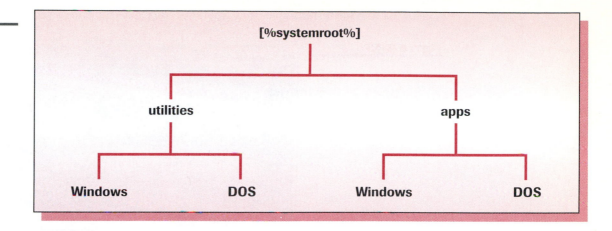

By now, you should have a fairly good idea of how to create this directory structure the long way. First, you might have to enter cd \ to make sure you're at the root of the partition. Then you can create the two subdirectories, utilities and apps, below the root. You would then change to each of those subdirectories and create the windows and dos subdirectories within.

The commands to do it the long way then might be:

cd \

md utilities

md apps

cd utilities

md windows

md dos

cd ..

cd apps

md windows

md dos

This is a total of 10 commands. Is there anyway to streamline it?

NOTES

Let's do it in four commands. Notice that I included the root of the drive in the command. In the example shown in Figure 3.12, I used C:. Writing DOS commands can be compared to programming. You need to be as specific as possible whenever you write code because you never know what your users will be doing or what partition they will be in when they run the code. By specifying the root, I am positive that the subdirectories will be created in the partition I expect to find them in.

We're able to create six subdirectories using four commands because DOS will also create the second level subdirectories, utilities and apps, if they don't already exist, when it creates the ones below them, dos and windows.

Figure 3.12

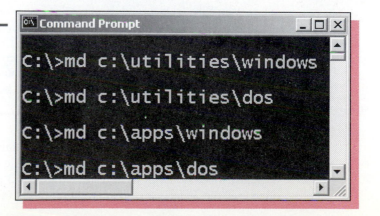

Now back to the first example. How would you create this directory structure with four commands?

Figure 3.13

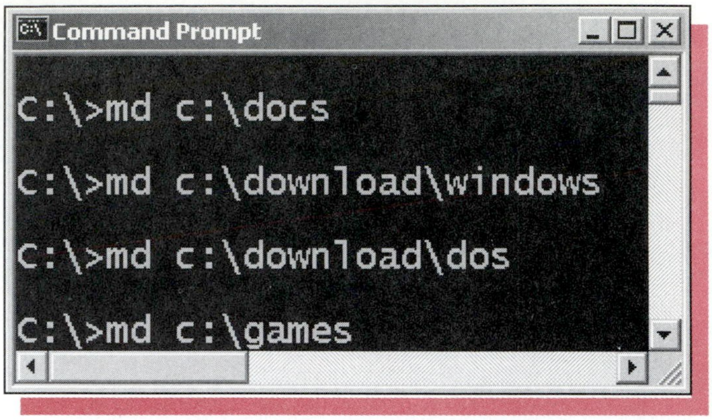

In the example shown, the commands are entered at the root of C:, so the commands would still work correctly if the reference to the C: drive were omitted—md docs versus md C:\docs. Retaining the C:\ reference is, however, a good habit to get into. Later in this chapter, you will be creating batch files. Since you never know what partition or directory the user will be in when they run the batch file, such careful attention to detail is important.

Figure 3.14

If you enter these commands now, you may get an error message telling you that the subdirectories already exist if you created them in the earlier example. Shortly, you will see how to avoid those messages.

Prior to GUI word processors, the DOS Edit command was pretty much your best option for creating a document. It is a simple text editor and you use it by typing in the command Edit. Generally, it is easier to name the file when you invoke the DOS Edit program.

CHECK IT OUT

Create a file called LETTERS.TXT in the subdirectory docs. In this example, the drive C: will be used but you should adjust accordingly if you are on another partition.

1. Change your path by entering cd C:\docs
2. Type Edit letters.txt
3. When the DOS text editor opens, key in a sentence such as "This is a sentence."
4. Notice that your mouse doesn't work in this editor but the arrow keys do. To save the file, hold down the Alt key and look at the menu bar. Certain letters in the menu options change color to reflect which ones you should use for each command. Press the F key to pull down the menu under File. Then the S key will save the document.
5. Alt, F, X will exit the program.

You can check your progress with the DIR command to see if your file is there. It should be called LETTERS.TXT. Notice that you had to specify the file extension; DOS does not append one for you automatically. Because users were restricted to an 8.3 naming convention in the early DOS days, people often used the 3 characters to the right of the dot to help keep track of their files. Long file names can now be 255 characters and it's a lot easier to name your files so they make sense and are easy to find. When you are restricted to a total of 11 characters, however, you need to be a bit more creative.

How would you copy the LETTERS.TXT file to the apps\dos subdirectory created earlier? You could do it with two commands as shown. How would you do it with one and ensure that the command would be successful no matter what partition or path the user was in when they ran it? The correct command for this would be Copy C:\docs\letters.txt C:\apps\dos

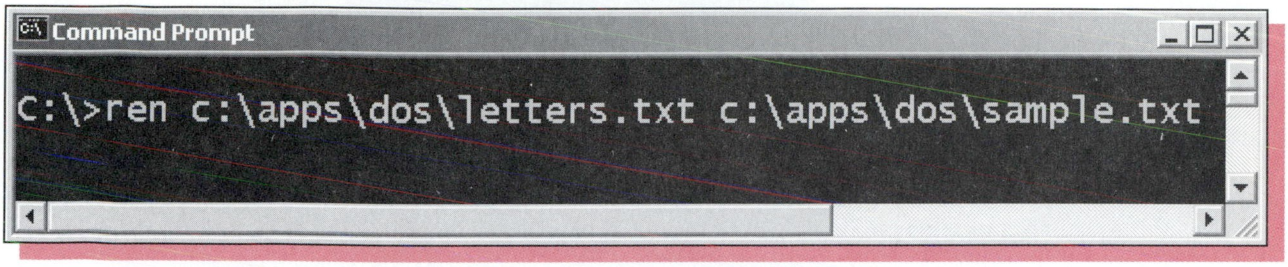

```
C:\>ren c:\apps\dos\letters.txt c:\apps\dos\sample.txt
```

Figure 3.15

By now you should have noticed that the commands in DOS are not case sensitive. That isn't true in all operating systems. UNIX and Linux, for example, do tend to be case sensitive.

After completing the Copy command, how many instances, or copies, should you now have of LETTERS.TXT? If you guessed two, you are correct. There should be one file in the docs subdirectory and one in the apps\dos subdirectory. If you had used the Move command instead of the Copy command, you would only have one copy and it would be in the apps\dos subdirectory. Remember, if you have a house key and get a copy made, you now have two keys. However, if you move your house key from one side of a table to another side of the table, you still have only one key.

To delete the original copy, the command is Del C:\docs\letters.txt. To rename the LETTERS.TXT file to SAMPLE.TXT file using DOS, the command is Ren C:\apps\dos\letters.txt C:\apps\dos\sample.txt.

Figure 3.16

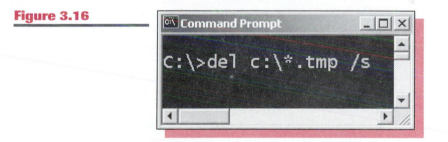

```
C:\>del c:\*.tmp /s
```

Using Wildcard Characters

Of course, that all works well if you are working with only one file and always know the name of it. Wildcards can come in handy when working with multiple files. There are two different wildcards that can be used, the question mark and the asterisk, but the asterisk is more commonly used. The question mark can be used instead of an individual character in a file name and the asterisk can be used to replace more than one character.

SAMPLE.?XT means the question mark is being used in place of any one character. Examples of valid matches include SAMPLE.AXT, SAMPLE.BXT, SAMPLE.2XT, and so on. You could also use SAMPLE.??? to represent any file extension, but the asterisk is more commonly used and is pronounced as "star." SAMPLE.* means any file named SAMPLE, no matter what file extension it has or how long it is. When you want to indicate all possible files, *.* is pronounced "star dot star" and means every file. If you wanted to copy all of the files in one subdirectory to another, the command would be Copy C:\docs*.* C:\download\docs. It works in Windows too. If you wanted to find all files on your computer with a .tmp extension, click Start > Find or Search, and then enter *.TMP. Temporary files such as this are often created by applications and are supposed to be deleted by the application after use but that doesn't always happen.

If you wanted to use a DOS command to delete all temporary files in a partition, the command is Del C:*.tmp /s. The /s switch stands for all subdirectories. Use caution anytime you are using a Delete command: You could wipe out all of the files on your drive. In addition, attempting to delete some .tmp files may cause problems if they are being used by the operating system at the time.

Figure 3.17

Make it a point to notice the direction of the slashes. A backslash is generally used in regard to a path and a forward slash is used as a switch. A switch means that you are turning on or off some additional parameter or setting to go along with the main command.

Redirecting Output

An old DOS command that isn't as useful as it used to be but is still fun to watch is the Tree command. It displays the directory structure of the partition you are in.

Figure 3.18

It isn't quite as useful as it used to be but old-timers often kept copies of the output in case they needed to rebuild a computer. It is still a handy command in terms of demonstrating redirection. The standard output for the Tree command is the screen and if you enter the Tree command at the prompt you will see the entire directory structure of your computer fly by. We can redirect the output to a file, however, using the > symbol and giving it the name of a file to redirect the output to. Any file name will do; the example uses TREEOUTPUT.TXT.

In addition to redirecting the default output, you can also use piping to filter the default output. The command Tree | more will pause after every screen. Pressing the Enter key will scroll one line at a time and pressing the spacebar will scroll one screen at a time. To quickly get back to the prompt, Ctrl+C should abruptly terminate the Tree command.

To check the contents of your new file, you can use the DOS editor to open it up. To open it, enter Edit TREEOUTPUT.TXT. Alt, F, X will get you out when you are done.

Figure 3.19

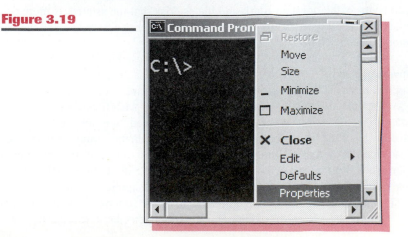

Customizing the Command Window Interface

By now you may be tired of looking at the white text on the black background and thinking that DOS is rather bland. Not to worry: We have some options. Right click on the title bar of the Command window.

Notice that the context menu has a couple of interesting options. Edit, for instance, will allow you to copy and paste from the DOS window. The Properties option will allow you to customize your Command window interface.

Figure 3.20

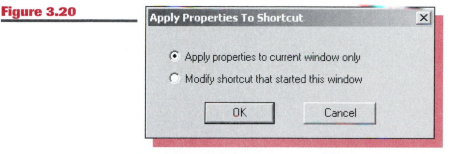

On the Options tab in the Properties window you can change the size of your cursor and have other display options for screen size, etc. On the Font tab you can change the size of your text. On the Layout tab you can change the size of your window and on the Colors tab you can make your DOS world a little brighter.

If you do make changes, it will ask if you want the new changes applied to the current window only or if you want the changes to be more permanent.

Figure 3.21

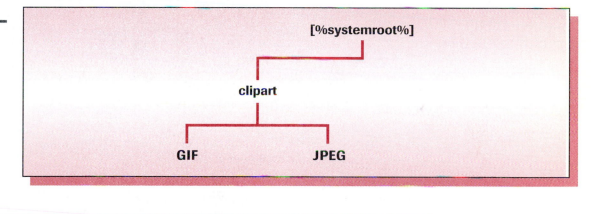

BATCH FILES

In most cases, the individual DOS commands you've worked with aren't really as useful now that we have GUI interfaces. It's much easier to drag and drop a file than to bail to a DOS prompt and key in a long command.

However, when you combine the commands and put them into a batch file they can still be very helpful. Batch files are written with text editors and contain line after line of code; each command is placed on a line by itself. If commands need to be repeatedly used, it is much easier to put them into a batch file and simply run it than to repeatedly type the commands.

To make a batch file from the commands, use either Notepad or DOS Edit. Actually, Microsoft Word or any other word processing application will work but you'd need to remember to save the file as file type plain text as opposed to a Word document and it needs to end with a .bat extension.

Figure 3.22

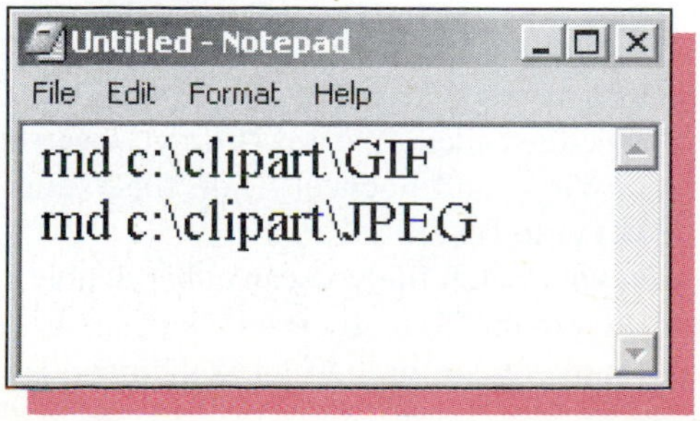

Untitled - Notepad

File   Edit   Format   Help

```
md c:\clipart\GIF
md c:\clipart\JPEG
```

For this example, Notepad will be used. Enter each command on a separate line. To create the directory structure shown, two lines of code can be used.

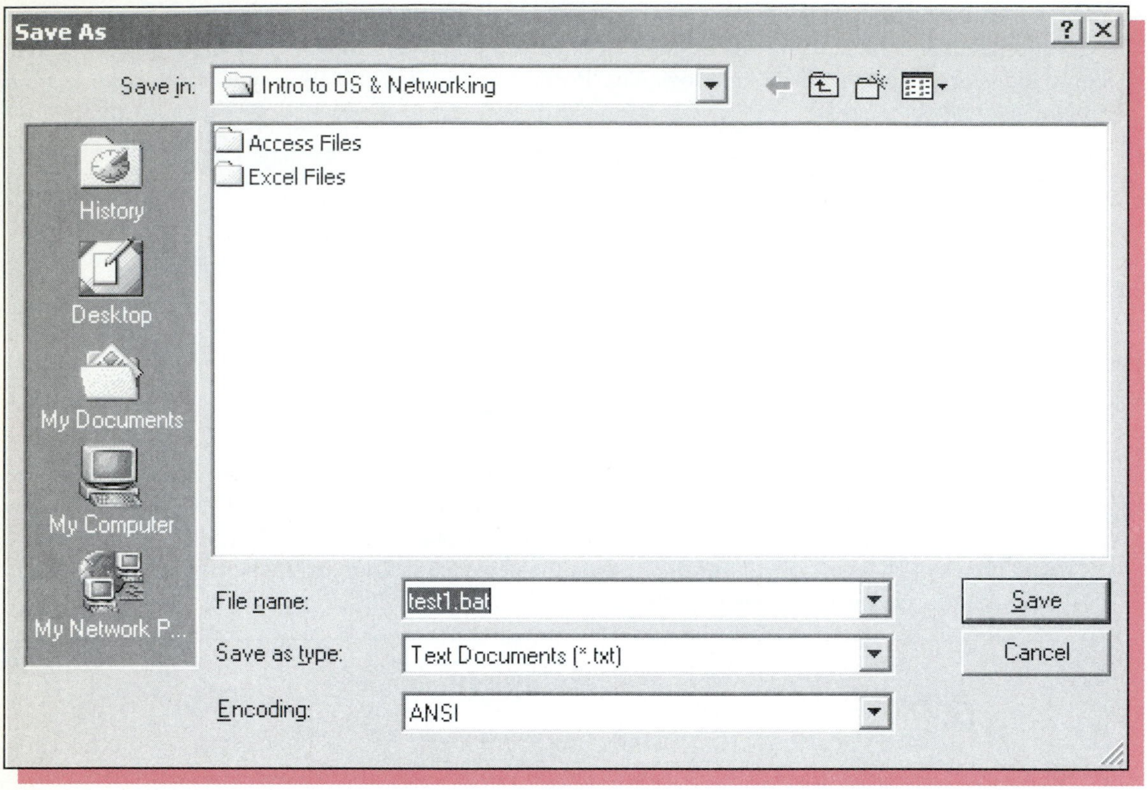

Figure 3.23

After entering the code, you need to save the file as a batch file. You do this by naming it and changing the file extension from the default of .txt to .bat.

Figure 3.24

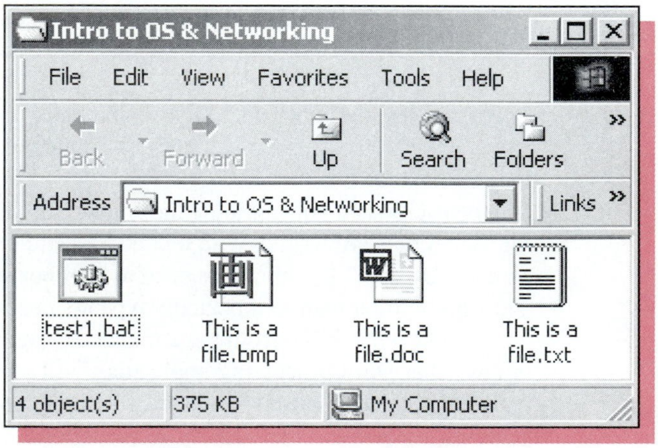

The icon for your new file, TEST1.BAT, should look like a program icon. If it is displaying a text file icon like the file called THIS IS A FILE.TXT, then you need to take two extra steps. Click on Tools > Folder options > View, and uncheck Hide file extensions for known types. Now rename your file from TEST1.BAT.TXT to TEST1.BAT.

To run your batch file you can either double click the icon or enter the name of your batch file at a Command prompt. To really test it and gain the most knowledge, use the Command prompt. You need to make sure you are in the same subdirectory you saved the file in and then you simply type in the name of the file. In this case, you would type in TEST1. The .bat part isn't required to run it; it works either way. The operating system searches for program files with the name TEST1. Other valid program extensions are .com and .exe. After running your batch file, check to see if the new subdirectories have been created.

If you saved the batch file on your desktop, what is the path to get to it using DOS commands? Windows 2000 Professional and Windows XP Professional keep different directory structures for each user who logs onto that computer so the path to the desktop will be different depending on your current logon name. If you are logged on as "administrator," for example, the path would be C:\documents and settings\administrator\desktop.

Knowing that, what would a batch file look like if you wanted to create two subdirectories on the desktop, Spring and Fall, and you are using Windows 2000 Professional or Windows XP Professional? See Figure 3.25 for the answer.

Figure 3.25

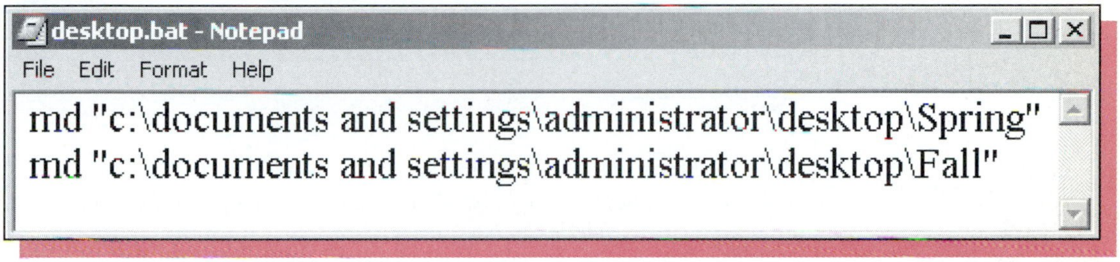

```
desktop.bat - Notepad                           _ □ ×
File  Edit  Format  Help

md "c:\documents and settings\administrator\desktop\Spring"
md "c:\documents and settings\administrator\desktop\Fall"
```

Notice the double quotes around the path. They are required because there are spaces in the part of the path for documents and settings. The double quotes tell DOS that it all goes together. A shortcut around that is to remember that the 8.3 naming convention still applies. That means that md C:\docume~1\administrator\desktop\Fall would also do the trick. The tilde (~) can be used to replace characters keeping within the 8 character restriction and is usually found in the upper left corner of the keyboard. Use the first six characters of the filename (not counting spaces) and then add the tilde and the numeral 1.

If you have two files with long names and the first six characters are the same, the second file will have a numeral 2 following the tilde. For example, if you have one file named THIS IS MY FALL HISTORY HOMEWORK.DOC and another named THIS IS MY FALL MATH HOMEWORK.DOC, the first file would be THISIS~1.DOC and the second would be THISIS~2.DOC.

NOTES   In Windows 2000 Professional or Windows XP Professional, make sure you are at the root of the partition and then change directories to Documents and settings with the command Cd documents and settings. Do a directory listing (Dir) to see what is there. Go back to the root with the cd \ command. Next, change to docume~1 with the Cd docume~1 command. Do a directory listing to see what is there.

Figure 3.26

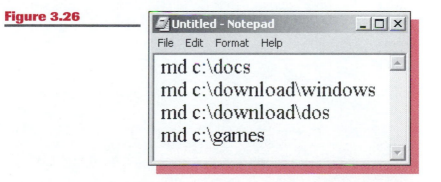

```
Untitled - Notepad                 _ □ ×
File  Edit  Format  Help

md c:\docs
md c:\download\windows
md c:\download\dos
md c:\games
```

In a previous example, you created a directory structure using four commands. Create another batch file called test2.bat using the same commands you used before.

Figure 3.27

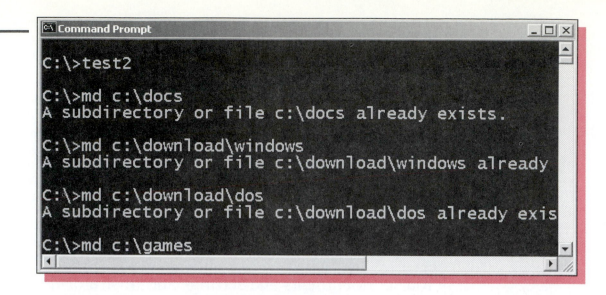

What happens when you run the batch file? You should get an error message saying that the directories already exist because you already created them in a previous example. Typically, you wouldn't want your commands to display an error message because it can be confusing. To avoid having an error message displayed, you can employ a little error checking in your code.

Edit your batch file and add some additional code in front of each of your commands as shown then run it again. You edit the batch file by right clicking on it and choosing Edit. If you double click the icon, you will run the batch file.

Figure 3.28

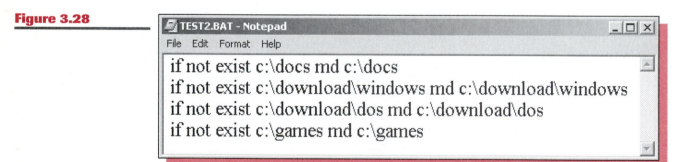

These commands are checking to see if the subdirectories already exist. If it doesn't currently exist, the end part of the command tells DOS to go ahead and create it.

Figure 3.29

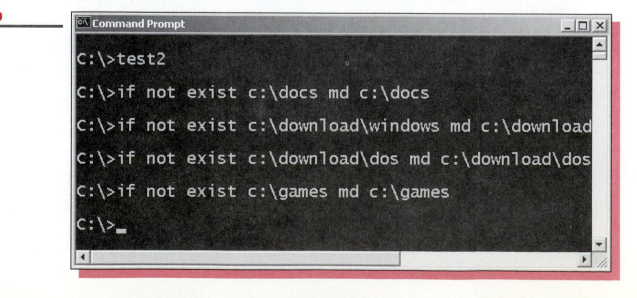

You should no longer have error messages but it does still display the code itself as it executes. This may confuse a typical user. To really have clean code, you might want to add another line, @echo off, which will stop the displaying of code as it executes. Where you place the @echo off command is important. It will only stop code from being displayed on the standard output device, usually the screen, from that point on.

This time when you run your batch file, it should not display any messages and should simply return you to a prompt.

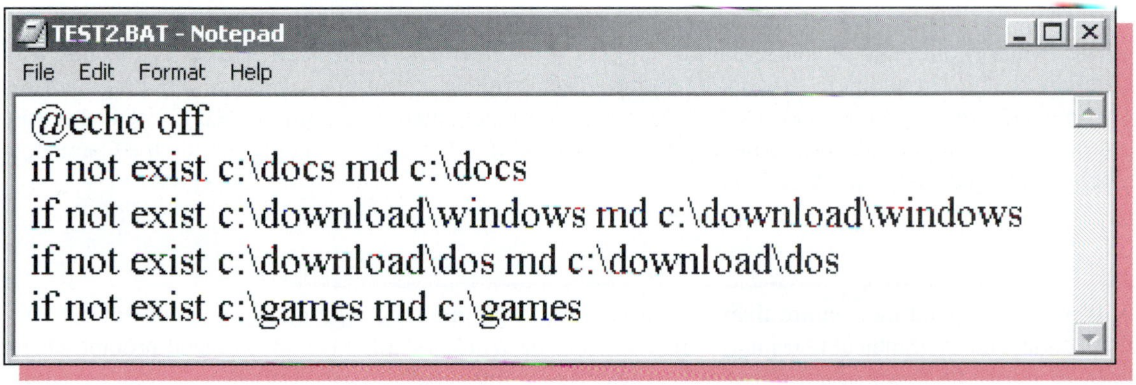

```
TEST2.BAT - Notepad
File   Edit   Format   Help
@echo off
if not exist c:\docs md c:\docs
if not exist c:\download\windows md c:\download\windows
if not exist c:\download\dos md c:\download\dos
if not exist c:\games md c:\games
```

Figure 3.30

THE TRUE POWER OF DOS

The true power of DOS really only becomes evident when you are working in the information technology field. You may be thinking that it was kind of nice to see what DOS commands and batch files are so you can astound and amaze your friends with your knowledge but other than that you may not be able to think of when you would need to use this knowledge. So let's think of some examples.

Picture a sunny day: you are the network administrator in a high school setting. Let's say a teacher has students working on their typing homework. They have to key in whatever is required and then print a hardcopy to receive a grade. The teacher isn't comfortable with them using floppies because it increases the chances for viruses so he has them save their documents in a class folder on the hard drive of each computer. Unfortunately, it didn't take the students long to figure out how to pull up the file from the class period before them, change the file name, print it out, and submit it for a grade. Then they'd get to play on the Internet as a reward for quick work.

One solution to this problem would be to create a batch file that deletes all documents in the class folder on the hard drive and place this batch file in the Startup folder to run each time the computer boots or a new user logs in. Click Start > Programs or All Programs and then right click on the Startup option in the Programs menu. From the context menu, choose Open. The Startup folder is just another special folder on the computer. Any files you place in here, even a Notepad document, will run when the computer boots or a new user logs in. Something else you can place in your Startup folder is a batch file to delete all of the cookies and/or temporary Internet files placed on your computer when you are on the Internet. I have also seen some schools place a copy of their AUP (acceptable use policy) in the Startup window to remind students of the rules they must follow when using the computer.

Having a good understanding of batch files is useful when you "image" a computer. Imaging a computer means that you make a copy of everything on the computer including the operating system, application files, and data files so that you can restore the computer to that state or so you can make copies of it onto other computers. Imagine that you maintain several labs of computers at a college campus and every semester you want to wipe all of the changes that have been made to them and put them back to their original state. You wouldn't want to go to each individual computer and install the operating system, then install each application, and necessary data files, etc. Rather, you would set up one computer the way you want it and then use an imaging application such as Symantec's Ghost or StorageSoft's Image Cast to clone it to selected other computers.

Often, the process of doing so requires that boot disks be made containing batch files and drivers and these sometimes need to be customized to your specific needs at the time (A boot disk is a floppy disk that has enough of an operating system on it to boot a computer.) There are also home editions of this software to allow you to take an image of your hard disk. You could archive it to a CD and if your computer crashes, you could more easily get back up and running in a lot less time.

Another example is using a batch file to easily back up your data files. Say you save all of your files in one folder as you work throughout the day. You could write a batch file that copies all of the files to a Zip or floppy disk and at the end of the day just double click the program icon to have a quick backup of your day's work.

In a networked environment, logon scripts use similar commands. A logon script runs whenever a user logs in. The network administrator writes the script and configures the account to run it at logon. The syntax is different, of course, but the concept is the same and knowledge of DOS commands will definitely help. In addition, network operating systems often have utilities that can only be run at the Command prompt. With Windows 2000 Server, for instance, there is a utility called CSVDE that can quickly produce user accounts from a comma-separated text file and it can only be run at a Command prompt using the appropriate switches.

Summary

Typical computer users will probably spend their entire lives never needing to know a DOS command. A graphical user interface, mouse, and a keyboard will suffice for now and it is probable that they will be replaced with voice commands in the future. However, if you plan to work with computers for a living, understanding and using DOS commands and other utilities entered at the Command prompt will give you an edge over others who do not.

Text-based DOS preceded a graphical environment but current versions of Windows still have a Command prompt where you can do everything that you can in Windows, including creating files and directories and passing commands to the processor. The key is understanding the syntax of the commands. Combining these commands into batch files to automate a process is where the true power of DOS and other command-line utilities show their importance in the world of computing.

ACTIVITIES

Review Questions

1. What command would you use to see a directory listing with the results shown horizontally?

2. What are two different ways to get to the Command prompt?

3. What does the RD command do? What is the correct syntax for the command? What switches can you use with it and what do they do?

4. In your own words, compare the COPY and XCOPY commands.

5. What is a wildcard?

Hands-on

1. Write a batch file to create two folders on your desktop: DATA and STUFF.

2. Use DOS Edit to create two text files and save them in DATA.

3. Write a batch file to move the files from DATA to STUFF and delete DATA.

4. Do a search for all files ending in *.txt.

5. Write a batch file to delete all of the cookies on your computer.

6. In the Command prompt, use redirection to create a text file from the Help command. This should result in a file that lists all of the DOS commands with a brief description of each command.

Important Terms

Using www.webopedia.com or another online technical dictionary, define:

backslash	path	standard output
batch file	prompt	switch
clone	redirect	syntax
forward slash	root	wildcard
GUI	shell or user	
partition	interface	

Multiple Choice Questions

1. **Usually, a backslash is used as part of a _____.**

   a. syntax

   b. command

   c. path

   d. switch

2. **Usually, a forward slash is used to denote a _____.**

   a. syntax

   b. command

   c. path

   d. switch

3. The role of the _____ is to take any commands you enter and pass it off to the operating system to execute.

   a. shell

   b. command interpreter

   c. user interface

   d. all of the above

4. To get a listing of all available DOS commands, type in _____ at the Command prompt.

   a. dir /p

   b. list

   c. help

   d. /?

5. To learn more about a particular command, key in the command followed by _____.

   a. dir /p

   b. list

   c. help

   d. /?

6. If you use the _____ command, you will have more than one instance of the file.

   a. Paste

   b. Move

   c. Copy

   d. Send

7. If you use the _____ command, you will have only one instance of the file.

   a. Paste

   b. Move

   c. Copy

   d. Send

8. This command will leave you in the current directory without giving an error message.

   a. cd /

   b. cd ..

   c. cd .

   d. cd \

9. This command will take you one level above, also known as the parent directory.

   a. cd /

   b. cd ..

   c. cd .

   d. cd \

10. This command will quickly take you back to the root of the partition.

   a. cd /

   b. cd ..

   c. cd .

   d. cd \

11. Based on Figure 3.31, what is the full path to the Windows subdirectory?

   a. G:\> cd download\windows

   b. G:/download/windows

   c. G:\docs\download\games\windows

   d. G:\download\windows

12. If your prompt is C:\docs and you enter the command Move letters.txt f:\apps\dos, what is the full path to the file letters.txt?

   a. C:\docs\apps\dos

   b. F:\apps\dos>letters.txt

   c. F:/apps/dos/letters.txt

   d. F:\apps\dos\letters.txt

13. If you searched for all files using this wildcard— Letters.?xt—what are valid filenames that would be found? Choose all that apply.

   a. Letters.6xt

   b. Letters.fft

   c. Letters.xxt

   d. Letters.txt

Figure 3.31

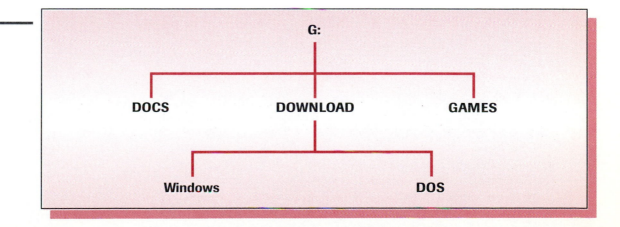

14. **If you searched for all files using this wildcard—Letters.*—what are valid filenames that might be found? Choose all that apply.**

    a. Letters.6xtempt

    b. Letters.fft

    c. Letters.1234

    d. Letters.txt

15. **In the world of computers, two dots signify _____.**

    a. past directory

    b. previous directory

    c. current directory

    d. up one directory

16. **In the world of computers, one dot signifies _____.**

    a. past directory

    b. previous directory

    c. current directory

    d. up one directory

17. **If you were several directories deep (e.g., C:\documents and settings\administrator\desktop) but wanted to quickly go back to the root (C:) of the drive, you could use the change directory command with _____.**

    a. cd .

    b. cd ..

    c. cd \

    d. cd /

18. **Which switches would have to be used with the Prompt command if your current prompt was C:\practice?**

    a. gp

    b. qp

    c. %g%p

    d. pg

Windows Utillties

After reading this chapter, you will be able to:

- Explain the importance of maintaining your computer
- List several maintenance tools that come with Windows and explain what each does
- Demonstrate the Disk Cleanup tool
- Demonstrate the Defrag tool
- Demonstrate how to back up and restore data
- Demonstrate how to boot a computer into Safe mode
- Explain how to create a boot disk
- Explain how to download and install software
- Demonstrate how to compress files and folders using WinZip
- Demonstrate how to compress files and folders using Windows
- Explain what viruses are and how to prevent them
- Explain what a hoax is
- Explain the function of a firewall
- List at least three security measures you can take to protect your computer

INTRODUCTION

A computer isn't a magical thing; it's a tool that needs to be maintained. Most operating systems, including Windows, come with tools that allow us to do that more easily. There are also a lot of other tools that can be used to help maintain our data and our security. Many can be downloaded from the Internet as shareware or freeware and these tools are generally adequate for minor maintenance. More powerful and easier-to-use tools need to be purchased.

Although we now have a lot more options for storing bigger files and transporting them, compressing them still comes in handy, especially in connection with the Internet. For a nonwork-related example, it is much easier to send one zipped file containing all of your family photos to a relative across the country than a couple dozen separate files. For maintaining your computer, the tools you download from the Internet are compressed (for quicker download) and consequently you will often need another tool, such as WinZip, to uncompress the files.

Of course, anytime you are sending or receiving files from the Internet, viruses become an issue. Viruses don't just happen by accident. They are programs designed to cause you difficulties that can range from mild annoyance to a total system failure.

Perhaps one of the most important issues in the field of information technology today is security. With the user explosion on the Internet, many people are excited about being connected but ill-informed about the potential risks they are taking. Although hackers used to focus on large corporations, they are now looking at the typical home user. The reason for this is most corporate networks have tightened security to fend off the hackers, whereas most home users haven't yet learned the potential dangers and taken sensible preventative measures.

MAINTAINING YOUR COMPUTER

There are several aspects of computer maintenance. For example, it is important to know what components are inside your computer in case you ever need to update hardware and software or reinstall the operating system. Often, when you use your computer, temporary files are stored on your computer and are not removed. You should be able to recover the used space to increase efficiency. Also, as you write files to your disk they aren't actually stored in contiguous chunks on the disk. As files are deleted, they leave gaps, or fragmentation, that causes your computer to work harder. You can use standard tools that come with Windows to keep track of your system components and maintain your data.

Tools that Come with Windows

System Info After spending quite a bit of money for a nice computer, you might feel a little sad when you learn it's outdated before you ever get it out of the box. Updating a computer is a fairly common thing. Certainly, it can be cheaper than buying a brand new computer. So it's important to know what components you already have in your computer. In addition to the hardware, you should also take a look at the versions of drivers and even the Service Packs. Service Packs are updates for the operating system and application software. Service Packs usually include security enhancements, fix buggy code, and sometimes include new features.

Figure 4.1

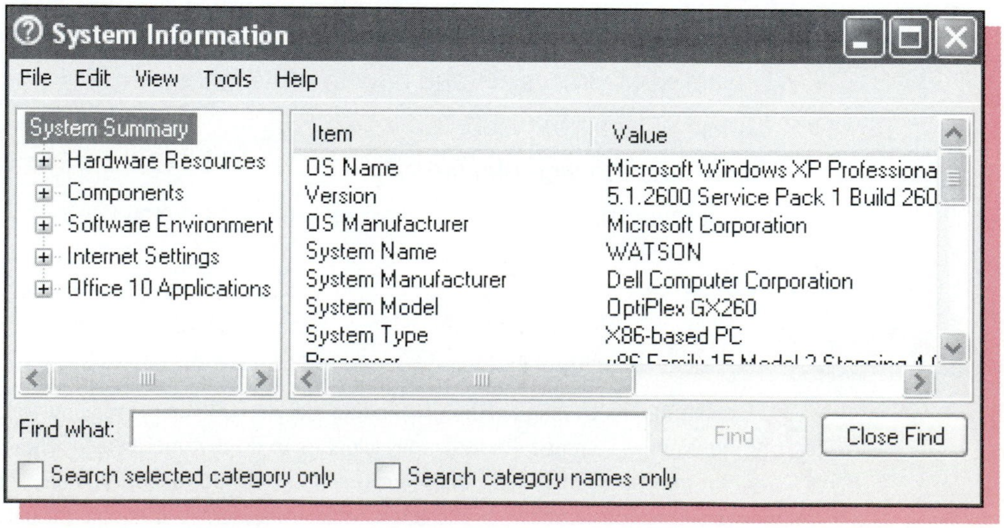

NOTES To view some of your system information, click on Start > Programs or All Programs > Accessories > System Tools > System Information. What is the name of the operating system on the computer you are sitting at? In Figure 4.1, the computer name is WATSON. Check if your Service Pack is current. The Service Pack installed on the computer is listed where it gives the version information. In the example shown, Service Pack 1 for Windows XP Professional is installed. You can compare the version on your computer with the current version offered on the Microsoft web site at http://windowsupdate.microsoft.com. Note that in addition to a link to update your operating system on the Windows Update site, there is also a link for the Microsoft application software. Application software also has Service Packs and should be updated regularly.

Under Components, what is the name of the display adapter on your computer? You have the option of printing all of this information or saving it as a text file. Choose Action in the Windows 2000 Professional snap-in or click File > Print in Windows XP Professional.

Figure 4.2

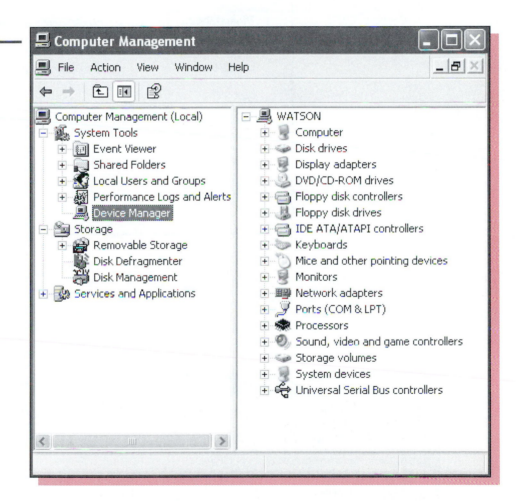

Local Disk Properties Another place to find information about your system is Computer Management. In Windows 2000 Professional, click Start > Settings > Control Panel > Administrative Tools > Computer Management, then click on Device Manager. In Windows XP Professional, click Start > Control Panel > Administrative Tools > Computer Management. In both Windows 2000 Professional and Windows XP Professional, you can also right click on My Computer and choose Manage.

In addition to listing all of the system components, you can also view the properties to get more information such as the version of a driver. If a hardware component isn't working, sometimes updating the driver will resolve the problem. That usually involves downloading a newer driver from the manufacturer's Web site. To do so, you need to know the exact make of the hardware component.

Figure 4.3

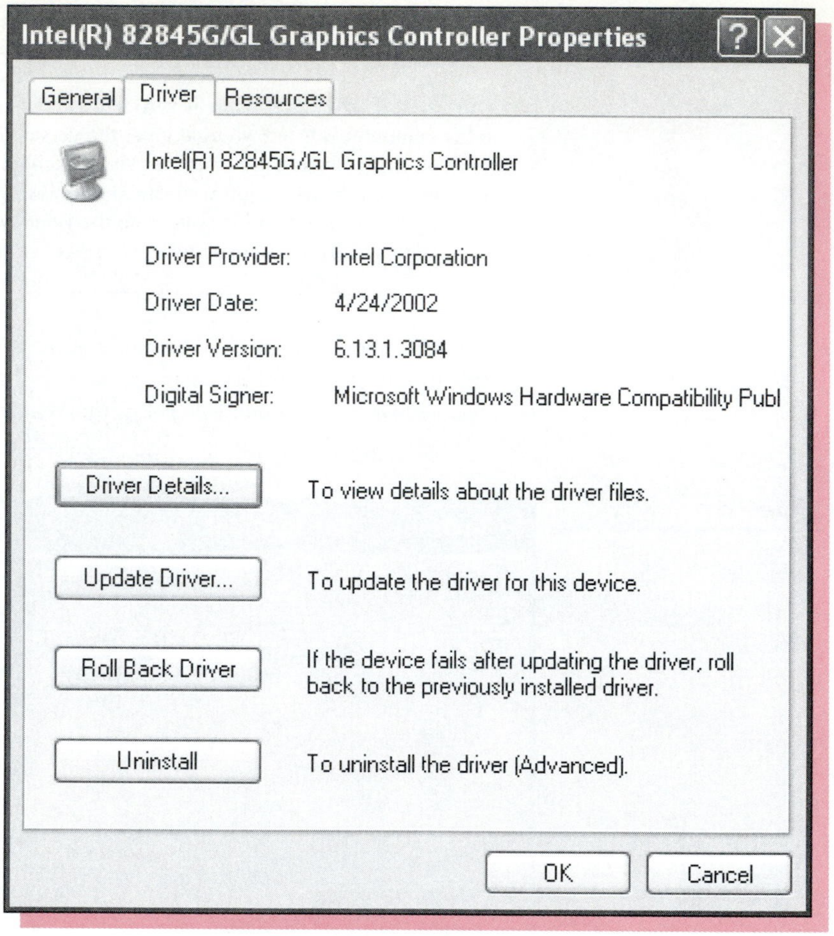

Notice that you also have an option called Event Viewer here. What kinds of information do you find there? You should find three different logs: Application, Security and System. These logs keep track of different activities on your computer.

When you view entries in the logs, you will notice that some of the entries are information, some are warnings, and others are alerts. Different icons are used so you can tell at a quick glance if an entry is just routine information or alerting you to a potentially serious system problem. Many of the entries are

Figure 4.4

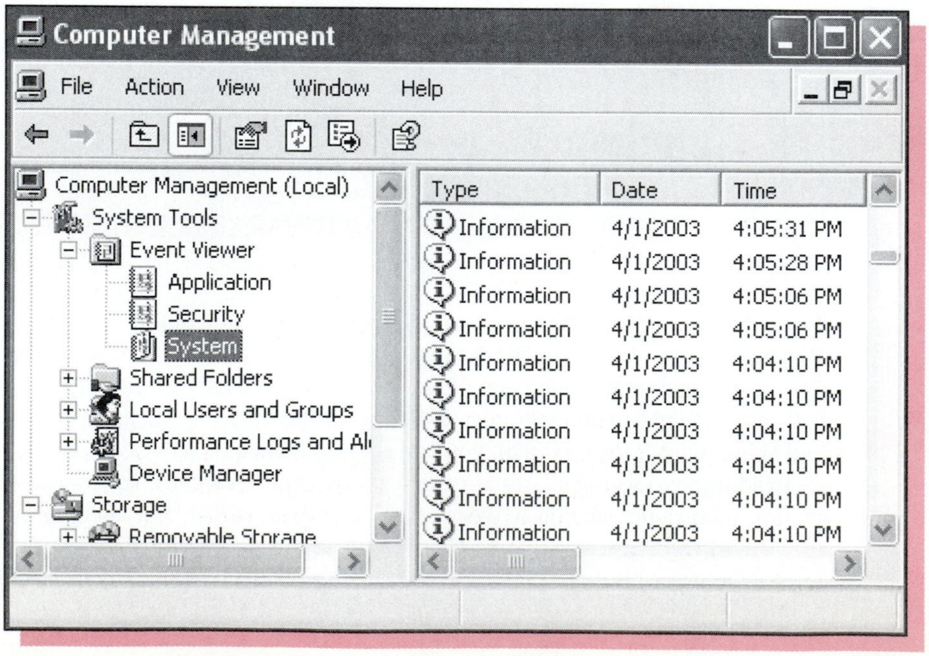

made as the system "boots" (starts up) or shuts down. You should see entries in both the Application log and the System log. Entries in the Security log are only made if you configure the operating system to track specific events.

Figure 4.5

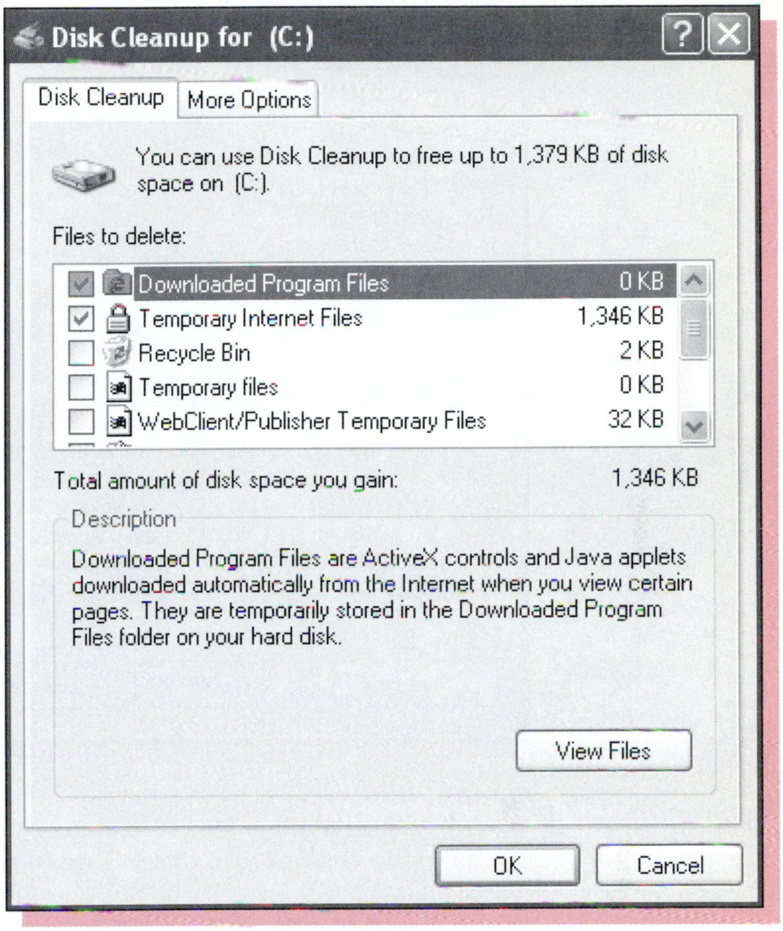

Disk Cleanup Disk Cleanup is a very handy tool that deletes temporary files that are no longer needed. You can find it by clicking Start > Programs or All Programs > Accessories > Disk Cleanup. Another way to get there is to open My Computer, right click on a hard drive or partition (e.g., C:) and choose Properties. The dialog box will have a button for Disk Cleanup and a host of additional information about your hard drive.

So what exactly is it cleaning up? For one thing, temporary Internet files are deleted. Any time you visit a Web site, Web pages, support files, and some graphics are stored on your computer. This is also referred to as "caching" and theoretically means that a Web page will display more quickly the next time you request it because it's actually pulling information from the local cache instead of downloading it again from the Internet. Of course, this is also another way to track what sites have been visited on a particular computer.

The folder that holds all of these temporary Internet files is a hidden folder and most people don't even realize that it is there. However, these files can begin to take up quite a bit of space if they aren't regularly purged from the hard drive. If hard disk space is limited, filling it up with these files can affect the performance of a computer as well.

NOTES   If you're using Internet Explorer as your browser, you'll find the temporary files stored under c:\documents and settings*your username*\local settings\temporary internet files. Local settings is usually a hidden folder so you may need to configure your computer to show hidden files. Do this in My Computer by clicking on Tools > Folder Options > View and select the radio button for Show hidden files and folders. If you right click on the Temporary Internet Files folder and choose Options, can you tell how much space is it taking up? How many files are listed there? Disk Cleanup will give you the option of deleting these files.

Figure 4.6

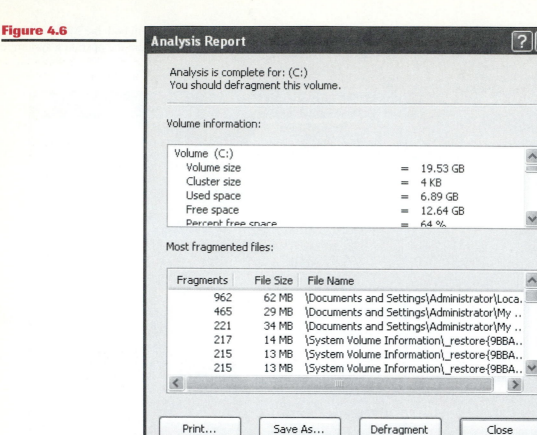

Defrag Another tool you can use to increase the efficiency of your computer is Disk Defragmenter. When files are stored on your computer they aren't stored in one block as a complete file. Each file is broken up into tiny bits and the bits are stored in blocks. The size of the blocks, actually called "clusters," is dependent upon the size of the hard disk. Larger hard disks usually have larger clusters. Some people, usually those heavily involved with gaming, partition their disks to increase performance because of this. If a disk is fragmented, the operating system has to work a lot harder to retrieve files, and this could slow an application down. If a file is smaller than the cluster, the rest of the cluster remains unused resulting in something called "slack space."

As you save files they are broken into bits and spread out in different clusters all over your disk. A lot of programs create temporary files when you use the program and then delete the temporary files when you're done. In addition, you often create and delete files. This means data is scattered in noncontiguous (nonadjacent) clusters all over the disk with a lot of clusters in between remaining empty. When you want to read a file, your computer has to work a lot harder to find all the bits of the file to put it back together.

Defrag is rather like taking a dust broom and sweeping all the bits of files back into one corner of the disk. More current versions of the operating system do a better job at organizing the bits in the clusters than older operating systems did but defragmenting your hard disk is still a good task to add to your overall maintenance plan. People who do intensive work with database files or use CAD (computer-assisted design) programs should defrag more often than others because those applications frequently create large temporary files.

You can determine how often you need to defrag your computer by establishing some sort of baseline. Start by checking if your computer needs to be defragmented once every two or three months. You can monitor how often it needs it and then adjust your maintenance schedule accordingly.

Error Checking No matter how hard we try to take care of our computers' disks, sometimes bad things just happen. Error Checking (previously called "Scandisk") is a utility you can use to attempt to recover bits of your file from portions of a disk that have been damaged. This damage is often caused by physical damage such as letting a floppy disk get too hot or too cold or putting it near a magnet or zapping a hard disk with an electrical spike. Some people would argue that all of those things don't really hurt floppy disks. Those are the people who eventually need to use a tool like Error Checking.

NOTES   To check your drive for errors, go to My Computer and right click the drive you want checked. Choose Properties > Tools, then Check Now. What happened? You should get a dialog box asking if you want to automatically fix file system errors or scan for and attempt recovery of bad sectors. Choose both options and then click Start.

Figure 4.7

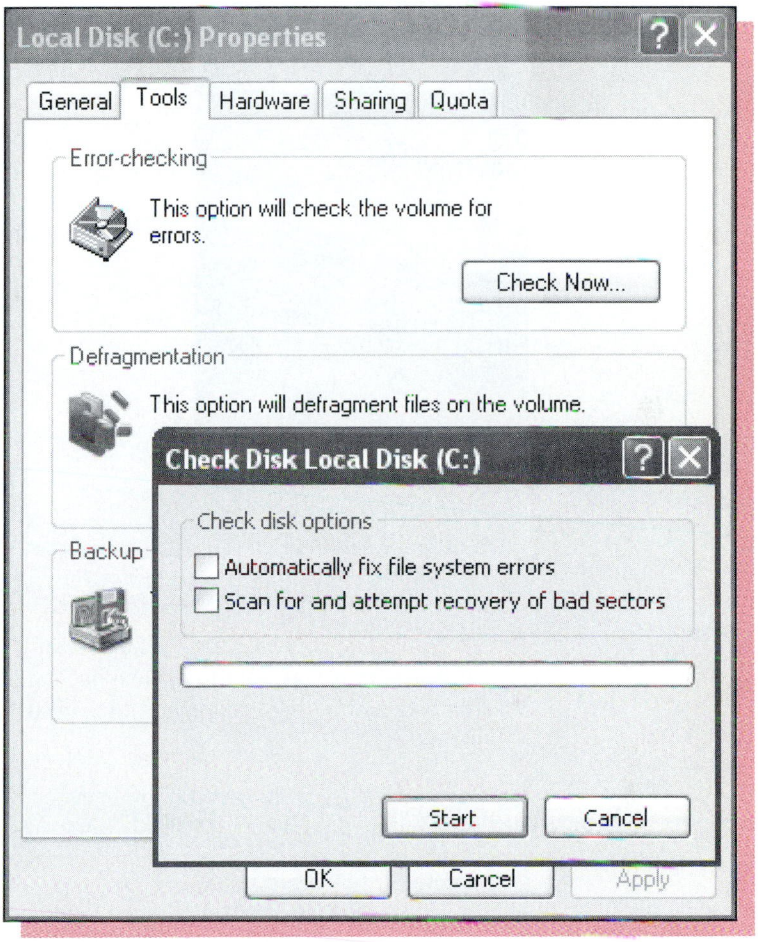

Backups From My Computer, select a drive and choose Properties > Tools. You will see an option to Backup Now. The word "backup" just means that you make copies of your important files and keep them elsewhere. Sometimes that simply means making a copy and putting it in a different folder on the same computer in case you accidentally delete the original or overwrite it with something else. Sometimes it means copying a file to a floppy, Zip disk, or CD. As a network administrator, you would be responsible for backing up one or more servers and would usually use a tape to back up to. Backing up servers is discussed further in Chapter 11—Network Maintenance.

Windows 2000 Professional and Windows XP Professional offer a tool to help you back up your files. As you can see, there's even a Wizard to walk you through the steps. Using this tool isn't the same as just copying a file to a disk. It can back up many files and stores them all as one file on a disk. You must use the Backup utility to restore files from the backup.

Since a typical computer doesn't have a tape backup unit like most servers do, your options to save your files would normally include a floppy disk, hard disk, Zip disk, a shared folder on another system, or CD-R.

You can also schedule your backups to occur at specific times. Backing up files using the Windows 2000 Backup tool is different than just making copies of your files because it actually stores it in a special format. To get your files back, you must use the Restore feature shown in Figure 4.9. Similar to creating the backup, a Wizard will walk you through the Restore process. Although the end result of your backup is usually one compressed file with a .bkf extension, when you use Restore it does let you see all of your files in that one .bkf file and you can extract an individual or several selected files as needed.

Figure 4.8

To begin a backup using the Backup Wizard, click the Next button as shown in Figure 4.8. The next screen is asking if you want to make a backup or if you need to restore a file (Figure 4.9). Choose the Backup files and settings option and click Next.

Figure 4.9

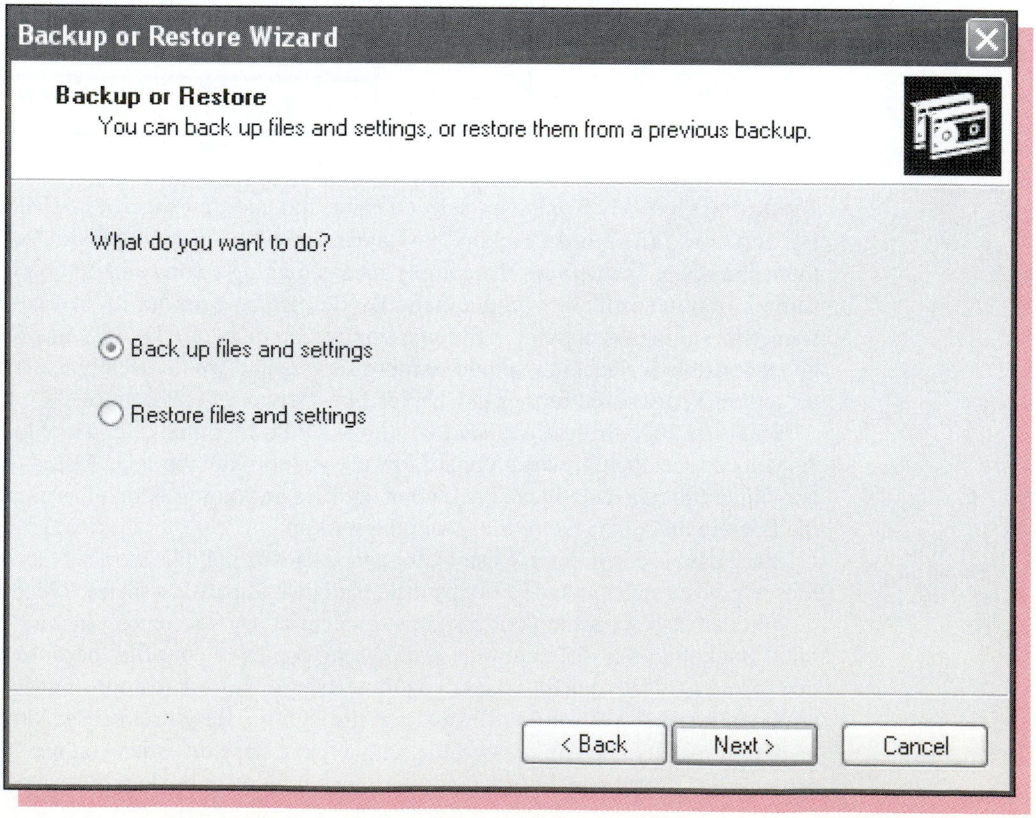

Figure 4.10

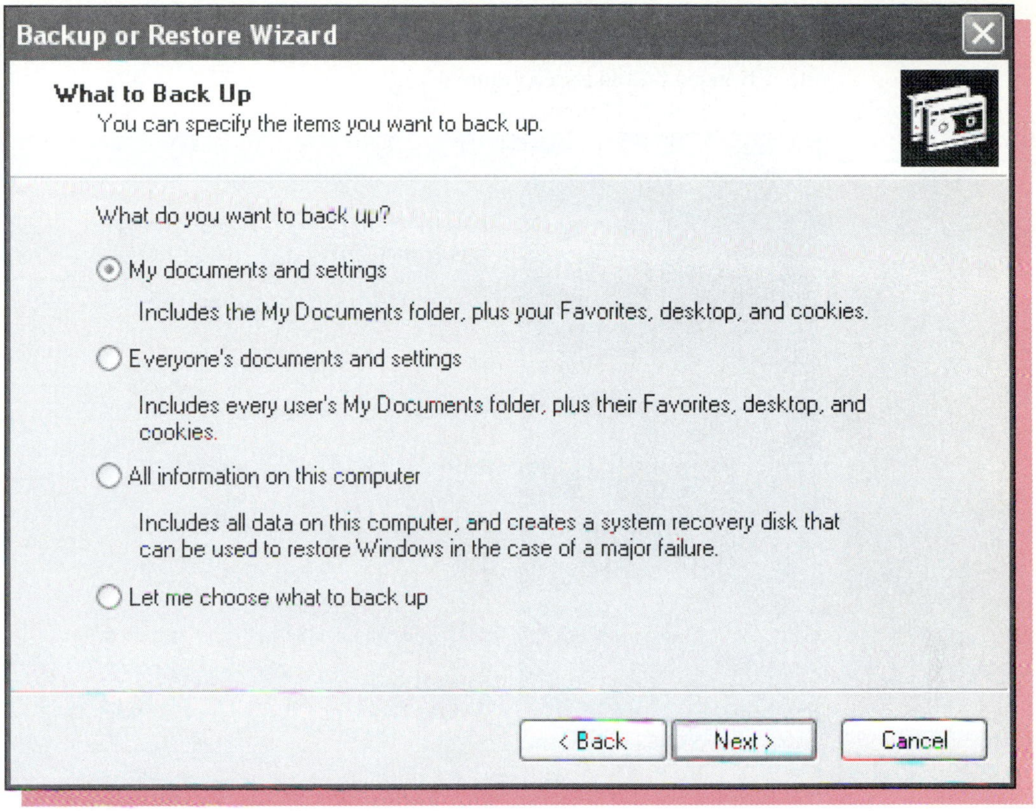

Figure 4.10 is asking what you want backed up. For this example, choose the default, My documents and settings, and click Next.

In Figure 4.11, the Backup Wizard is asking where the backup file should be saved and what it should be named. Choose a place to save the backup file on your computer (e.g., the Desktop), accept the default name for the backup (Backup), and click Next.

Figure 4.11

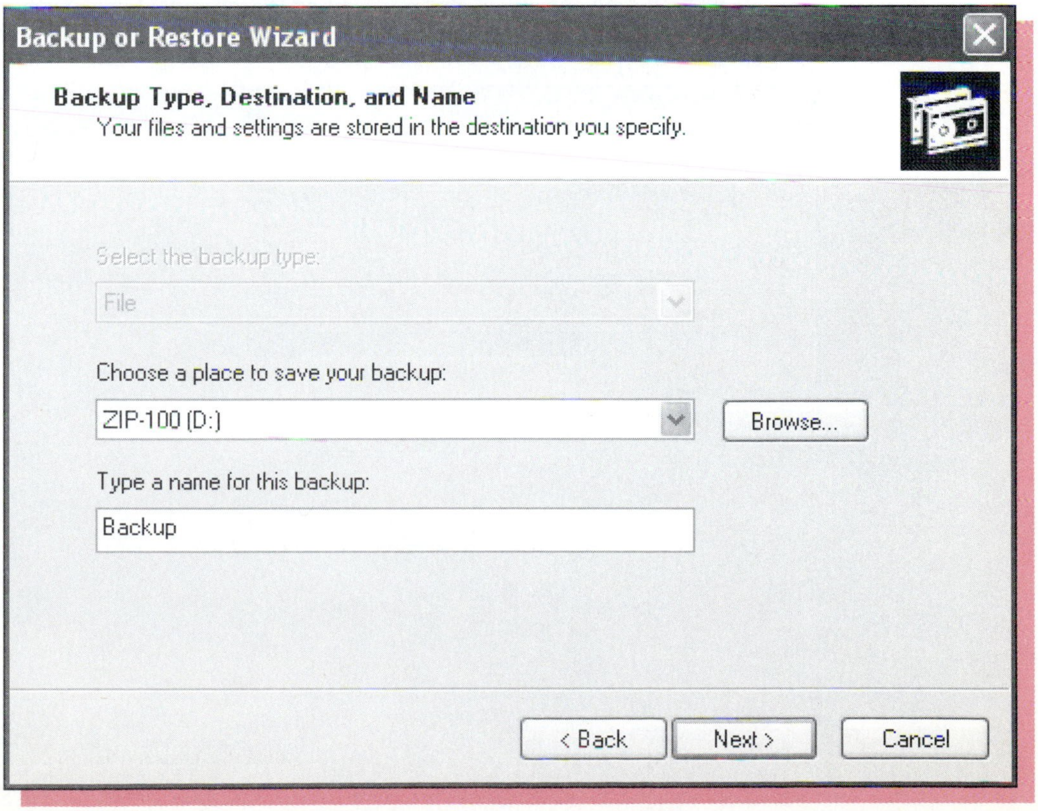

Figure 4.12 is confirming the selections made so far. If you click Finish, the Wizard will create the backup but there are additional selections available when you click the Advanced button. Click the Advanced button to see Figure 4.13.

Figure 4.12

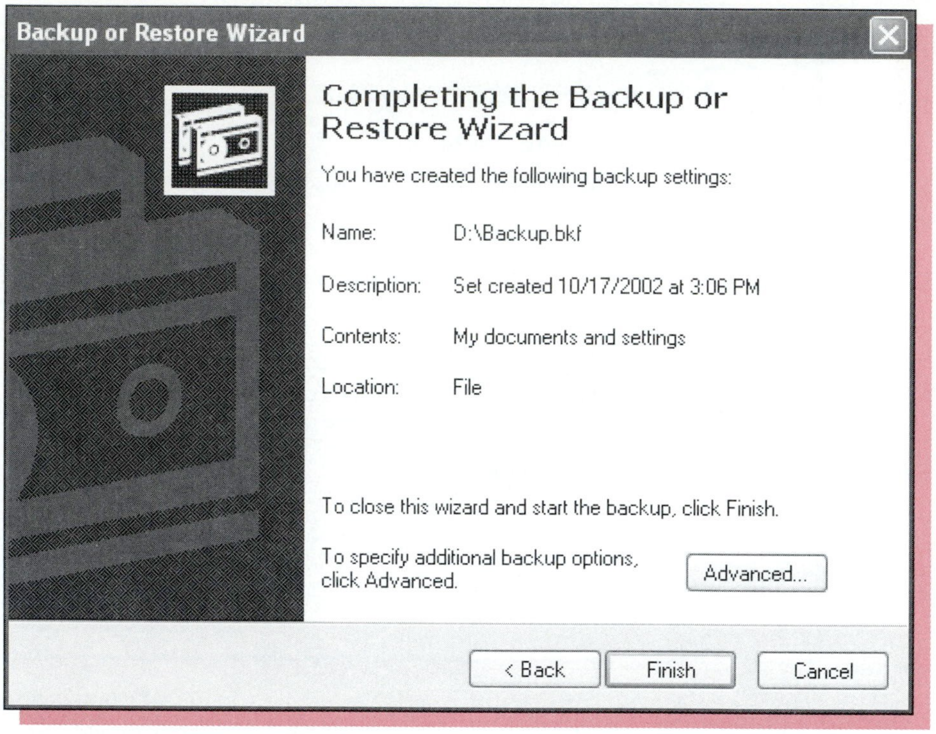

Figure 4.13 is asking which type of backup you wish to perform. Microsoft lists five different options to choose from. The differences between the types of backup determine which files are backed up (e.g., all files or only those which have changed since the last backup) and if the archive bit is cleared from the file. Removing the archive bit from a file signifies that it has been backed up. The archive bit is placed on a file when a file is newly created or modified to signify that changes have been made since the last backup. Defining the five different backup types is left as an exercise.

Figure 4.13

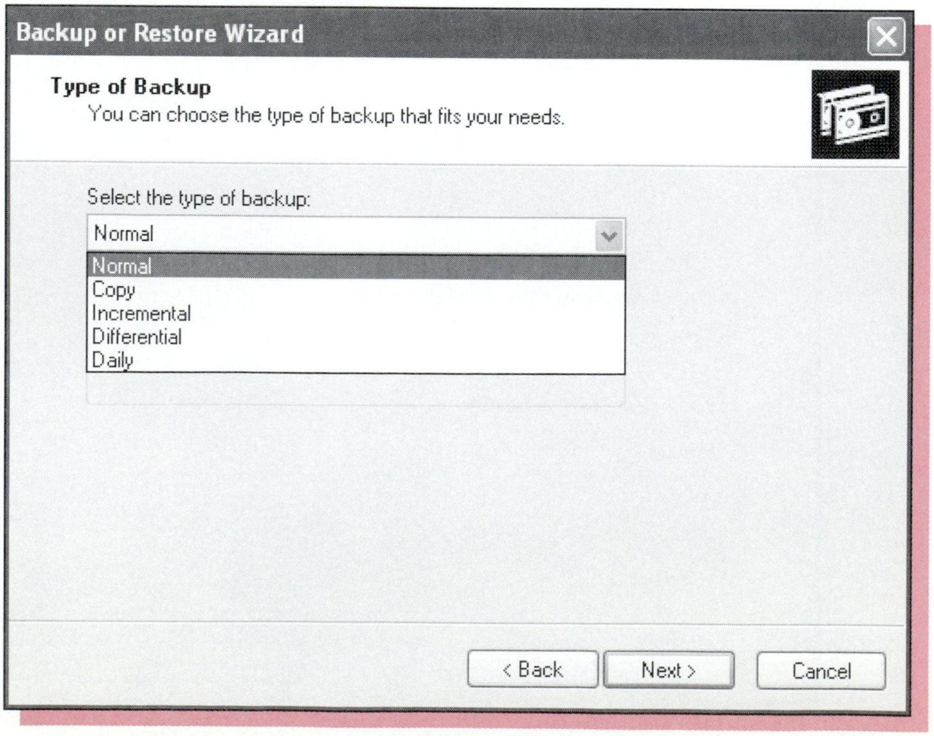

Choose the Normal backup option to back up all of the selected files and then click Next.

The next window, shown in Figure 4.14, offers options for verification, which verifies that every file copied is the same as the original; compression, which saves space; and shadow copy, an option in Windows XP Professional but not Windows 2000 Professional. Disabling shadow copy may force the backup tool to skip files that are in use. For this example, accept the default settings and click Next.

Figure 4.14

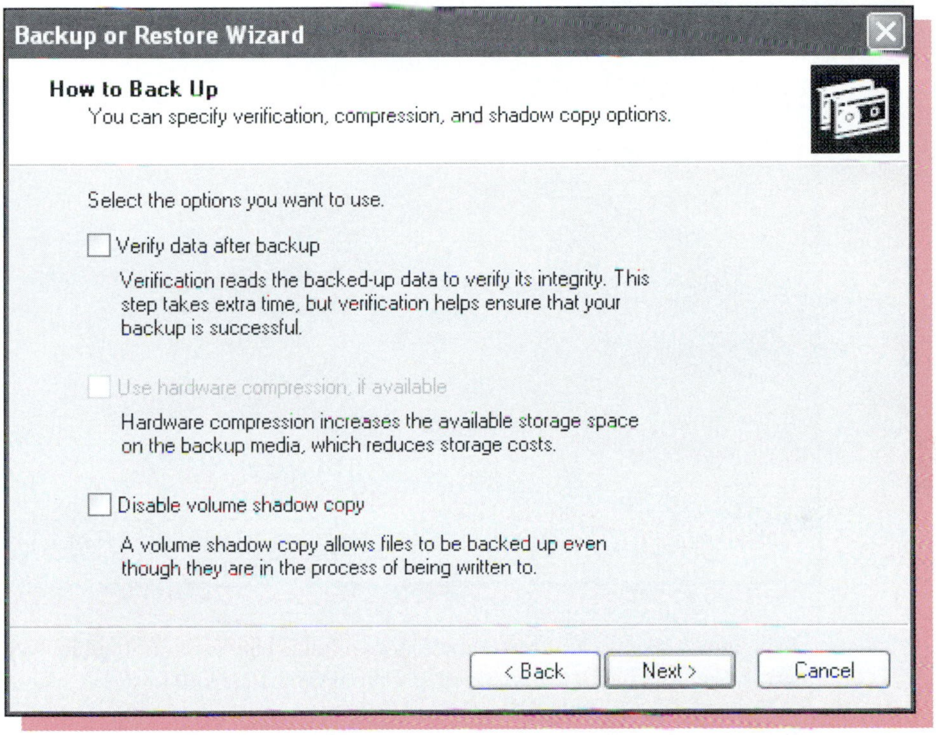

The window shown in Figure 4.15 gives the option of appending (adding) the data to an existing backup or replacing (overwriting) an existing backup. Accept the default setting and click Next.

Figure 4.15

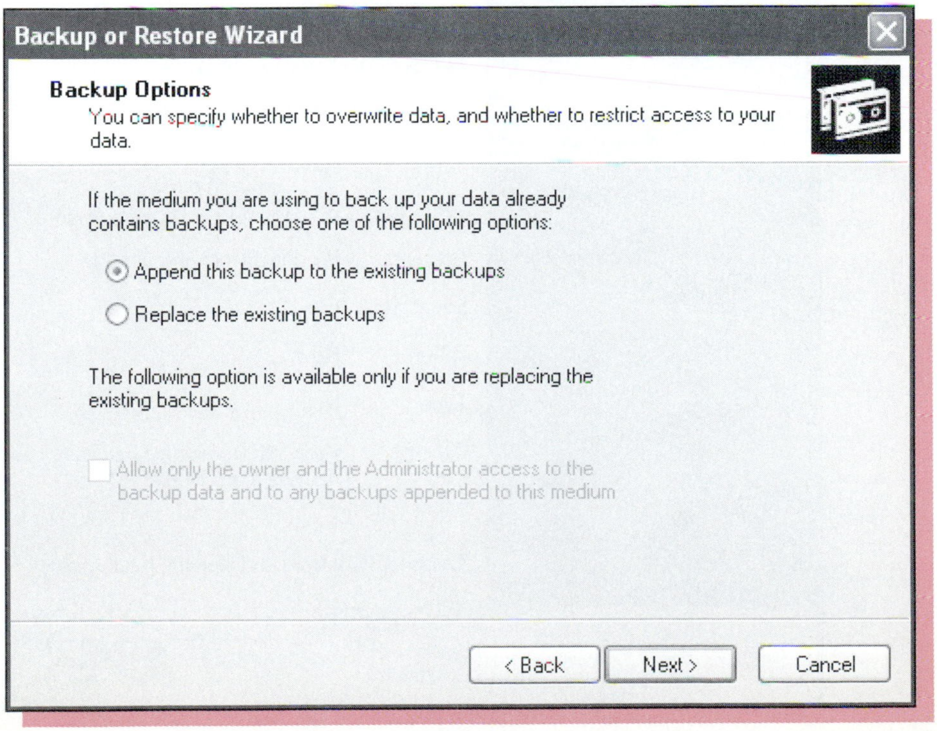

Figure 4.16

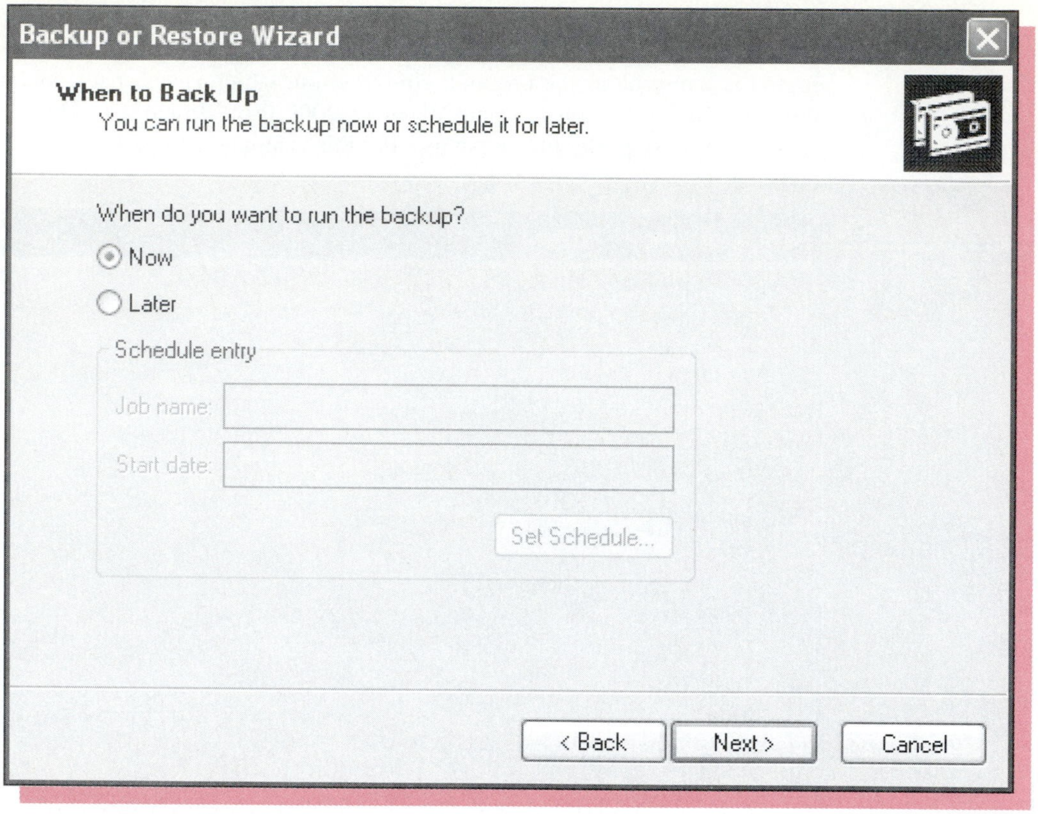

Backup or Restore Wizard

When to Back Up
You can run the backup now or schedule it for later.

When do you want to run the backup?

◉ Now

◯ Later

Schedule entry

Job name: _____

Start date: _____

Set Schedule...

< Back   Next >   Cancel

The next window (Figure 4.16) offers the choice between running the backup now or scheduling it for later. If you schedule it for later you can program the backup to run at specific days and times. For now, accept the default and click Next.

The last window (Figure 4.17) confirms your selection. When you click Finish the Backup utility will perform the requested backup and create one file with a .bkf extension.

Figure 4.17

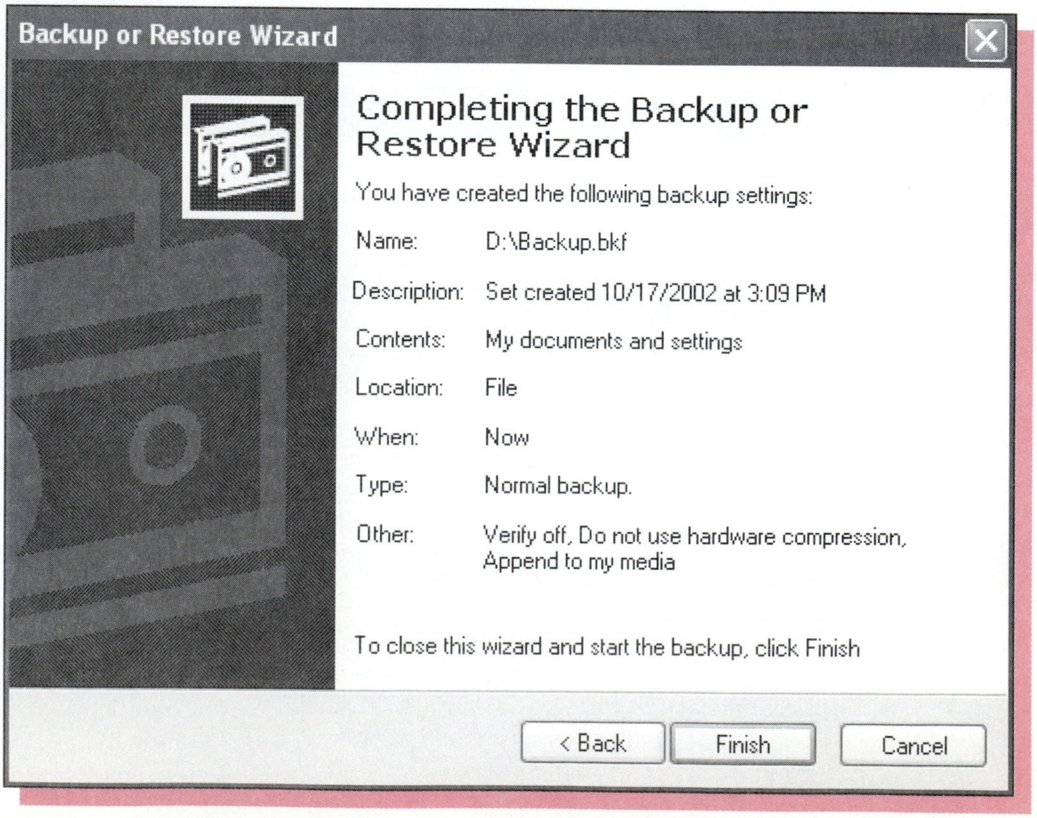

Backup or Restore Wizard

Completing the Backup or Restore Wizard

You have created the following backup settings:

Name: D:\Backup.bkf

Description: Set created 10/17/2002 at 3:09 PM

Contents: My documents and settings

Location: File

When: Now

Type: Normal backup.

Other: Verify off, Do not use hardware compression, Append to my media

To close this wizard and start the backup, click Finish

< Back   Finish   Cancel

Additional Tools

Safe Mode Sometimes in the process of installing a new driver or some other software or hardware device, bad things happen. Suddenly the computer or the server no longer boots correctly. What can you do?

If you have just installed a new driver and the computer now refuses to boot, the best thing to do is boot the computer into Safe mode and remove the new driver. Safe mode boots a computer without loading all of the device drivers for the components in your computer. This usually allows you to first remove the offending driver and then reinstall another driver to get the computer working again.

To boot a computer into Safe mode, restart the computer and press the F8 key as it is booting. When a computer boots, it performs the POST(power on self test). You may see a message about the version of the BIOS (basic input/output system) that is loaded and then the computer usually checks its drives. You can start tapping the F8 key around this time. Don't hold the key down constantly; just tap it every second or so until you see the menu with the option to go into Safe mode. If the computer boots into Windows you didn't catch it in time with the F8 key and you need to start over.

If the problem isn't due to a bad driver, you may need to try something a little more intense and that's when boot disks may come in handy.

Boot Disks In Windows XP Professional, you can create a boot disk in the same window where you format the floppy disk. In addition to booting the computer, this boot disk will also have generic CD-ROM drivers so you can access the CD-ROM drive. If a computer doesn't have an operating system on it or the operating system has been damaged and isn't booting properly, you may need access to the CD-ROM drive to reinstall or attempt a repair of the operating system.

In Windows 2000, creating boot disks requires four floppies. These disks are used in conjunction with the Windows 2000 install CD to attempt to repair an installation. Looking for these disks usually means you are having a really bad computer day. You create the boot disks from the install CD using a Makeboot utility on the CD. You use these disks to start the computer if it doesn't support booting directly from the CD. If it does support booting directly from the CD, try that first.

Either way, the process looks like you are going to install the operating system but at some point the Wizard asks if you want to do a "clean install" or attempt to repair an existing installation. No matter who the network administrator is or how much experience they have, this is not going to be a fun day for them. To help prepare for such a day, a prospective network administrator should take classes that include some hands-on experience working with hardware and installing operating systems.

Tools You Can Download

Installing Software You should be able to install software applications on your computer. Some of these applications will be purchased and some will be downloaded from the Internet for free. In addition to free software on the Internet, there is also "shareware." You can try a shareware application out for free for a limited time but if you decide to continue using it, you are supposed to pay the author for it.

In most cases, the software you download from the Internet will be compressed. It may be in the form of a self-extracting executable or it could be in "zipped" format. If it is in zipped format, you'll need an application like WinZip to uncompress it. While WinZip may not be considered a utility to maintain your computer, you may need to know how to use it if you download tools from the Internet. If you are installing software from a disk, the software may also be compressed but will already have whatever it needs to extract the files as it installs them.

From the Internet. Step One is to find the software. A good place to start might be Tucows.com or shareware.cnet.com. A word of caution, however: any software that you download from the Internet will most likely not have any guarantees that it will work, that it will work with your computer, or that your computer will continue to work after you install it. If you are considering installing software from the Internet, ask around to see if anyone you know is using it or has previously downloaded software from the same site.

Once you have downloaded the compressed file to your computer, you may need to use WinZip to uncompress it. Once the files are uncompressed, you should find a Setup or Install file. If it is a self-extracting executable, you would run the .exe file. It may launch the installation process or it may simply uncompress the files and you'll then need to run an install or setup file. Either way, nearly all applications should have a README file. Usually, the README file gives some clues to what you're supposed to do.

Most software applications have default directories that they wish to install to but most give you the option of changing the default directory. Why might you want to change it? If your computer has more than one hard disk or partition, you may want to install your applications on one partition and use another partition for something else.

From a Disk. If you are installing software from a disk or CD, no doubt instructions have been included. If you are installing from a CD, once you put the CD into the drive it usually autoruns the CD and either starts the installation or offers a screen that allows you to choose what you want to do.

It should have a default directory for installation but should offer you the option to change it. If you were installing the Microsoft Office suite, for example, what default folder will it want to install into? Almost all software applications try to install themselves in the Programs file folder.

Usually there are no issues of viruses or problems caused for your computer when you install software from a CD purchased from a well-known company. You will still need to make sure, however, that your system is compatible with the new software based on the application's minimum system requirements. Some programs require a minimum level of hardware such as memory or storage space to run correctly.

Of course, it should also be for the correct operating system. All applications don't just run automatically on any operating system. They must be specifically written for an operating system. That means that application software vendors have some say in how popular an operating system is. OS/2 by IBM is an example. When OS/2 first came out it was considered a stable operating system but didn't become immediately popular because for a long time there wasn't any application software to run on it.

From the Microsoft Update Site. If you are using any type of Microsoft software including the operating system, you should periodically visit their update Web sites. In addition to bug fixes, you can update your operating system and applications for security issues. They have Web pages where you can selectively download updates or add-ons but they also have a page that checks your operating system for you and determines what updates you need (http://windowsupdate.microsoft.com). It is strongly recommended that you do this often as part of regular maintenance.

Uninstalling Software. The nice thing about using WinZip to install software is that it has a CheckOut feature. If you use the CheckOut feature, install the software, and test it, you can easily uninstall it when you close WinZip because WinZip then asks you if you want to keep the new software or not.

You can always uninstall any software, however. If the software does not have an Uninstall option on the Start menu, you can usually uninstall it from the Control Panel using Add/Remove Programs. Simply deleting the application folder in My Programs isn't the recommended way to uninstall a program. While that may delete the application, it does not remove any entries regarding the application made in the registry at the time of the application installation. The registry is a database used by the Windows operating system to keep track of specific information including installed applications, desktop colors, hardware configurations, and much more.

File Compression If you want to download a new screensaver or game from the Internet, you won't want to download all of the files separately. Or if you need to send files to someone via e-mail attachments, it is often best if you compress multiple files into one file. You can also compress files to more efficiently manage space on a computer.

When you compress a file, one goal is to make it smaller. That isn't the only advantage of file compression, however. You can also compress several files into one file. That makes them a lot more portable. There are many different kinds of compression algorithms to make files smaller. Fortunately, the typical user doesn't really need to understand how they work because there are tools that do the work for us.

But generally speaking, a simple compression algorithm might take a text file and find instances of repeated text and replace it with a smaller representation. For example, if the word "anomaly" was used several times in a document, it could be replaced with @ or some other smaller symbol to represent it.

Using WinZip. An example of an application that compresses files for you is WinZip. You can find it at www.shareware.cnet.com and a million other places. If it isn't already installed on your computer, download the executable file and then double click the icon to install it. The Install Wizard will walk you through the steps. Typically, an Install Wizard will ask you where you want to install the application and possibly offer some options to customize the software. When you install WinZip, it asks which interface you plan to use. The examples shown here are using the Classic interface. Another option is to use the Wizard mode.

Figure 4.18

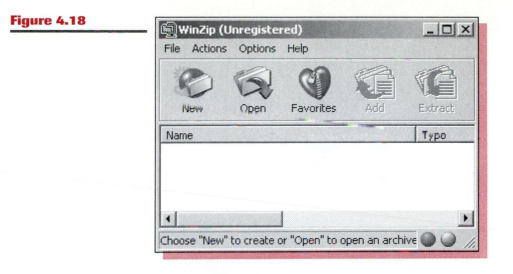

At first, WinZip seems a little backward. Typically when you create a file such as a Word document, you would open Word, type some text, then save the document. WinZip, like Microsoft Access, requires you to save it first and then add the files you want zipped.

You want to create a new zipped file, so select the New button. It prompts you to give it a file name and tell it where you want to save it. WinZip will append the file extension .zip to denote that it is a zipped file. Keep in mind the fact that you are zipping files doesn't have anything to do with a Zip drive; the terminology just happens to be the same.

Figure 4.19

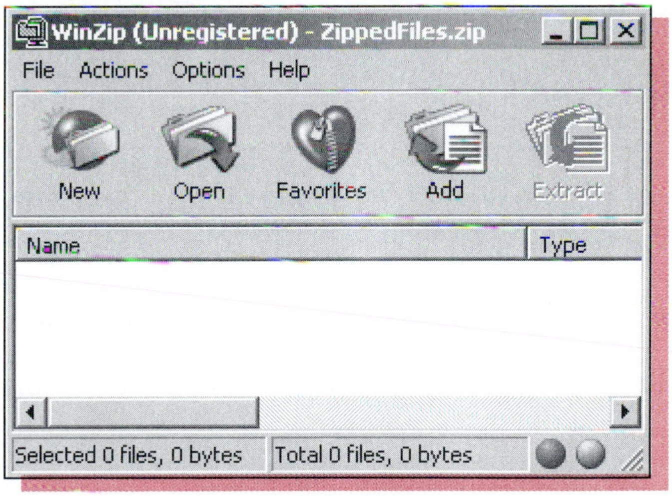

Once you've named the new file, it doesn't seem like much happened. You're returned to Figure 4.19. Notice the difference at the bottom when compared to the graphic above, however. Figure 4.18 is telling you to choose New or Open. Figure 4.19 is waiting for you to add files and also has whatever you named it at the top. So click the Add button and select the files you want to include.

Remember, you can select noncontiguous files by holding down the Ctrl key when you click. You can select a range of contiguous files by holding down the Shift key when you click. Once you have selected the files you can typically just use the default settings for everything else here. An exception to that is if you are also compressing folders. If you are, you'll probably want to select the Include Subfolders option. If you don't, all files are placed together; if you do, the files remain in the folders you have them in and the directory structure is recreated on the destination computer when the file is unzipped.

Figure 4.20

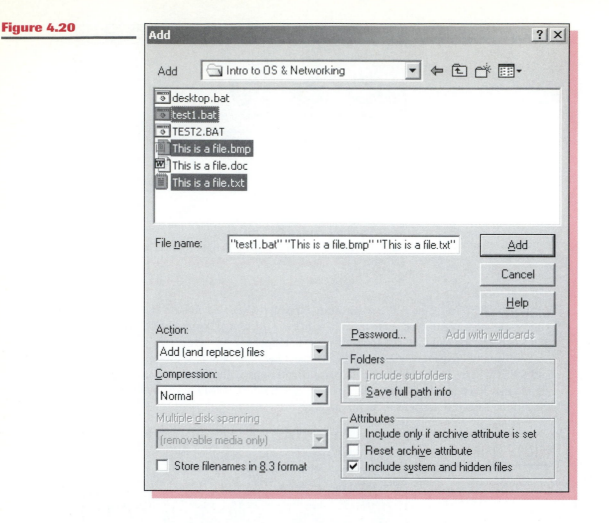

Once you have added all of the files you want to the zip file, you can just close WinZip. No other action is necessary. At the instant you add the files to WinZip they are compressed. Some types of files can be greatly compressed whereas compressing others might not yield any benefit whatsoever.

NOTES Create a graphics file and a text file, then compress them. What is the compression ratio for the graphics file versus the text file?

WinZip also has the ability to create a self-extracting executable (.exe) file from the zipped file. To give an example, if I wanted to distribute data files for a class and the students weren't very comfortable with computers, creating an executable file could make things easier. In addition to making it a self-extracting executable, I can also tell WinZip what I want to happen when the .exe file is run. For instance, I could tell it to create a folder on the hard drive and unzip the files in that specific folder. Then, in my instructions to my students, I can tell them exactly where to look for the files. To create an .exe from a zipped file, click on Actions, Make .exe.

To make it easier on the person receiving the files, you can enter a default folder for the files. This might make it a bit easier for them to find them on their machine once they are unzipped. When you do this, you will have a .zip file and an .exe file. The real bonus to this is that the recipient will not need to have WinZip on their machine if you send them an .exe file. They will just need to run the .exe and the files will be unzipped into the folder you have listed.

Another example of why you might want to do this is if you send digital pictures to a relative. Certainly it is best to send them compressed. Rather than explaining to Cousin Howard how to download and install WinZip, you can just explain to them that they should double click the icon and where they will find the uncompressed files on their computer. Of course, it is a good idea to e-mail them in advance telling them that you will be sending a virus-free file attachment.

Figure 4.21

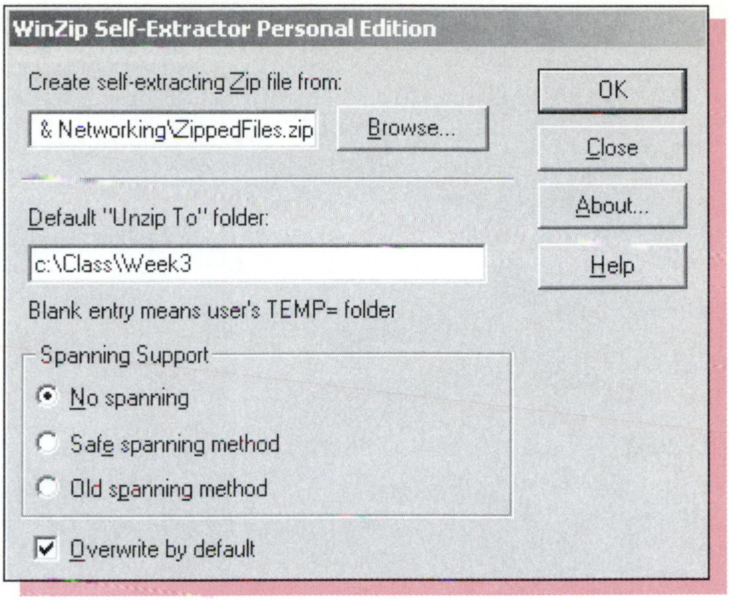

WinZip Self-Extractor Personal Edition

Create self-extracting Zip file from:

[& Networking\ZippedFiles.zip]   Browse...

Default "Unzip To" folder:

[c:\Class\Week3]

Blank entry means user's TEMP= folder

Spanning Support
- ⦿ No spanning
- ○ Safe spanning method
- ○ Old spanning method

☑ Overwrite by default

OK
Close
About...
Help

Windows Compression. Windows 2000 Professional and Windows XP Professional also have a compression option to more efficiently manage space on a computer. The disk must be formatted with the NTFS file system. Right click on My Documents and choose Properties. On the General tab, click the Advanced button. You will see an option to Compress the contents to save disk space (Figure 4.22). Choose this option wisely. When you access a file that has been compressed, the operating system must uncompress it on the fly (immediately when needed) and compress it again when the file is closed. This causes the operating system to work harder.

Figure 4.22

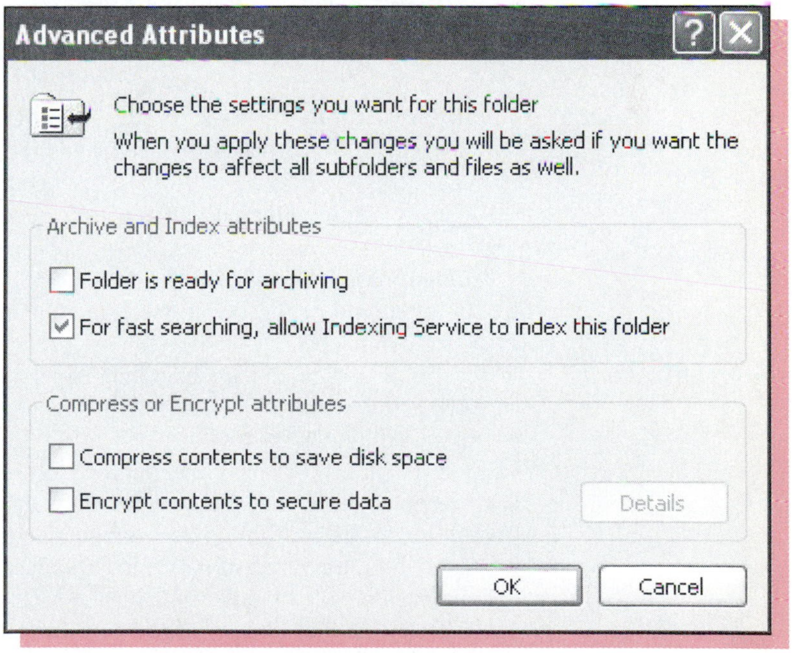

Advanced Attributes   [?] [X]

Choose the settings you want for this folder
When you apply these changes you will be asked if you want the changes to affect all subfolders and files as well.

Archive and Index attributes

☐ Folder is ready for archiving

☑ For fast searching, allow Indexing Service to index this folder

Compress or Encrypt attributes

☐ Compress contents to save disk space

☐ Encrypt contents to secure data   Details

OK   Cancel

When you compress the contents of a folder you can't really tell by looking at the files if they are compressed or not. To give a visual cue, Microsoft changes the color of the file or folder name to indicate that the contents are compressed. In Windows 2000 Professional, you have to configure the settings to display the different color by clicking Tools > Folder Options > View and selecting the option to Show compressed files in color. In Windows XP Professional, the default is to show compressed files in color (Figure 4.23).

Figure 4.23

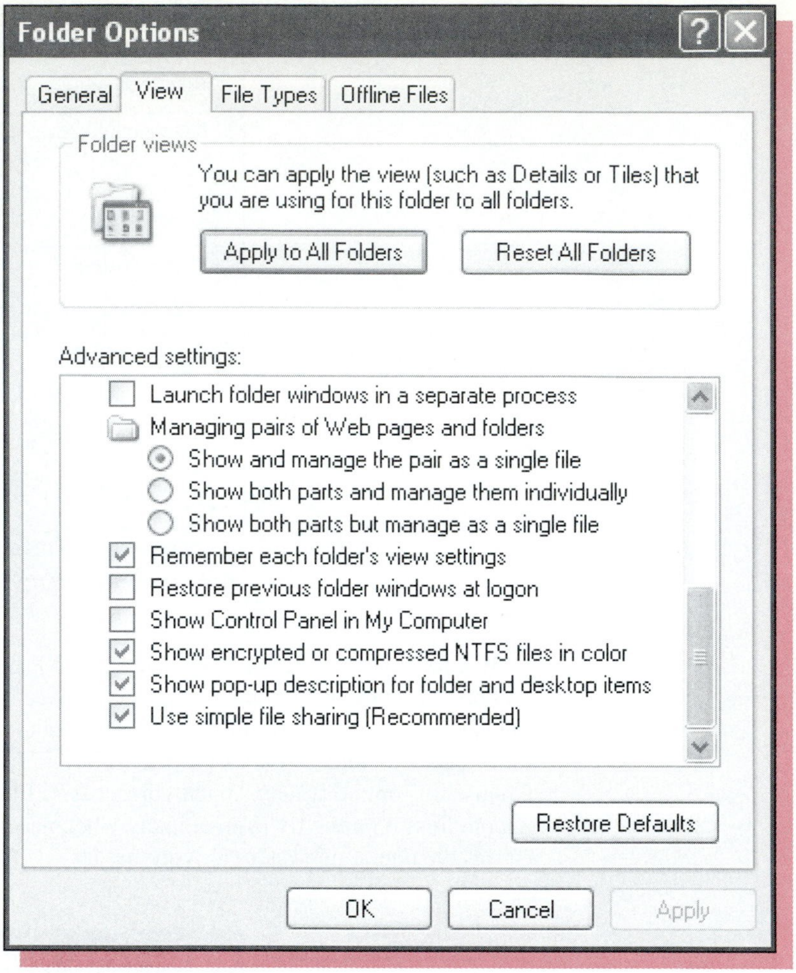

Preventing Viruses Viruses are usually programmed to have three phases: they need to get onto your computer, do their dastardly deed, and then somehow get onto someone else's computer to share the wealth. So how do you get a virus, what can a virus really do to your computer, and how can you take steps to ensure you aren't an unwitting accomplice who infects someone else—usually someone you know?

Getting a Virus. Seems like whenever we go where there are a lot of people, we increase our chances of catching a cold or the flu. In fact, some places seem to present greater opportunities than others. Catching a computer virus tends to follow the same trend. If you use a floppy disk at home and never use it anywhere else, then you are less likely to get a virus on it. If you take that same floppy disk to school and work and use it in several different computers that are often accessed by several different people, you are more likely to get a virus.

You can also get a virus on your computer if you use the Internet. You might get an e-mail message from someone—even someone you know—with a file attachment. Wondering what it is, you click on it. Usually it is in the form of an .exe (executable file) that launches a program. This program may even look like it didn't do much of anything but in fact it has written a virus to your disk.

Sometimes people download shareware such as screensavers or games. When they install the software it does what they expect it to so they don't really think about the possible problems they could be causing themselves. They don't realize that in addition to installing the new software, they may have also installed an additional file in the form of a virus. Think of it—if you were writing a virus, you would want to tempt as many people as you can to become infected by packaging your payload in something that looks appealing and you would want to be stealthy about it. You can write code to run an application in stealth mode. Only a knowledgeable person would be able to find it running in the background. Of course, a knowledgeable person wouldn't have installed it in the first place. They would be called in after the fact when the user complains that their computer is "acting funny."

Detecting a Virus. So, you've been called in because someone's computer was "acting funny." Where would you begin to look for signs of a virus? Obviously, you should try running an antivirus software utility. Make sure that the software is as updated as it can be. There are usually two parts to antivirus software: the engine that does all of the work and the signature files. The engine is the actual application that you run. New versions do come out periodically. Certainly, as the operating systems evolve, the antivirus software will also have upgrades.

The second part is updated more frequently, however. The signature files are data (.dat) files that contain information about every known virus in the wild. In this case, think of it as the World Wild Web. These data files must be updated as soon as the antivirus software vendor comes out with them. The antivirus software companies must come out with new data files whenever someone detects and reports a new virus. Typically, this is a daily occurrence. In most cases, your engine does a search for new signature files whenever you boot your computer, typically every couple of days or some other schedule that you set.

Depending on what virus outbreak is occurring in the world at the moment, you may need to update once a week or once a day. Your antivirus software will have a Web site for you to monitor current virus activity in the world. They usually also have pages that explain the virus hoaxes. There always seems to be someone who will believe anything they hear and stories about viruses are no different.

If you ever get a warning that some terrible virus has been unleashed on the world, check to see if it is true. Sites such as Symantec (http://securityresponse.symantec.com/avcenter/hoax.html) also give information on hoaxes and you'll want to know for sure before you e-mail all of your friends to warn them.

Let's get back to real viruses and detecting them. No matter how good an antivirus application is, it won't detect every virus. Some people even run more than one antivirus engine and have found that one might be good at picking up some viruses and the other might be good at picking up other viruses. None are perfect, however, so you might still need to do a little detective work on your own as part of a periodic maintenance procedure.

Checking the Processes tab in Task Manager to see if anything is running that you don't recognize is another good idea. If you find anything that you don't recognize, don't just start deleting. Check it out first. Do a keyword search on the Internet or at Symantec's site at http://www.symantec.com/avcenter/ to learn more about the file. Usually the user who called you in because their computer was acting funny can give you some clues. They may tell you that everything was working fine yesterday but today it is not. Try to retrace their steps in that time period. Did they get an odd e-mail or did they update their screensaver, etc.? Fair warning: most end users won't really know what they did. If you ask them if they downloaded a file, they will usually say "no" because they won't think you mean "did you update your screensaver?"

Therefore, using the Search option is also a good idea. Click Start > Search, and then look for all files and folders modified in the last *x* number of days, depending on when they first noticed the computer was acting funny. Another clue they might give relates to the actual virus. Each virus acts differently, has its own "signature," so to speak, its own *modus operandi*. They may tell you that they saw an icon or a text box or something appear immediately before the computer started acting funny. Try to get them to tell you as much as possible about the occurrence. Then go to http://www.symantec.com/avcenter/ and do a search using key words based on what you were told. This part is a lot like being a detective. Based on what the user told you, you're trying to find a virus with a signature that matches.

Getting Rid of a Virus. If you're lucky and actually find it, Symantec will tell you all about the virus, including what you need to do to get rid of it. If the antivirus software doesn't detect it and inoculate your system, you usually have to do some pretty intensive work to get rid of it. This can include working in the registry, tracking down files that have been placed on the computer and deleting them, or restoring the original file that should be there.

To explain that a little more clearly, some viruses overwrite system files with the virus itself. Every time you turn on the computer and the system boots, it's actually invoking the virus. You'll need to delete the corrupted system file and restore the true version of it. To be honest, this is where DOS comes in handy. If it's a system file for Windows, Windows won't usually let you delete it while the computer is running Windows. Booting the computer in DOS should allow you to delete the file since Windows won't be using it. To do this, you'd really need to be in DOS, not just a Command Prompt window with Windows running in the background.

Symantec does do a nice job explaining the steps but if you don't feel comfortable going into the registry, extracting system files from the operating system installation CD or system folder on the hard disk, etc. you might want to call in a knowledgeable friend for backup and just assume you're going to owe them one.

Not Getting a Virus. Of course, the smartest thing to do is to not get the virus at all. Keep your antivirus .dat files updated whenever your antivirus software says you should update. That also means that if your software prompts you about checking for upgrades whenever you boot your computer, you shouldn't tell it not to prompt you anymore when you get tired of seeing the message.

If you hear of an outbreak, go to the Web site of your antivirus software vendor and check for updates and advice. In some cases, people are accessing your system and placing viruses there because of known issues with the operating system or software application (e.g., Microsoft Outlook or Netscape Navigator). If you keep current on your operating system and application patches, you can avoid a lot of problems.

If you're running Microsoft software, Microsoft has an update site that will check your system for you and install whatever it needs to keep it current, or you can check the version yourself and install a new patch if needed for all of your applications and the operating system. You'll find it at http://windowsupdate.microsoft.com. There is a link for product updates for your operating system and there is also a link to do the same thing for your Microsoft applications. Often, your system is compromised based on known holes or security issues with the operating system and the application software. You need to constantly update the patches for both.

Something else that most people don't think of is file and printer sharing. By default, this is usually turned on and is configured in the dialup or network connection settings. Most people don't need it. Most security experts would suggest that you turn it off if you're sure you're not sharing files on your computer with others. Hackers can potentially exploit the file and printer sharing and place Trojans on your computer. A Trojan is yet another type of virus but deals more with compromising the security of your computer. A Trojan specializes in giving someone access to your computer; in essence, it opens a back door for intruders.

How does it work? Think about it: how does a computer communicate? Every service or application running on your computer uses a different input or output port to communicate.

NOTES

Open your DOS Command prompt window and key in NETSTAT—AN. Although this topic will only be introduced in this book and not covered in depth, this command will show you all of the ports currently being used on your computer to communicate. There is a column for the local ports being used (that's your computer), and a column for remote ports that you are communicating with.

For instance, if you just looked at a Web page, your computer will open up a session with the remote Web server. It will select an available port number on your computer and will typically use port 80 on the Web server. There are over 65,000 available ports on a computer. They are broken up into three categories. The first 1024 ports are called well-known ports and typical services and applications on your computer use these. Any additional applications or services then use the middle range of ports. Trojans typically use a port that is very high in the range, such as 30,000 or above.

When a Trojan is installed on a computer, potential hackers can use port scanners to see if there are any computers on in the world with a Trojan on them. If they find one, they can usually get into that computer. So in essence, having a Trojan on your computer is an open door for any hacker, not just one.

What Can a Virus Do? The effects of a virus can range from proving mildly annoying to causing a total system failure. Some viruses only flash you a message to let you know that someone else feels smarter than you are because they managed to get the virus onto your computer. Some viruses, like macro viruses, might cause an application to become unstable meaning it stops working unexpectedly at the worst moment, causing you to lose data. At the very least, having an application crash on you all of the time and having to restart it every few minutes is annoying.

Worst of all, of course, some viruses reformat your hard drive and cause you to lose everything on it. That can be more than mildly annoying. A virus is code written by someone in the world and the code is designed to do something to your computer without your knowledge and/or permission.

Don't Be an Accomplice. Don't click on e-mail attachments, even if you know the sender. In most cases, a virus is sent from someone's account without their knowledge. Usually it's because they got an e-mail attachment from someone they knew and clicked on it. After delivering the virus payload on their computer, the virus was also programmed to find their e-mail address book and send an e-mail to everyone in it with the file attachment so the infection can spread. If you do need to send a file to someone, work out some sort of system between you to contact each other in advance.

Saving documents in rich text format (RTF) is usually a good idea as well. Microsoft Word and other applications use macros a lot and some very common viruses are macro viruses. The RTF format does allow some document formatting such as bold, centered, etc., but is still a watered down text version and doesn't save the macros. Therefore, it doesn't offer as much access for potential viruses. When you save your document, in addition to giving it a name, check where is says "Save as Type." You should see a drop down button with several options. Choose RTF.

Keeping Your Knowledge of Viruses Current. Pay attention when you hear of outbreaks, keep your operating system and applications updated with patches, and check Web sites like Symantec to learn about what is going on in the world of viruses. When you hear about an outbreak, don't assume it can only happen to someone else. Take action to protect your computer immediately.

Desktop Security Securing your computer doesn't just mean making sure it won't grow feet and walk away. Once you are connected to a local area network (LAN) or the Internet, perhaps the biggest potential threat is unauthorized access to your computer and data files from a remote intruder.

Given the amount of publicity surrounding successful hacker intrusions into high-profile organizations such as the FBI and even the Microsoft Corporation, the possibility of your system being hacked should be taken seriously. Keep in mind, Microsoft and the FBI have some smart, well-paid people working for them and they still cannot keep out some hackers. So why should you care if anyone hacked into your computer and why would they want to, anyway?

Why Would You Care? Actually, you might be amazed at the personal information you have on your computer. In addition to possibly doing their taxes on their computers, a lot of people store resumes, address books, etc. If someone wanted to steal your identity, it really wouldn't be difficult. What do you have on your computer? Find out. Do a search for files containing text and enter your street address or your phone number or your social security number and see what turns up. And there are other things hidden on your PC, like passwords, that hackers know how to find. They can then go to your favorite Web sites pretending to be you.

Worse still—true story—ever see the little cameras you can attach to a computer? A college student who happened to be the daughter of a IT professor had one but a hacker broke into her computer and took control of it. He would leave messages on her computer telling her what she was wearing. Her dad freaked out, reformatted the computer, and took the camera back to the store.

Why Would They Want To? A lot of hackers aren't really interested in information about you. They're more interested in "The Big Hack," like a bank, the FBI, etc. and they need to disguise their identity. So they hack from machine to machine, making it more difficult to follow the trail back to them. Nonetheless, if the FBI thinks your computer tried to hack into their network, who do you think they'll blame first?

How Are They Doing It? Too many ways to count and new ways are being devised every minute. For the most part, however, they are usually exploiting a known issue with your application or operating system software. When the software is initially written, it may be sold before it has been truly tested for all possible issues. Hackers will work until they find a way into a specific application or operating system and then share the information so other hackers can do the same thing. Often, they take an extra step and write little scripts (programs) to make it even easier for others to get into your computer. They then post the scripts on the Internet for anyone to download. A typical computer user is usually unaware of this and uninformed about what protective maintenance measures they should practice regularly.

Another common way to access a computer is through lax practices by most computer users. For instance, do you have file and printer sharing turned on? If you aren't really using it, you shouldn't. Hackers love to find shares with easy to hack passwords or—even worse—no password. Moreover, a lot of hackers are aware that people, if they have to use a password, will use something that's easy to remember. Usually, people select some ordinary word or name. So hackers have devised hacking utilities that use word lists and name lists to crack your password.

Certain software applications and even some hardware devices, like routers, that require user names and passwords to run or configure them often have generic passwords out of the box and it's up to the network administrator to change them. If the network administrator does not change them from the default when they install the software because they aren't aware of the potential security risks, a hacker can access the network easily. They can also "sniff" data as it passes along the network and decipher your username and password. And, in some cases, they can place small applications on your computer that capture your keystrokes, for instance, so they can see what you're typing.

Remember, a Trojan is something that seems like a gift but has an evil payload to it as well. If you've ever installed anything on your computer from the Internet, you are susceptible to this. For instance, you might download a new game or screen saver, not realizing that a hacker's tool is installed at the same time. Once it's on your machine, any hacker can get to you by using a port scanner to see who is vulnerable. Hackers don't need to create all of these tools themselves. They are all readily available from the Internet. Anyone can download the code, or scripts, to hack into computers.

But how do they find your computer? They don't actually search one by one. Rather, they enter a range of addresses and scan them all at once. Places such as large Internet Service Providers and universities are easy targets because of this. There are lookup tools on the Internet that allow you to enter the name of an organization and they return the range of IP addresses used for the organization. The hacker simply has to enter the range into one of the scripts or programs they have downloaded and it will scan for open ports on all of the computers within the range it can find. These open ports may be there because of a Trojan or because file and printer sharing is turned on, etc.

The best way to help prevent unauthorized access to your computer is to install a firewall. A firewall will block any attempts to access the ports on your computer. More importantly, it hides them from tools like port scanners. You can buy firewalls, such as Norton from Symantec, or you can download them for free, such as Zone Lab's free version of their ZoneAlarm for noncommercial use. Usually the ones you download for free don't have as many features as the ones you purchase. ZoneAlarm also has a more enhanced version that you can purchase.

Hackers can also use something called "wrappers" to render a good application into an evil one. Wrappers take an existing application, such as calc.exe, the calculator for Windows, and they wrap additional code around it. The calculator still works but every time you use it you are also running the other code. The other code might be a Trojan, some other virus, or may even create a new user on your computer for the hacker.

So-called "social engineering" is another common way to learn someone's password. If your network administrator calls you ands asks for your password, should you give it to them? Why or why not? The answer is "no." A network administrator has total power; they don't need to ask you for anything. You may be talking to an imposter trying to elicit your password.

Another method that hackers use is to capture data submitted via the Internet. If you visit a Web site that asks for critical information such as a credit card number, make sure the URL starts with "https": The extra "s" on the http is very important. It means that the web site is using SSL (secure socket layer). Remember the communication ports on your computer? When your computer communicates with another, it uniquely identifies the communication by appending the port number to the IP (Internet Protocol) address. IP is one half of the TCP/IP protocol and deals with addressing. The othe half, Transmission Control Protocol (TCP), deals with end-to-end transmission of the data packets. Every computer on the Internet must have a unique IP address. When a port is appended to it, the channel of communication it opens is called a socket. SSL is a technology that secures that socket so information can be transmitted securely. Otherwise, information is usually sent simply as clear text and anyone can intercept it.

Lastly, some free e-mail sites do not encrypt the e-mail messages when they are transmitted. They are sent instead as clear text. There are encryption techniques that have been developed and are considered industry standards for encrypting e-mail. When you select a free e-mail site, be sure to check on the encryption technology they use, if any.

What Measures Can You Take To Protect Yourself?

- When a software company is made aware that there is a security breach, they usually issue a software patch or fix. You need to regularly check for updates and apply them to your computer.
- Be cautious about the software you download from the Internet.
- Never tell anyone your username and password.
- Turn off file and printer sharing if you aren't using it:
  - In Windows 2000 Professional, Start > Settings > Network and dial-up connections > Local area connections > Properties
  - In Windows XP Professional, Start > Control Panel > Network Connections then right click and choose Properties
  - remove file and printer sharing.
- don't make online transactions unless the address starts with https.
- consider using an e-mail application that encrypts.
- Most important—install a firewall.

Summary

In the same way you expect to perform routine maintenance on your car to keep it running at its best, you also need to develop a routine maintenance schedule for your computer. This will include things like defragging your disk, scanning for viruses, updating your virus signatures to ward off infection by the newest threats, cleaning up unnecessary files, and checking for any errors on your disk. Of course, backups are equally important in case of a disk failure, total system failure, or accidental deletion of files.

Windows operating systems come with utilities that you can use to perform routine maintenance but you can also download freeware or shareware applications as well. In addition, you can purchase third party applications from other companies. Generally speaking, the applications you purchase are more robust and secure than ones you download for free from the Internet. Downloading software also increases the possibility of exposure to viruses, as well. If you do plan to download software, check with friends and colleagues first to see if they have used the application and if it ever caused them problems.

You should also know how to compress and uncompress files using utilities like WinZip. It is very easy to use and it makes a lot more sense to compress files that you intend to e-mail or post on a Web page for download.

ACTIVITIES

Review Questions

1. Explain what you need to do regularly to protect yourself against viruses.
2. List three good security practices to follow to secure your computer.
3. Give two reasons why a hacker might want to hack into your computer.
4. What is a port scanner?
5. What is a hoax?

Hands-on

1. Use Disk Cleanup on your computer. How much space is being taken up by the temporary Internet files?
2. Use the Backup Wizard to back up a folder containing documents and store the backed-up image in My Documents. List the steps and describe the outcome. How would you extract a single file? Using Windows Help, define the five backup types (normal backup, copy backup, incremental backup, differential backup and daily backup).
3. List 5 different firewalls available from http://shareware.cnet.com.
4. Using http://www.symantec.com/avcenter/, list three of the bad viruses wreaking havoc today and give a brief explanation of what they do.
5. Create a folder called CLASS and place three files into it. Create another folder inside of CLASS and call it DATA. Place 3 files inside the DATA folder. Create one zipped file from the CLASS and DATA folders and their contents and make a self-extracting executable from it. Have it unzip to a folder called TESTFILES off the root of the drive or partition. Explain your steps.

Important Terms

Using www.webopedia.com or another online technical dictionary, define:

algorithm	freeware	socket
cluster	hacker	software piracy
defragment	port Scanning	spyware
encryption	Pretty Good	SSL
file compression	Privacy (PGP)	Trojan
firewall	shareware	virus
fragmentation	sniffer	

Multiple Choice Questions

1. Often when you use your computer, _____ are stored on your computer and are not removed.
   a. broken links
   b. temporary files
   c. clusters
   d. sectors
2. Use _____ to easily view the versions of the drivers and service packs on your computer.
   a. Error checking
   b. Defrag
   c. Disk cleanup
   d. System info
3. Use _____ to delete temporary files that are no longer needed.
   a. Error checking
   b. Defrag
   c. Disk cleanup
   d. System info

4. Use _____ to reorganize the data on your hard disk more efficiently.

   a. Error checking

   b. Defrag

   c. Disk cleanup

   d. System info

5. If your disk has been damaged, you can try using _____ to recover a file from a damaged disk.

   a. Error checking

   b. Defrag

   c. Disk cleanup

   d. System info

6. Using the Windows Backup tool will compress many files and/or folders into one file with a(n) _____ file extension.

   a. .bak

   b. .brk

   c. .blk

   d. .bkf

7. In order to use a file that has been backed up, you must use the _____ tool to extract it.

   a. Remind

   b. WinZip

   c. Restore

   d. Recycle Bin

8. Different compression _____ use different techniques to make a file smaller.

   a. ratios

   b. aliases

   c. pseudonyms

   d. algorithms

9. A(n) _____ is code that someone has written usually to do harm to someone else.

   a. virus

   b. antivirus

   c. hacker

   d. hoax

10. To protect yourself from viruses, you must update your _____ signature files regularly.

    a. virus

    b. antivirus

    c. hacker

    d. hoax

11. If you receive an e-mail warning you of a virus, you should first check someplace like Symantec's Web site to see if it is a _____ before you pass the information along.

    a. virus

    b. antivirus

    c. hacker

    d. hoax

12. If you suspect a Trojan, one place you should check is _____ to see if it is running as a service.

    a. Task manager

    b. System manager

    c. Device manager

    d. System information

13. A computer uses _____ to communicate.

    a. ports

    b. states

    c. docks

    d. windows

14. There are _____ on the Internet that allow you to enter the name of an organization and it returns the range of IP addresses used for the organization.

    a. freeware sites

    b. shareware sites

    c. antipiracy sites

    d. lookup tools

15. A URL that begins with https:// indicates that the site is using _____.

    a. Javascript

    b. SSL

    c. PGP

    d. SMTP

CHAPTER 50

Customizing Your Environment

OBJECTIVES

After reading this chapter, you will be able to:

- Demonstrate how to customize your desktop, including:
  - Changing your background
  - Creating your own background
  - Using a screen saver
  - Changing the appearance of icons and other desktop items
  - Changing the screen resolution
  - Rearranging desktop icons
  - Customizing the Taskbar
- Demonstrate how to use the Windows Media Player
- Demonstrate how to use the Sound Recorder
- Demonstrate how to adjust Volume Control

INTRODUCTION

Using a computer isn't always all work and no play. Configuring your desktop to better reflect your personal taste can make your work on the computer less of a chore. It can also lessen eye strain, an important factor in ergonomics. The Microsoft Windows family of operating systems also has some entertainment applications installed by default.

CONFIGURING YOUR DESKTOP

If you have to look at your computer for eight hours a day while at work, it might be a good idea to check out different color schemes and possibly a customized screen saver. Some people argue that colors have an effect on moods. That may or may not be true, but I don't think many people would argue that colors could definitely affect your eyes. Testing a few color combinations under various lighting conditions should prove that some cause more strain on the eyes than others. For this reason alone, you may wish to make some configuration changes on your computer to make it more ergonomically suitable for your needs.

A lot of people use screen savers simply because they are entertaining, but they can also be used for security. Either way, one serious cause for concern is where you get the screen saver. If you are interested in installing a screen saver, check with friends and colleagues who use one and ask if they've ever had a problem with their computer after installing the screen saver. It isn't uncommon for a screen saver to cause your computer to "hang" (freeze up). It also isn't uncommon to be enticed into installing a cool screen saver only to unwittingly install a virus or Trojan along with the screen saver.

Display Properties

To customize your desktop, minimize everything by clicking on the Show Desktop icon in the lower left corner next to the Start button and then right click anywhere on the desktop where there isn't an icon. Then choose Properties from the context menu.

Choosing a Desktop Theme   A theme has preconfigured settings for the background, icons, sounds, and other objects related to the desktop settings in Microsoft Windows XP Professional. The two main themes available allow you to choose between the new look for Microsoft Windows XP Professional or revert to desktop settings that reflect the earlier Microsoft Windows 2000 Professional appearance, which is referred to as Classic. You can choose a theme as a basis and then customize individual desktop components also. If you do so, the name of the theme will be Modified Theme as shown in Figure 5.1.

Figure 5.1

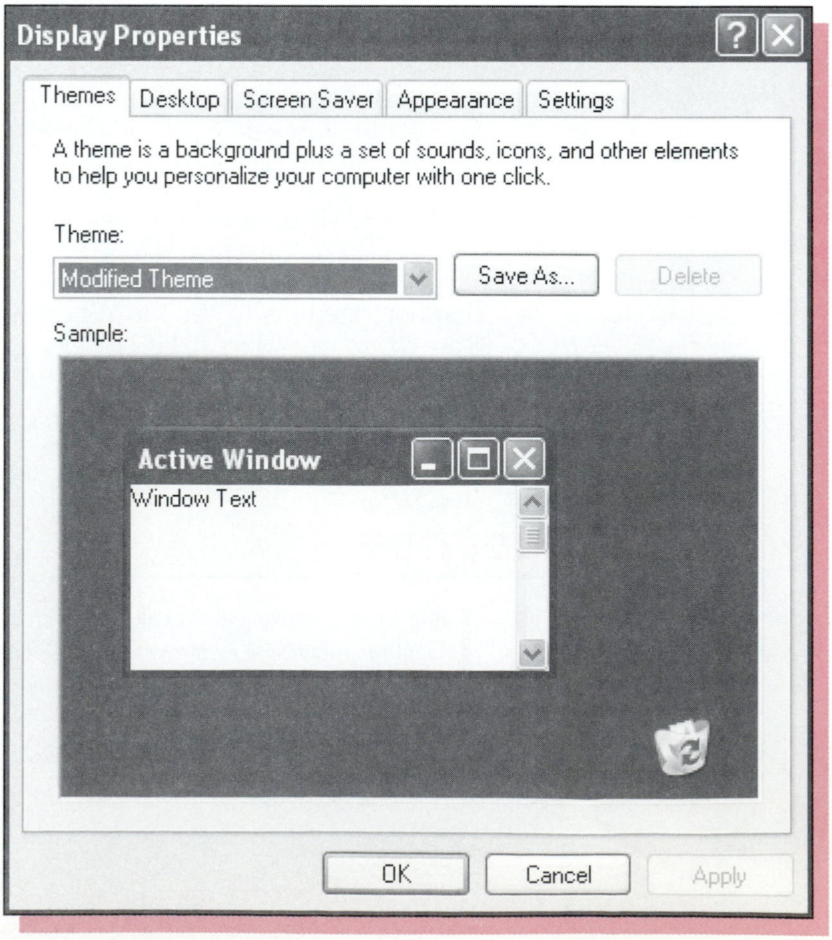

Figure 5.2

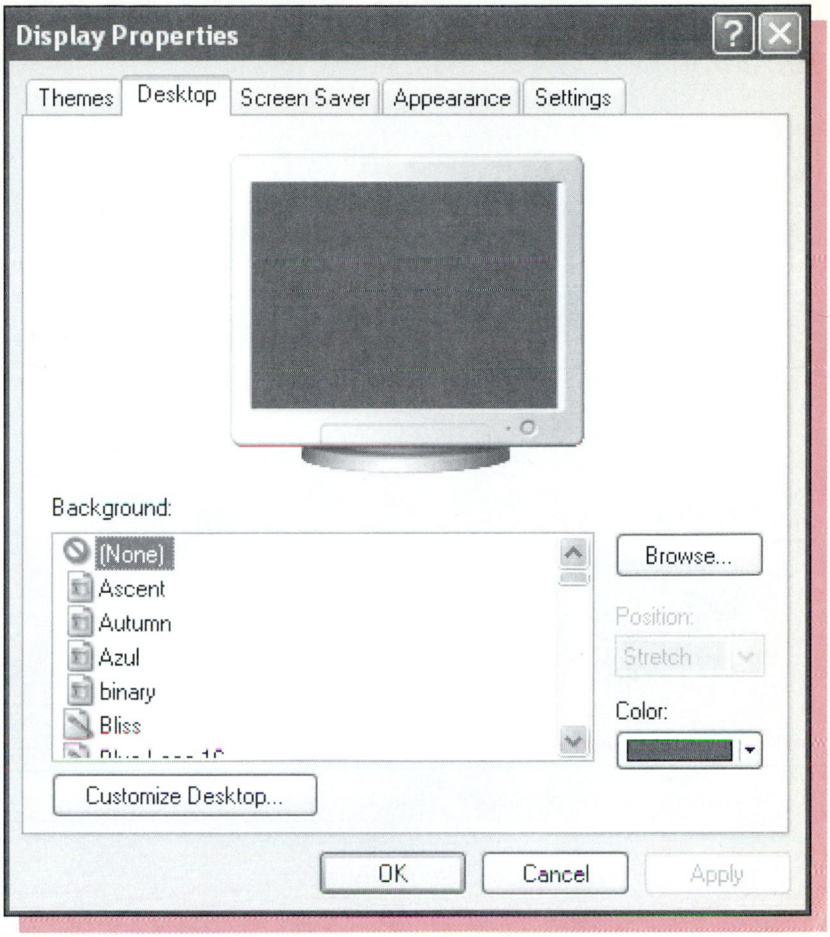

Choosing a Desktop Background You can choose from some of the preinstalled backgrounds to customize your desktop. Microsoft refers to these as "Wallpaper" in Windows 2000 Professional and "Background" in Windows XP Professional. Another option is "None" if you want a solid color for the background versus a graphic (Figure 5.2). If you click one time on any of the wallpaper options listed you will see a preview above it. You can also set any graphic that you find on the Internet to be the background for your desktop.

NOTES   Find a Web site that has graphics and right click on a graphic. Choose the option Set as Background or Set as Wallpaper from the context menu. Open up your Display Properties window again and check to see how your downloaded image is referred to in the Background list.

Creating your own Desktop Background If you find or create your own graphic, you can use that as your desktop background as well.

NOTES   Create a simple graphic using Paint. Save it in the My Pictures folder. Click the Browse button in the Desktop tab (in Windows XP Professional) or the Background tab (in Windows 2000 Professional) of the Display Properties window. Browse to find your graphic.
Click Open and then Apply.

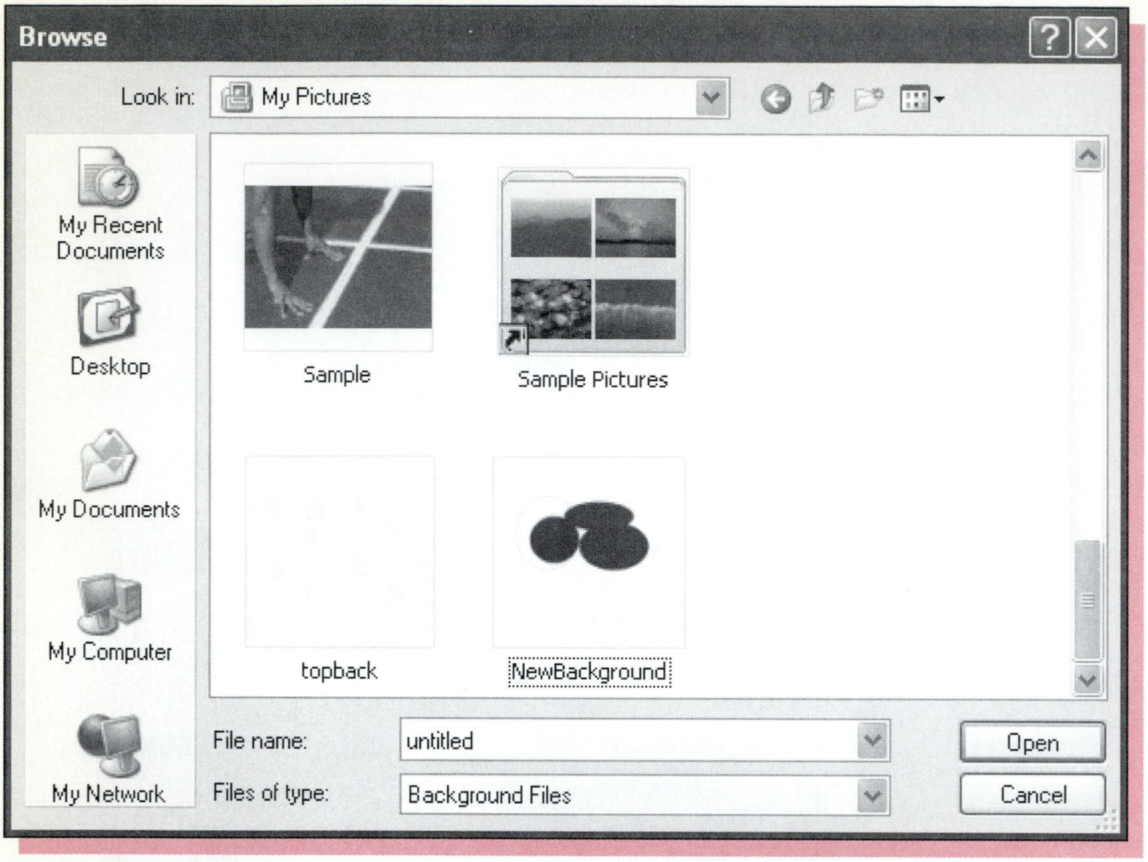

Figure 5.3

Some graphics will look better displayed in the center whereas others should be set to the stretch mode. You configure that under the Picture Display option in Windows 2000 Professional and under Position in Windows XP Professional. When you are done, you may wish to change the colors around your icons for readability. One way to do that is to change the color of the desktop in the Appearance tab (discussed later).

There is also a button in Windows 2000 Professional that says Pattern. You do have some options to use or create a pattern for your desktop background but with all the other settings you can use now this isn't a very popular option anymore and isn't included in Windows XP Professional.

Additional Desktop Settings To see additional desktop settings options in Windows XP Professional, click the Customize Desktop button shown in Figure 5.2. On the General tab, you can change icons for My Computer, My Documents, etc. You can also schedule a Desktop Cleanup to remove icons that haven't been used recently. In Windows 2000 Professional, some of these options are usually found under the Effects tab.

The Web tab in Figure 5.5 will allow you to view Web content on your desktop. You can configure it to show any Web page and the objects on it are clickable, just like a Web page. You can also configure it to update the Web page periodically so that you have the most current content. If you have a favorite sports or news site, this might be an interesting option. In Windows 2000 Professional, the Web settings may have a separate tab in the Display Properties window like the Screen Saver, Desktop, and Appearance options.

Screen Savers A lot of people think that you should leave your computer on 24 hours a day, seven days a week (24/7). After all, what is the screen saver for? But in reality, the typical computer is not designed to run 24/7. You don't leave your car running when you're not using it, for example. The computer is made up of electronic components that can fail after prolonged use, the same way the components in a car engine can.

Figure 5.4

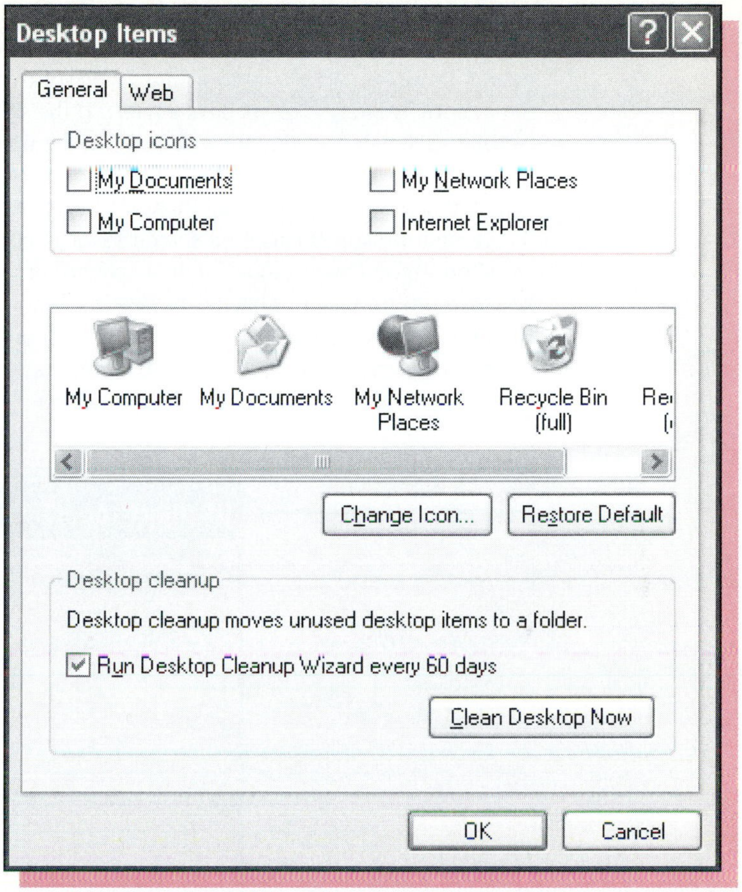

Figure 5.5

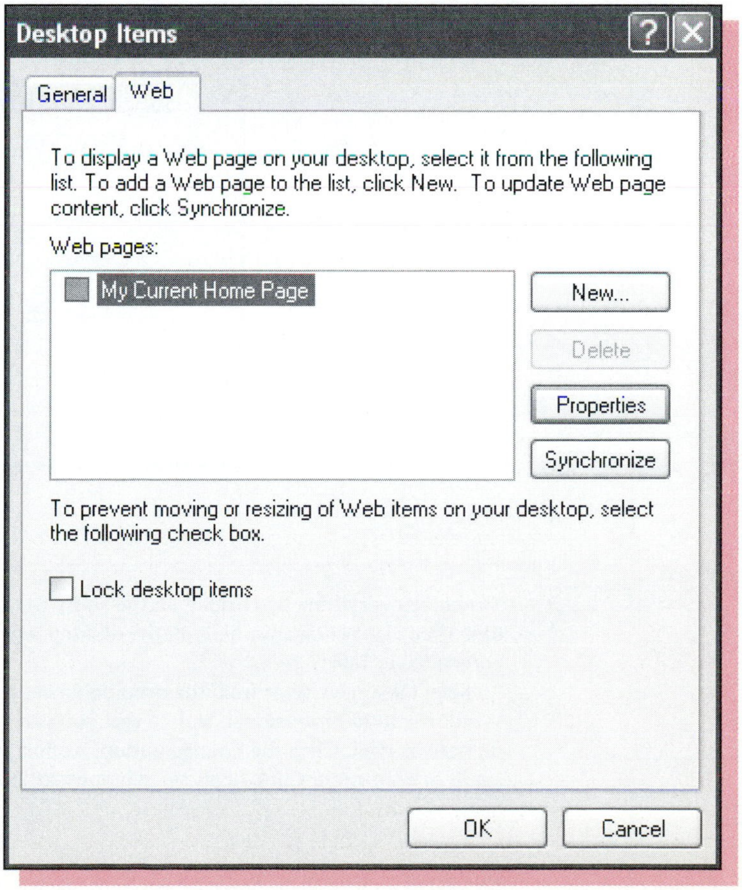

A screen saver isn't really necessary for a typical home user. If you're only using a computer for a few hours and then turn it off until the next time, you don't need a screen saver. In some cases, it can come in handy, however. An example would be a work environment where the same screen is displayed from 8A.M. until 7P.M., five or six days a week. If the same screen is left on the monitor for a prolonged period of time such as every day for a year or so, the image may burn into the monitor. You'll know when this has happened because even when the monitor is turned off you can still see a ghost-like image of the screen that would be displayed there if turned on.

Another reason for using a screen saver is security. You can set your screen saver to automatically come on if you haven't touched the keyboard or mouse for a specific period of time and you can set it to be password protected. That means that if someone tries to access your computer if you've stepped away for a few minutes, they'll need to know your password to clear the screen saver. No matter where you get your screen saver software, they all basically do the same thing but some may have some added features and the screen savers that come with Windows also allow you to set a password.

Figure 5.6

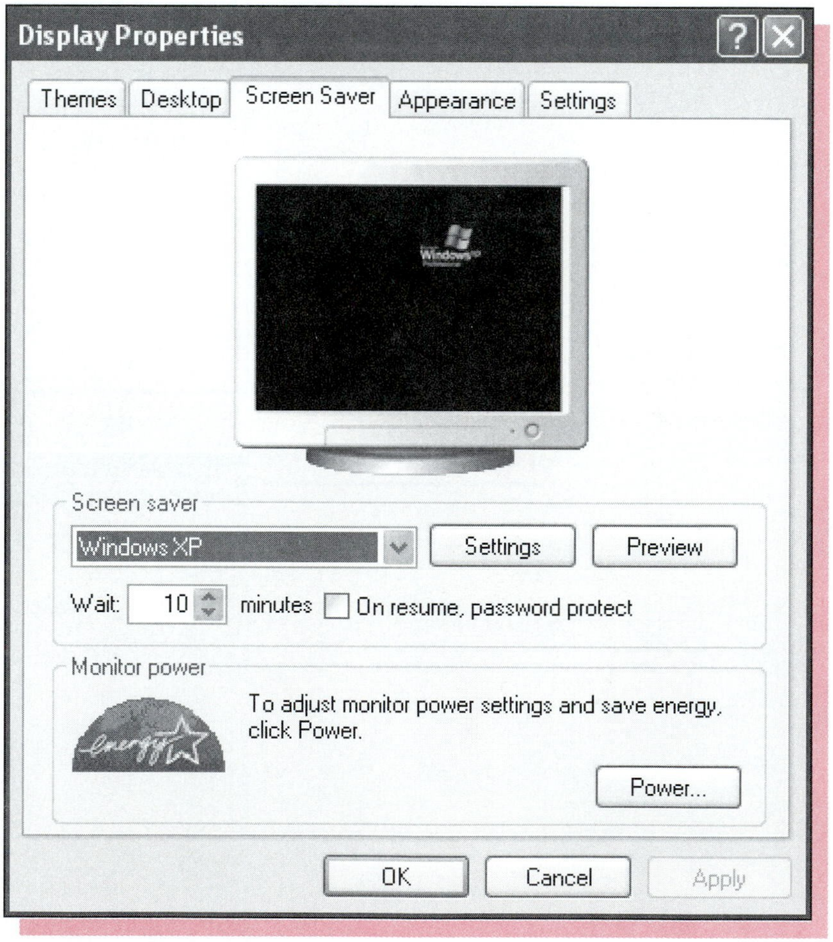

NOTES Minimize everything by clicking on the Show Desktop icon in the lower left corner next to the Start button. Then right click anywhere on the desktop where there isn't an icon. Choose Properties and then the Screen Saver tab.

Select a screen saver from the drop down list and then check the Password Protected checkbox in Windows 2000 Professional. Notice that you can set the number of minutes before the screen saver comes on here as well. Click the Change button. At that point you would enter a new password and then type it again to confirm it. Click Apply. In Windows XP Professional, the option to set a password is called On

Resume, Password Protect. It doesn't ask you to create a password. To unlock the screen saver, you would use the password you use to log in to the computer.

What is another way to get to the Display Properties window? Check Start > Control Panel or Start > Settings > Control Panel. There is an icon there for Display.

Other Screen Saver Options Of course, you can also download or purchase applications that will not only act as a screen saver but will also give you a different desktop each day. Again, check with friends and colleagues to see if they've used any applications you are considering and ask if they've had any problems after installation.

Figure 5.7

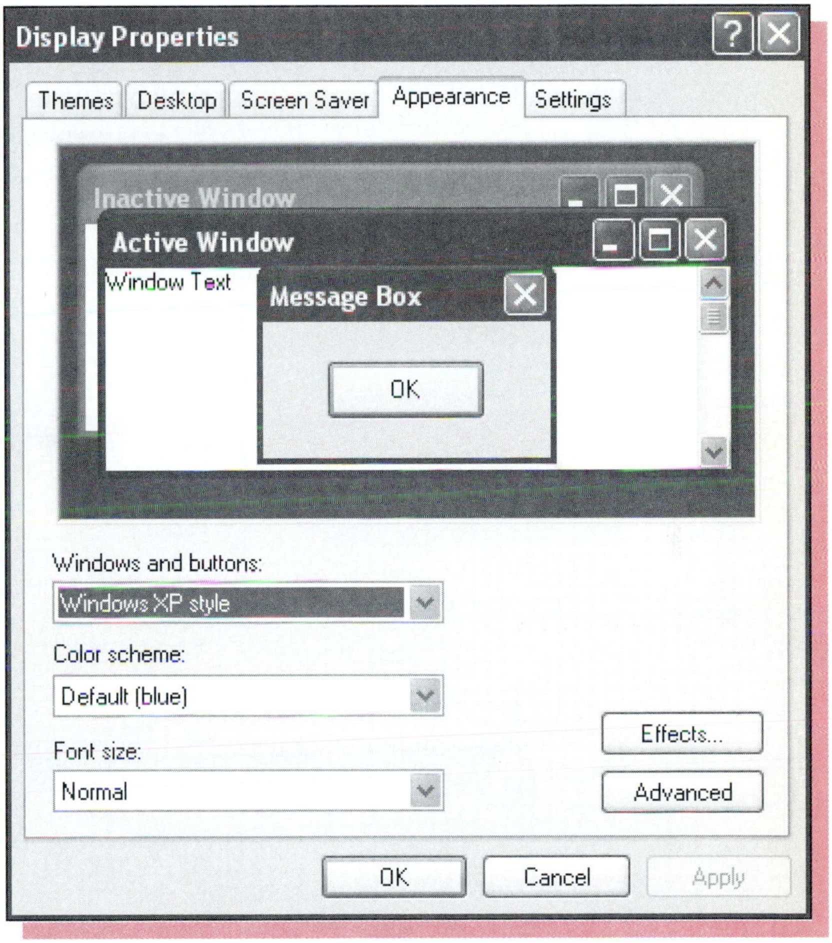

Appearance In the Display Properties window, you have some options to configure the individual objects on your desktop.

NOTES   Go to the Appearance tab and select a scheme for your desktop in Windows 2000 Professional. A scheme is a preconfigured setting for all of the items that make up your desktop. In Windows XP Professional, you can choose between the XP and Windows Classic style for the windows and buttons as well as the color scheme. You can also set the color individually for each item. In Windows XP Professional, you need to click the Advanced button to see the list of individual items. In the drop down list for each item, select a different color. For some items, you will also have the option of changing the font attributes (Figure 5.8).

Look closely at the items you have to choose from. Remember that Windows has a graphical user interface for you to point and click. Every item that you can click on is an object. You can customize exactly how you want each of these objects to appear.

Figure 5.8

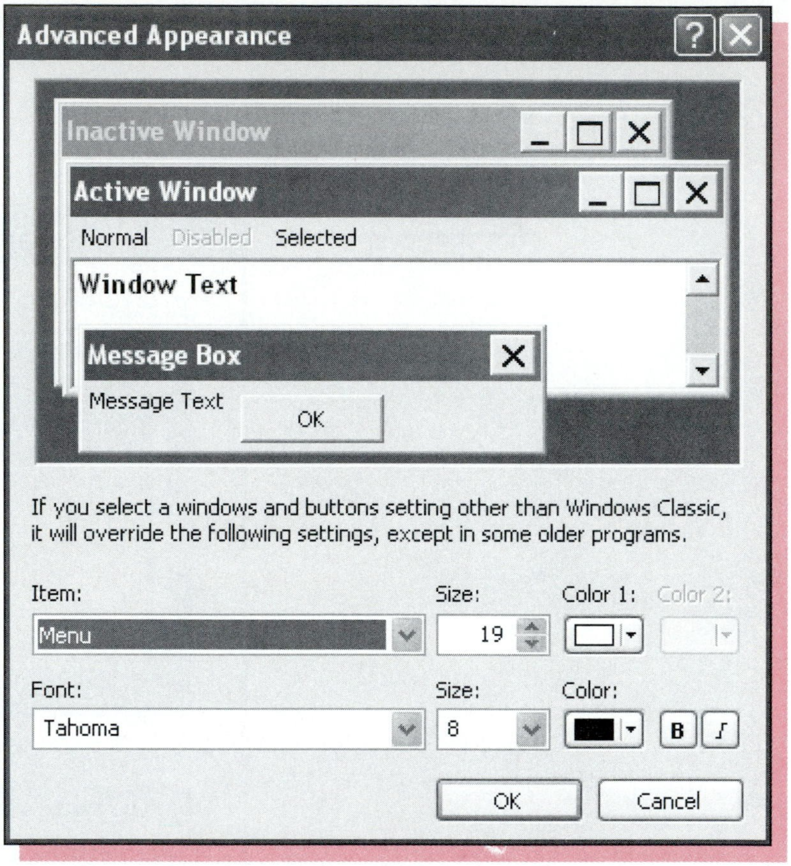

Figure 5.9

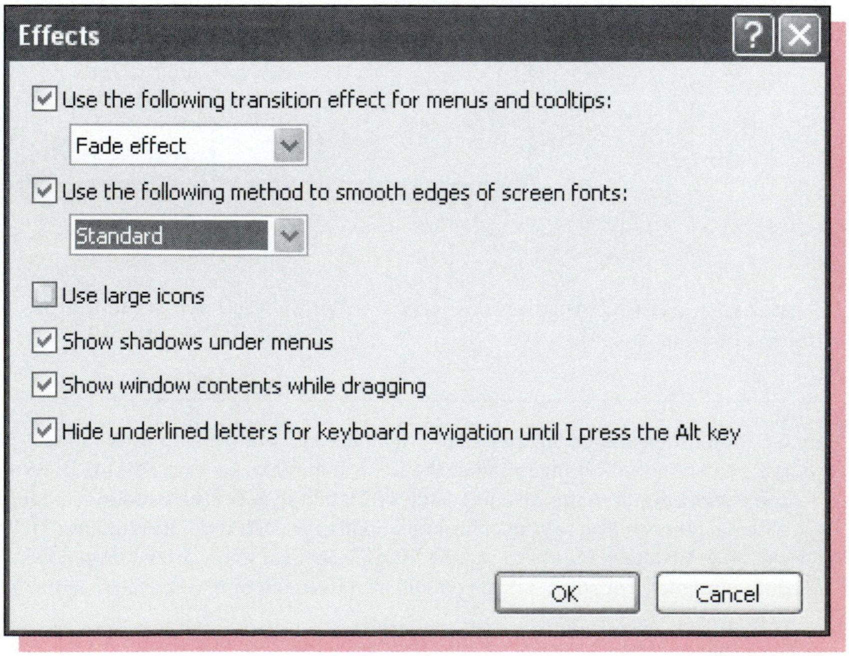

Effects This allows you to customize things like the icons that will be used on your desktop and any special effects that may be used when you open a menu. Choosing the option to use large icons may be helpful for someone visually impaired. Use caution when choosing some of these options, as they tend to be resource-intensive. If you do not have a powerful computer, you may not wish to make any changes here at all.

As an example, whether or not you can view the contents of a window when you are dragging it across your desktop isn't really going to have much effect on your productivity but takes a little more work on the computer's part to do it. A fairly new computer shouldn't have any problems handling the additional load but a very old, slow computer may.

To configure effects in Windows XP Professional, click the Effects button on the Appearance tab. In Windows 2000 Professional, there may be a separate tab for Effects along with the Appearance, Screen Saver, etc. tabs.

Settings Depending on the software you use, you may need to reconfigure the size of the screen area and the number of colors displayed. Some applications, such as games, will make the changes automatically when you run them. Video-intensive games often prefer to run at 640×480 with only 256 colors, for instance.

You may find that changing these settings will make it easier or harder to see the text on your computer. Imagine that a computer monitor is like a spreadsheet. Adjusting your screen resolution determines how many columns and rows you can see at one time. Setting your screen resolution to 640×480 allows you to see 640 columns and 480 rows at a time. If you change your settings to 1024×768, you can see more columns and rows but the icons and everything else being displayed will be proportionately smaller to accommodate it.

Figure 5.10

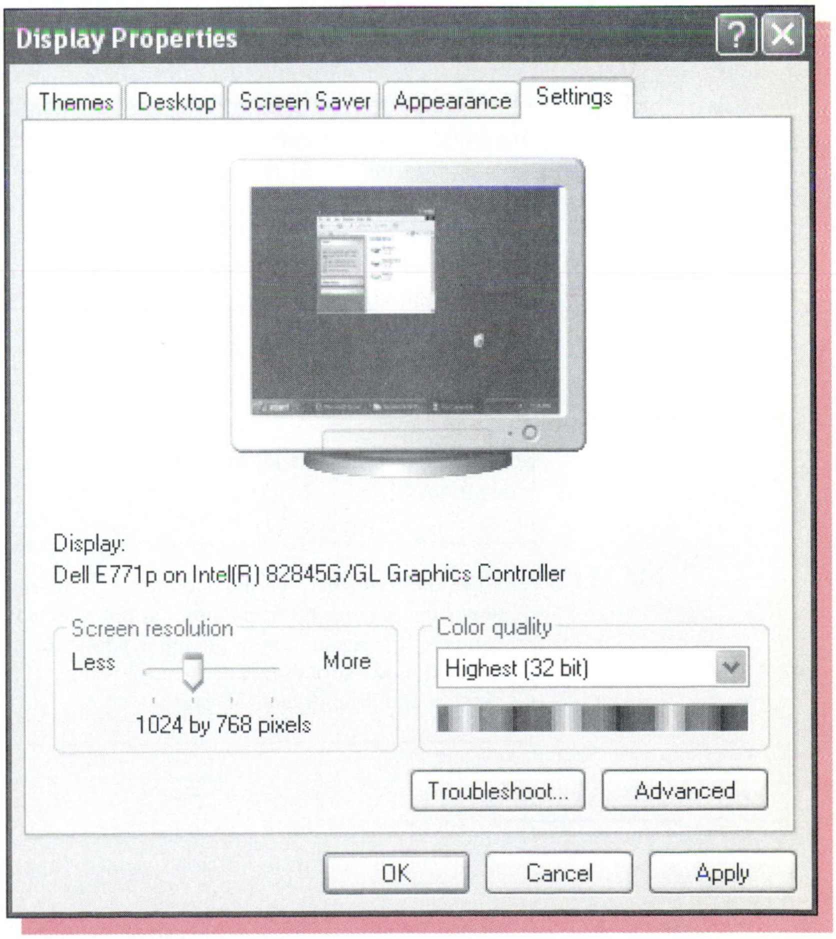

NOTES   Change your screen area to 640 × 480. Then change it to 800 × 600. Finally, try 1024 × 768. Which did you prefer? You may find that if you leave it at 640 × 480, you have to scroll a lot, even when using applications such as Microsoft Word. If you leave it at 1024 × 768, you may find yourself squinting more and straining your back as you lean over the desk to get a closer look.

Like Goldilocks, you need to find the settings that are just right for you. But when might your personal decision be important to others? If you are a Webmaster, you will design Web pages on your computer with the settings you have chosen. If you design a Web page to look good at one setting, it may not look good at another. This is a design issue that you will need to consider. After creating your Web pages, it is considered a good practice to view them on other computers with different monitors, settings, browsers, and operating systems. Programmers will face similar issues. If you design a Visual Basic form, for example, to look better at 1024 × 768 your users may not be pleased if they prefer 640 × 480.

What setting do you think is more common currently? You can test your theory by changing the settings and then visiting some of your favorite Web sites. Can you tell if the pages look better using one setting versus another?

Let's go back to the Display Properties. What color options do you have? If you change to 256 colors, do you notice a difference? You should. Even your desktop icons should look less clear and attractive. Any Web page you view will probably be downright ugly. When would you ever want to use only 256 colors? Whenever you have an application that uses video, such as a game, for example. Video is pretty resource-intensive and the compression algorithms for them aren't as good as most hardware would like them to be. A clip created using millions of colors would be huge and really isn't practical just yet.

You can install an additional video card in your computer and connect a second monitor. Windows does support multiple monitors but you do need a separate video card for each monitor. If you did have two cards and two monitors, you could have a different application showing on each monitor. If you have a second video card and monitor installed, you will see an option in Windows 2000 Professional under your color choices that says "Extend my Windows desktop onto this monitor." In Windows XP Professional, you would click the second monitor icon in the Settings tab to select it and then choose Extend my Windows desktop onto this monitor. You could then display one application split across both monitors or two separate applications—one on each monitor.

Usually you would not need to click on the Advanced tab, but if your computer wants to reboot whenever you change the size of your screen area you can change the setting there. Click on Advanced and under the General tab you should find a setting that lets you make changes without rebooting (Figure 5.11). Under the Monitor tab you will also see the refresh rate that your monitor uses. You monitor constantly refreshes the images it is projecting onto the screen and this value is measured in megahertz.

Desktop Icon Arrangement

Some people prefer to let Windows align the icons on their desktop and others prefer to position the icons themselves.

NOTES   Right click anywhere on the desktop where there isn't currently an icon and make sure that Auto Arrange under the Arrange Icons By option is not selected (Figure 5.12). Choose Arrange Icons by Name. What happened? Drag an icon to the other side of the desktop and drop it. Does it stay there?

Next, make sure that Auto Arrange is selected. What happened? Drag an icon to the other side of the desktop and drop it. Does it stay?

Customizing the Taskbar

Your Taskbar is generally at the bottom of your desktop but you can customize its location also. To do so, point to the Taskbar, hold down the left mouse button, and then drag and drop. You can resize it by grabbing the edge and dragging your mouse. Actually, these two things are some of the common

Figure 5.11

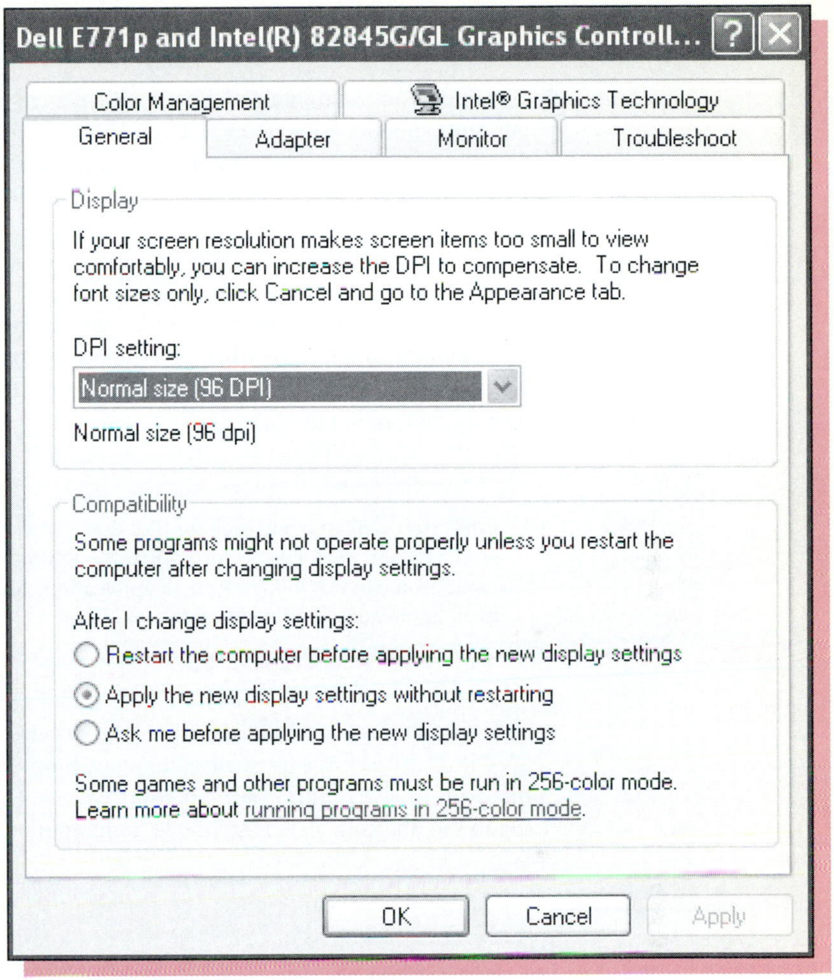

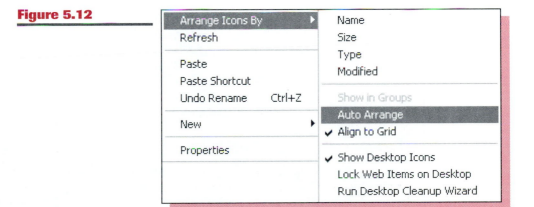

Figure 5.12

mistakes that new computer users make all the time but have no clue about what they did wrong and how to get it back to normal.

You can also add folders to the Taskbar. As an example, drag the My Documents folder and drop it on the Taskbar. You may need to resize the Taskbar afterwards to see the new contents. Whenever you want to get something off the Taskbar, right click on the Taskbar and choose Toolbars. Unselect any toolbars you do not want included on the Taskbar.

ENTERTAINMENT

Although you can download other media players to listen to your favorite music, your operating system has some applications already. Even if you have no interest in listening to music or watching movies using your computer, you should at least know how to configure your sound settings. To see what entertainment applications Windows has, click Start > Programs > Accessories > Entertainment.

Windows Media Player

The Windows Media Player should launch automatically when you try to stream some multimedia content from the Internet or when you attempt to play a sound or video file from your computer. Do you have any? The media player supports a lot of different media file types including wav, snd, au, mpg, mov, qt, avi, mdi, etc.

NOTES   Click Start > Search and look for files that end in .wav. What other extensions are valid? In Windows Media Player, click File > Open > Browse and then click on the drop down arrow where it says "Files of type." You can use this trick on all applications to see what types of files they support. Trying to "Save as" in an application would also give some clues.

The Windows Media Player also plays your music CDs. It should launch automatically when you put a music CD in your CD-ROM drive. The Windows Media Player has controls similar to the controls on a VCR or cassette player such as the Play, Stop, Pause, Previous, and Next buttons (Figure 5.13). If you rest your mouse on the control buttons, you will see what each one does. You have the option of listening to the tracks in a standard mode, random mode (shuffle), etc.

Figure 5.13

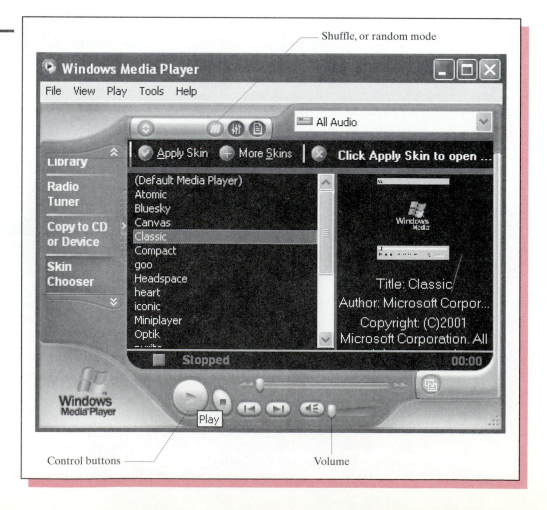

Shuffle, or random mode

Control buttons

Volume

On the left side of the Media Player window are some menu options including Now Playing, Media Guide, and Skin Chooser. You can choose the Classic media look if you prefer the older look for the Media Player or you can choose different "skins." A skin is just a way to customize the look of the Media Player.

Figure 5.14

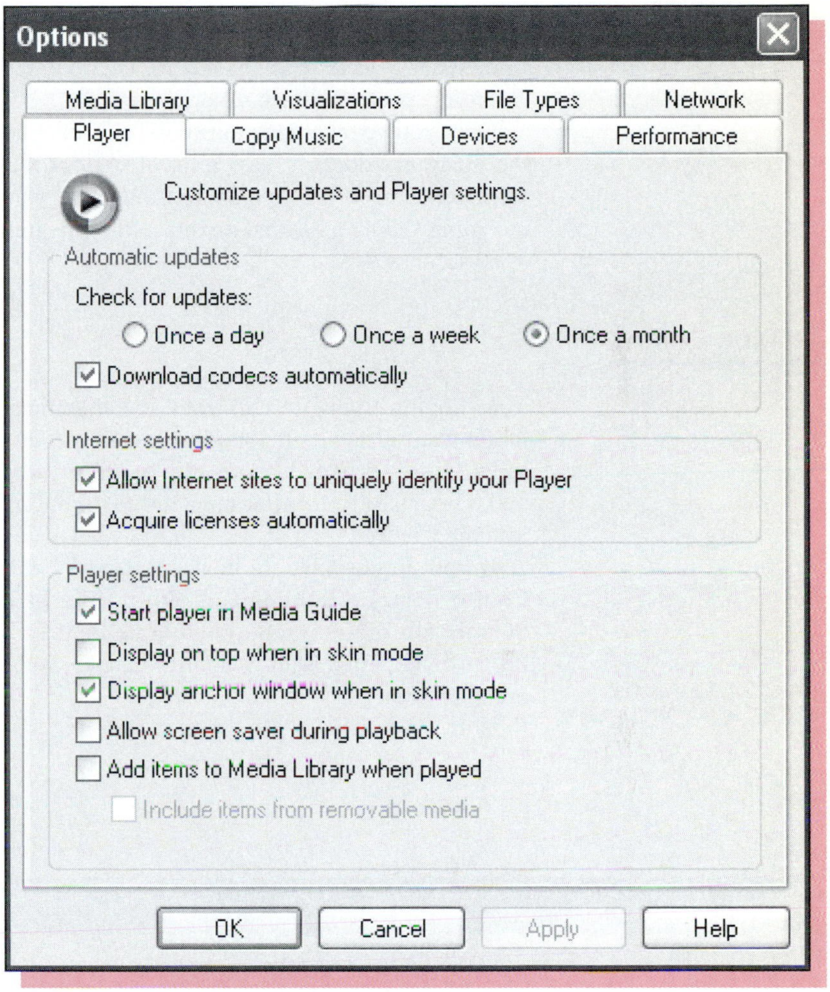

If you click Tools > Options you can see that you also have some default configuration settings. For most, the default settings are probably fine but they include how often the Media Player checks for new updates and what view the Player should start in (e.g., Media Guide).

Figure 5.15

Sound Recorder

The sound recorder is a simple way to create a short .wav file of your own. It might be used to send a short message across the Internet—grandchild to grandparents, etc. You can also insert sound files into files such as Microsoft Word documents or PowerPoint slideshows. This might come in handy for transcription reasons, giving additional information about certain passages or slides, etc. The Sound Recorder also allows you to play .wav files.

To create your own .wav files, you'll need a microphone and your computer must have a sound card in it. When you're ready to record, click the red button or click File > New. When you want to stop recording, click the black square.

Once you've recorded your sound clip, click File > Save to name your .wav file. The effects option on the menu bar doesn't have a lot of options but you can add an echo, increase/decrease the speed, increase/decrease the volume, or reverse the .wav file. You do have some minor editing options as well, including adding a file and mixing a file. One limitation is that you can only create short .wav files of up to 60 seconds.

Volume Control

You shouldn't have to edit your sound settings, but on occasion it is necessary. For instance, you might want to mute all sound temporarily. You may have a shortcut icon to the Volume Control that resembles a speaker in your tray on the Taskbar. Double click it to get Figure 5.16 where you can make your configuration changes. To mute all sound, check the Mute all box in the column for Volume Control.

If you do not have an icon in your tray and would prefer to have one, click Start > Settings > Control Panel > Sounds and Multimedia in Windows 2000 Professional. Check the box on the Sounds tab that says Show volume control on the Taskbar then click Apply. In Windows XP Professional, click Start > Control Panel > Sounds and Audio Devices, then select Place volume icon in the taskbar.

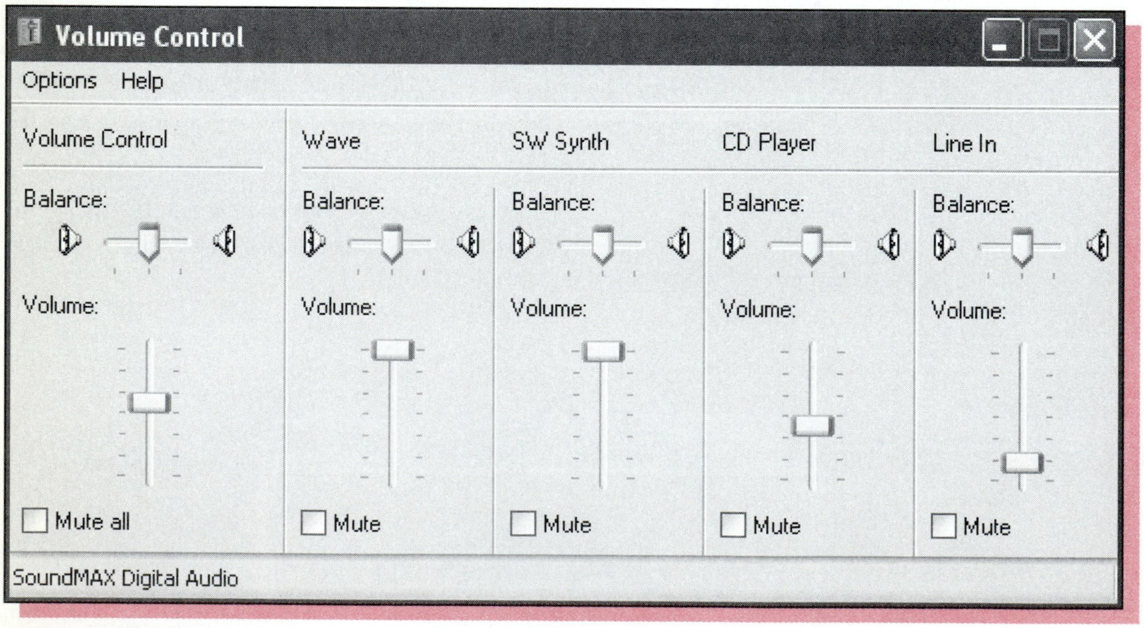

Figure 5.16

Figure 5.17

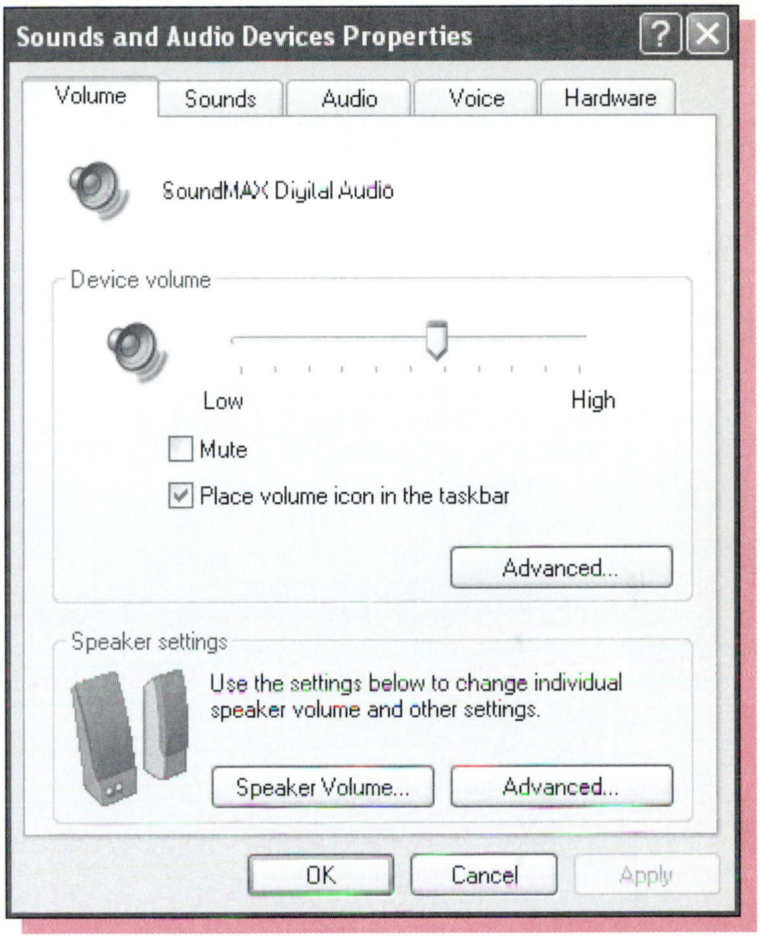

Sounds and Audio Devices Properties

Summary

It's easy to lose track of time when you are working or playing on a computer. At the end of a long session you may notice that your shoulders, wrists, back, and eyes are bothering you. Ergonomics may become more important as one ages, but proper placement of fingers and wrists, proper seat height in relation to the keyboard, and even the colors you use will have some affect on you at any age.

The screen resolution, font size, and colors can all affect eye strain. You should customize your environment to your own tastes to lessen that strain. Screen savers, on the other hand, are mostly used for entertainment. Since most computers are not designed to run 24/7, there really isn't a need to use a screen saver unless you're also using the feature that locks the screen when you step away from your computer for any length of time. Customizing your Taskbar and creating shortcuts can help reduce the strain on your wrists by minimizing the amount of clicking you need to do to launch an application.

Of course, it isn't a matter of all work and no play. You can also enjoy your favorite music, videos, and streaming content on your computer either using the players that come with Microsoft Windows or downloading your own from the Internet.

ACTIVITIES

Review Questions

1. Explain how ergonomics may play a role in customizing your desktop.

2. Under the Appearance tab on the Display Properties window, list five different items that you can customize. In Windows XP Professional, choose the Advanced button to see the items.

3. What is a scheme and what are three examples?

4. What does it mean to say that a monitor's resolution is 800 by 600?

5. What is the path to the default folder that contains the graphic files used for the background or wallpaper?

Hands-on

1. Resize your Taskbar until it fills about 1/3 of your screen. Right click and choose Toolbars > Desktop. What happens? What do you need to do to restore it to the previous settings?

2. Configure your computer to use the 3D Maze screensaver. Click Settings and choose different graphics for the wall, floor, and ceiling by using the arrow buttons to the right of the sample textures. Test your screen saver. What steps would you take to use your own graphics for the textures?

3. Create your own appearance scheme by altering properties for several items and save your new scheme. Explain what you altered and how you saved it. How would you return it to the original Windows scheme?

4. Select a different image for each of the icons in the Effects tab in Windows 2000 Professional or by choosing Customize Desktop in the Desktop tab in Windows XP Professional. How do you return them to their default settings?

5. Configure your desktop to show Web content. Explain the steps.

Important Terms

Using www.webopedia.com or another online technical dictionary, define:

avi	midi	resolution
digital audio	mp3	streaming
ergonomic	pixel	wav
MHz	refresh rate	

Multiple Choice Questions

1. _____ deals with your physical health and safety in the workplace.
   a. Phototonics
   b. IEEE
   c. Ergonomics
   d. Economics

2. One way to set your _____ is to right click on a graphic in a Web page and choose the appropriate option.
   a. screen saver
   b. screen resolution
   c. favorites
   d. background or wallpaper

3. There are three different choices for the picture display of your background: _____, _____, and _____.
   a. square, circle, rectangle
   b. small, medium, large
   c. center, top, bottom
   d. center, tile, stretch

4. A _____ is a pre-configured setting for all of the items that make up your desktop.
   a. scheme
   b. desktop
   c. display
   d. screen saver

5. Every item that you can click on your desktop is a(n) _____.
   a. icon
   b. effect
   c. object
   d. tool

6. In the _____ tab of the Display properties, you can configure your desktop to display web content.
   a. HTML
   b. www
   c. Effects
   d. Web

7. Your monitor constantly refreshes the images it is projecting onto the screen and this value is measured in _____.
   a. kilowatts
   b. amps
   c. megahertz
   d. gigahertz

8. If you are unable to place your icons on your desktop where you want them, chances are the _____ option is selected.
   a. Stationary
   b. Left justified
   c. Arrange icons
   d. Auto Arrange

9. The Sound Recorder supports _____ files.
   a. au
   b. wav
   c. snd
   d. mpg

10. The _____ should launch automatically when you try to stream some multimedia content from the Internet.
    a. Windows Media Player
    b. Sound Recorder
    c. Web browser
    d. Volume Control

Computer Hardware

OBJECTIVES

After reading this chapter, you will be able to:

- Explain the difference between RAM and ROM
- Explain the difference between RAM and storage
- Explain what a motherboard is
- Explain what a processor does
- Explain what RAID is
- Explain what a UPS is
- Demonstrate how to write-protect a disk
- Explain the difference between a partition and a disk
- Explain the role of the boot.ini file
- Explain why binary math is important to computers
- Explain the difference between a modem and a network interface card
- Explain the difference between a parallel and serial connection
- Identify at least four different ports by sight on a computer
- Demonstrate how to clean a mouse
- Explain what a driver is
- Explain what an interrupt is

INTRODUCTION

We all know that our computer is comprised of hardware and software. How does the hardware know what to do? How does the computer receive input from the user and transmit the user's requests to the processor?

People receive input from five senses and process that information with a brain. They can output information in several ways including speech, gestures, and the written word. Computers receive input via the keyboard, mouse, and other input devices and can output the results via the monitor, printer, sound card, etc. It is the operating system that coordinates all of this.

SURVEY OF INTERNAL HARDWARE COMPONENTS

The central processing unit (CPU), utilizing a combination of random access memory (RAM) and virtual memory to temporarily store data, commands, and results, processes the necessary commands to do whatever the operating system says the user wants to do. If the computer were compared to a human, the processor would be the computer's brain.

It is the role of the operating system to act as an intermediary between the user and the hardware and to interpret what the user wants to do into a language that the computer understands. You may physically touch the computer when you insert a floppy disk, but it is up to the operating system to handle the hardware when you say you want to copy a file to the floppy disk and actually move the physical components inside the floppy drive.

Ever notice the metal shield on the floppy disk? It is there only to protect the round, mylar-coated disk, sometimes called a cookie, inside. The cookie is where the data is written to and read from. When you insert a floppy disk into the drive, a mechanism pulls the metal cover to the side so the cookie is exposed. Another mechanism spins the cookie inside the floppy disk and the read/write head inside the floppy drive is moved across to access it. That metal cover is not required for the disk to work. If it ever bends you should tear it off, copy your data to another disk, and then throw the damaged disk away. Do not try to use the disk with the metal cover still on it if it is bent. It will become wedged inside the floppy drive and require some intense moments with a pair of needle-nose pliers to get it out. The floppy drive can be damaged in the process and you may possibly void a warranty.

As you can imagine, the components that make up a personal computer can be rather complicated. Here you will receive only an introduction to some of the major components of a computer system.

Case and Motherboard

If you were to build your own computer, you would need to consider every component, including the case. Usually, when you buy a case, the power supply is included but nothing else. So you would next move on to the motherboard. Usually when you buy a motherboard, you can buy it with a processor (CPU) already installed on it or you could buy the processor separately. The motherboard is what all of the internal components connect to. Many of these components need power; hence the power supply on the case. The power supply has a bunch of cables attached to it and you connect these cables to the individual components inside the computer. Examples include the hard drive, the floppy drive, a CD-ROM drive; all of these components need power to operate because they have moving parts.

The components inside the computer are either inserted into a slot on the motherboard or they're connected to the motherboard via a cable. For instance, a video card might be inserted into a slot on the motherboard, whereas a floppy drive is connected to the motherboard with a 34-pin ribbon cable. There are usually tricks to connecting the cable, including what direction a red stripe on one edge of the ribbon cable should be facing. This may vary with different manufacturers and you may need to check the documentation. If you connect the floppy drive cable with the red stripe on the wrong side, for example, your floppy drive won't work and the green indicator light may stay on constantly.

When you purchase a motherboard and a case separately, one thing you need to be concerned with is making sure the motherboard will actually fit into the case correctly. To connect various components such as the video monitor, the mouse, the keyboard, etc., you must plug various cables into the back of your computer. The ports you're plugging these into may be physically on the motherboard and your case must have the appropriate opening in just the right spot so that all of those ports are accessible from the outside the case.

Processor

There are different vendors who sell processors but the most commonly known company is still Intel. Intel has an entire family of processors and some are considered more appropriate for desktop computers while others are more powerful and are considered more appropriate for servers. Processors are coded with instructions to handle all of the operating system needs. Different processors are coded with different instructions and one may be more suitable than another depending on what you plan to do with the computer. For instance, the MMX processor had special instructions to better handle multimedia technology.

In addition, you can also have more than one processor inside a computer. This is most commonly done in a server. Typical desktop computers do not have dual processors. A machine that has dual processors is capable of processing approximately twice as many instructions at one time.

Although all of the components inside a computer are important, arguably one of the most important components is the processor, sometimes also referred to as the CPU or central processing unit. In addition to Intel, another company that manufactures processors is AMD (Advanced Micro Devices, Inc.). These two companies have a healthy competition and constantly work toward developing better and faster processors: This competition is usually good for us, the consumers. Remember that while the processor uses RAM and virtual memory, it is still the processor that does all the real work as it completes millions of instructions per second. Therefore, the speed of the processor is extremely important and is now commonly measured in gigahertz.

Processors have evolved over time beginning with the 8086 and 8088, then the 286, 386, 486, and then on the Pentium-class computers. It is rumored that one reason why Intel stopped using numbers to name the processors is because a number cannot be copyrighted, whereas a word, such as Pentium or Itanium, can. So while Intel may sell the Pentium processor, AMD has different names for their processors, including Athlon and Duron.

Storage

In the beginning, personal computers did not have hard drives. Instead, most had two floppy drives, an A: drive and a B: drive. You booted the computer with an operating system, usually some version of DOS, on a floppy disk in the first floppy drive and you stored your data on the floppy disk in the second floppy drive.

If you wanted to run an application program, you waited until after the computer was booted and then you took the first floppy disk out with the operating system on it and replaced it with the application disk that you wanted to run. You stored your data files on the second floppy disk. These floppy disks were 5-1/4 inches and were definitely very floppy. The 3-1/2 inch floppy disks used now are still called floppy even though they are contained inside a less flexible cover.

Storage on the computer is very important. The storage space you have on your computer comes in many different forms and the information you store on your disks stays there until you delete it. Without storage space a computer would not be able to run the huge applications that are common today. While operating systems and applications used to fit on single floppies, they now can take up large amounts of storage space.

At first, storage space was very expensive. The first computer lab I remember helping to set up had Intel 286 processors, 3 1/2″ floppy drives, 40 MB hard drives and, if my memory serves, 4 MB of RAM. By the standards of the day they were screaming fast and had more storage space than anyone would ever need! Applications in the DOS days were typically very small, primarily because they were not graphic intensive, and so were the files they produced. Because our operating systems, applications, and uses for computers have changed, we now have several more options to store applications and data. It is not uncommon for computers to have Zip drives, CD-ROM drives, CD-writable and rewritable drives, floppy drives, and huge hard drives.

To learn more about the storage options on your computer click Start > Settings > Control Panel > Administrative Tools > Computer Management in Windows 2000 Professional. In Windows XP Professional, click Start > Control Panel > Performance and Maintenance > Administrative Tools > Computer Management. In both Windows 2000 Professional and Windows XP Professional, you can also right click on My Computer and choose Manage.

In Computer Management, left click on Disk Management. Here you can see all of the storage devices available on your computer and see additional information such as their storage size and the file system they are using. Typically you choose the file system when you format the disk but you can also convert from FAT/FAT32 to NTFS using a convert utility that comes with Windows 2000. You cannot, however, convert from NTFS to FAT/FAT32.

Figure 6.1

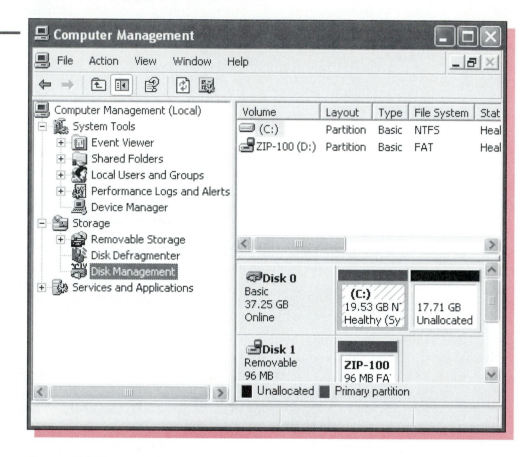

Types of Disks The hard disk is the most popular place to save applications and data. Saving data to a hard disk usually has the fastest transfer rates as compared to saving to a floppy or Zip disk. One of the things that determines the speed of a hard disk is the controller card. A controller card connects your disk(s) to the motherboard. Most hard drives in typical home or office computers are called IDE ("Intelligent Drive Electronics" or "Integrated Drive Electronics") drives. With IDE drives, the controller is actually integrated with the drive. SCSI (pronounced *scuzzy*) is another type of controller and is capable of much faster data transfer rates. SCSI is short for "Small Computer System Interface." Typically, because it is more expensive, a SCSI solution is used on a server and not on a regular desktop computer.

Because a server is usually storing important data and applications necessary for an organization to operate smoothly, maintaining the integrity of that data is very important. If a SCSI solution is used for high data transfer speed, an additional option to ensure the integrity of the data is to couple that with a RAID solution.

RAID stands for "redundant array of inexpensive disks" or "independent disks," depending on what source you read. Either way, RAID technology uses multiple disks or, depending on which level of RAID is used, will either just speed up write times or will offer fault tolerance. Fault tolerance is the capacity for a system to continue to perform despite an unexpected hardware or software malfunction.

Microsoft Server operating systems can handle three different levels of RAID: 0, 1, and 5. Level 0 requires at least two disks and is called disk striping. It is used to increase speed but offers no fault tolerance. Data is striped across the disks, which also offers load balancing on the disks. Remember, this would be done on a server that is typically used to store data for a lot of people. They would be spending most of their time reading files from and writing files to the disk (I/O). Load balancing means you are spreading the work load out across the disks.

Level 1 is disk duplexing or mirroring and simply means that you have two disks (and one or two controllers) and you make an exact copy onto the second disk. If one disk fails, you always have an up-to-the-minute copy. Level 1 has slower write times because it must write everything to both disks but it does offer fault tolerance because you can recover the data if one disk fails.

Level 5 is called disk striping with parity and also offers fault tolerance because the parity is used to rebuild the data if a disk fails. It requires at least three disks and you lose the storage space equivalent of $1/n$ where n = the number of disks. If you have three 5-GB disks, $5 + 5 + 5 = 10$ GBs of storage space because you lose 1/3 in this case.

Because this course is intended to be introductory and the topic of RAID is very advanced, at this point you should only remember that there is such a thing as RAID and assume that you may learn more about it in future classes. Keep in mind that RAID would be used in addition to backups, not as a replacement. Having fault tolerance means you always have a fairly current copy of your data but doesn't help if a colleague wants you to recover a file from today's tape backup that they accidentally deleted off the server two weeks ago.

It is now very common for a personal computer to have some form of a writable compact disk such as CD-R ("Compact Disc–Recordable"), CD-RW ("Compact Disc–Rewritable") or DVD-R ("Digital Video Disc–Recordable") for a mass storage option but Zip drives are becoming very common for portability as file sizes increase beyond the limited storage space on a typical floppy disk (1.44 MB). You may not wish to burn a CD if your combined data size is 10 MB but you also wouldn't want to save it across several floppy disks. Zip drives can be either external or internal. In most cases, hard drives, floppy drives, and CD-ROM drives are internal. Zip disks can hold anywhere from the equivalent of several dozen floppy disks up to the equivalent of a little over a hundred floppies.

Care of a Disk Both hard disks and floppy disks can be physically damaged. With a hard disk, damage is often caused by an unexpected spike of power. This can damage certain portions of the hard disk and any data stored there may not be retrievable. If unexpected power fluctuations, including those caused by storms, are an issue, an uninterruptible power supply (UPS) should be used. A UPS is a battery backup. It is not designed to keep a computer running for long periods of time. Rather, a UPS typically is designed to keep a computer running about fifteen minutes until either power is restored or the computer can be shut down correctly. If the computer is being used as a server, it is considered a best practice to have a UPS but even desktop computers may warrant the use of a smaller UPS depending on the circumstances.

A UPS is not usually a large device; typically they are about the size of a bread box but they are fairly heavy. They have several electrical outlets on them and you plug the monitor and computer power cord into the UPS and then plug the UPS into the wall outlet. Often, there is also a serial cable between the computer and the UPS that allows for communication and there is software that is installed on the computer to monitor the UPS. Usually you configure the software to shut the computer down correctly during an extended power loss but often it can also be configured to notify the network administrator that there is a problem.

Computers use a certain amount of power measured in watts when operating but, depending on how many devices the computer has (e.g., CD-ROM drives, tape backups, additional hard drives, etc.), that amount is different. The UPS must be capable of handling the needs of a specific computer. There is a formula to calculate what is needed but usually when you purchase a server the vendor suggests an appropriate UPS for an additional cost and bundles it with the server.

It is much easier to damage a floppy disk. They should not be exposed to extreme heat or cold conditions, magnets, and fluids, they shouldn't be dropped or physically abused and they shouldn't be stored on top of your monitor. You might be thinking that you never do such things but putting a disk near a magnet is a very common event if you carry your disks in a purse. Often, purses have magnetic clasps.

Formatting a Disk In the old days, prior to using a disk you had to format it. This prepared the disk for use by placing information about the file system onto the disk. Specifically, it created a table to keep track of the files. Floppy disks often now come preformatted so you usually don't have to worry about formatting a new floppy disk. However, you may still wish to do it if you find an old floppy just to clean it off and reset the table. To format a floppy, open My Computer and right click on the floppy icon. Choose Properties from the context menu and then Format.

Figure 6.2

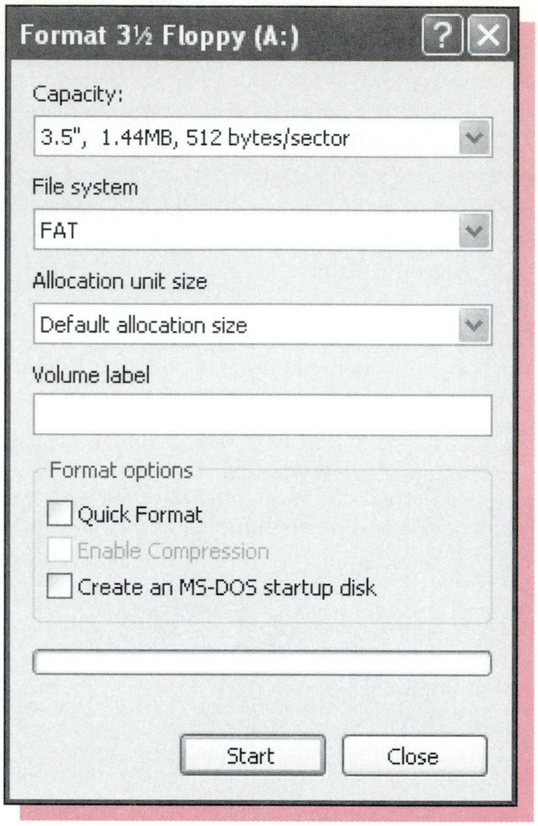

Notice that you have the option to do a full format or a quick format. A full format erases all of the data and resets the table. A quick format simply deletes the pointers in the table to the files and the data is still there but then is overwritten as needed when you save more files to the disk.

When you look at a floppy disk you may see the number 2.0 on it. It says that it can hold 2.0 MB of data unformatted and 1.44 MB when it is formatted. Of course, it can't actually hold any data until it is formatted. Where does the difference between 2.0 MB and 1.44 MB go when you format? Remember, when it is formatted it receives information about the file system and puts an index table on it to keep track of your data. Although Windows 2000 understands both the FAT and NTFS file systems, the only option you have when you format the floppy disk is to format it with the FAT file system. That is because the file system information for NTFS is so big it doesn't fit on a floppy. File systems are discussed further in Chapter 7—Introduction to Networks.

Since you are already looking at the floppy disk, turn it over and look at the back. You should see a little tab in the lower corner and it should be in the closed position. That tells the computer it is OK to write to the disk. If you flip it to the open position, you will be unable to write to the disk but you will still be able to read from it. Why would you ever want to do that? Remember the discussion about viruses. If you do need to carry data on a disk, write-protect it to protect yourself against viruses.

On occasion, you may even need to format a hard disk. Certainly, you should do it at some point just for fun so you can say you did it. For experience, you should format a hard drive and then install the operating system on it and application software. If you can get to a DOS prompt on the computer, you should be able to issue the infamous Format C: command. If you are unable to boot the computer to any operating system because it is damaged beyond that point, you will most definitely need a boot disk.

Needless to say, you wouldn't want to do this to a computer that has important data on it until you have backed it all up and you make sure you have all of the disks you need to get everything back onto the computer. Remember, when you format you lose everything on a disk or drive.

Multiple Drives Often people want to put another hard drive in their computer to add another operating system or to have additional space for more applications or data. The disk with the main operating system (the system disk) will be the master drive and the other disk(s) will be a slave. You configure the disks per the manufacturer's instructions depending on the intended role and that usually means you are flipping switches of some sort on the disks themselves prior to installing them.

If you do have more than one hard disk, each one usually has its own drive letter. However, if you have only one disk and it is partitioned into smaller sections, they also have their own drive letters. So you cannot tell at a quick glance if a computer has only one physical disk or multiple hard disks.

One place you can tell is in the Properties window for a disk. Right click on the drive letter in My Computer and choose Properties. On the Hardware tab, you will see a list of the storage devices in the computer. In the example shown, the desktop computer has only one hard disk in addition to the floppy drive, Zip drive, CD-ROM drive and CD-RW drive.

Figure 6.3

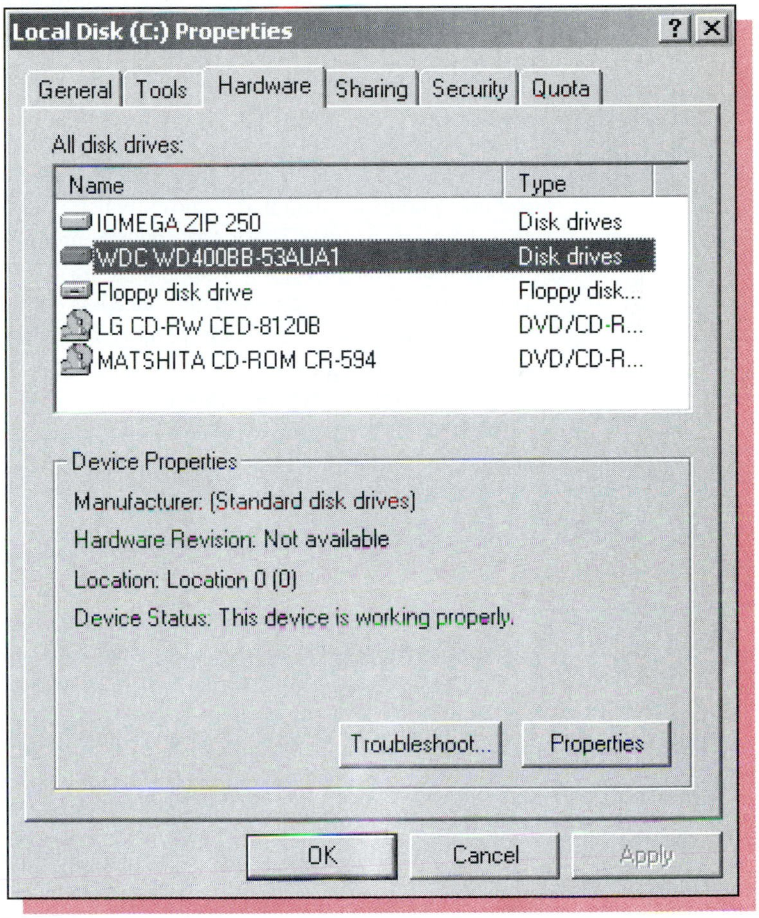

Partitions In addition to adding more physical hard drives, you can also slice up one large hard drive into partitions. If you plan to install more than one operating system, they prefer to be in separate partitions. When you have separate disks or partitions, you can also format them with different file systems should you wish to.

You can create different partitions in a few different ways. If you are installing Windows 2000 on a computer without any other operating systems on it, you first designate a size for the partition you are installing it in. You can choose to use the whole disk or enter a number smaller than the whole disk. This will leave unallocated space on the disk. During the installation, you could then create additional partitions from the unallocated space and format them or you can wait until Windows 2000 is installed and then use Disk Manager to further partition and/or format the rest of the unallocated space.

You couldn't do this with previous versions of Windows. Windows 2000 has an additional routine that the older operating systems didn't have that allows you to partition a disk, even one with the NTFS file system. Fdisk is an old DOS routine that allows you to partition disks but it doesn't recognize NTFS formatted disks.

There are other third-party tools you can purchase to partition as well. Partition Magic by Software Oasis will not only let you partition a disk, even if it has been formatted with NTFS; it will also allow you to resize a disk with an existing operating system. Fdisk and Windows 2000 do not have this feature. If you use them to create partitions on a disk, anything currently on the disk is lost.

If you have an operating system already on a disk but you want to have a separate partition to add another operating system without losing everything you have on the computer, you either need to add a new, separate hard disk or use something like Partition Magic to resize an existing disk.

Boot Options If you have multiple partitions, a file called the boot.ini file is responsible for creating the boot options that you see when you first turn the computer on. The boot.ini gives you the option of going into the different operating systems you have installed on the computer. You can edit the boot.ini but should only do so if you know what you're doing. It can be found in the root of C: but it is a hidden file so if you don't see it, you'll need to show hidden and system files.

Types of Memory

When it comes to a computer, the brain is actually the CPU, the central processing unit. It receives input, processes it, and stores it in short-term (RAM) or long-term (storage) memory. RAM (random access memory) holds the data that is currently being processed by the CPU and it is considered volatile, meaning that if you lose power the RAM contents are gone forever. Any programs that you run or files that you access must first be copied from storage (disk) into RAM. RAM is memory but it is not the same as the storage space on a computer. This concept is confusing to most beginning computer users. When you ask a new computer user how much memory they have they are likely to say something like "80 gigabytes" because they thought you meant their hard disk space. In a way, they are right. RAM is considered primary memory or primary storage and hard disk space is considered secondary memory or secondary storage.

If there isn't enough RAM available, virtual RAM can help out. It's actually part of your secondary storage that is used to hold data while it's being processed. How much of the hard disk is being reserved for virtual memory on your computer?

NOTES In Windows 2000 Professional, right click My Computer, then select Properties > Advanced > Performance Options. In Windows XP Professional, open My Computer. In the left pane, choose View system information. Then click the Advanced tab and choose Performance Settings. Click on the Advanced tab in the Performance Options window. At the bottom there is a section for Virtual Memory. Click the Change button. The default size is 1.5 times your RAM.

ROM, "read only memory," is yet another kind of memory. This kind is generally "burned in" on a chip at the factory and includes information that your computer needs to boot. Without an operating system, a computer is just a really big paperweight. Before the computer has fully booted and loaded the operating system, it needs some information to tell it what to do and also gives information about itself. Rather like some people before getting their morning coffee, a computer isn't fully aware and functional until the operating system has completely started. ROM has enough instructions and information to get the computer started until the operating system can take over.

Although many people refer to the memory of the computer in terms of the storage capabilities, it's important to understand that these are really two separate things. Your computer's primary memory is the amount of RAM in your computer in the form of one or more memory modules that hold data as long as it has power (electricity). The instant you turn off the computer, the data or instructions are gone. It's only held temporarily while it is being processed. Your hard disk is your storage space that permanently holds data until you delete it. Virtual memory, physically stored on your computer as pagefile.sys, does use a portion of your hard disk to also temporarily process data.

Data Transfer and Format

The data travels inside the computer along a bus. The bus is a series of pathways that connect the hardware components to the processor. This is also a factor in determining how quickly your computer can process instructions. The wider the pathway, the faster the data moves. When data transfers, it is in the form of electrical signals represented by one of two states—on or off.

Figure 6.4

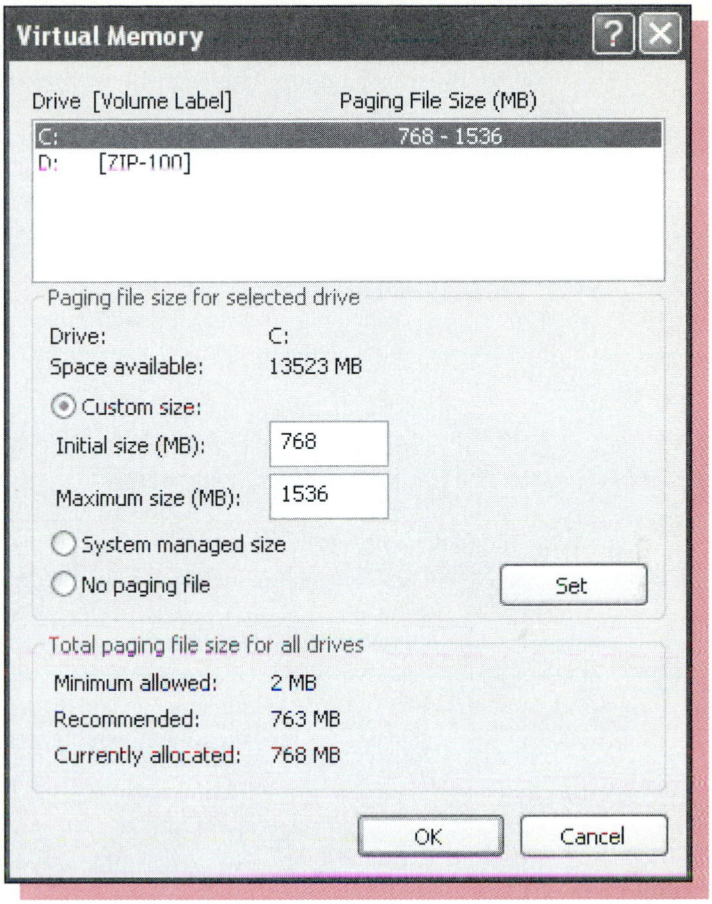

Binary math is associated with computers because it only has two states, 0 or 1, off or on and that simply makes it convenient for the computer. However, humans don't typically want to converse with their computers using binary math so there are other intermediate levels of communication that allow us to use a language we want to use and still allow the computer to understand us.

ASCII ("American Standard Code for Information Interchange") is used to help translate something a human can understand into the 1s and 0s that the computer understands. If you press the capital A (Shift + a on the keyboard), the ASCII equivalent of 65 is converted into the binary equivalent of 1000001 which is then converted into electronic signals of off or on. There are many Web sites that still display the sets of ASCII character tables. For every key and character on the keyboard there is an ASCII equivalent number associated with it.

With the advent of GUI interfaces and object-oriented programming, programming is a lot easier now than it used to be. A programmer now might create an OnClick event to handle a user's action. Prior to GUI interfaces, a programmer had to know the ASCII equivalent of the key that might be pressed so it could be included in the code. Now, of course, most computer users don't even think about ASCII, let alone memorize the tables of characters and their decimal equivalents, but they should at least have an understanding of binary math.

Binary math is actually not as difficult as it might sound. Most of us use the decimal system known as Base 10 (0-9 which totals 10 numbers). Binary is Base 2 (0 or 1). Remember that a 1 is turned on, a 0 is turned off. Also remember, in the Base 10 numbering system that you're more accustomed to, the numbers are representatives of 1s, 10s, 100s, 1000s, etc.

$$\begin{array}{r} 136 \\ +12 \\ \hline 148 \end{array}$$

If we were adding numbers, we would make sure that the places line up correctly in order to add the one's column, the ten's column, and the hundred's column. The Base 2 numbering system also has proper placement of the digits but different values for them.

128		64		32		16		8		4		2		1		
1		1		1		1		1		1		1		1		
128	+	64	+	32	+	16	+	8	+	4	+	2	+	1	=	255

So the decimal equivalent of the binary number 11111111 is 255 and the decimal equivalent of the binary number 1011 is 11 because $8 + 0 + 2 + 1 = 11$. Getting tired of calculating it by hand? Cheat: Use Windows' Calculator accessory. First open the Calculator and choose Scientific from View on the menu to expand your calculator to give you more advanced features.

Then make sure you're in the right numbering system to start. Let's suppose you want to enter a binary number, 11110000, and convert it to decimal. First, switch to binary mode by clicking the BIN (binary) radio button, enter the 1s and 0s, click the DEC (decimal) radio button and it automatically converts it to 240. Obviously, if you want to find the binary equivalent of a decimal number (e.g., 240), you would make sure you're in DEC mode, enter the number 240, and then click the BIN radio button to automatically convert.

Notice that when you are in the binary mode, the only numbers on the keypad available to you are 1 and 0. A common mistake is to forget which mode you are in and get frustrated because you try to enter a decimal number and they are "grayed out." To enter a number, you can either use the mouse to click on the numeric keypad on the calculator or you can use the keys on your keyboard. It is a good idea to get into the habit of using the numeric keypad on the keyboard rather than the numbers going across the top of the keyboard. It is less stressful on your wrists.

Figure 6.5

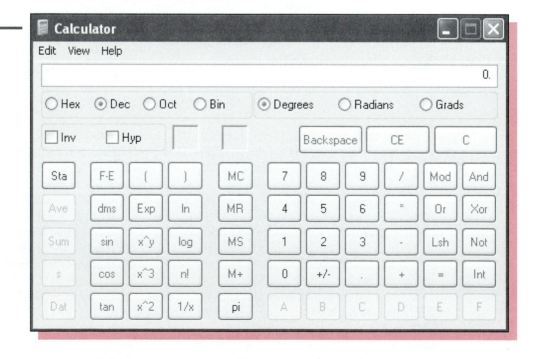

Network Interface Cards and Modems

Having Internet access is extremely important now, so most computers will have either a modem or a network interface card. A modem connects your computer to the Internet using phone lines or a cable connection. A network interface card (NIC) connects you to a local area network. It also has a port that looks like a phone jack but is slightly larger. The connector used for the NIC is referred to as an RJ45 connector. Typically a phone line has two twisted pairs of wires inside and a network cable has four twisted pairs of wires. The connector for a phone line is referred to as RJ11.

An internal modem or NIC is plugged into one of the slots in the motherboard. These slots are called expansion slots and the favorite technology for them now is PCI ("Peripheral Component Interconnect"). When you purchase a NIC or modem, you must check the type of expansion slots your motherboard supports and ascertain how many slots of each type are still unoccupied by some other device so you purchase the correct type of card. Older expansion slots were called ISA ("Industry Standard Architecture") and were larger than the PCI slots. PCI is faster and if you have a newer computer it no doubt has PCI expansion slots but may also include some ISA slots.

ADDITIONAL COMPONENTS

The world of computing isn't restricted to just the physical hardware inside the computer. There are also external components, such as printers, speakers, etc. that must be installed, updated, configured, or maintained. In addition, you may need to install or update the drivers for internal and external components. You should also begin to get an understanding of how the components interact with the processor (CPU).

Peripheral Devices

The peripheral devices can either input data or output data and are often connected to the computer via a special port. Common peripherals are devices like scanners, digital cameras, printers, etc.

Types of Connectors and Ports
If you ever need to move a computer, you will need to know how to get connected devices plugged back into the correct ports. Some common ports are the 25-pin LPT1 port used for a local printer, a 15-pin video port for the monitor, various com (communication) ports, and universal serial bus (USB) ports.

Some of the external components are connected to your computer via a serial cable and some via a parallel cable. A mouse is an example of a serial connection and a printer is parallel. Why is that? Well, a serial connection allows only one bit to be transferred at a time and therefore is slower but more accurate. A parallel connection can handle more than one bit at a time. It is faster, but potentially less accurate.

What ports are on your computer? Poke around the back of your computer and look. After blowing off the dust balls, you should see the LPT1 (pronounced "L-P-T-one") port for the printer, the video port for the monitor, and the ports for the mouse and keyboard. They may even be color coded. You should also see a place to attach the power cord. This connects to the power supply, which is kept somewhat separate from the rest of the components. Notice that it is usually within a special container inside the case.

If you have an audio card installed, you should also see ports to plug in a microphone and a headset or speakers. And you should have a couple of 9-pin ports called com (communication) ports. While the video port is designed for a male connection, anything connecting to the com ports will be female. It used to be common for the mouse to be connected to one of the com ports but now a mouse has a PS/2-style connector. You could also have converters that allow you to plug a PS/2-style mouse into a com port. Keyboards also have a PS/2-style connector now but the older styles of keyboards used to have a larger connector called a 5-pin DIN. The PS/2 connector has six pins but is still smaller than the older 5-pin DIN.

Newer computers have one or more USB ports. This does make more sense. Instead of having a confusing array of different ports on a computer, a universal connector makes life much easier. Any device that supports a USB cable can be attached to your computer. Another port that may be on a computer is called by its IEEE reference, the 1394 port, which is designed for high-speed transfer rates. IEEE is the Institute of Electrical and Electronics Engineers, an organization that sets standards for technology.

On a related note, you should keep your computer free of dust balls as much as possible. For routine maintenance, you may wish to purchase a can of compressed air and use it to periodically clean behind the computer and possibly even inside the case. I have seen computer cases from homes with cats and the amount of fur inside was amazing; in some cases, enough to make a whole new cat. Follow standard safety procedures and unplug the computer prior to attempting this kind of maintenance.

Keyboards

A keyboard presents a serious ergonomic issue that should not be overlooked. Until we can talk to our computers, the keyboard will remain the most popular way to communicate but potentially the most painful. Like all technology, keyboards have evolved over time. In the beginning, for example, they were smaller. No doubt you are using an extended keyboard. Look at the numeric keypad. It has a second function for most of the keys. For instance, if the Num Lock key isn't on, the seven key functions as the home key. On earlier keyboards, the set of navigation buttons to the left of the numeric keypad was not there. You had to turn the Num Lock key on the numeric keypad off and on as needed and either use it for navigation or numbers.

There is more than one option for the layout of the keys on a keyboard. Currently the most common keyboard is the QWERTY keyboard, so called for obvious reasons. The first six letter keys on the left side of the keyboard spell QWERTY. It is considered the most stressful to use in terms of ergonomics. If you rest your fingers on the designated home keys for proper positioning when you type, you'll notice that all of the most used keys are in difficult to reach places.

Another layout often compared to the QWERTY keyboard is the Dvorak keyboard, named after the man who designed it. Dvorak placed the commonly used letters in easy to reach places. This not only makes typing less stressful on the wrists and fingers but also allows faster typing.

In addition to having the key placement altered, some keyboards are considered more ergonomically correct because of the physical design of the keyboard. It may be split, for instance, one side for the left hand and one side for the right, in an attempt to change the positioning of the hands and wrist to something less stressful.

For maintenance, a can of compressed air can be used to clean the keyboard as well as the case and motherboard. Clearly, you should avoid dumping liquids into the keyboard.

Mouse

Your computer receives input from several different sources, including your mouse. Like the dust balls that accumulate over time behind the computer and even inside the case, a mouse is very prone to becoming dirty. How would you clean it? How does it actually work? What is a trackball and why would you use one?

Turn the mouse over and notice that there is a cover around the mouse ball that can be removed. Turn it in the direction indicated by the arrow to remove it and carefully take the mouse ball out. Notice that inside there are small wheels, called capstans, which surround the ball. As you move your mouse around the pad, these capstans move also and send signals to the processor. In very simple terms, it uses the X Y coordinates on the monitor to convey the location of your mouse clicks. Using a Q-tip dipped in alcohol, clean any dust or dirt you see inside the cover where the ball was. Then put the ball back in and secure it in place with the cover. Obviously, you should use a clean mouse pad as well.

You can tell when a mouse is dirty because it becomes more difficult to position it or click on things and sometimes it just seems to have a mind of its own. I was in a middle school computer lab years ago and the mouse was not cooperating. When I tried to click on anything the pointer went everywhere except where I wanted to be. I flipped it over to take the ball out and clean it but was unable to get the cover off. The teacher explained that the students would take the balls out as a prank and take them with them when they left for another class. So the teacher glued them shut.

Track balls are also pointing devices like mice but turned upside down. They are used primarily for people who require specialized assistive technology due to some physical difficulty. They plug into the computer the same way a mouse does but may use one of the com ports instead of the PS/2 port unless it has a converter. So the ball is on top and the mouse buttons surround it and are usually larger for easier access. Usually, no special driver is needed and you can swap the mouse for a track ball on any computer without any additional steps.

Drivers

A driver is a piece of software code used to act as an interpreter between the computer and another device, such as a mouse, a printer, or sound card. A manufacturer includes a driver with their own proprietary technology adapted for different operating systems. When you add a new device, you must also install the driver that is appropriate for the operating system on your computer.

If you are unable to find a driver disk or you update your operating system and need a new driver, nearly all hardware manufacturers have Web sites that allow you to download them. You do need to know the exact brand and model of the hardware and the correct version of the operating system.

Periodically, you may experience hardware trouble on a computer and updating the driver will help. There is more than one way to update a driver. Sometimes you run a Setup or Install program (executable) and it handles everything else. Sometimes it is just a file or files that need to be copied over to the computer and you can usually do that through the Device Manager.

To get there, click Start > Settings > Control Panel > System > Hardware > Device Manager in Windows 2000 Professional or Start > Control Panel > System > Hardware > Device Manager in Windows XP Professional. Then choose one of the components, such as the mouse, and right click on it. Choose Properties from the context menu. You should see a tab for the driver and there you will find a button to update the driver. Device Manager simply asks you for the location of the driver and then handles the rest.

Figure 6.6

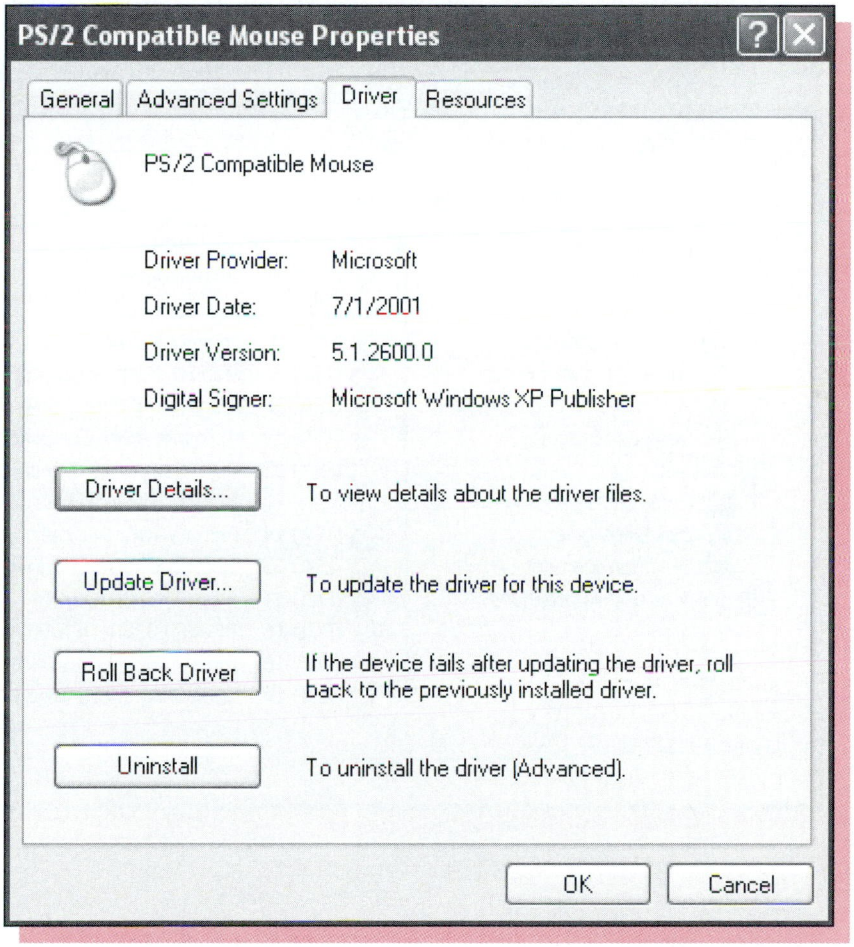

Interrupts

When the computer receives input from a particular device, it's comparable to the CPU being tapped on the shoulder and asked for attention. An interrupt isn't a bad thing; the operating system is designed to work with interrupts. The processor busily handles any request and only pauses when it receives another interrupt—a sign that something else needs attention. For example, if the CPU receives a request from IRQ 1, it is the keyboard. Software can interrupt the processor for attention as well. It may need input or additional instructions in the form of another module of code.

Interrupt signals travel to the processor along interrupt request lines (IRQs). Although some devices are designed to share an IRQ, most of these interrupt request lines are dedicated to one device. It is the interrupt request line (IRQ) for the keyboard that is numbered as a 1, not the interrupt itself. When the processor receives a request from IRQ 1, it knows that the interrupt traveled along the request line for the keyboard.

NOTES To see which IRQs have been reserved for your devices, go back to Device Manager. You can also access the Device Manager in Computer Management. This time, click View > Devices by Type, and then expand the listing for Interrupt Request (IRQ). The internal and external hardware components send interrupts to the processor whenever they need something or need to do something such as input or output and all of the components need to be uniquely identified so the processor knows exactly what to do.

Problems can arise when hardware is added and tries to use an interrupt that has already been assigned to another device. This is known as a conflict and usually means that one or both of the devices won't work until you change the IRQ for one of them. It doesn't happen as often as it used to because the operating system is better able to manage its devices with something called Plug and Play (PnP). With plug and play, the operating system makes sure there are no conflicts. Most problems only occur if you install a device that isn't Plug and Play-compatible. If there is a conflict, the offending device is usually flagged in the Device Manager with a question mark or an exclamation point.

Figure 6.7

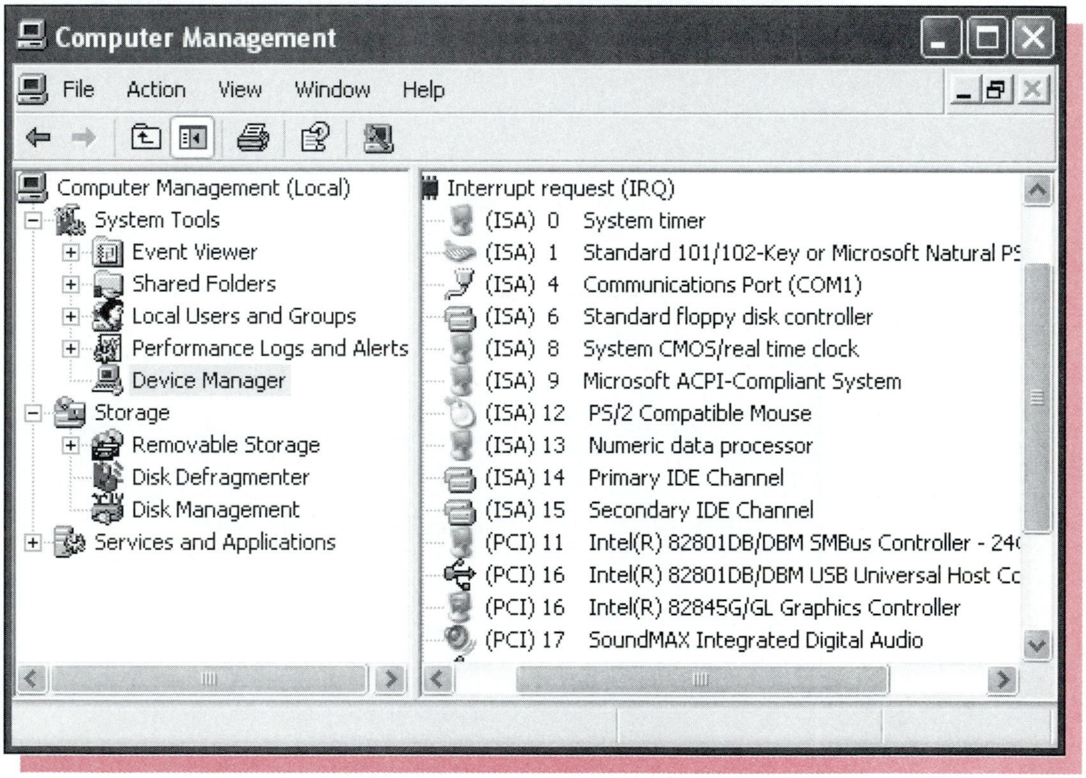

Installing Hardware

When you drive a car, no one expects you to be able to take it apart, describe in detail each component and how it works, and put it back together again. For some reason, computer users are often made to feel stupid if they cannot do this with a computer. It can be intimidating to listen to people explain that they upgraded their memory or added another hard drive if you have never done it.

Plug and Play does make installing or upgrading hardware easier, however. While there are things you will need to consider, such as hardware compatibility, you can usually get that information from the manufacturer's Web site or documentation you received with your computer or new hardware. If you plan to upgrade your memory, for instance, it must be the type of memory the motherboard supports. Once you have the correct type, you usually just need to unplug the computer, take the case off, and swap out or add more memory sticks. When you put everything back together and reboot, the operating system is aware of the new memory. Most computer technicians would suggest that you wear an antistatic wrist band to do such work to avoid doing damage to the internal components.

Speaking of memory, there is an important consideration to be made when you purchase a computer. Often, there are two slots on the motherboard to hold memory sticks. If you want 512 MB of RAM, you can either order it with one 512 MB stick or two 256 MB sticks. It costs a little more to go with one RAM stick versus two but makes it a lot easier to upgrade later on. If both slots are full when you want to upgrade, you have no choice but to take out what is there and then try to get rid of it after you replace it. If you ordered the computer with only one memory stick, you can later add another one much more easily.

Other hardware components can be added using the Add/Remove Hardware Wizard found in the Control Panel. The Wizard will help you along by asking if you want to add/troubleshoot a device or if you need to uninstall a device. If adding, it will next search for any new Plug and Play hardware to install. If you did add new Plug and Play-compatible hardware, you usually don't even have to start this Wizard yourself. Usually, after adding new Plug and Play hardware, the next time you boot the computer the operating system immediately launches the Wizard for you and installs the necessary driver or requests a driver disk from you.

If no new Plug and Play hardware is found, the Wizard assumes you want to troubleshoot a device and offers a list of the components inside your computer. It also has an Add a New Device option so you can continue to install something the operating system didn't detect. If you choose this option, the next screen asks if you want the operating system to search for it (again) or if you simply want to choose something from a list. If it didn't find it the first time, it's best to choose from the list. The Wizard offers you a list of different types of hardware and, after you choose the appropriate one, continues in the same way it would have if the operating system had found it. The goal is to install the correct driver for the hardware.

Summary

There is a funny thing about computers. You can drive a car or use a microwave without anyone expecting you to take it apart and put it back together again. With computers, however, we are often made to feel stupid if we don't know how to add another hard drive or more memory. While that may not be fair, depending on what aspect of information technology you plan to work with, knowledge of hardware may help give you an edge in getting the job.

Some areas of IT will expect you to know more about hardware than others, but most expect at least a basic knowledge. Certainly, you should understand the role of the processor, know what ROM is, and be able to explain the difference between RAM and storage space. The file system your hard disks are formatted with will determine what level of security you have available. Understanding the difference between a partition and a disk is also important.

The newer operating systems do a much better job of making sure there aren't any interrupt conflicts but you should know where to look if you suspect one exists. While you're there, you can also think about updating drivers. Often, manufacturers come out with new versions of drivers with enhanced capabilities and you can take advantage of them if you know where to find them and how to update them. Think in terms of your favorite game and how an enhanced video driver could make it even better.

ACTIVITIES

Review Questions

1. What is the difference between RAM and ROM?

2. What is a bus in computers? What is the difference between a 16-bit bus versus a 32-bit bus?

3. What is the current Intel processor recommended for a desktop computer? Give the processing speed and provide some information on its current capabilities. Try http://www.intel.com/home/desktop/index.htm for information.

4. AMD (Advanced Micro Devices) also has a current processor. What is the name of their current processor and what are some of the features? Try http:// www.amd.com/us-en/ for more information.

5. Explain two different ways to find out how much RAM is in a computer.

Hands-on

1. Using the calculator,
   a. convert the following numbers from binary to decimal:
      0101101
      10110
      11101001101
   b. convert the following numbers from decimal to binary:
      145
      278
      1056

2. Go to the Hewlett Packard Web site (http://www.hp.com) and download and install the printer driver for an HP LaserJet 5000N. List the steps you had to take.

3. Try booting a computer with a regular floppy disk in it. What happens? Why?

4. Go to the Control Panel and configure your mouse for a left-handed user (or right-handed if currently set to left). List the steps you took. Also, what other configuration options do you have for the mouse in terms of pointers, speed, and motion? Remember to reconfigure the mouse to the original settings when done.

5. Write-protect a floppy disk and then try to save a file to it. What happens?

Important Terms

Using www.webopedia.com or another online technical dictionary, define:

ASCII	hard disk	network
bus	IDE	interface card
cluster	IEEE	parity
com port	IEEE 1394	partition
connector	interrupt	PCI
controller	I/O	Plug and Play
CPU	IRQ	port
DIN	ISA	RAM
driver	master/slave	ROM
Dvorak keyboard	memory	SCSI
EIDE	microprocessor	sector
floppy disk	modem	virtual memory
gigahertz	motherboard	Volume Control

Multiple Choice Questions

1. It is the role of the _____ to act as a go-between the user and the hardware and interpret what the user wants to do into a language that the computer understands.
   a. processor
   b. CPU
   c. central processing unit
   d. operating system

2. The _____ inside a computer is what all of the internal components connect to.
   a. motherboard
   b. CPU
   c. power supply
   d. RAM

3. One of the tricks with installing a floppy drive is knowing which side the _____ should

face on the ribbon cable that connects to the motherboard.
   a. twisted pair
   b. red stripe
   c. yellow stripe
   d. blue stripe

4. The _____ has a bunch of cables attached to it and you connect these cables to the individual components inside the computer.
   a. motherboard
   b. RAM
   c. CPU
   d. power supply

5. _____ is/are coded with instructions to handle all of the operating system needs.
   a. RAM
   b. ROM
   c. Processors
   d. Buses

6. Typically you choose the _____ when you format the disk.
   a. operating system
   b. amount of RAM
   c. type of CPU
   d. file system

7. _____ means that if a disk fails, the data can be recovered.
   a. Fault tolerance
   b. SCSI
   c. IDE
   d. Mission critical

8. A(n) _____ is a battery backup but is not designed to keep a computer running for long periods of time.
   a. AMD
   b. hard disk
   c. unsuspended power supply
   d. uninterruptible power supply

9. A(n) _____ erases all of the data and resets the table. A _____ simply deletes the pointers in the table to the files and the data is still there but then is overwritten as needed when you save more files to the disk.
   a. backup/deletion
   b. Fdisk/format
   c. partial format/full format
   d. full format/quick format

10. If you do need to carry data on a disk, _____ it to protect yourself against viruses.

    a. erase
    b. format
    c. write-protect
    d. tab-protect

11. In addition to adding more physical hard drives, you can also slice up one large hard drive into _____.

    a. sectors
    b. partitions
    c. clusters
    d. pies

12. _____ is an old DOS routine that allows you to partition disks but it doesn't recognize NTFS formatted disks.

    a. Ide
    b. Pdisk
    c. Edit.Com
    d. Fdisk

13. _____ holds the data that is currently being processed by the CPU and it is considered volatile.

    a. RAM
    b. ROM
    c. A disk
    d. The operating system

14. The _____ is a series of pathways that connect the hardware components to the processor.

    a. bus
    b. highway
    c. cache
    d. vehicle

15. The decimal equivalent of the binary number 1011 is _____.

    a. 8
    b. 10
    c. 11
    d. 15

16. A _____ is a piece of code used to act as an interpreter between the computer and another device, such as a mouse, a printer, or sound card.

    a. screen saver
    b. thread
    c. process
    d. driver

17. The processor busily handles any request and only pauses when it receives another _____—a sign that something else needs attention.

    a. CPU
    b. interrupt
    c. disruption
    d. series of code

18. Interrupts travel to the processor along _____.

    a. VQRs
    b. TSRs
    c. USBs
    d. IRQs

19. Problems can arise when hardware is added and it tries to use an interrupt that has already been assigned to another device. This is known as [a] _____.

    a. confusion
    b. interruption
    c. conflict
    d. terminal

20. _____ means that the operating system should recognize the new component and a Wizard should help you install the driver.

    a. Add/Remove
    b. Adding hardware
    c. USB
    d. Plug and Play

7 Introduction to Networks

OBJECTIVES

After reading this chapter, you will be able to:

- Differentiate between a peer-to-peer network and a client/server network
- Explain the importance of the choice of file system
- Differentiate between a client computer and a server
- List at least three different server services
- Explain the difference between centralized and decentralized administration
- Explain the difference between workgroup and domain membership
- Explain why the NTFS file system is more secure than the FAT file system
- Define topology
- Describe the four main topologies
- Differentiate between a network topology and a network technology
- Demonstrate how to configure Local Area Connection properties
- Describe the role of the network interface card

INTRODUCTION

It is very rare in today's business world for an employee to work on a stand-alone computer. A stand-alone computer is one that is not connected to other computers and/or a server in order to share resources. No matter which Information Technology (IT) area of concentration you might choose for your career, the chances of you working in a networked environment are almost 100%. So what is a local area network (LAN) and why is working on a LAN different than working on a stand-alone computer? Working in a networked environment does add an extra layer of complexity. Often, security becomes an issue and to help secure data, the choice of a file system can be important.

Just as computers aren't magical things, local area networks don't function on magic either. When designing networks, there are specific guidelines to follow for their physical structure and for how the data access the media and are transmitted along the media. The physical structure of a LAN includes not only the computers but also the network interface cards, protocols, transmission media, hubs, switches, routers, etc. While this kind of hardware is needed to connect the LAN, a network technology determines how the data access the media and traverse it.

NETWORK SCOPE

There are actually different kinds of networks that can be categorized by the scope and type. In terms of scope, or size, there are local area networks (LAN), wide area networks (WAN), and metropolitan area networks (MAN), to name a few.

A local area network is the smallest of the three and is usually confined to a floor of a building, an entire building, or a small (square mile) geographic area. It may include several buildings and several servers and anywhere from one computer to several hundred computers. It could, perhaps, be as small as one room. A LAN is comprised of resources such as computers and printers that are connected together via some media such as cabling, and other components.

A wide area network is two or more LANs connected together. Technically, the Internet is one big WAN. All WANs require additional components to connect them together and a router is one such component.

A metropolitan area network (MAN) consists of computers in a large area, such as a city, connected together to share and maintain resources. Imagine being able to configure all of the traffic lights in a city, or the subway schedules or the sewer system, from one central location.

In terms of network types, examples for a local area network would be peer-to-peer or client/server. Many people are networking their computers at home as well.

TYPES OF NETWORKS

One of the main reasons that local area networks became popular in the 1980s was because they enabled a company to share printers. Rather than buy one expensive laser printer for each computer, networking the computers and printers together saved money. It also allowed users to share other resources such as folders and files and gave the ability to communicate easily via e-mail. This connectivity resulted in a lot of time-saving. Prior to the advent of networks, if you wanted to share a file with someone you had to put it on a floppy and walk it over to them—hence, the term "sneakernet." Since you are in a networked environment, how many different ways can you think of to share a file with someone else in the room or elsewhere without using a floppy or Zip disk?

Peer-to-Peer

Peer-to-peer networks are popular for smaller environments and relatively easy to set up. There is a lot of maintenance involved for each user in a peer-to-peer environment, however. Typically, there is no dedicated network administrator. It is the responsibility of each user to maintain resources and give permissions to other people to use them. There is also no dedicated server in a peer-to-peer environment so every computer can act as a server providing resources but also act as a client when accessing someone else's resources. Peer-to-peer networks are relatively small, with perhaps up to 10 computers.

Problems occur if a computer that is supposed to be sharing resources isn't turned on, for example, or if a shared printer is locked in the office of an employee who has taken time off work. Bottlenecks are also an issue. If you share a printer from your computer for others to use, your computer suddenly has a lot more work to do. If your computer isn't particularly powerful, it can become a bottleneck and slow things down. Security is yet another serious issue because each person is responsible for allowing access to the resources on their computer and may not always be trained to do it correctly.

If the number of computers you need to connect is small, a peer-to-peer network may be the best solution. Low cost is a plus since you don't have to buy a dedicated server or hire a network administrator. However, it does put more of a workload on the individual users and a peer-to-peer network would be an absolute nightmare to maintain and secure in a larger environment.

Client/Server

In contrast, client/server networks typically have one or more dedicated network administrators who maintain not only the server but also the client computers. Client/server environments have one or more computers dedicated as a server. A server has a special network operating system (NOS) installed that is designed to provide resources to clients in a multiuser environment.

An example of a client operating system is Microsoft Windows 2000 Professional. Examples of a network operating system are Microsoft Windows NT and 2000 Server. Microsoft Windows 95, 98, and Me are also client operating systems and for the most part were developed to be backwards-compatible with DOS. When Microsoft developed Windows NT they started from scratch and did not attempt to keep NT backwards-compatible with DOS because they were hoping to develop a more secure, stable operating system. So Windows NT, Professional, XP, and Server are from one side of the family and Windows 95, 98, and Me are from the other side of the Microsoft family.

Windows 95, 98, and Me use the FAT32 file system whereas Windows NT, Professional, XP, and Server can use either the FAT32 or NTFS file system. NTFS allows for much greater security and explains why Windows NT, Professional, XP, and Server are typically used in a business environment.

Problems in a client/server environment include access, security, and integrity of the data. Since most of the data is located in a central place, if the server fails the users no longer have access to the resources they need. If there are no current backups, the situation is even worse. Correctly configuring the permissions to access the resources will directly affect the level of security of the data and it can be a complicated task. Additionally, viruses can spread a lot easier in a networked environment and this is an issue for both peer-to-peer and client/server networks.

At least one dedicated server will also be needed and can be expensive. Prices can range from thousands of dollars to tens of thousands for each server.

Servers   You can install a network operating system on any desktop computer but this never works out well. A regular desktop computer is not designed to run all day every day for years but a server is. Computers built to be servers have special cooling features and typically other redundant features built in such as an additional power supply should the first one fail. Servers are usually designed for faster data access rates and other enhanced features that make them a more appropriate choice for a multiuser environment. Usually, a server has a lot more RAM than a typical client computer and more processing power, including multiple processors. In fact, you determine where and how to spend more money on a server depending on what you will be using it for. A file server will be used to store files and the users will need to either place a file on the server or retrieve a file from it. It makes sense then that data transfer is important and you would want your server to be able to transfer data quickly. SCSI drives can transfer data at incredible speeds and are often used on file servers.

Your choice of a network operating system is dependent on what features it supports. Not all operating systems can address multiple processors, for instance, and certainly not all of them support multiple users simultaneously. You can't have more than one person logged into a computer with Windows 98 at the same time, for example. The level of security they provide is also an important consideration, as is the stability of the operating system. You might find an operating system that is really cheap or even free but if your server crashes on a daily basis because it isn't compatible with the hardware inside your server or the operating system code is still buggy, it probably isn't a good choice.

Servers run special programs, or services, that handle various needs in a local area network. As an example, the DNS service (Domain Name Service) interprets from domain name to IP address and vice versa. When you visit a Web site, you key in the domain name (e.g., www.microsoft.com) but computers and other devices such as routers don't understand names, they want numbers. The DNS handles that translation.

The Web site you visit is running another special service, the WWW (World Wide Web) service. On a Microsoft server, IIS (Internet Information Services) is the main service that contains the WWW service, and could also have the FTP (file transfer protocol) service, and SMTP (simple mail transport protocol). Apache is another well-known Web server software.

There are many other services that can be installed on a server and they often determine the role of a server. Some servers, called file servers, are strictly used to store files and may not need to be as powerful as a server that acts as an e-commerce Web site with thousands of Internet users visiting each day. The role of the server figures into the cost because you would purchase different components depending on the need. A file server would need a lot of storage space and definitely a tape backup unit but the processor and perhaps even the amount of RAM isn't as important, depending on the number of users supported. A popular Web site's server, however, may need to be more powerful and several important components may determine the best choices for serving up the data in a timely fashion to the remote visitors.

Home Networks

A popular new trend is to install a home network. Previously, homes that did have computers probably only had one. Lower prices and the increased speed at which newer models are coming on the market have resulted in homes with multiple computers that all want access to the Internet, to shared printers and other resources, and to interactive gaming. Since it wouldn't be economical to pay for multiple Internet connection fees, a home network is a great solution.

Home networks are typically peer-to-peer and do not have a dedicated server. What they might use is a device that acts as a router. All of the computer's requests for Internet content are sent to the router and vice versa. The router keeps track of all of the computers inside the home network and knows which one requested the data. When you pay an Internet Service Provider (ISP) for Internet access, you are allotted one IP address. Since every device on the Internet must have an IP address, having multiple computers means they must share one address. In most cases, the router is configured with that address. Each of the computers is configured with a "fake" IP address, one that falls within a range of reserved addresses not recognized on the Internet. It allows them to communicate with each other but not with the Internet. To communicate on the Internet, they pass through the router, grab the real IP address, and use it temporarily.

Routers for home networks are sold by most office supply stores and the setup is fairly straight forward. It is important to note that a router is a device that routes data packets. When you send an e-mail, for instance, the message is broken up into smaller data packets. Routers forward the data packets to their proper destination, where they are reassembled. That does not necessarily mean that a router secures your computers as well. Although some routers can also be configured to act as a firewall, it is not safe to assume that all routers are configured that way. If you have a home network or are considering installing one, be sure that a firewall is part of the installation.

Centralized versus Decentralized Administration

A client/server environment would usually require one or more network administrators to install, configure, and maintain the network. Much of the work involves creating and maintaining accounts, granting appropriate permissions to access resources, performing backups, etc. In a client/server environment, this type of work is done at the server or at a client computer configured with a "client administrator console." This allows for more centralized administration versus the decentralized administration that a peer-to-peer environment offers.

In a client/server environment, resources can also be centralized. Rather than having shares on individual client stations, they can be on the server. This makes backing up much easier. Users can save their data on shares and these shares can have different levels of permissions or other users can be blocked from them altogether. These shares would be available to the appropriate user no matter which computer they used to log onto the network.

A client/server environment can also help in terms of profiles. Profiles keep track of an individual user's environment (desktop, etc.). A roaming profile can allow a user to see exactly the same thing no matter which computer they log into. This means that the profile is typically stored on the server (centralized) so it can be accessed from any computer on the network the user may be logging onto rather than storing or configuring it on each computer the user may use (decentralized).

Workgroup versus Domain Environments

What configuration is currently in your computer lab: peer-to-peer or client/server? Are you logging into a network or into your local computer? Is your computer part of a workgroup? What is a workgroup? Who can you see in Computers Near Me? What happens if you change your workgroup?

To begin answering these questions, let's start by determining if your computer is configured as a member of a domain or a workgroup. Right click on My Computer and choose Properties. In the System Properties window, choose the Network Identification tab in Windows 2000 Professional and the Computer Name tab in Windows XP Professional. Next, click the Properties button in Windows 2000 Professional and the Change button in Windows XP Professional. You should see your computer name and domain or workgroup membership. In the example shown, the computer is part of a workgroup called ONLYME.

Figure 7.1

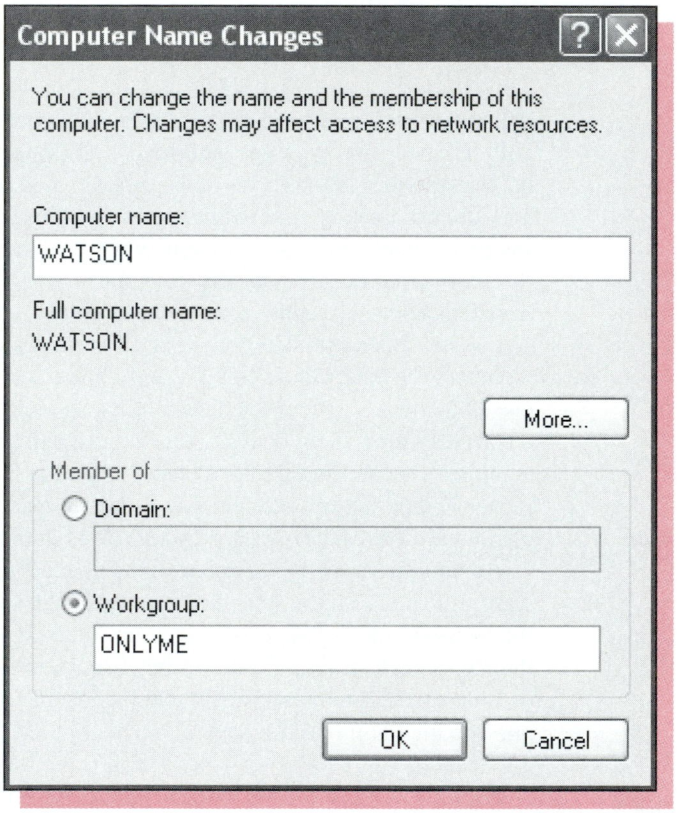

Workgroups are used primarily in a peer-to-peer environment and are designed to help users find the resources, such as a shared printer, in the peer-to-peer network more easily. Anyone in the same workgroup will find each other in Computers Near Me in My Network Places. The name of the workgroup doesn't matter; you get to make it up. However, you must all be in the same workgroup in order to see each other.

NOTES

Split the computer lab into two groups and change your workgroup membership. After taking note of your membership before the change, half of you should join a workgroup called LEFT and the other half join a workgroup called RIGHT. To join the workgroup, make sure the Workgroup radio button is selected and simply type in the name of the new workgroup. Notice that it doesn't ask you to introduce or authenticate yourself when you join the workgroup but it does welcome you to the workgroup and then tells you to reboot.

After the reboot, go to My Network Places and check in Computers Near Me. In Windows XP Professional, first open My Computer and then choose My Network Places listed in Other Places. Choose View Workgroup Computers in Network Tasks. Who do you see? It may take several minutes for the other computers to show. When done, reconfigure your membership the way it was.

Workgroups can be effective for small environments but don't offer the security that a domain environment offers. "Domain" is a Microsoft term. Other network operating systems have similar concepts but call it something different. A domain requires one or more domain controllers. A domain controller is a server that has been configured to authenticate users and keep track of the resources they are permitted to access. Rather than having access to a few resources in a workgroup environment, a domain user potentially has access to all of the resources in an entire domain,

In a workgroup environment, the user is typically authenticated by the local computer they are using. The account is local to that computer. Say you have an account on the computer you use in the lab and the username is your last name. If you get to class late someday and someone takes your seat before you get there, will you be able to sit at another computer and log into it? Not if an account for you was only created on the other computer you usually use.

In a domain environment, the account is on the domain controller, not the local computer. The user can log into the domain from any computer within the domain. As an example, think of a college campus. The network administrator certainly isn't going to sit at each computer and create an account for every potential user on each computer. Rather, they create all of the accounts one time on the domain controller and the students, faculty, and staff can access their resources in the domain no matter which computer they use to log on. The network administrator has control over all of the resources within the domain but cannot manage someone else's domain just because they are a network administrator.

Joining a computer to a domain is similar to joining a workgroup but you select the radio button next to Domain and then enter the domain name. You must know the correct name of the domain but it also asks for a valid username and password. Configuring your computer to join a workgroup did not require this; it let anyone in. To join a computer to a domain, you must have an account in the domain.

The default setting on a Microsoft 2000 Server is to let anyone with a valid account join a domain. It is possible to restrict this for security reasons, however, and only let certain members join computers to a domain. As an example, the network administrator might configure your computer for you using their account and you would then have access to the domain resources using your account once it was done. For security reasons, this might be done to reduce the risk of unauthorized access.

FILE SYSTEMS

Different operating systems use different methods of keeping track of files and folders. DOS and older versions of Windows use the FAT (File Allocation Table) file system. When files are saved to a disk, they are broken up into tiny pieces and scattered throughout the disk wherever they can find an open space in the form of clusters. A file system allows you to organize your files by creating a directory structure and it also keeps track of the directories and files.

Microsoft Windows 2000 has an additional, much more secure option called NTFS (New Technology File System). In fact, NTFS was originally developed to meet a certain security level for an operating system required by the U.S. government for consideration of its use. It isn't the only operating system to meet these requirements. It is a sort of status symbol for operating systems to be able to display this seal of approval.

When you format the main hard drive prior to or during installation of the operating system, you designate which file system you want to use. Which file system(s) are being used on the computer in the lab?

NOTES   Right click on the C: drive in My Computer. Choose Properties from the context menu. In addition to how much space is free and how much is being used, it also lists the file system. If you have more than one partition, repeat the steps for each. Another way to find out is to use the Disk Management feature in Computer Management.

Choosing a File System

There are several hundreds, if not thousands, of file systems to choose from. Each operating system has its own native file system designed for it but some operating systems can use more than one file system. Currently, a common file system for Linux is ext2 but a newer file system called ext3 is also available.

Windows 2000 prefers NTFS but FAT32 can also be used. A file system determines how your data can be organized, managed, and secured. FAT32 has very few security features whereas NTFS has such "granularity" you can configure access permissions at the individual file level. The main categories of permissions include the ability to write a file, read it, execute it, modify it, delete it, or have full permission to do all of these things. However, with NTFS you can break those main categories down into even finer detail. The Read Permission is actually broken down into four separate parts of the whole as shown by the check boxes in the example.

Figure 7.2

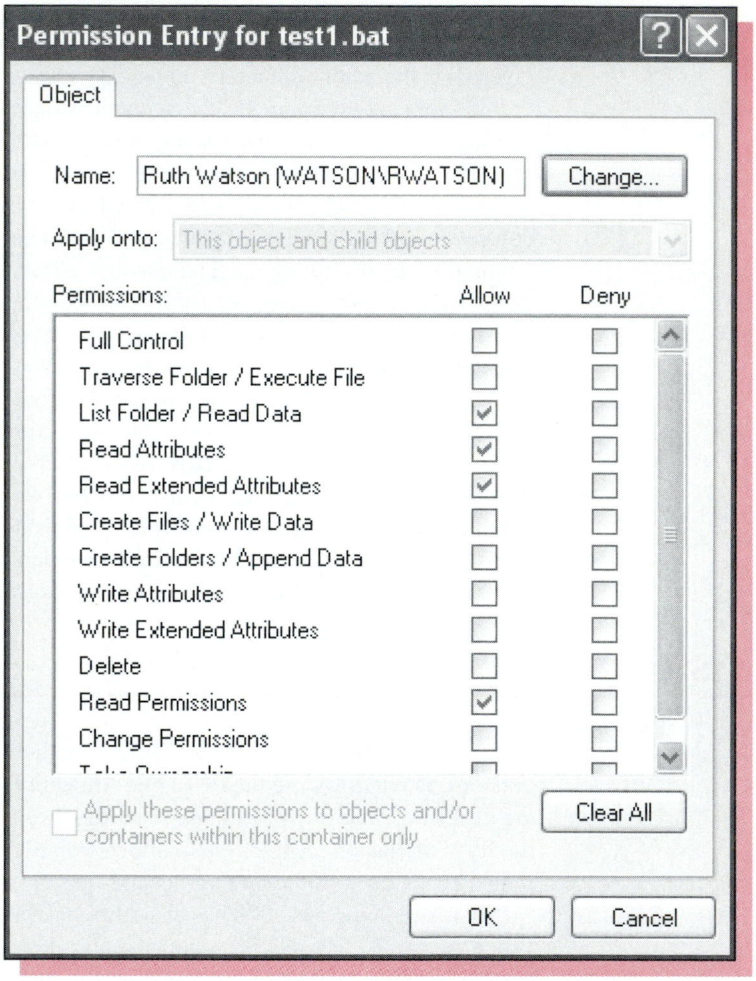

Think of granularity as a grain of sand. Rather than securing the whole beach with one set of access permissions, you can secure each individual grain of sand with different parts of permissions as needed. Understanding permissions and how to correctly apply them to resources is an important part of a network administrator's job.

To view permissions of a file or folder in Windows 2000 Professional, right click on the file or folder > Properties > Security. In Windows XP Professional, you may need to first configure your folders to allow you to view the permissions. In Control Panel, open Folder Options. Click View and in the Advanced Options list, clear the entry that says "Use Simple File Sharing (Recommended)." You can then view the permissions of a file or folder by right clicking on it and choosing the Security tab.

File systems also determine how files can be named. For instance, in the beginning DOS was restricted to the 8.3 naming convention because the only file system DOS could use was FAT. That meant that you could only have up to eight characters to the left of the dot and three to the right. Back then, to help make the file name meaningful under those restrictions, we often used the three characters to the right of the dot as well instead of letting the application append its normal extension. So a secretary who has to type hundreds of letters might adopt a naming convention to help figure out what's what.

In a college environment, for instance, that might mean using the three characters to designate a semester (e.g., filename.F03).

One difference between FAT and FAT32 is that FAT32 can handle long file names but FAT32 was also developed to recognize larger disks. However, FAT32 still offers no real security options.

Deciding which file system you should use is an important security consideration with the Windows 2000 operating system. The NTFS file system is the recommended file system for use with Windows 2000. NTFS has better file security, better disk compression, and also offers support for large hard disks, an important consideration for a file server.

If you're using a dual-boot configuration with different file systems, however, you may not be able to gain access to files on NTFS partitions from another operating system on your computer. Say you have Windows 98 on the first partition and Windows 2000 on the second. You can configure the first with FAT32 and the second with NTFS and it will function perfectly fine. If you are booted into the Windows 2000 partition, you will be able to access the data files in both partitions because Windows 2000 is capable of understanding both file systems.

If you are booted in the Windows 98 partition, you will only have access to the data files on the first partition. For this reason, you should probably use FAT32 on both partitions if you want a dual-boot configuration and you want to be able to access files them both no matter which operating system you have loaded. If you don't need to access all of the data at all times, having different file systems is fine.

You already know that disk partitioning is a way of dividing one hard disk into two or more logical sections of the physical disk. You might create separate partitions to organize data or to dual boot with another operating system. Once you have created the partition, you decide what file system you want to use to format it. Your decision will be based on the different operating systems on your computer and whether or not you want to be able to access all of the partitions no matter which operating system you are in at the time. Do you have access to the data on all of the partitions on the computers in the lab you use for this class? Can you save a file to them all?

Security The decision you make regarding the file system you use will also be dependent on the level of security you need. If security isn't an issue at all because your computer is not connected to a LAN nor to the Internet and it is housed in a locked room and you are the only person with a key—then you could format it with the FAT/FAT32 file system. If one or more of these conditions doesn't apply to you, then you should seriously consider NTFS.

In a network, determining who has the ability to back up your files and where the backups are stored is also important. Once your data has been backed up to tape, does NTFS still protect it? The answer is "maybe." It depends on what options were selected during the backup. Usually you can configure it to only allow the administrator or the owner of the file to have access or restore it.

If you copy a file secured with NTFS permissions from the server to a floppy disk, is it still secure? The answer is "no." Since you can't format a floppy disk with the NTFS file system, it is no longer protected.

NETWORK TOPOLOGY

The word "topology" is used in many different fields. In elementary school, you may have looked at topology maps. Depending on what math courses you took, you may have also discussed topologies. A network topology is the physical design of the network and describes how the computers are connected together physically and logically. There are four main topologies: bus, star, ring, and hybrid. In the early days of local area networks, the bus topology was commonly used simply because that was the only existing technology at the time but the most used topology currently is the star. That doesn't mean you could not install a new network using a bus topology now. You choose a topology based on issues such as cost, ease of installation, ease of maintenance, and data integrity. Each of the main topologies has advantages and disadvantages that need to be considered prior to installation.

Any topology can be used with a peer-to-peer or client/server environment. What determines the type of network is the presence or absence of a dedicated server. Either network type, peer-to-peer or client/server, can use the bus, star, or ring topology. In addition to the three main topologies mentioned, there are also variants of each but let's start with the main three.

Bus

A bus topology was commonly used in the 1980s. It is considered the least expensive topology as well as the easiest to implement. It uses a coaxial cable that looks similar to the coax cable you would have at home for cable access to your television. In a bus topology, computers are daisy-chained together, which explains why this topology is referred to as the linear bus topology. Data packets are sent along the coax cables. When computers wish to communicate, the network interface cards send the data out onto the lines and every computer hears it. That only makes sense: they're trying to figure out if the data is for them. This is also referred to as broadcasting and is a quick and dirty way to scatter data out onto the LAN. The opposite of broadcasting is routing. As you can imagine, when you broadcast data to every device on the line it is comparable to a roomful of people all talking at once, and often the data packets collide. Imagine yourself talking to a friend and you both start speaking at the same time. Usually, you both stop and wait for the other to continue. The bus and star topology do the same thing when collisions occur. The only difference is, they wait a precise mathematically calculated time and then they start transmitting data again.

Figure 7.3

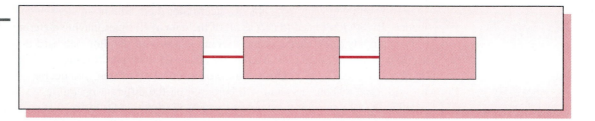

It isn't actually one long cable that connects the computers together. Picture a computer lab using a bus topology. Let's say the teacher station is the server, and a printer in the back of the lab is the last device to be connected. The network interface card (NIC) used in a bus topology has a connector called a BNC (British Naval Connector) and there are more pieces of hardware needed to connect the cabling to it. One piece is a tee connector and one length of cable will be attached to one side of the tee on the server with either a twist-on or crimped-on end and it will run from the server to the closest student computer. The other side of the tee connector on the server will have a hardware piece called a terminator. It signals the beginning of the line. Another terminator will be used on the printer to signal the end of the line.

A tee connector will be used on the back of each student computer and one length of cable will run to the computer on either side of them. Each of the computers is connected together in a daisy-chain fashion with a terminator at the beginning and end of the line. So it appears as one long line of cable but is actually several shorter pieces connected with hardware to each network interface card.

A bus topology could still be used today. Bus topology networks do have one inherent problem, however. If there is a break anywhere in the line, none of the computers on that line can communicate. Distance is also a problem and results in attenuation, which is a loss of signal strength. A device called a repeater can be used to boost the signal.

Star

If you were to install a LAN today, the chances are almost 100 percent that you would use a daisy-chained star topology. In most cases, you would use a cable similar to a phone line but with four extra wires inside. The cable used for voice (phone) is typically Category 3 with only four wires inside and the cabling used for data is currently Cat 5, although new categories are planned for the future and Cat 6 is on its way. The difference between them is the speed at which the data can transfer. Because Cat 5 is very common, it is not that expensive to install (as compared to using fiber optic cable) and it is also easy to install. A hybrid topology combines the bus topology and the star topology and joins groups of star-configured networks with a linear bus backbone.

Many new networking students believe that only the bus topology suffers from problems with data collisions but that is not true. The star topology uses the same technology to transmit data packets that the bus topology uses and therefore also is designed to deal with data collisions.

It was easy to figure out why the linear bus topology is named as it is but why is this called a star topology? It has to do with the way the computers are concentrated into a star pattern using hubs or switches. Hubs are designed to broadcast the data to all of the devices attached to it, including other

Figure 7.4

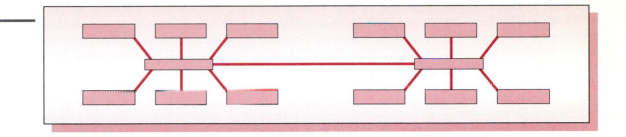

hubs. A more intelligent device, called a switch, can be used instead of a hub but it is more expensive because it has enhanced capabilities. One of the best features of a switch is its ability to help segment traffic. The switch builds and stores a database table that keeps track of the network devices (computers, printers, etc.) and remembers where they are so it can get the data packets from one device directly to another without having to broadcast to every computer. Obviously this results in a lot less data on the lines and fewer collisions as a result.

Figure 7.5

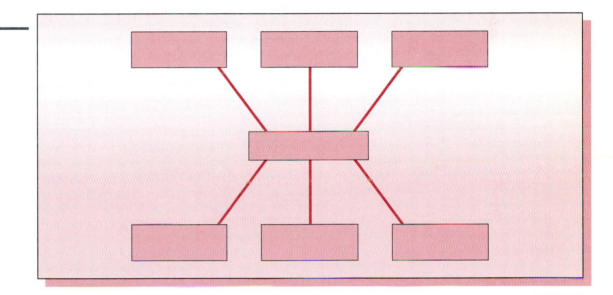

Your computer lab is no doubt using a star topology. Every device in the lab has one end of a cable attached to the network interface card and the other end plugged into a port on the hub or switch. Your lab may have patch panels on the wall or floor and you may not see where the hubs or switches are actually housed. However, the port on the patch panel that you plug your cable into has more cable coming out of the back of it that you can't see because it is in the wall or floor. It is that cable that runs back to the hub or switch and the patch panel is just a convenience like electrical outlets. You want electrical outlets in more than one place in a room in case you change you mind about where you want to place things or wish to add additional components. Just as the electrical outlets in the wall run back to a fuse box, ultimately each of the computers in the lab is using one port on the hub or switch.

Using the previous example of networking the lab, if the teacher station is a server it also is plugged into one of those ports. It is a common misperception to think that all of the computers in a LAN must somehow connect back to the server; actually, the server is just another device. If all of the devices are connected to a hub or switch, they can potentially all communicate no matter what role they play.

A star topology network doesn't have the same problem the bus topology has. If there is a break in the cable that connects a computer, only that one computer is affected. Star topology networks do have an issue with attenuation if the cable runs are too long, however. All cables commonly used inside a local area network to connect the devices have a maximum length limit. Fiber optic cable is the exception but it is still usually too expensive to consider connecting all of the devices inside a LAN using "fiber" and it is more commonly used for long distances such as connecting buildings together.

If you are using Category Five cable, the connector you will use is called an RJ-45 connector. A phone line uses a slightly smaller RJ-11 connector. You can purchase the cables with the connectors already on them or you can make your own. My students, after several frustrated attempts to make them, usually announce that they plan to buy their own. It can be very difficult to get the eight little different colored wires into the RJ-45 connector exactly right. There are tiny little chutes inside; one for each thin wire, and the wires must go in a specific order depending on what the cable will be used for. In addition, they must touch gold connectors at the end of the chutes. So you cut back the outer sheath about 1/2 to 5/8 of an inch to expose the eight wires inside, untwist them enough to straighten them out, pinch the eight wires tightly, keep them in the right color order, make sure you cut them all to the same length so they touch the gold connectors correctly, and then get them into the correct chutes. The last step (at this point my students are usually muttering things under their breath) is to use a tool to crimp the RJ-45 connector onto the main wire while making sure that none of the eight wires inside is disturbed from its correct position before doing so.

Ring

The third main topology is called the ring topology. Why are there different topologies? For the same reason there are different protocols, hardware, software, etc. All over the world there are very smart people who come up with their own solutions to a problem. In the case of the ring topology, the engineers wanted to get data from one device to another without any collisions. So the integrity of the data was more important to them than the speed of transmission.

The ring topology is not used as often as the star topology. It uses different hardware to connect which is not as commonly sold so it is more expensive and, because of the complexity, it is considered more difficult to install. Just as a star topology uses hubs or switches, the ring topology also has a concentrator called an MSAU or "multistation access unit."

Figure 7.6

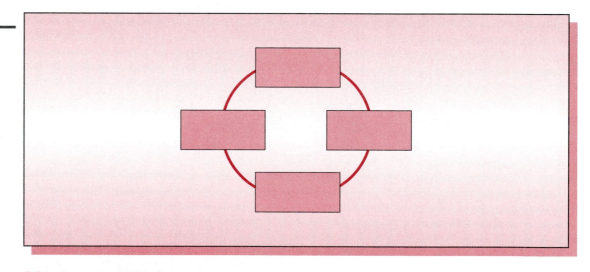

Advantages and Disadvantages

Bus Topology
- least expensive to install
- easy to install
- easy to get line breaks, difficult to troubleshoot, effects all computers on the line

Star Topology
- relatively inexpensive to install but requires hubs/switches
- not difficult to install
- very stable, break in line/connection usually effects only one computer

Ring Topology
- most expensive to install
- most difficult to install
- best at passing data with fewest collisions, difficult to troubleshoot, problems effect all computers in the ring

NETWORK TECHNOLOGY

The difference between a network topology and a network technology is important. A network topology is the physical layout of the network. A network technology is not a physical thing and is not dependent upon a specific type of cable. A network technology defines how the packets traverse the network, each using a set of rules (network protocols) to get data from Point A to Point B.

Ethernet

The most common network technology in local area networks today is Ethernet, which was developed by Bob Metcalfe and D.R. Boggs at the Palo Alto Research Center (PARC) in the early 1970s. Ethernet is the technology that defines how the data packets are constructed and transmitted across the LAN.

Ethernet isn't dependent on a specific type of cable or protocol; it actually allows multiple protocols to be used. That means it can allow different kinds of networks to be connected such as Windows, Macintosh, Novell, and UNIX. Each of those platforms might be using different protocols to communicate among them or may be using a common protocol, like TCP/IP, to communicate with each other.

Also, these different networks might be connected using different kinds of media, or cabling. Ethernet permits the use of different transmission media including coax, twisted pair, and fiber and also different topologies including the bus and star. Wireless technologies are also becoming a more stable option but still have a way to go.

Token Ring

Token ring is another network technology that uses a different access method. Only one device on the network can transmit at a time and uses a token to pass around the ring. As the token passes around the ring, a device can take the token if it isn't in use and attach its data to the token with additional info such as the intended destination. Each device checks the token to see if it's for them. Once the data reaches its destination, it is removed from the token and the token is sent along its way.

PROTOCOLS

In the beginning, people wanted to connect computers together so they could communicate and share resources. In order to do this, some rules had to be agreed upon to allow the devices to communicate using the same language, so to speak. Protocols are the agreed-upon rules that networked devices use to communicate with each other. The problem is, different organizations came up with different types of protocols in their quest to connect their computers together. It wasn't until the Internet became an issue that everyone realized their computers could communicate with each other but not with everyone else's. TCP/IP resolved that but meant that everyone had to agree to the standards being used rather than develop their own.

What protocols are being used on your computer?

NOTES In Windows 2000 Professional, click Start > Settings > Network and Dial-up Connections. In Windows XP Professional, Start > Control Panel > Network Connections then right click and choose Properties. Click the icon called Local Area Connection. If you have more than one network interface card in the computer, you will have more than one icon. Each NIC is configured separately. Click the Properties button in the Local Area Connection Status window.

Another way to see the protocols is to right click on My Network Places, choose Properties from the context menu, right click Local Area Connection and choose Properties from the context menu.

The protocols in use on your computer are listed in the box where you see TCP/IP (see Figure 7.7). TCP/IP (Transmission Control Protocol/Internet Protocol) is the most common protocol in use today because all computer platforms understand it and they can all communicate using it.

You shouldn't install additional protocols that you aren't using in your network because they just use up system resources but you should know where you would install a new protocol if you must. To add protocols, click the Install button.

Figure 7.7

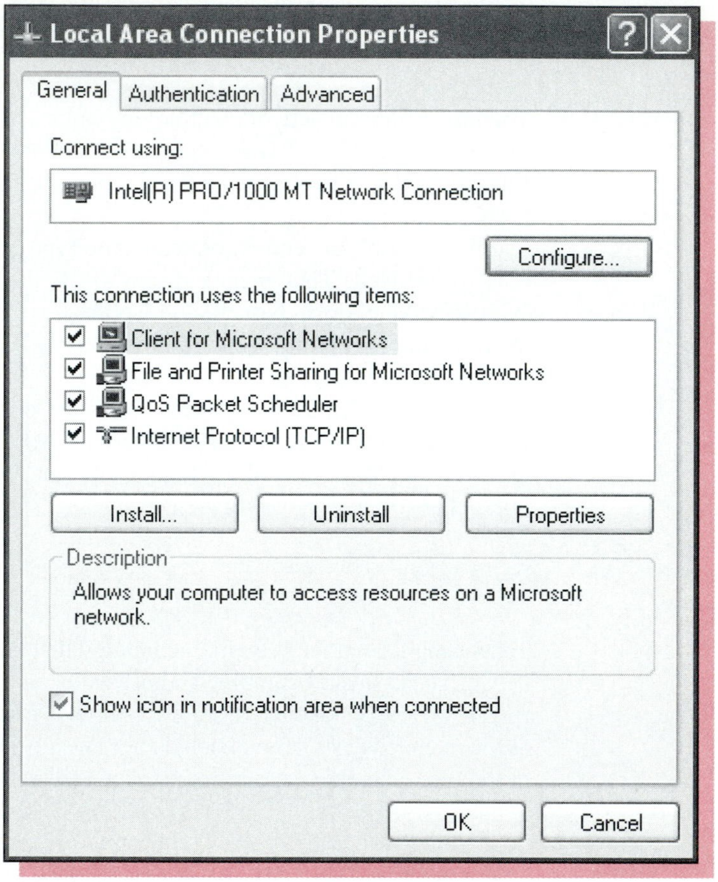

Notice that you have three options (see Figure 7.8). In addition to adding a protocol, such as TCP/IP, you can also add a client or a service. If your computer is in a Windows LAN environment, your client will be Client for Microsoft Networks. The other option is a client for a Novell network. As you can see, an example of a service that can be added is file and printer sharing.

Figure 7.8

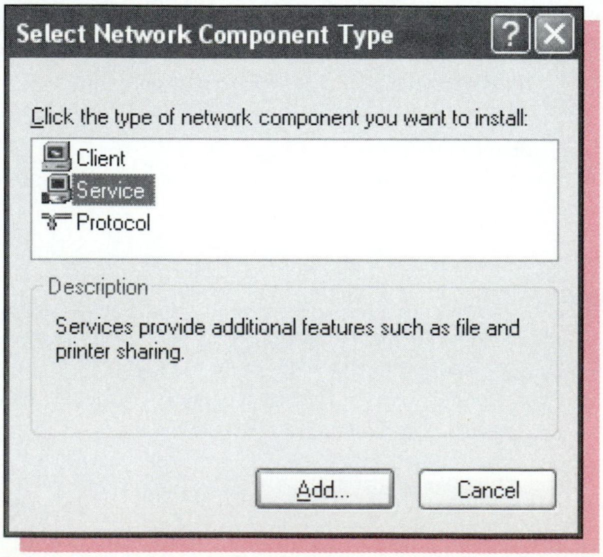

LAN COMPONENTS

When you have more than a couple of computers, you'll need some additional hardware to connect everything together. Common components used to extend a LAN are repeaters, hubs, switches and routers.

Local area networks are comprised of computers and other devices that are connected together with some medium such as cabling. Because the transmission technologies used to move the packets around the network often cause collisions, or noise, on the cables, it is often best to break the network into smaller segments. In some cases, we want to segment traffic to improve performance on the network and at other times to improve security. In addition, if we want to connect two or more local area networks together to form a wide area network (WAN), we need special equipment to facilitate the proper transfer of the data to its intended destination.

If we are using a bus topology and the length of cable is so long attenuation becomes an issue, a repeater is used. A repeater amplifies the signal and sends it along its way.

If you were planning to install 100 computers in a client/server environment using a star topology, you wouldn't run every cable from each computer directly back to the server. Hubs act as concentrators in that several computers are connected to the hub. Instead of using hubs, another option is to use a device called a switch. Switches are more intelligent than hubs and can help segment traffic to alleviate collisions but they also cost more.

A router is even more intelligent than a switch. In order to have access to the Internet, you must have a router. In fact, if you run a Tracert to a host, you will see every router that it passes through. Routers keep track of the LANs in the world in a routing table so they can forward the data using the next best path to get the data its proper destination.

NOTES
> Open the Command prompt and enter TRACERT and a URL. What happens? The addresses you see are the routers that your data packets are passing through to reach their intended destination.

Figure 7.9

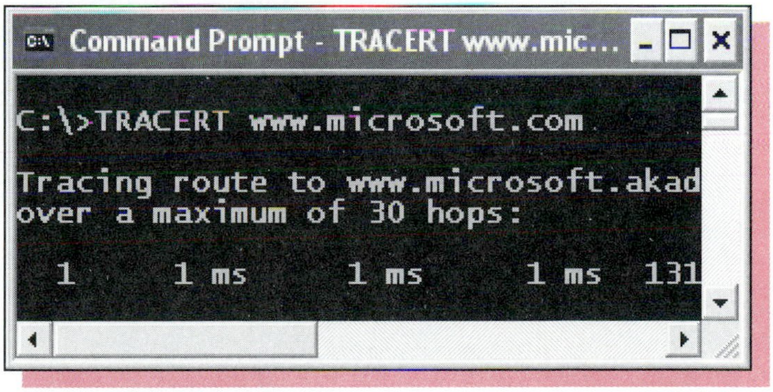

Network Interface Card

In order to facilitate communication, your computer has some unique identification. In addition to having a unique IP address whenever you want to access the Internet, your network interface card also has a unique identifying number called a MAC (media access control) address. This MAC address is burned into the card at the manufacturer. Companies who manufacture network interface cards are given a range of MAC addresses they are allowed to use so all network interface cards in the world should be unique. What is your MAC address?

NOTES
> In the Command prompt, type IPCONFIG. What do you learn? Next try IPCONFIG/ALL. Do you see the MAC address? It is in hexadecimal format, a Base 16 system. Hexadecimal numbers range from 0–9 and A–F.

People often get confused and think that the MAC address is the IP address. It is not. A MAC address uniquely identifies a network interface card and is static; the address always stays the same because it is burned in. The IP address is dependent upon the range of IP addresses that has been allocated to your Internet Service Provider. An IP address also helps to identify your computer but may be static or dynamic depending on how your network connection has been configured.

NOTES   In Windows 2000 Professional, right click on My Network Places > Properties > Local Area Connection > right click and choose Properties. In Windows XP Professional, Start > Control Panel > Network Connections > Local Area Connection > right click and choose Properties. Either double click TCP/IP or click it once to select it and then click the Properties button. The default setting is to obtain an IP address (see Figure 7.10) and that is considered dynamically configured since you may not always get the same address. The other option is to statically assign an address by keying the information into the window shown here.

Figure 7.10

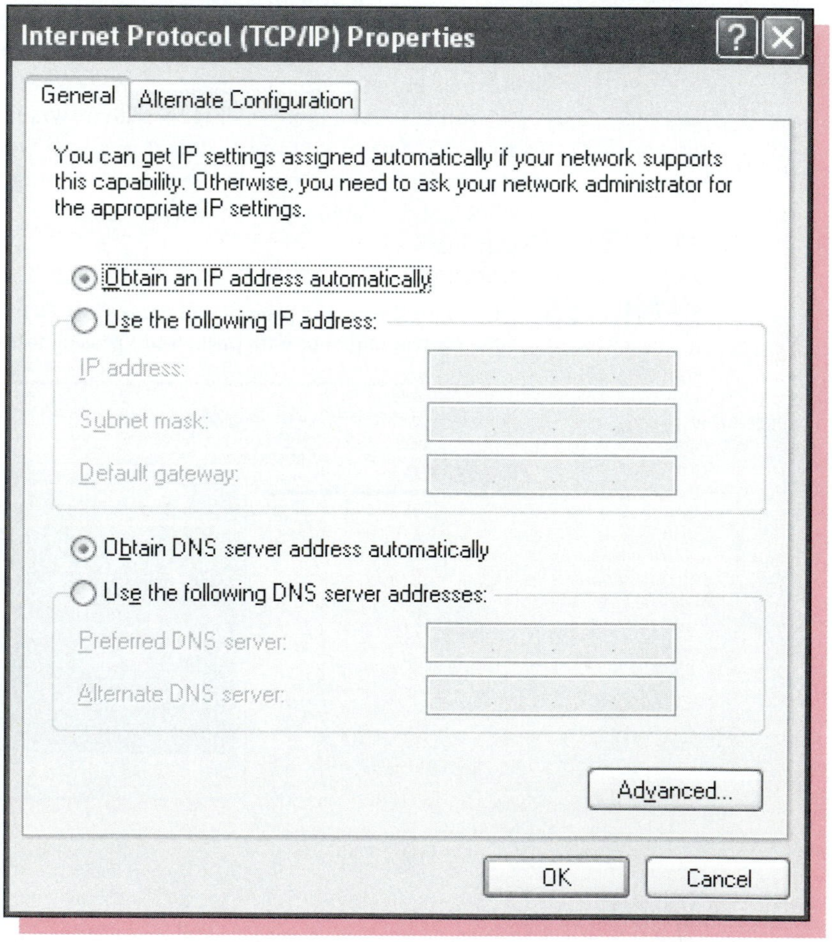

If your computer is configured to obtain an IP address automatically, where does the IP address come from? In a Microsoft LAN, it is usually a server with the DHCP (dynamic host configuration protocol) service installed. On the DHCP server, you key in the range of IP addresses you are allotted and any additional information you wish to provide such as the DNS (domain name service), subnet mask, and default gateway. A subnet mask helps determine if the data packets can be broadcast because the two devices communicating are on the same network segment or if they need to be routed to another network segment. A default gateway is the first router on the network segment that data packets would pass through if they need to be routed. Whenever a computer in the network boots, it checks for a DHCP server and then pulls the information from it. This is also something you might see in detail in future courses.

Summary

It seems that everyone is interested in networking. Even if you don't have aspirations to become a network administrator, you've probably at least thought about connecting your computers at home to share an IP address so they can all access the Internet. No matter where you go, there is almost always a network in place.

The types of networks range from small to very large and may or may not include special computers acting as servers. A server has a special operating system on it that allows multiple users to log in at the same time and also has special services that provide various resources.

Peer-to-peer networks require no server but security is often an issue. This is usually because everyone has to maintain their own computer and make files, printers, and other resources available. Often, these users are not trained or experienced. At any time, all of the computers in a peer-to-peer environment can be either a client or a server depending on what they are doing at the time. They are a server if someone else is accessing a file on their computer. They are a client if they are accessing a resource on another computer.

A client/server network does have at least one dedicated server and almost always has at least one dedicated network administrator. A client/server network is more complex to configure and maintain but is considered more secure than a peer-to-peer environment.

No matter which type of network you choose, the four most popular ways to connect them together are the bus, star, ring, and hybrid. At this point in time, the star is by far the most common. These are known as topologies. A topology is the physical layout of the LAN.

The devices in every network communicate using something called protocols. Protocols are the rules that computers and other devices like printers use when they communicate. The most common protocol in use today is TCP/IP.

ACTIVITIES

Review Questions

1. List three characteristics and three potential problems of a peer-to-peer environment.

2. List three characteristics and three potential problems of a client/server environment.

3. Explain the difference between centralized and decentralized administration.

4. Explain the difference between a workgroup and a domain environment.

5. Compare and contrast the four main LAN topologies.

Hands-on

1. In the Local Area Connections properties in the Network and Dialup Connections window, configure your NIC to show an icon in the Taskbar. Once the icon appears, point to it with your mouse. What does it say the transmission speed is?

2. Unplug your network cable from your computer. What happened to the Network Connection icon in the system tray?

3. Change your workgroup membership to a new workgroup. Since you get to make up the workgroup name, use your last name. Whom do you see in Computers Near Me? Explain the steps you took to change your workgroup and check Computers Near Me.

4. Using the Internet for resources, find an average price for a 12-port hub and a 12-port switch. Remember to cite your sources as well as the price.

5. Using your computer lab as a guide, sketch a diagram of a local area network. Assume your lab needs a server, a printer, and the student computers. Explain which topology you are using and why and make sure your choice is evident in your drawing by placing the cables and other necessary components correctly.

Important Terms

Using www.webopedia.com or another online technical dictionary, define:

attenuation	MAN (metropolitan area network)	peer-to-peer
bus		repeater
client/server	media	ring
cluster	network	router
Ethernet	NIC (network interface card)	slack space
FAT32		star
file system	NOS (network operating system)	switch
hub		token ring
LAN (local area network)	NTFS	WAN (wide area network)

Multiple Choice Questions

1. **In terms of _____, there are local area networks, wide area networks, and metropolitan area networks to name a few.**

   a. network scope

   b. network types

   c. network topologies

   d. network technologies

2. **In terms of _____, examples for a local area network would be peer-to-peer or client/server.**

   a. network scope

   b. network types

   c. network topologies

   d. network technologies

3. There is a lot of maintenance involved for each user in a _____ environment.

   a. peer-to-peer

   b. client/server

   c. WAN

   d. MAN

4. _____ networks typically have one or more dedicated network administrators who maintain not only the server but also the client computers.

   a. Peer-to-peer

   b. Client/server

   c. WAN

   d. MAN

5. A server has a special _____ on it designed to provide resources to clients in a multiuser environment.

   a. controller

   b. cluster of disks

   c. network operating system (NOS)

   d. tape backup unit

6. _____ allows for much greater security and explains why Windows NT, Professional, XP and Server are typically used in a business environment.

   a. Fxt2

   b. FAT

   c. FAT32

   d. NTFS

7. One thing that differentiates a network operating system from a desktop operating system is the specialized _____ that can be installed on the server to provide resources such as a DNS.

   a. services

   b. attributes

   c. controllers

   d. managers

8. A _____ network is an example of centralized administration whereas a _____ network is an example of decentralized administration.

   a. peer-to-peer, client/server

   b. client/server, peer-to-peer

   c. WAN, LAN

   d. MAN, WAN

9. _____ are used primarily in a peer-to-peer environment and are designed to help users find the resources in the peer-to-peer network more easily.

   a. Domains

   b. Servers

   c. Workgroups

   d. Firewalls

10. A _____ allows you to organize your files by creating a directory structure and it also keeps track of the directories and files.

    a. memory management system

    b. file system

    c. virtual memory manager

    d. data manager

11. Disk _____ is a way of dividing one hard disk into two or more logical sections of the physical disk.

    a. management

    b. controlling

    c. partitioning

    d. scanning

12. A network _____ is the physical layout of the network.

    a. topology

    b. topography

    c. technology

    d. protocol

13. A network _____ defines how the packets traverse the network, each using a set of rules to get data from point A to point B.

    a. topology

    b. topography

    c. technology

    d. protocol

14. The most common network _____ in local area networks today is Ethernet.

    a. topology

    b. topography

    c. technology

    d. protocol

15. _____ are the agreed-upon rules that networked devices use to communicate with each other.

    a. Topologies

    b. Topographies

    c. Technologies

    d. Protocols

16. When designing a network, the distance of a cable run is an issue and can result in _____ which is a loss of signal strength.
    a. intensification
    b. augmentation
    c. escalation
    d. attenuation

17. Your network interface card also has a unique identifying number called a _____ address which is burned in at the manufacturer.
    a. IP
    b. MAC
    c. DNS
    d. DHCP

18. A _____ server interprets name to IP address and vice versa.
    a. SMTP
    b. FTP
    c. DNS
    d. DHCP

19. A _____ server is configured with the range of available IP addresses and other information that is passed on to client computers.
    a. SMTP
    b. FTP
    c. DNS
    d. DHCP

20. _____ are more intelligent than _____ and can help segment traffic to alleviate collisions but they also cost more.
    a. Hubs/switches
    b. Switches/hubs
    c. Hubs/routers
    d. Repeaters/hubs

CHAPTER 8

Network Administrator

OBJECTIVES

After reading this chapter, you will be able to:

- Describe the role of a network administrator
- Explain what the administrative tools are
- List at least three administrative tools and explain what they are used for
- Explain what an MMC is
- Differentiate between a member server and a domain controller
- Explain the importance of ethics
- List at least two different jobs in the IT field and explain what characteristics might be a good match

INTRODUCTION

In a previous chapter, we determined that a client/server environment would have one or more network administrators. What does a network administrator do all day?

Many people would argue that a local area network is comprised of computers connected together to share resources. While that certainly describes some of the components of a LAN, it doesn't mention the most important part. Without the users, the people who need to access the resources to facilitate productivity at their workplace, there is little need to have anything else. While technical skills are very important to the success of finding a network administrator job, the ability to communicate on an appropriate level with the users will often determine how long that employment will last.

ROLE OF A NETWORK ADMINISTRATOR

Picture it's a sunny day and you've just been hired as a network administrator. Your new company wants you to install a local area network. How would you make your decisions? You're the expert. You already know what a server does, what the client workstations are for, and all about operating systems. Do you simply make all the decisions on your own? The answer is "no."

Usually a network administrator would evaluate the needs of the organization by interviewing many of the users to determine the actual need versus a perceived need. For instance, everyone might think they should really have a color laser printer, but in reality many could do with something less expensive. Also, in some conditions, several employees could share a printer rather than each having their own.

Only after gathering information would the network administrator consider the server and other equipment to be purchased, the network operating system, the client computers, their operating systems, and the application software, all based on the outcome of a needs assessment. Another crucial factor will be any monetary limitations they may have. Sometimes decisions may need to be made regarding short-term goals and long-terms goals. What must you buy now and what can wait? However, any future purchases should be factored into the design of the network early on so they can easily be integrated later without a major overhaul of the network when they are eventually purchased.

The design of the network must be considered before any equipment is ordered. A diagram of the area to be networked will help visualize the placement of each component and will help determine the components that need to be ordered. The number of computers and other network devices will determine how many hubs or switches will be needed because each device will take one port. The placement of them will help determine how much cabling will be needed and where it will be installed.

When the equipment is received, the network administrator would physically set up the server and client computers by taking them out of the boxes and may need to install the operating system and application software if it didn't come preinstalled.

If the network interface cards or the media (cabling) aren't installed, the administrator would need to do that as well. If a great deal of cabling needs to be installed, the organization may contract with an outside company to do the installation. However, the network administrator would still need to make most of the decisions about where to run the cables, where to place any wiring closets if needed, etc.

Once the physical components have been identified and are out of the boxes, the next step is to configure the network. Typically there are several key issues that a network administrator needs to worry about: installation, maintenance (including backups), creating and maintaining accounts, giving appropriate access to resources, security, training, and supporting the users. Often, that means that a network administrator needs to know a little about what each of their users does. This enables the network administrator to offer suggestions on hardware, software, and solutions to make the users' jobs easier. For instance, are they currently doing something by hand that could be done much more easily with a database? Are several users doing similar tasks, like keeping track of addresses, when one user could do it and place the file in a central location on the server for all to access?

Once the network operating system has been installed on the server, the network administrator needs to develop a directory structure on the server so the users can get access to shared resources and/or can store their data. The users would need to store their data files either on their client computers or on the server. If the data files need to be backed up regularly, it makes more sense to have a copy of the data files on the server.

The directory structure on the server is often a reflection of the organizational structure. There may be a folder that everyone has general access to and then each department may have their own. Inside each departmental folder might be folders for each member of the department. This just makes it convenient if they are working on projects together or need to access each other's files when someone is on vacation or an extended leave. There is no prescribed way to configure a directory structure on a server. The correct way will depend on the needs of each organization.

Individual directories for each employee are usually referred to as home directories. A home directory is simply a place where the user has access to store files but typically no one else does. An exception to that may be the network administrator. It is not unusual for the network administrator to have access to everything.

Security is always an issue and doesn't just include making sure the hardware doesn't grow feet and walk away. Making sure that only your authenticated users are gaining access to the appropriate network

Figure 8.1

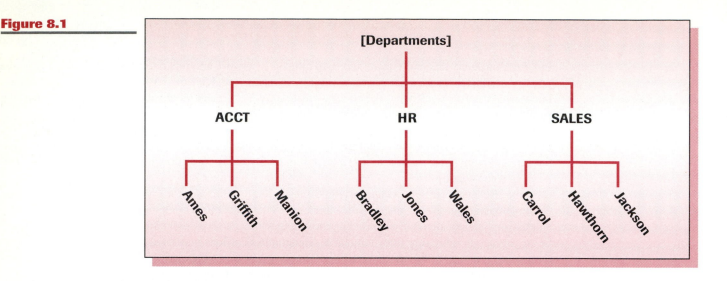

resources is also very important. Users are authenticated on a network by supplying two very important pieces of information: a username and password. Once authenticated, users can then access resources that the network administrator has given them permission to access. Typically, decisions about who has access to resources and what level of access they have are made by supervisors and administrators in the organization with input from the network administrator.

It's up to the network administrator to design and implement the best security model and then train and support the users. Training is probably one of the most important aspects of being a network administrator. Not only does it enable the users to be more productive, it also often frees up the network administrator as well. Would you prefer that someone call you every time they need to put paper in the printer or would you prefer they do it themselves? Being a network administrator is similar to being a teacher in this regard: You always have two options; you can either choose to foster ignorance, or you can choose to educate.

This is where "techies" often get into trouble. They realize that they know more about technology than many people they know and they will often assume that their coworkers are incapable of understanding or learning something that may be complicated. Please remember, though, that while your network users may not have as much experience as you do with technology, they are usually extremely knowledgeable about other aspects of life. Either way, a little patience will often make everyone's day go a lot more smoothly.

On the flip side, if you are one of the users in a networked environment and experience a problem that requires you to call in the network administrator for assistance, try to be as helpful as possible. Reporting that the computer did "something funny" isn't really helpful. If there is an error message, write it down or make a screen shot. Try to remember what you were doing just before the problem occurred. Troubleshooting a problem is a lot like detective work and it can be a lot easier to solve a problem when you have all the clues.

NOTES   You can capture a screen shot of the entire desktop by pressing the Print Scrn button located above the Insert key on the keyboard. To capture only the active window, hold down the Alt key while you press the Print Scrn button (Alt+Print Scrn). Once you have made the screen shot you can paste it into a document and save it or print it out.

Network administrators spend a lot of time supporting their users. For instance, a user may need to keep track of a lot of information for reporting to various agencies. That user may ask for advice on the best software application to use, how to create the formulas to calculate the information, and how to generate the reports. Often, this is something you would work on together to accomplish because you know what the applications are capable of doing and they know what needs to be accomplished.

The level of technical knowledge of the users in an organization will vary from none to expert level. Troubleshooting problems will range from something not being plugged in to much more complicated things. A consistent office environment is very helpful when it comes to troubleshooting. If all of your users have the same office applications and even hardware, you'll identify common problems much more quickly.

Upgrading and installing new software applications involves not just the actual task of installation, but could include giving permissions to use the application. In some cases, you may be installing the application on the client computer, in some cases on the server. If it is on the server, you may need to give permissions to the appropriate people to use the application. For example, you may have an application installed that creates the paychecks for the employees. Should everyone have access to use it? Probably not.

You'll need to monitor the software licensing to ensure that there are enough legal copies based on the licensing for each specific application. They can be very different when it comes to the wording of the licensing, so you'll need to read each one. Some are per computer and you can install x number of copies. Some are per concurrent use and you can have the application everywhere as long as only y number of people use it at any given time. Once the software is installed you will often need to train the users to use it effectively or arrange to bring a trainer in.

The role of a network administrator will vary depending on the size of the company and the number of network administrators employed. If it is a very small company and there is only one network administrator, chances are he or she will do a little bit of everything. If it is a very large company with several network administrators, the tasks may be split among them and their individual roles will be much more focused. Perhaps one only creates and manages accounts while another is responsible for the backups and another department handles training or software acquisition.

There are several tools automatically installed with the operating system on both the client computers and the server that a network administrator can use to implement and maintain the entire network. You should find them by clicking on Start > Programs > Administrative Tools in Windows 2000 Professional. In Windows XP Professional, click Start > Control Panel > Performance and Maintenance > Administrative Tools. In Windows 2000 Professional you can also access the Administrative Tools icon in the Control Panel.

Figure 8.2

NOTES   If you do not see an option for Administrative Tools in the Start menu, right click the Taskbar and choose Properties from the context menu. On the Advanced tab in Windows 2000 Professional there is a list of Start Menu settings. Check the box to include the administrative tools. In Windows XP Professional, right click the taskbar > Properties > Start Menu > Customize > Advanced. In the Start Menu items list, choose either Display on the All Programs menu or Display on the All Programs Menu and the Start Menu.

Figure 8.3

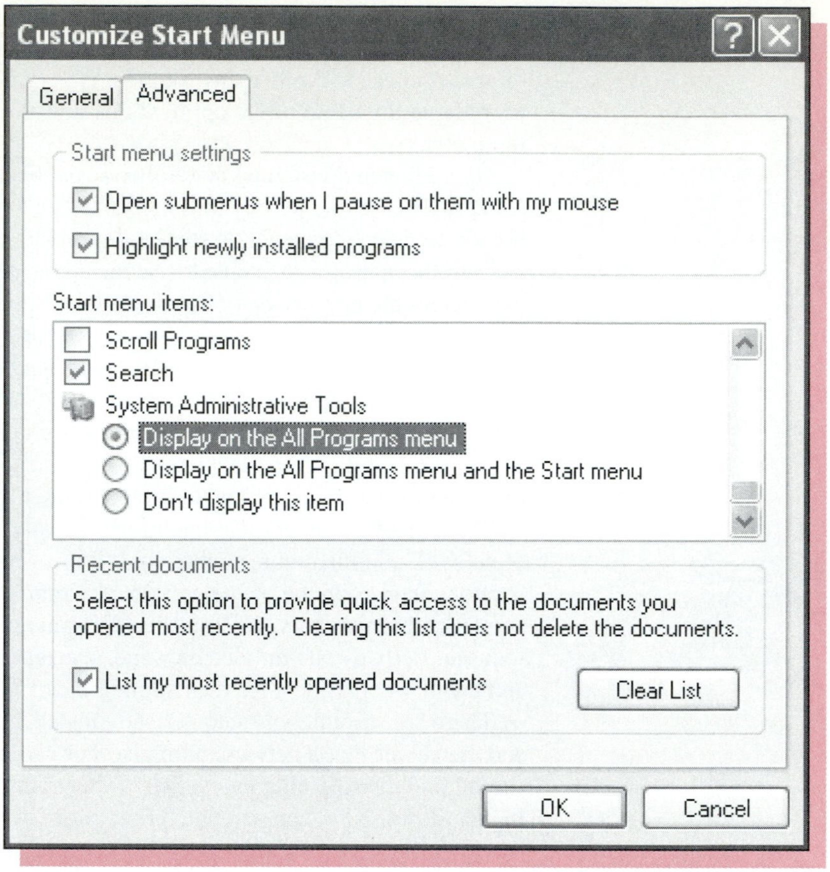

ADMINISTRATIVE TOOLS ON A WORKSTATION

There are fewer tools available on a client computer than there are on a server because a server is capable of doing a lot more. Of the tools you have available, there are a few that you will use more often and several can be used either on the local computer or a remote one. This means you can sit at your computer but configure or monitor someone else's.

Computer Management

Computer Management is one of the most important tools. It is an interface that contains tools to manage your disks, create accounts, monitor activity and performance, defrag the disk, and manage the services. This interface is known as an MMC (Microsoft Management Console). The console is just a window, or interface, that gives you access to tools. The console is designed to look similar no matter which tool you are using to make it easier to find things or to figure out how to do something. A console can be thought of as a toolbox; it contains important tools that you need to manage and maintain your computer and they all have a consistent look.

Many of these tools can be accessed elsewhere as well, but they are gathered in Computer Management because they may be most helpful to manage the computer. It has three main categories of tools: System Tools, Storage, and Services and Applications.

System Tools Event Viewer has three different logs, Application, Security, and System, that keep track of what is happening to the computer. The Security log will not contain any entries unless you configure your computer to track events such as success or failure of logons. You should see several entries in the Application and System logs, however. Each entry has an icon related to it as a visual cue of importance. Some entries are just informational whereas others are warnings or problems.

System Information is the same tool you looked at in an earlier chapter. It provides detailed information about your computer's components including the operating system, service packs, drivers, installed applications, etc.

Figure 8.4

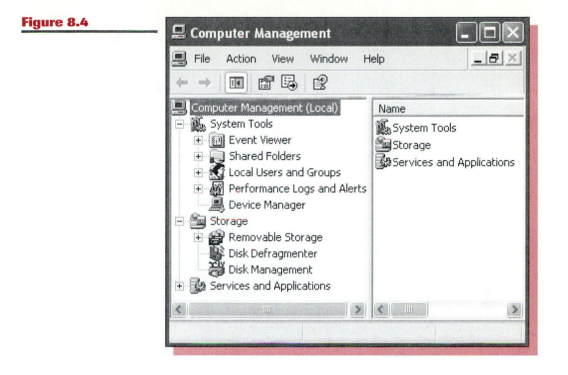

Performance Logs and Alerts contains the results of any monitoring you have configured using the Performance Monitor tool. You can monitor hardware use such as processor and memory and select counters for them to measure on both local and remote computers. An example would be the number of interrupts per second that the processor receives. This kind of information is very useful when trying to establish a baseline. A baseline is a snapshot of what a computer looks like when it is typically operating under a normal load and you get one by checking for results at different times of the day. You may wish to see how a server handles everyone logging on in the morning, and then you might check again at certain other times in the day. Eventually, you gather enough data to get a clear overall idea of how well the equipment is handling the requests being made of it.

You need to establish a baseline before you can really troubleshoot a problem. If you don't know what "normal" is, how do you know when something is wrong? This kind of information also helps determine if you need to upgrade. If the server becomes a bottleneck because it can't handle the load, Performance Monitor can help you determine if it is caused by the RAM, the processor, etc.

Shared folders displays any shares that have been created or exist, who is connected to your computer, and any open files.

Device Manager is the same tool discussed in a previous chapter. It allows you to view information about and configure your hardware devices.

Local Users and Groups is the tool you use to create local accounts and groups. This is discussed in more detail in Chapter 9—Accounts and Groups. If your server is a domain controller, this option is not available. Local accounts cannot be created on a domain controller; only domain level accounts can be created.

Storage Disk Management displays your disk configuration information for your hard disks, partitions, and other storage media such as a Zip drive and CD-ROM drives. You can use this tool to do things like delete and create partitions, format them, and view information about them. If you are using Disk Management on your computer and you see that you only have one partition, your operating system is installed on it. You cannot slice up that one partition without losing everything on it using Disk Management. You can only add additional partitions if you have unallocated space or add another hard drive. If you do wish to repartition your computer without losing the operating system and everything else, you'll need to purchase a third-party application such as Power Quest's Partition Magic.

Disk Defragmenter is the tool that gathers together the pieces of files stored all over your hard disk(s) and makes it easier for your operating system to find them when needed.

Logical drives shows you all of your local and mapped drives and you can view and edit their properties. Removable storage deals with your removable storage media, like tapes.

Services and Applications WMI Control deals with remote management and the Indexing Service keeps track of words in your documents so you can find them using the Search utility. Services shows you all of the services installed on your computer and their current state which could be started, stopped, or paused. It can be confusing the first hundred times or so that you look at it but it is worth monitoring. Over time, you should try to become familiar with the services on your computer. Look it up on the Internet if you can't readily identify what a service is. If you do get hacked, you may find a service here that the hacker installed, possibly as a backdoor so they can get back in.

ADMINISTRATIVE TOOLS ON A SERVER

The tools you have available on a server will depend on the role of the server. If your server is just a member server in your network that provides resources and is not a domain controller that authenticates users, your list of available administrative tools will be similar to those on a client workstation with Windows 2000 Professional installed. There will be some additional options; again, it depends on the services such as DNS or DHCP that have been installed. Remember, a DNS interprets from name to IP address and vice versa, and the DHCP service dynamically allocates IP addresses and other information so the network administrator doesn't have to manually configure each machine.

However, a domain controller typically will have a few more options to manage the additional services that are installed on a domain controller. The example shown will be from a domain controller that should also cover any tools that would be installed on a member server. A brief overview of some of the tools is covered here.

Figure 8.5

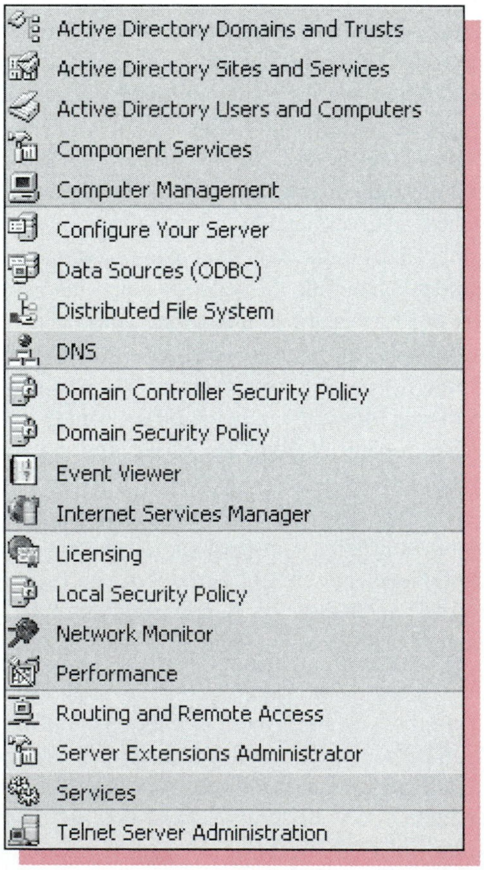

Active Directory Domains and Trusts
Active Directory Sites and Services
Active Directory Users and Computers
Component Services
Computer Management
Configure Your Server
Data Sources (ODBC)
Distributed File System
DNS
Domain Controller Security Policy
Domain Security Policy
Event Viewer
Internet Services Manager
Licensing
Local Security Policy
Network Monitor
Performance
Routing and Remote Access
Server Extensions Administrator
Services
Telnet Server Administration

Overview of a Domain Controller

Converting a member server into a domain controller is done by running a utility that comes with Windows 2000 Server called Dcpromo. This utility is used to promote a member server to a domain controller. Doing so means that you install directory services to keep track of your users and other resources. Microsoft calls their directory services Active Directory.

Figure 8.6

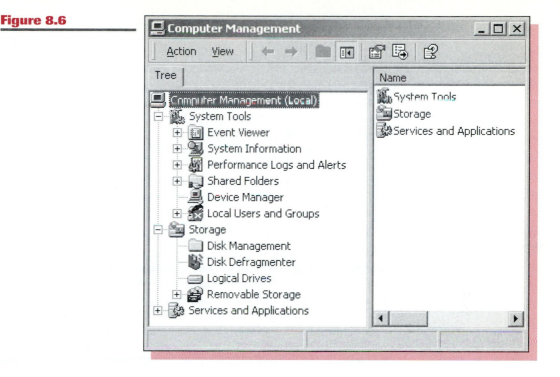

In the menu shown in Figure 8.5, the first three options deal with managing resources using the directory services (Active Directory). Directory services are just a database that organizes the resources in the domain. When you want to add a new user you would use Active Directory Users And Computers rather than creating them in Computer Management. Notice that on a domain controller Local users and groups is not an option in Computer Management (Figure 8.6). The red X signifies that it is not active. However, all of the rest of tools that were available on a client computer are still available on a server.

You can only create domain accounts on a domain controller and these accounts will be able to log in to the network from any computer that has been joined to the network.

There are also several options from the menu that deal with security. DNS, the Domain Name Service, is also installed in the example shown and has a tool to manage it as well.

You will continue to work with some of these tools throughout this course.

ETHICS

Perhaps one of the most important aspects of a network administrator's job is his or her ethical conduct. Obviously, they have complete access to anything in the network. Often, this includes sensitive documents, information, and possibly access to e-mail. In addition, it is up to the network administrator to ensure that the organization's practices remain legal in regard to software licensing.

Ethics and Access

You might be thinking that you're a pretty honest person and this isn't going to be an issue. What would you do if you are backing up files one day and come across a personnel listing that includes current salaries? On the list you see the name of a person who has a reputation for not working very hard and once they even took your parking space. You see that they are making $5000 more per year than a friend of yours who you know works very hard (and would never take your parking space). You consider this to be wrong. Do you tell your friend?

Let's say that you also have a mail server in your organization that you maintain. Just like the U.S. Postal Service, an e-mail service also has a postmaster account. When e-mail is misdirected because of an incorrect e-mail address, it can potentially end up in the postmaster account if enough of the e-mail address is correct. For instance, if the e-mail address is BSmith@north.acme.com and someone entered BESmith@north.acme.com, the postmaster account at north.acme.com could receive the e-mail and notification that the address was wrong.

What if such a thing happen to you and the e-mail is from the supervisor of a colleague whom you happen to know fairly well? The e-mail says that the supervisor is displeased with the amount of time your colleague has missed from work recently. It goes on to say that if it continues, the supervisor plans to fire your colleague. Should you warn your colleague?

What if you also maintain the Web server and one day during routine maintenance you realize that one of your colleagues is using the Web server to post their fantasy football league results. Knowing that this has nothing to do with the mission of the organization, should you tell anyone? Should you speak to the colleague who posted the Web pages?

As a network administrator, you'll often be placed in situations that have gray areas that appear to have no clear yes or no answers. Understanding a code of ethics is what will help you through. Many organizations and professional groups have their codes published. If in doubt, check. Keep in mind that you may also get into trouble if you are aware of a situation and you don't report it.

Ethics and Licensing

It never fails: As soon as someone in the organization finds out that you installed new software for someone else, they will want it too, even if they don't really need it. What do you do if someone begs you to install a copy when you don't have enough licenses? It's easy enough to answer if you don't happen to like the person, but if they are a friend or even a friendly colleague it gets a little tougher.

It isn't unheard of for an organization to be audited for the software they legally own. It is up to the network administrator to ensure that an organization is in compliance. Often this includes keeping track of the paperwork so that you can quickly prove how many licenses the organization has for all of its software, including operating systems. Your organization may suffer downtime until you can confirm your licensing.

There are many Web sites that allow people to anonymously submit names of organizations they believe to have used software illegally. Software piracy is an extremely important issue for the makers of the software and they take it very seriously. It is always possible for a disgruntled employee, current or previous, to submit the name of the company you work for. Would you be ready for it?

CAREERS

You may still be trying to decide which area of concentration in the information technology field is right for you. Here are some questions that may help you decide:

- Are you the type of person who likes to move around a lot or do you prefer to spend most of your day in one place?
- When you were young did you take a radio apart to see the people inside?
- Do you like to work with your hands, take things apart, see how they work, and put them back together again?
- Do you like working with databases?
- Do you have an eye for detail?
- Do you like working with puzzles and other brain teasers?
- Do you find yourself keeping track of the latest new processor or operating system or programming language or whatever—just because you can?

The information technology field encompasses a lot of different areas. This includes hardware technicians, database administrators, programmers, and network administrators, just to name a few. You'll know the perfect career for you when it matches up to what you do "just because you can."

Anyone who wants to see how things work and likes to take things apart just because they can may enjoy working with hardware. Anyone who has an eye for detail, especially if they already know they enjoy working with databases, should look into database administration. People who like working with brain teasers may enjoy programming. Typically, a programmer or database administrator tends to spend most of their time in one place. Network administrators, on the other hand, tend to move around a lot during the course of the day.

No matter which concentration you choose, all of them will require you to have good written and oral communication skills. The day of the "nerd," who only works with the mainframe computer and isn't expected to interact with humans, is gone. Today's organizations are looking for team players with solid technical and communication skills.

Summary

Network administrators spend much of their time dealing with the end users. Of course, setting up servers and other computers, installing software, securing data, and preventing viruses are also on the "to-do" list. There are many tools available on both the server and client computers that an administrator will need to use.

Knowing how to do all of these things will factor into *getting* the job. However, people skills, also called "soft skills," are usually the deciding factor in *keeping* the job. In addition to working with the end users, a network administrator may also work closely with management and will need to have a solid understanding of a business environment.

Responsibility and understanding the role of ethics in a work place is very important. A network administrator by definition has access to everything within the network, including every computer, every server, and every file on them. These files often contain sensitive information. Following rules of appropriate software licensing also plays into this. When a company hires a network administrator, they assume and expect that the person they hire will follow any rules to ensure the company is legally abiding by any laws.

ACTIVITIES

Review Questions

1. What are all of the Administrative Tools you have available on the computer in the lab?

2. Using the Help button in each of the Administrative Tools consoles, give a brief explanation of each administrative tool.

3. In your own words, explain what a code of ethics is.

4. You are the network administrator at Acme Manufacturing. You have been receiving complaints that the network is running incredibly slowly at certain times of the day and your users can not get access to their resources. After some investigation, you find that two of your colleagues have been playing video intensive interactive games in the afternoon and they appear to be the culprits. How should you resolve this situation?

5. What is a baseline?

Hands-on

1. Using Event Viewer, check the top three (most recent) messages in the System log, double click on them, and write down the description.

2. In Computer Management, right click on Computer Management (Local) at the top of the left pane and choose Connect to Another Computer. What do you think you would need to have in order to connect to and manage someone else's computer?

Figure 8.7

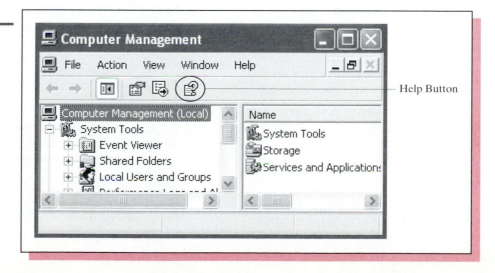

Help Button

3. Using the Internet, investigate three different jobs in the IT field. Give a brief description of the job and a typical salary if available. http://jobsearch.monster.com/ may be a good place to start.

4. In Computer Management, look up three different services under Services and Applications and give the name of each service and a brief description. You may wish to use a search engine such as http://www.google.com/

5. Using http://www.acm.org/constitution/code.html, list five of the imperatives.

Important Terms

Using www.webopedia.com or another online technical dictionary, define:

ethics	system
software piracy	administrator

Multiple Choice Questions

1. The _____ of the network must be considered before any equipment is ordered.
   a. age
   b. design
   c. epoch
   d. client workstations

2. The number of computers and other network devices will determine how many hubs or switches will be needed because each device will occupy one _____.
   a. port
   b. range
   c. hub
   d. switch

3. The _____ on the server is often a reflection of the organizational structure.
   a. accounts
   b. security
   c. operating system
   d. directory structure

4. A _____ is simply a place where the user has access to store files but typically no one else does.
   a. directory structure
   b. folder
   c. home directory
   d. departmental folder

5. Users are _____ on a network by supplying two very important pieces of information: a username and password.
   a. authenticated

   b. replicated
   c. created
   d. passed

6. A network administrator needs to monitor the software _____ to ensure that there are enough legal copies.
   a. equipment
   b. performance
   c. licensing
   d. piracy

7. Computer Management is an interface, known as a(n) _____, that contains tools to configure, manage, and monitor a computer.
   a. CMI
   b. CMM
   c. MCI
   d. MMC

8. Event Viewer has three different logs, _____, that keep track what is happening to the computer.
   a. Security, System, and Events
   b. Application, Security, and System
   c. Application, System, and Events
   d. Application, Security, and Events

9. Performance Logs and Alerts contains the results of any _____ you have configured using the Performance Monitor tool.
   a. licensing
   b. accounts
   c. monitoring
   d. baseline

10. A(n) _____ is a snapshot of what a computer looks like when they are typically operating under a normal load and you get one by checking for results at different times of the day.
    a. license
    b. account
    c. monitoring
    d. baseline

11. _____ displays your disk configuration information for your hard disks, partitions, and other storage media such as a Zip drive and CD-ROM drives.
    a. Disk Defragmenter
    b. Performance Logs and Alerts
    c. Disk Management
    d. Performance Monitor

12. _____ is the tool that gathers together the pieces of files stored all over your hard disk(s) and makes it easier for your operating system to find them when needed.

a. Disk Defragmenter

b. Performance Logs and Alerts

c. Disk Management

d. Performance Monitor

13. _____ shows you all of the services installed on your computer and their current state, which could be started, stopped or paused.

a. Services

b. Performance Logs and Alerts

c. Disk Management

d. Performance Monitor

14. A _____ interprets from name to IP address and vice versa and the _____ service dynamically allocates IP addresses and other information so the network administrator doesn't have to manually configure each machine.

a. DHCP/DNS

b. SNMP/DNS

c. DNS/SNMP

d. DNS/DHCP

15. _____ are just a database that organizes the resources in the domain.

a. Fields

b. Permissions

c. Shares

d. Directory services

9 Accounts and Groups

OBJECTIVES

After reading this chapter, you will be able to:

- Explain what authentication is

- Demonstrate how to create an account

- Demonstrate how to create a group

- Explain the role of groups

- Explain what built-in accounts are and list at least two

- List at least three password policies that can be configured

- Explain the role of a container

INTRODUCTION

In order to access a properly configured network, users must provide verification of who they are. Without the proper authentication, the user will not be permitted access to the network or its resources.

In a local area network, authentication is in the form of a username and password. Network administrators create an account for each user and place the accounts into groups. When the user attempts to log into a network by keying in a username and password, the first thing the network operating system does is determine if the user is permitted entry. Once appropriate identification in the form of a username and password is provided, authentication has occurred. The network operating system then takes additional steps beyond this point. First, it determines your group membership. Next, it determines what resources you have access to depending upon that group membership.

AUTHENTICATION

Continuing with the example in the previous chapter, picture it's a sunny day and you are the new network administrator. You have done your needs analysis, purchased the equipment, and set up the server and client computers. You need to create accounts for your users. What naming convention should you use? Can you just name each account with the user's first name? Or their last name? What problems might you run into? Is it possible that you might have two Joyces or two Smiths? Can you have two accounts with the same name? The answer is "no."

Accounts

A user account (username) must be unique and it's a good idea to follow a standard naming convention for all of your users. The naming convention you devise may depend on the size of your organization and the number of users. If your LAN is very small with only a handful of users and turnover at your organization is rare, it may be possible to use just the first name of your user to create their account.

Larger environments require a little more thinking, however. In addition, there are certain characters that cannot be used when creating an account. In a Microsoft environment, usernames can be up to twenty characters but may not contain the reserved characters " \ / [ ] : ; | = , + * ? < >

Let's say you have about 100 users. What naming convention would you suggest? There is no right or wrong answer. You could opt for a combination of their first and last names. An example might be first initial last name (e.g., Tom Jones would be tjones). This seems like a workable solution. Can you think of any problems that might occur?

With 100 users, is it possible to have more than one employee named Jones? Yes, but the account is still unique unless you have more than one Jones with a first name that begins with a "T." You could also use a middle initial to help ensure an account is unique. Another option might be to use the last name first and then a combination of the first name and/or middle initial. Why might it matter? Is it easier to find Tom Jones in a list of 100 users by searching under J for Jones or T for Tom? What if Tom's real first name is Delmas and he prefers people use his nickname, Tom, derived from his middle name, Thomas?

Another option might be to use a full name such as TomJones or Tom.Jones. For professional reasons, using a full name makes more sense in terms of their e-mail address. And would you use nicknames or legal names (e.g., Robert Smith instead of Bob.Smith)? It may depend on how many users you support. Often, in a larger environment you receive information about a new employee from some other non-IT department requesting that you make an account for them and you have no clue what their nickname is unless they actually use it when signing legal documents such as employment papers.

There are several issues to consider when determining what naming convention you will use. However, you may also wish to have a contingency plan. Even if you go with a full name such as Thomas.Jones you may still have duplicates. What will you do to resolve this problem?

Local Accounts

When you first install the operating system, some accounts and groups, called Built-in, will automatically be created. With Windows 2000 Professional, the two accounts are Administrator and Guest. In Windows XP Professional, there are some additional accounts that deal with remote tech support. Accounts are a method of identifying individual users. Groups are used to cluster users who need access to similar resources. What do you see listed for the built-in groups? Click on the Groups container in the left pane. You should see a listing of the built-in groups with a brief description of each. Groups are discussed shortly.

As you can see in Figure 9.1, the Guest account has been disabled. The Guest account has historically been a prime target for hackers. In previous versions of the operating system, you had to know to disable the account manually. It wasn't done automatically. In Windows 2000 Professional, it is automatically disabled for you. In Windows XP Professional, if you are not using the Guest account you may wish to disable it. To disable the Guest account, right click on the Guest account > Properties > choose Account is Disabled.

Figure 9.1

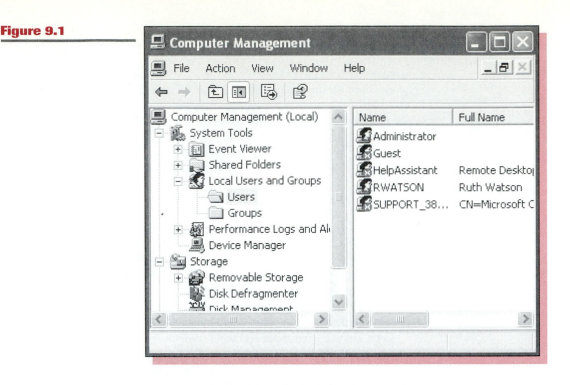

The Administrator account is all-powerful. It is used to configure and maintain a computer. It can also be a frequent target for hackers because every Microsoft computer is known to have an Administrator account. Other operating systems do as well but they call them something different. For example, Linux refers to the administrator account as Root. Typically, even if you are the network administrator, you would log into the computer using a regular end user account, someone without special privileges. If you need to do anything that requires you to be logged in as an Administrator, you use the Run As option.

NOTES In Windows 2000 Professional, click Start > Programs > Administrative Tools. In Windows XP Professional, click Start > Control Panel > Performance and Maintenance > Administrative Tools. Right Click on Computer Management. Choose the Run As option.

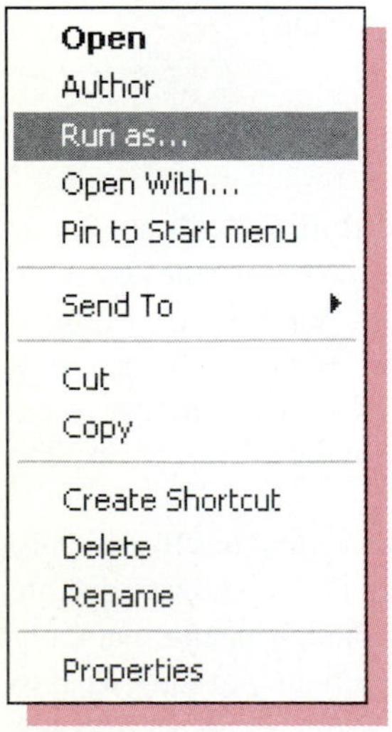

Open
Author
Run as...
Open With...
Pin to Start menu
Send To ▶
Cut
Copy
Create Shortcut
Delete
Rename
Properties

It will prompt you to log in as the Administrator. This is a security feature to reduce the chances of the Administrator account getting hacked into. Think of it as playing the odds. If you are always logging into an Administrator account, even just to type a Word document or stay logged in all the time, the chances of a hacker getting your password are greater. If you only log in using Run As on rare occasions when you actually need to do an administrative task, the chances are less.

If there is more than one person in the organization who logs in as the Administrator, you would typically create administrative equivalent accounts for each of them. You do that by creating an account and placing that account in the Administrators group (discussed in detail shortly).

The Guest account is used for any transient user. That would be someone who doesn't typically need an account but might need network access for a very short period of time, such as someone who is giving a presentation or auditing a company and plans to only be there one afternoon.

You must create any additional accounts yourself. Generally, that means creating one account for each user who needs to log into the computer. You can also use generic accounts but it isn't recommended. If you have one account, called Student, for all of the students on campus, how would you keep track of who was accessing the resources?

Figure 9.2

Figure 9.3

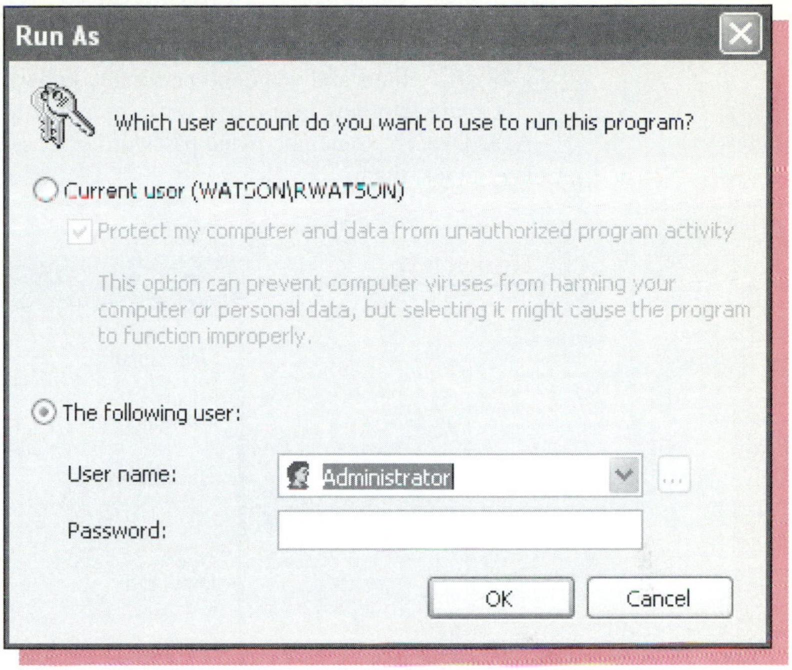

Creating Local Accounts A local account will only be able to log into the computer on which the account has been created. This may not be feasible in a larger organization but makes sense if there is more than one person using a computer at home, or perhaps for a LAN that has workstations that do specific tasks such as operate milling machines in a steel mill.

You create a local account by right clicking on the Users container in the left pane or anywhere there is white space in the right pane. Choose New User from the context menu. You will be presented with a window asking for some information.

Figure 9.4

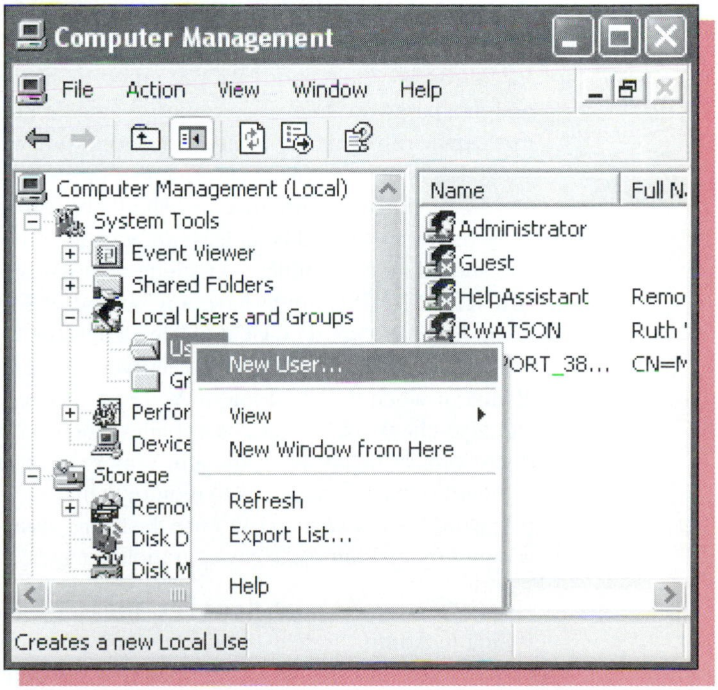

The username (account name) is what the user will use to log in. The full name and the description are not required. It does make it easier to find people in the list of users, however, especially if there are a lot of accounts and you don't personally know them or their roles in the organization.

Create two new users, one with username MICKEY.MOUSE and another with username DONALD.DUCK. Remember what password you assign to each account. You will need to use the accounts later to test them.

Figure 9.5

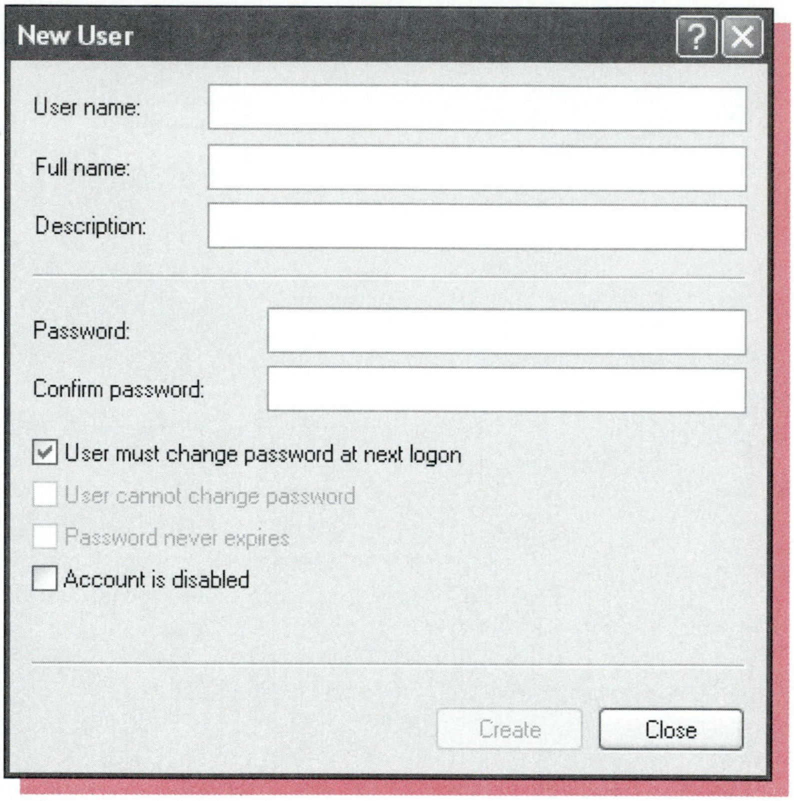

Passwords A password isn't required to create an account but it is a common security practice to assign a password to every account. There are little programs that can be downloaded from the Internet that can be run against a computer and they will easily find any account with a blank password or a password that is the same as the username. For security sake, you should always require passwords for every account and also require that they should be difficult to guess or hack.

A password should be at least eight characters, should include upper case and lower case characters, and should include numbers and letters. Passwords do not have to be unique. For instance, user account MICKEY.MOUSE might have a password of M8I7C6K4E9Y and that doesn't prohibit another username (e.g., DONALD.DUCK) from also using the same password.

You can assign a password when you first create the account. The default setting is to make users change it when they first log in. You can uncheck that box if you don't want your users to do that. You can also check a box that doesn't allow them to change it or forces the password to never expire. That doesn't make much sense, though. Why require passwords at all if they keep the same one for years? A standard security practice is to require them to change their password every 30 or 40 days and to keep a password history so they can't use the same password all the time. To do that, you need to customize the account by making some configuration changes.

Customizing a Local Account To change the default password policies, choose Local Security Policy in Administrative Tools. Here you can enforce the password history and set a maximum number of passwords for the operating system to remember. This means a user won't be able to use a favorite password over and over again. The maximum password age determines the time period within which

Figure 9.6

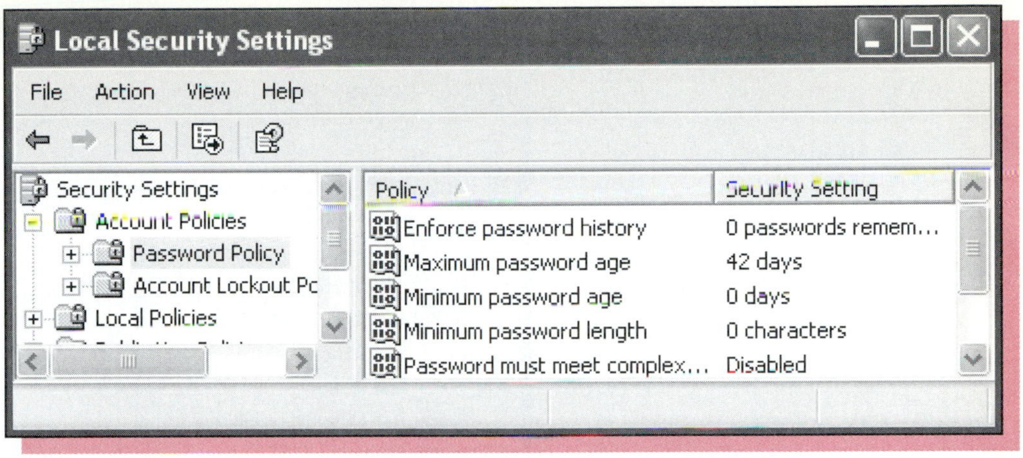

they must change it again. The default setting requires users to change it after 42 days but you can change that number. The minimum password age determines when they are permitted to change their password voluntarily.

The example shown is set to the default of zero. Why might you change that? Think of your pesky users who want to use their favorite password. If you set the history to remember the last five passwords and leave the minimum password age at zero, they simply need to quickly reset their password five times to get to the one they really want and then they'll get to keep using it for the next 42 days.

The minimum password length is very important. If I ask you to guess a number between one and ten, what are the odds you will pick the right number? It would be easy to guess the correct number because there are only ten possible correct answers. As you increase the number of digits, however, it gets harder. Can you guess what letter I am thinking? What are the possible answers, A to Z? Keep in mind, however, that passwords in Windows 2000 are case sensitive, so a–z and A–Z are different characters. This doubles the odds from 26 to 52. Any characters that are not numbers or letters can also be used. When you combine all of these different characters, referred to as complexity, with a password of sufficient length, you are promoting a more secure environment.

There is no one recommended minimum length that is agreed to be the best by all network administrators but you may find several knowledgeable people at least suggesting similar numbers. When I first started working as a network administrator, the minimum that many agreed to was five. It next moved to six and a few years later it moved to eight, where it is now. You will see some recommendations that it be even longer. Technically, they are correct but realistically getting your users to remember 25 character passwords that look like G7f$d(myy3`=)f%s*<\&kw?^4 isn't as easy as it sounds.

The Account Lockout option under Account Policies is also an important security issue. No matter how good your passwords are, they can be hacked if a determined intruder is given enough time and opportunity. Hackers can run programs against a password attempting to crack it. You can configure the Account Lockout option to stop that by limiting the number of unsuccessful logon tries that are permitted on an account. For instance, you can set it to disable the account for 30 minutes if there are three unsuccessful tries within a five minute period. Of course, the easiest way to figure out someone's password is to check the side of their monitor. Many users jot it down and tape it there.

Maintaining Accounts It isn't unusual for users to go on extended vacations, be called to active military duty, have name changes, or forget their passwords. Maintaining accounts isn't the most glamorous part of the job but it is easy enough to do and can also be important in terms of security. If a user will be gone for an extended period of time, it is best to disable their account. If a user is fired, it is also best to disable the account rather than delete it. They may come back, for one thing, but you can also use the account as a template and copy the disabled account to create the new account for the employee who replaces them. That will put them in the same groups the previous employee was a member of, so they have access to all the resources they need. To disable a local account, right click on it and choose Properties. On the General tab, check the box to disable the account.

To rename an account or change the password, right click on the account and choose the appropriate option in the context menu.

Figure 9.7

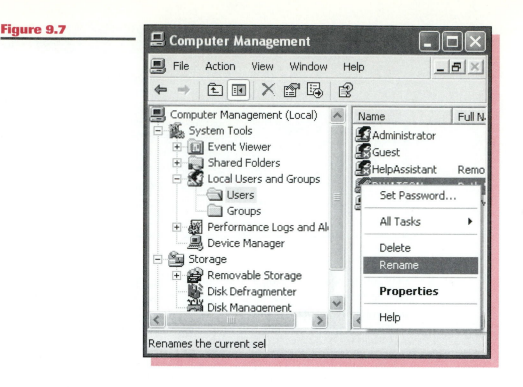

Active Directory Users and Computers

If you are working on a member server, your options will be fairly similar to working in Windows 2000 Professional. On a domain controller, however, you do have several more options available to configure. Rather than working in Computer Management to create accounts, you will use Active Directory Users and Computers.

Each of the manila folders in the left pane is referred to as a container. They contain objects such as users and groups. You can visually tell the difference between a user object and a group object because of the icon next to it. A user shows only one head while a group displays two. A domain controller also has built-in accounts but there are more of them on a domain controller than there are on a member server or Microsoft Professional. We will make some brief comparisons between local accounts and domain accounts here.

Figure 9.8

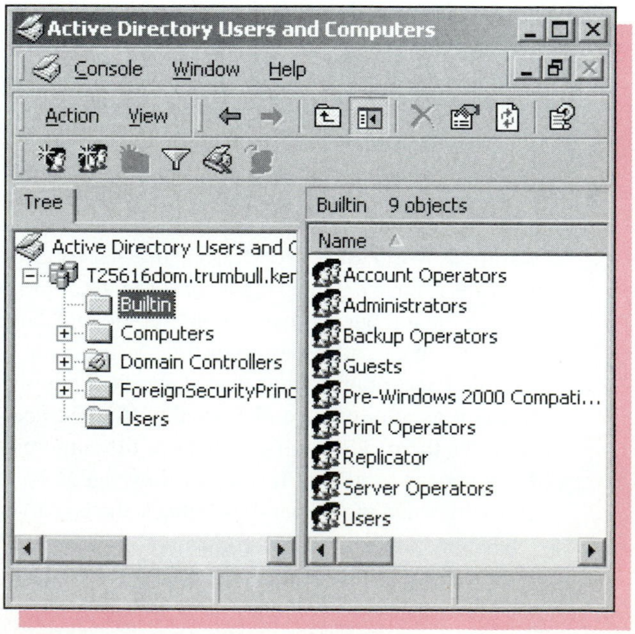

Creating Accounts in AD Users and Computers Right click on the Users container and choose New User (see Figure 9.9). A Wizard steps you through the process and asks for information similar to that needed for creating a local account. This account, however, will be a domain account and the user will be able to log into the domain from any computer in the domain.

Figure 9.9

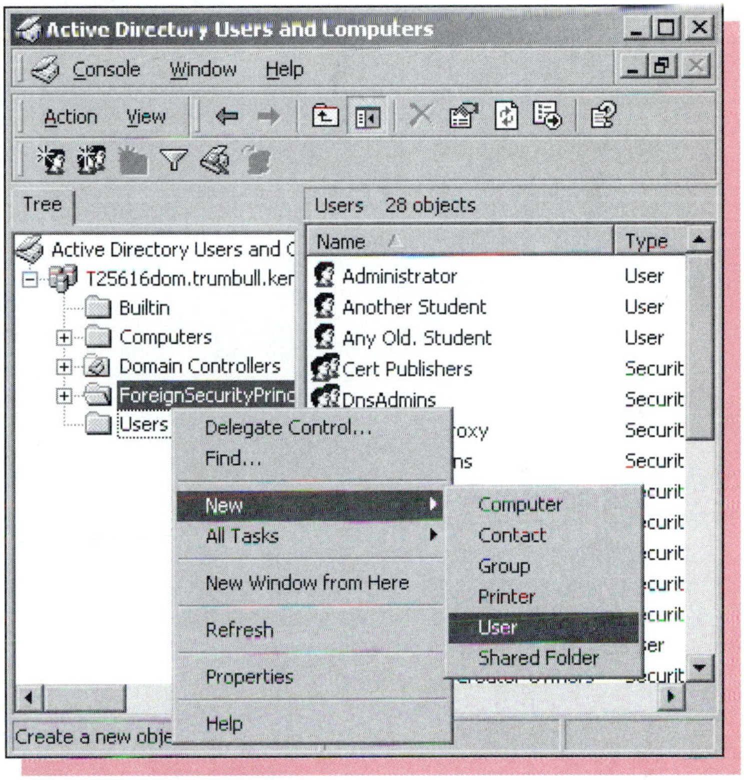

The user logon name is what the user will key in for their username (see Figure 9.10). You do have to give it a full name before the Wizard will let you move on. The domain information to the right of the username is listed automatically.

Figure 9.10

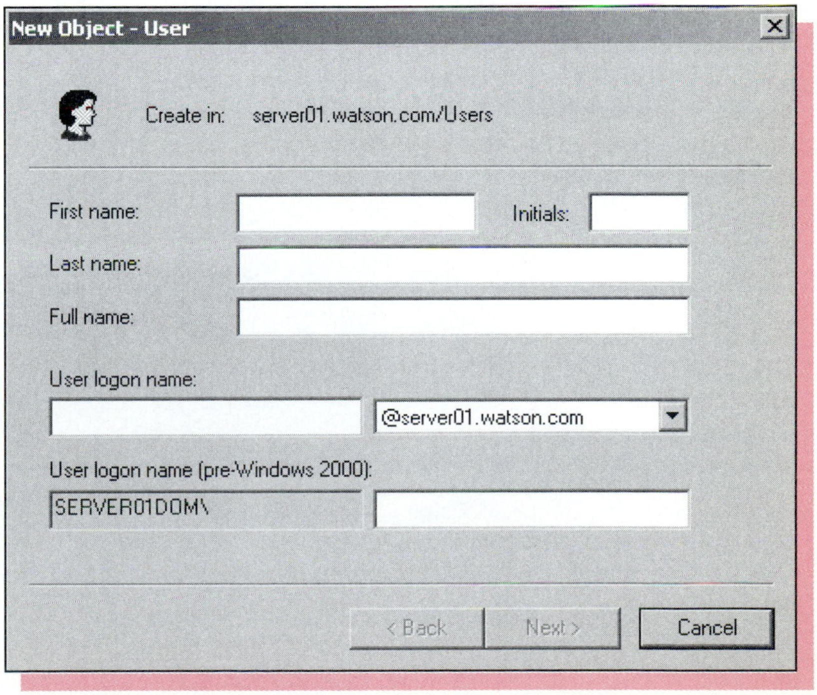

The next window (see Figure 9.11) is asking for password information and you can also require them to change their password the next time they log in, not allow them to change their password, force the password to never expire, or disable the account.

The final step of the Wizard confirms your choices, and when you click Finish the account is created. You should then see your new account in the right pane of the Users container. The next step is to make the account as secure as possible.

Figure 9.11

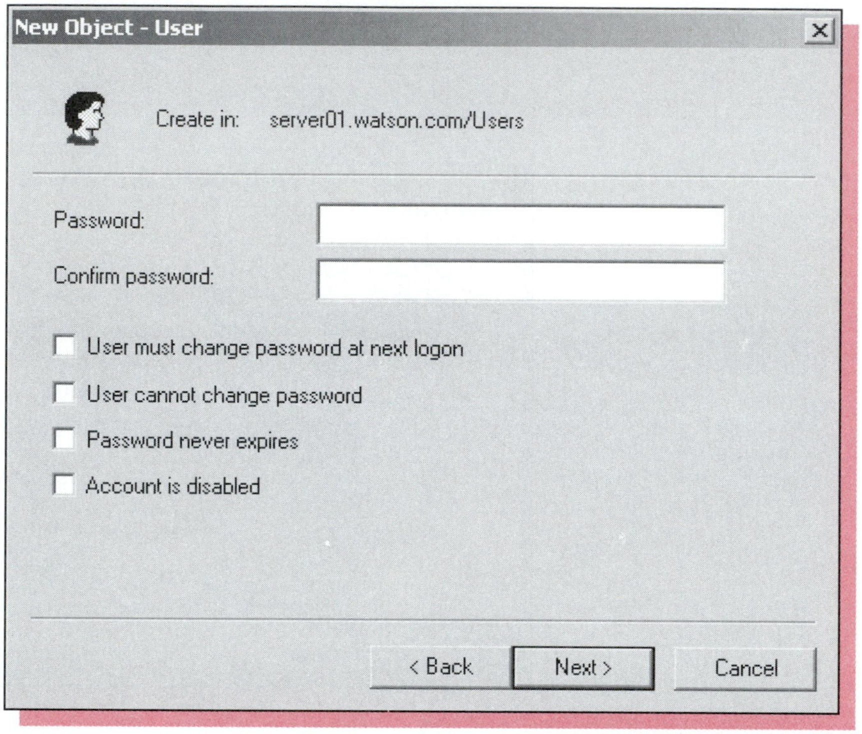

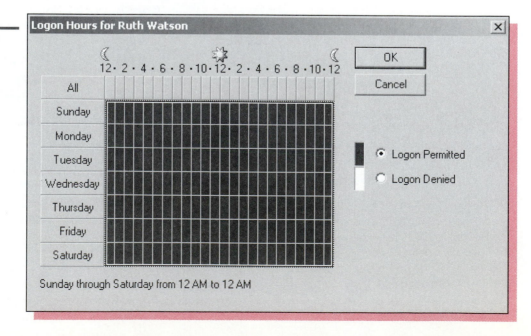

Customizing an Active Directory Account Double click the new user or right click and choose Properties. Here you have several tabs where you can make changes such as restricting the day or time a user is permitted to log into the network (see Figure 9.12). This is not an option when you create a local account.

There are many more advanced options that can be configured to secure a domain account and you will see those in future courses.

Figure 9.12

Maintaining AD Accounts You may need to reset passwords or disable an account. The steps are similar to those discussed previously for a local account. If you right click on a user, the context menu has options to reset a password, rename or disable an account.

Figure 9.13

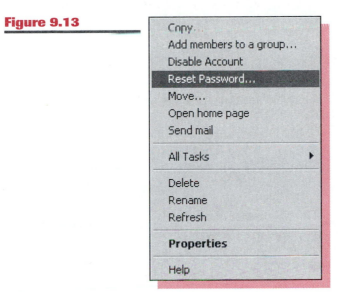

Groups

It is a common practice to group like objects to make the job of a network administrator easier. For instance, if there are 2,500 students, 100 faculty, and 25 administrators, you wouldn't try to manage the accounts individually. You would probably create three groups and place the users in the appropriate groups. It would be much easier to work with three objects than 2,625 separate objects.

Once you have logged into the network, your group membership determines what permissions you have to access the resources on the network. By default, every user belongs to the group Users (or Domain Users in Active Directory). Members of the Users group have a typical end user account and they are restricted when they log in. For example, typically an end user can use the software that is installed on the computer but they can't install software themselves.

Other groups include Administrators, Account Operators, Backup Operators, Guests, and Print Operators. These groups have different levels of access to the network and in some cases could assist the administrator in managing the network. What groups are currently on your computer? If you are in Windows 2000 Professional or a member server, you may also have a Power Users group. Members of this group have much of the same power that an administrator does. A domain controller does not have a Power Users Group.

NOTES   In Windows 2000 Professional or Windows XP Professional, click one time on the Groups container in Computer Management. You will see a listing of the built-in groups that were created when the operating system was installed.

Microsoft recommends that you use the existing groups if they fit your needs but you must create any additional groups yourself. Right click on the Groups container and choose New Group. First you give your group a name and then click the Add button to add members to your new group. In Windows 2000 Professional, you should see a list of usernames and you select the users you want in the group. In Windows XP Professional, you key in the usernames and it performs a lookup to confirm your entry.

Network administrators create additional groups depending on the needs of the organization. For instance, on a campus it would be common to have a group called Students. Earlier, you created two

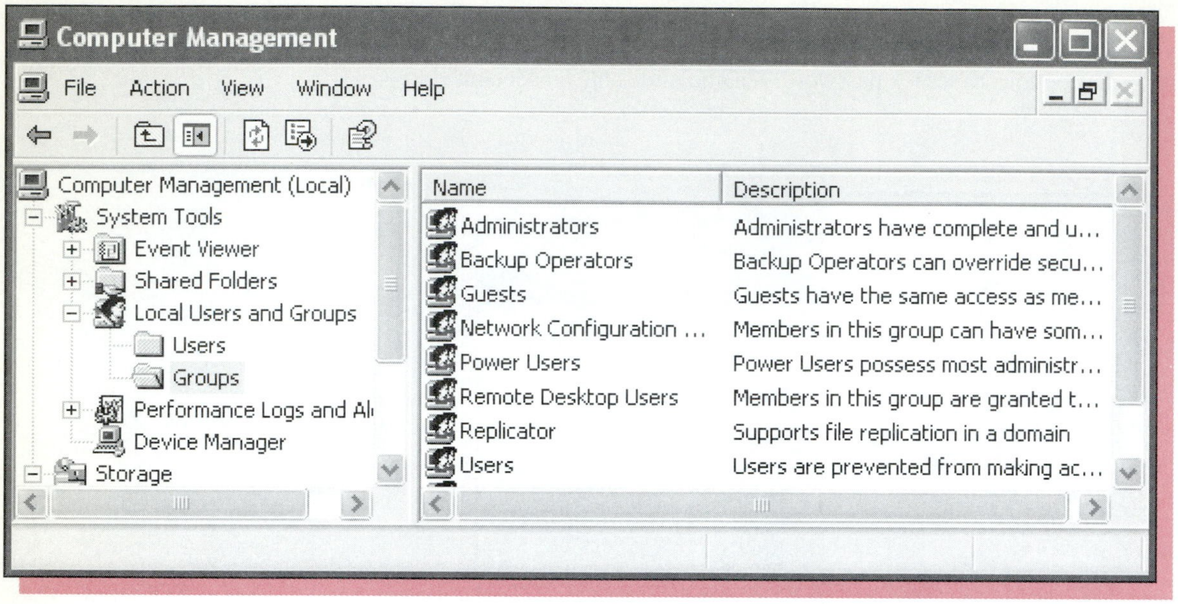

Figure 9.14

Figure 9.15

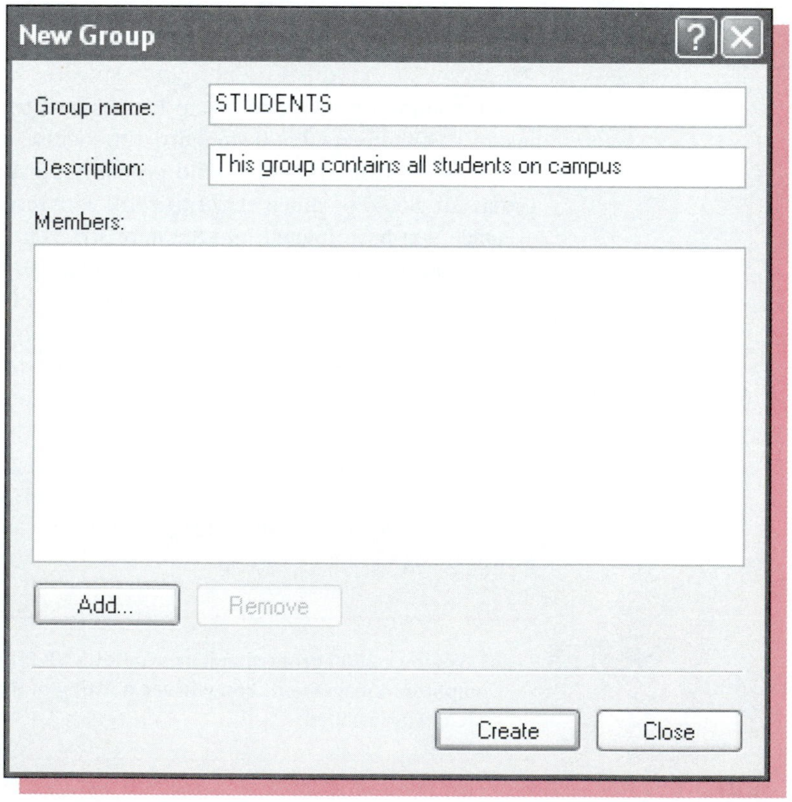

accounts, MICKEY.MOUSE and DONALD.DUCK. Add them to the new group Students. When you are done adding them and have clicked all of the Create or OK buttons you need to click, find one of the Student accounts in the right pane of Computer Management and double click the account to see the properties. Your Student accounts should have membership in two groups now, Users and Students (see Figure 9.16).

Figure 9.16

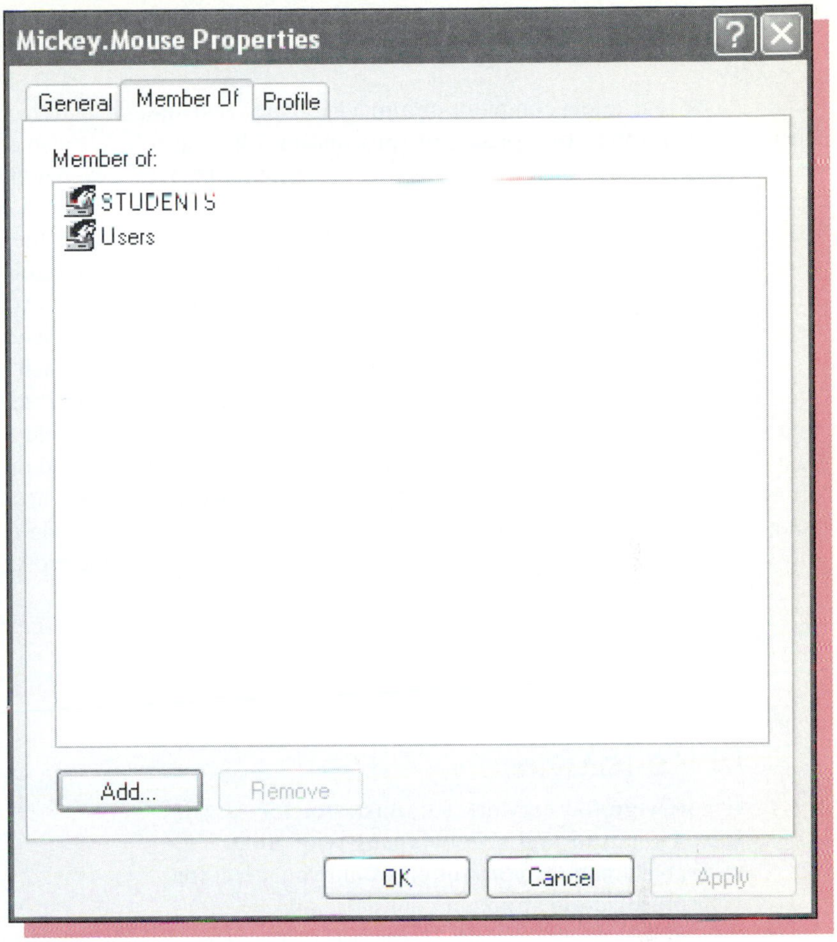

Notice that you can also add your users to groups this way as well. So you can either open the properties of a group and add members to it or you can look at the properties of a user and add them to a group.

Knowing this, how would you make an account Administrator-equivalent, one that has all the power of an administrator but logs in using a different username? You can do this by adding the user to the administrator's group.

CHECK IT OUT

1. Create an account for yourself using your last name.

2. In Windows 2000 Professional, click Start > Shut Down > Log Off your current account. In Windows XP Professional, click Start > Log Off.

3. Log into the computer using your new account (your last name). Can you change the system time?

4. Log back into your previous account and add your new account to the Administrator group.

5. Log back into your new account (your last name) to test it. Can you change the system time now?

When an account has membership in more than one group, the account inherits the permissions of all of the groups. So while the Users group restricts a user, adding them to the administrator's group overrides any restrictions. The account combines the permissions of all of the groups they are a member of and the permissions accumulate, with the most powerful taking precedence.

Once you have created your groups and added the members, you give access to the resources on the network to these groups; we will do that in the next chapter.

Summary

When a user logs into a computer or into a local area network, they usually provide two pieces of information: their username and a password. This is known as authentication. You are verifying your identity in the same way you might by using a PIN (Personal Identification Number) with a debit card. In the same way you wouldn't give out your card and PIN number, you should not tell anyone your username and password.

A username and password is determined when a user account is created. In addition, other parameters can be configured for a user account including a minimum length for a password, how often a password should be changed, how often a password can be reused, and what day of the week or hour of the day a user can log in. These are all security measures that should be carefully considered.

To help manage access to resources, the network administrator also creates groups. A group isn't an actual container, *per se*, even though the terminology makes it sound like it is. When you place a user account into a group, the account doesn't disappear from the list; it isn't now housed inside the group. Groups are used to associate users with specific resources. If I have a shared directory and I want all of the students in an Accounting 101 class to access it, I would not individually configure permissions for each user. Instead, I might create a group called ACCT01 and make all of the appropriate students members of that group. I would then give the group ACCT01 permission to access the shared directory. When the next semester rolls around, I would take the old students out of the group and put the new ones in. I wouldn't have to reconfigure permissions to the share because the group ACCT01 is ready to go.

ACTIVITIES

Review Questions

1. If you were the network administrator for ACME Inc., a small to mid-size company with about 300 users, what naming convention would you select for your organization? Explain your decision.

2. ACME Inc. has a president, vice president, and several departments including Human Resources, Sales, and Tech Support, which comprise the 300 users in addition to the line workers who never access the LAN. What groups would you create? Explain your decision.

3. List each built-in group on your lab computer and give a brief description of what it is for and what it can do.

4. Explain why and how you would use Run As.

5. What group does Windows 2000 Professional, Windows XP Professional, and a member server have that a domain controller does not?

Hands-on

1. Create four accounts using your own naming convention for Lawrence Jones, Robert Smith, Deborah Sue Murphy, and Kenneth Vince. Remember the passwords you select. List the steps you took to create the accounts.

2. Create two groups, Faculty and Tech, and place Lawrence Jones and Kenneth Vince in the Faculty group; place Robert Smith and Deborah Sue Murphy in the Tech group. List the steps you took.

3. Log into each new account and customize your desktop by changing colors or the wallpaper, etc. List the steps you took.

4. Check to see if the changes stay. As you log into the different accounts, do the settings follow you correctly? How can you tell? Where are those settings stored for each user? List the path for each.

5. Write a batch file to copy a file from the root of a floppy disk to each of the folders you listed in your answer to Question 4.

Important Terms

Using www.webopedia.com or another online technical dictionary, define:

account   group   password
authentication

Multiple Choice Questions

1. **Once authentication has occurred, the network operating system next checks your _____ so it knows what resources you have access to.**

   a. name

   b. username

   c. group membership

   d. profile

2. **When creating accounts, you should follow a predetermined _____.**
   a. named system
   b. naming convention
   c. caucus
   d. duplicate

3. **When you first install the operating system, some accounts and groups, called _____, will automatically be created.**
   a. Standard
   b. Guest
   c. Administrator
   d. Built-in

4. **By default, the _____ account is disabled when the operating system is installed.**
   a. Standard
   b. Guest
   c. Administrator
   d. Built-in

5. **The _____ account is used to configure and maintain a computer.**
   a. Standard
   b. Guest
   c. Administrator
   d. Built-in

6. **The _____ account is used for any transient users.**
   a. Standard
   b. Guest
   c. Administrator
   d. Built-in

7. **Although not required in order to create an account, it is a common security practice to assign a _____ for every account.**
   a. password
   b. Guest group
   c. naming convention
   d. profile

8. **Requiring that passwords have mixed characters including uppercase and lowercase is referred to as _____.**
   a. difficult
   b. serious
   c. complexity
   d. intricate

9. **Password _____ is when the network operating system keeps track of the previous passwords used.**
   a. History
   b. Maximum age
   c. Minimum age
   d. Account lockout

10. **Password _____ is the amount of time that must pass before a user can change their password.**
    a. History
    b. Maximum age
    c. Minimum age
    d. Account lockout

11. **Password _____ is when the user is forced to change their password.**
    a. History
    b. Maximum age
    c. Minimum age
    d. length

12. **You should configure the _____ option to limit the chances a hacker has to figure out a password.**
    a. History
    b. Maximum age
    c. Minimum age
    d. Account lockout

13. **If a user will be gone for an extended period of time or fired, it is best to _____ their account.**
    a. delete
    b. recreate
    c. disable
    d. obliterate

14. **When an account has membership in more than one group, they _____ the permissions of all of them.**
    a. inherit
    b. forbid
    c. deny
    d. forsake

15. **To create an account on a domain controller, you use _____.**
    a. Computer Management
    b. Active Directory Computer Management
    c. Active Directory Sites and Domains
    d. Active Directory Users and Computers

10 Shares and Permissions

OBJECTIVES

After reading this chapter, you will be able to:

- Demonstrate how to create a shared folder
- Demonstrate how to access a shared directory in a workgroup
- Demonstrate how to create a hidden share
- List at least two default hidden shares
- Explain the importance of permissions in a network
- Explain the difference between DOS permissions and NTFS permissions
- Demonstrate how to apply permissions
- Demonstrate how to map a drive
- Demonstrate how to join a computer to a domain
- Demonstrate how to disconnect a mapped drive
- Demonstrate how to move a share

INTRODUCTION

In Chapter 7—Introduction to Networks, you learned that workgroups are used primarily in a peer-to-peer environment and are designed to help users find the resources in the peer-to-peer network more easily. Computers and users who need to share resources are grouped together by placing them in the same workgroup. You create local accounts for each user as described in Chapter 9—Accounts and Groups and the account is only valid on the computer on which it was created. In contrast, a domain account is created on a domain controller and the user can log into any computer that has joined the domain.

When you log into a local computer, you give it two pieces of information, the username and password. When you log into a domain, there is a third piece of information required, the domain name. In this chapter, you learn how to give your users access to resources in both a workgroup environment and a domain environment.

SHARED FOLDERS

The reason we network computers together is to give users access to resources. These resources include things like shared printers and shared folders. Once you have created a shared folder, you specify exactly what permissions a user has to it, if any at all. If you don't give a user or a group permission to a share, they typically can't access it. If you do give them permission, you determine exactly what level of permission. It'll start to make a little more sense once you do it—so let's start.

Creating a Share

First, create a folder on your desktop called CLASS. Right click on the new folder. Your context menu should have an option called Sharing. What is the reason you would not have the Sharing option in your context menu? How does it get there?

It depends how your local area connection is configured. File and Print sharing is one of the services you can install. It is installed by default but many security experts recommend you turn it off if you know you aren't using it.

The context menu should also have a Properties option. What is the difference between choosing Sharing and choosing Properties from the context menu when you right click on the folder CLASS?

CHECK IT OUT

1. First, right click on CLASS and choose Properties (see Figure 10.1). What do you see?
2. Next, right click on CLASS and choose Sharing (see Figure 10.2). What is the difference?

Figure 10.1

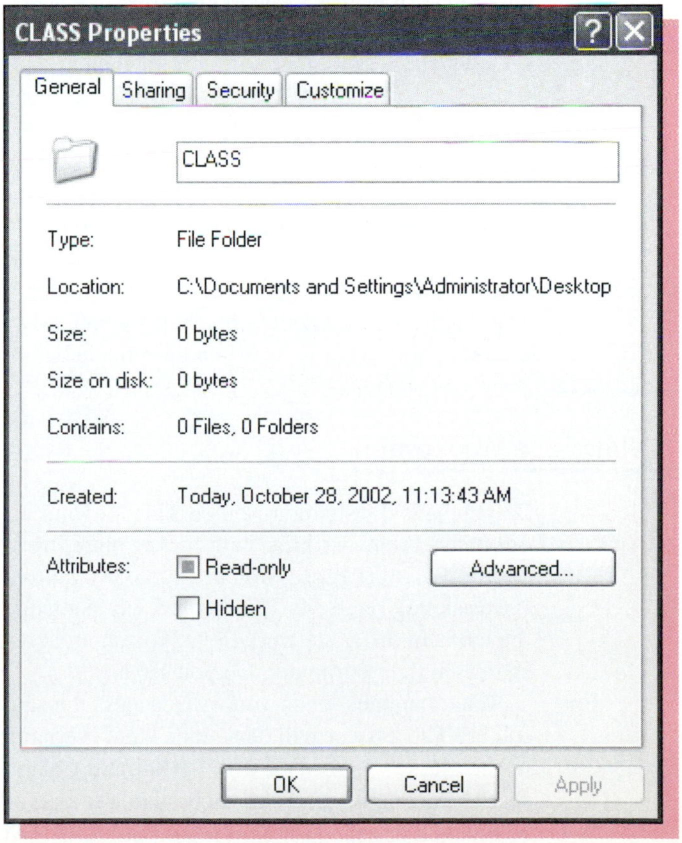

CLASS Properties

General | Sharing | Security | Customize

CLASS

Type: File Folder
Location: C:\Documents and Settings\Administrator\Desktop
Size: 0 bytes
Size on disk: 0 bytes
Contains: 0 Files, 0 Folders
Created: Today, October 28, 2002, 11:13:43 AM
Attributes: ☐ Read-only   [Advanced...]
               ☐ Hidden

[OK] [Cancel] [Apply]

Figure 10.2

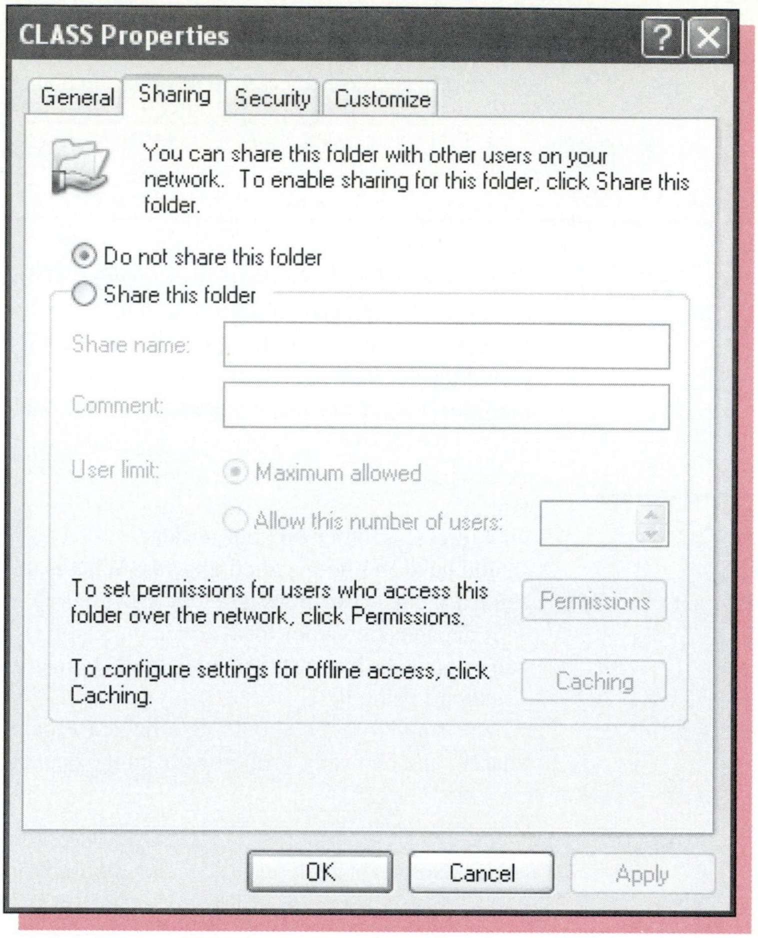

CLASS Properties   [?] [X]

| General | Sharing | Security | Customize |

You can share this folder with other users on your network. To enable sharing for this folder, click Share this folder.

◉ Do not share this folder

○ Share this folder

Share name: [   ]

Comment: [   ]

User limit: ◉ Maximum allowed

○ Allow this number of users: [   ] ▲▼

To set permissions for users who access this folder over the network, click Permissions.   [Permissions]

To configure settings for offline access, click Caching.   [Caching]

[OK]   [Cancel]   [Apply]

Both options bring you to the Properties window for the folder. The only difference is which tab is set by default. With the Properties option you are taken to the General tab and with the Sharing option from the context menu you are taken immediately to the Sharing tab.

To share the CLASS folder, click the radio button next to Share this folder. By default, it will offer to name the share with the same name as the folder. Although the folder is called CLASS, you don't have to use the same name for the share. You'll see an example shortly. Typically, I accept the default and use the same name for the share name.

After you share it, click the Apply button in the lower right. Move the Properties window so you can see the folder on the desktop. You should see a hand under the folder (see Figure 10.3). This designates that the folder is shared. What is the difference between clicking the Apply button and the OK button? The Apply button applies any changes you have made but leaves the Properties window open. The OK button applies any changes you have made but closes the Properties window. Create a file and save it in your new share.

Figure 10.3

Accessing a Share in a Workgroup

So you have the shared resource. How do your users get to it? As always in Windows, there is more than one way. First, working with a classmate, try to find each other's share in Computers Near Me. In Windows 2000 Professional, go to My Network Places > Computers Near Me. In Windows XP Professional, open My Computer > My Network Places > View Workgroup Computers. If everyone in the lab is in the same workgroup, you should see each other's computers. Double click one and look for shares on their computer. Do you see any?

What happens when you try to access the share and the file inside? Can you save files in the shared folder? The answer will depend on what username and password you are all currently using. If everyone in the class is logged in with the same username and password (e.g., the Administrator account) you should have total access to each other's folders. If you are logged in using different accounts, you may be blocked or asked for a username and password.

Exactly which username is it asking for? If you are sitting at the first computer in the lab (LAB01) and you are trying to access a share on Computer Number Five (LAB05) and it asks for a username, which computer must the account be created on?

If the resource is on computer LAB05, the account you use for authentication must also be on LAB05. It doesn't have to be the same username and password you are using at your own computer. In a peer-to-peer or workgroup environment, each user must act like a network administrator by creating the resource and giving access to it. So Chris, the student sitting at LAB05, must create an account on her computer for Paul, the student on LAB01. In addition, Chris must create a folder, share the folder, and then give permission for Paul's account to access the folder. Giving permissions is discussed shortly. First, let's finish with shares. There are two special kinds of shares, hidden and default.

Hidden Shares   Even if you may not have access to the shared folder, you can easily see shares in Computers Near Me. What if you don't want others to find your resources so easily? For security reasons, you may want to make your shared resources a little more difficult to find. You do that by hiding a share. Once a share is hidden, it can still be accessed by a user with the appropriate permissions. A hidden share won't be seen in Computers Near Me, however. To access a hidden share, the user or network administrator mapping the drive must know the exact name of the share.

When you clicked the radio button to share the folder, it automatically used the same name for the share that you named the folder, CLASS. You hide a folder by appending a $ to the end (e.g., CLASS$). The $ becomes part of the share name and must be included when you map a drive to it.

NOTES   Create a second folder on your desktop called SECRET. Share SECRET but don't just accept the default share name, call it SECRET$.

Next try to find each other's hidden share in Computers Near Me. Do you see them?

Figure 10.4

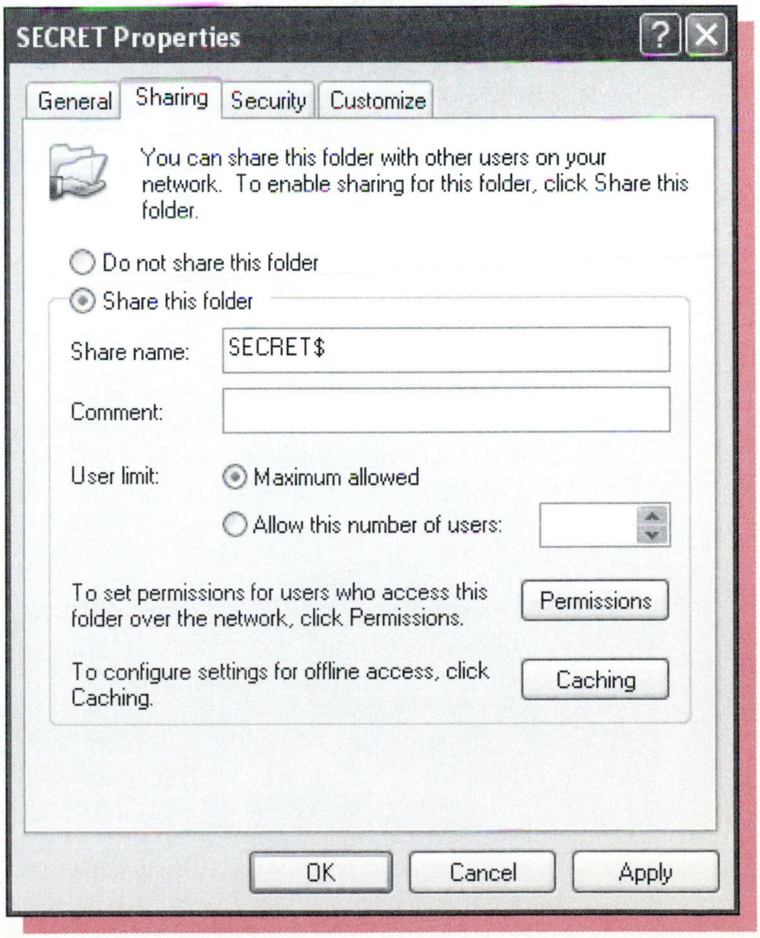

Default Shares Actually, there are already several hidden shares created by default on a computer with Microsoft Windows 2000/XP.

Figure 10.5

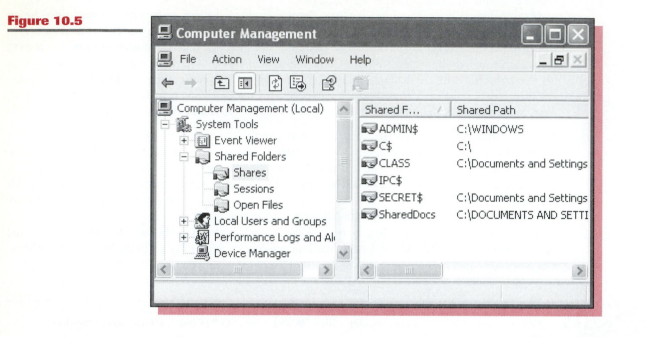

NOTES In Computer Management, click on Shared Folders and Shares. Notice that the WINNT folder, which stores all of the system files, is shared but not with the default name of WINNT. Instead, the share name is ADMIN$. The $ makes it hidden. The administrator might use this hidden share to remotely access the files there but the correct path to map a drive to it would reference the share name, not the actual name of the folder (e.g., \\LAB05\ADMIN$ not \\LAB05\WINNT). The root of each partition is also a default share that is hidden. Any shares you create will be listed here as well.

So who has access to all of these shares? That depends on which permissions have been applied.

PERMISSIONS

Permissions are how we control how much access a user has to the network resources. There are two kinds, the old DOS permissions and NTFS permissions. If your partition is formatted as FAT/FAT32, you only have DOS permissions.

Those are the permissions set on the Sharing tab. If your partition is formatted with NTFS, you should also have a Security tab. It is recommended that you use NTFS permissions to secure your resources so if you do have a Security tab, leave the DOS permissions alone. The old DOS permissions don't allow you to do much anyway. You can secure a folder and its contents, but not an individual file, for example, and the only levels of permissions you have to work with are Full Control, Change, and Read.

Full Control gives them the same access to the folder as an administrator would have. Change allows them to modify and delete the contents of the folder. Read means just that. They can only read the files in the folder.

NTFS permissions are much more flexible. Right click on the CLASS folder, select Sharing, and click the Security tab (see Figure 10.7). Add MICKEY.MOUSE, an account created from an earlier chapter, by clicking the Add button to the right of the list and browsing for him in the list. The default permissions Mickey has are Read & Execute, List Folder Contents, and Read. Basically, Mickey can open any file in the CLASS share and read it or copy it somewhere else but he can't delete it or modify it. What does "execute" mean? Remember a program file that ends with an exe extension because it is an executable? When you run a program, you are executing it. What permissions would a user typically need?

Figure 10.6

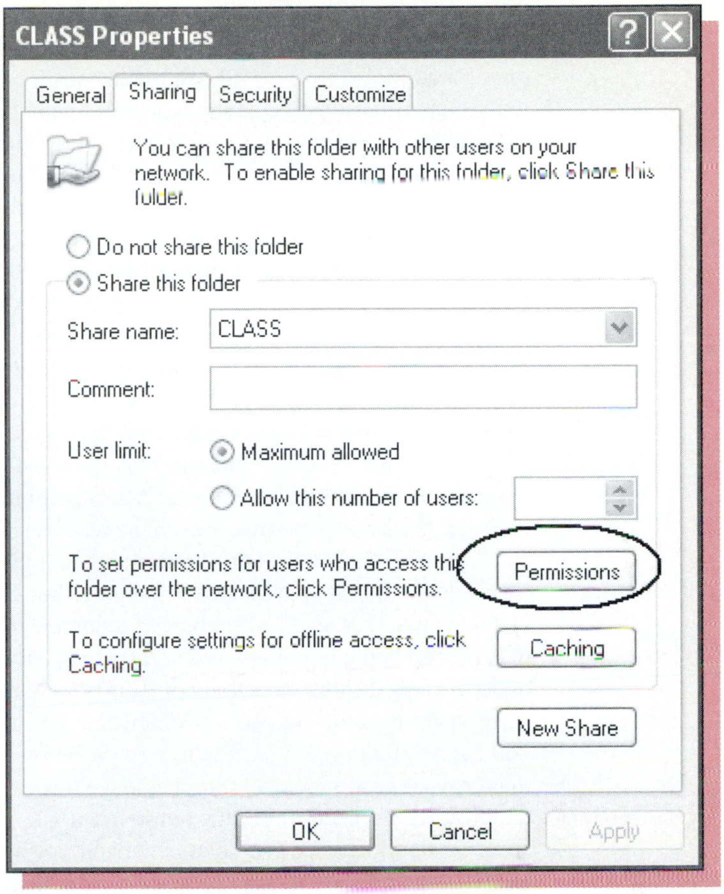

CLASS Properties

General | Sharing | Security | Customize

You can share this folder with other users on your network. To enable sharing for this folder, click Share this folder.

○ Do not share this folder

◉ Share this folder

Share name: CLASS

Comment:

User limit: ◉ Maximum allowed

○ Allow this number of users:

To set permissions for users who access this folder over the network, click Permissions.   [Permissions]

To configure settings for offline access, click Caching.   [Caching]

[New Share]

[OK]   [Cancel]   [Apply]

Figure 10.7

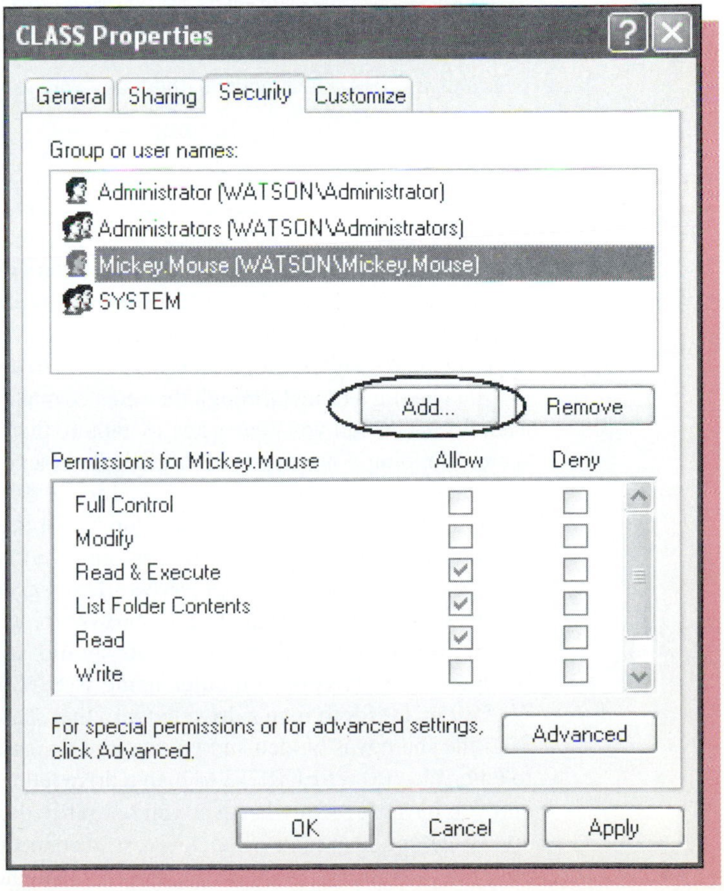

CLASS Properties

General | Sharing | Security | Customize

Group or user names:

Administrator (WATSON\Administrator)
Administrators (WATSON\Administrators)
Mickey.Mouse (WATSON\Mickey.Mouse)
SYSTEM

[Add...]   [Remove]

Permissions for Mickey.Mouse	Allow	Deny
Full Control	☐	☐
Modify	☐	☐
Read & Execute	☑	☐
List Folder Contents	☑	☐
Read	☑	☐
Write	☐	☐

For special permissions or for advanced settings, click Advanced.   [Advanced]

[OK]   [Cancel]   [Apply]

The highest level I would ever give is modify. That allows them to do everything listed under modify (e.g., read, write, delete, and change) but does not give them the Full Control that should be reserved only for administrators. "Full control" means a user is allowed to do exactly what we are doing now, play with the permissions. Typically, you don't want them to be able to do that.

In some cases, you don't want users to modify files either. A secretary might be in charge of maintaining a database of addresses used by several different departments. Rather than allowing anyone else to accidentally delete the file or modify an entry, you would give the secretary Modify permissions and everyone else would be given the ability to read.

In addition to Mickey, who else has access to the share CLASS? The group Everyone is listed also. Should they be? Do you want everyone in the world to have access? The answer is "no." So you add the group or user you want to have access and remove the groups or users you don't want to have access. In fact, as discussed earlier, it is best to use groups to give access and not individual users because it is usually less work.

Notice that we have only discussed the check boxes in the Allow column and haven't mentioned the check boxes for the Deny column. This is a topic for a future course but, typically, you give or don't give permissions to a resource using the Allow column only. If the Allow box is checked for Modify, the user or group has Modify permissions to the resource. If you do not give any user or group permissions by not checking the Allow box, you are implicitly denying them access. "Implicit" means "understood." If they aren't on the list, it is understood that they shouldn't be able to use the resource.

Over time, however, users have a tendency to move around an organization, change positions, and may end up being members of several groups on your network. They will inherit any and all permissions of the groups they are members of. It is possible that you will lose track of all those permissions and at some point those users end up somewhere on the network they shouldn't be. On some rare occasions, you can explicitly deny access to a resource by checking the boxes in the Deny column for a user. No matter what group membership they have, they will never be permitted to access the resource. It is rare that you would need to do this but perhaps you would give only the Personnel Department access to a share containing sensitive documents and you would explicitly deny some other user(s). "Explicitly" means "clearly" or "openly"; you are clearly denying someone access no matter what.

At this point, you have created an account, and a resource, and given appropriate permissions to the account to access it. They can wander through My Network Places and eventually find all of the resources. In a very small environment, that might suffice but with several computers and resources, it becomes more of a headache. Is there any way to make it easier for account members to find everything?

MAPPING DRIVES

Our local disk drives are designated with letters of the alphabet and you find them in My Computer. We map drives (drive letters) to disks or shares on other computers for our users to make it easier for them to find the resources in the network. Mapping a drive is like building a road or pathway. It doesn't have anything to do with giving a user permission to a resource.

You can dig a tunnel through the snow or make a brick walkway all the way to your neighbor's house. That doesn't mean you have a key to get into their house. You simply have a more convenient way to get there. Mapping a drive for a user gives them a convenient way to get to a resource. There is more than one way to do it. We'll start with mapping the drive on the local computer. Right click on My Computer or My Network Places and choose Map Network Drive.

You can map a drive to a shared resource in a local area network or anywhere in the world as long as you have a valid username and password on that computer and the permission to access the folder. If the folder is not hidden, you can usually browse for it. If it is, you need to enter the path to it using the proper syntax. Even if it isn't hidden, you should still learn the proper syntax. The example shown is \\server\share. If your computer name is LAB05 and the share name is CLASS, you would enter \\LAB05\CLASS to map a drive letter to that shared folder.

If the share was hidden and your computer name is LAB05 and the share name is SECRET, you need to enter \\LAB05\ SECRET$ to map a drive letter to that shared folder. The $ becomes part of the name and you have to use it whenever you reference the share.

Notice you also have a check box to reconnect at logon. If the user always uses the same computer, always needs access to the share, and the computer with the share is always available leave it checked.

Figure 10.8

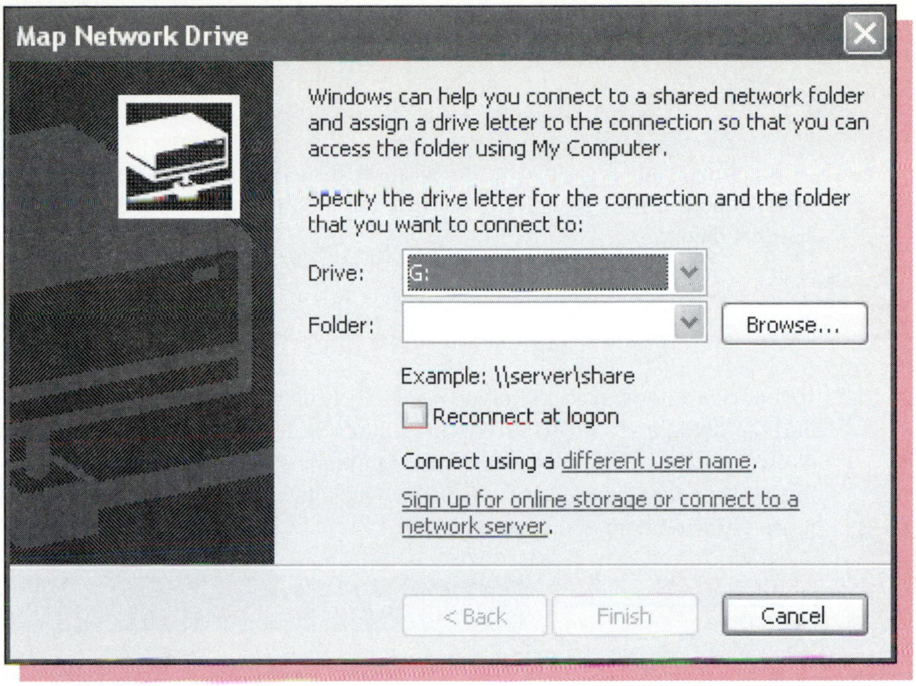

Otherwise, you should uncheck it. Can you access a share on a computer that isn't turned on? The answer is "no," and if you try this you would get an error message telling you that the resource isn't available.

In the example shown, the letter G is going to be used for a drive letter. Why? Can you use X or Z or B? You can use any drive letter not currently being used on that computer, the one you're sitting at when you map the drive. What uses up drive letters? Floppy drives, hard drives, CD-ROM drives, Zip drives, etc. The letter G happened to be the next available drive on this particular computer (the user's computer, not the computer with the resource), but you can choose any other letter of the alphabet that is available.

What if LAB05 has a share called GRAPHICS and two computers, LAB01 and LAB02, are mapping drives to it? Do they both have to use the same letter? No, they can use any letter available on their computers. LAB01 can map drive letter G: to \\LAB05\GRAPHICS and LAB02 can map drive letter Z: to \\LAB05\GRAPHICS. The drive letters are just variables, like you use in algebra.

Here's a word of advice, however, if you are the one mapping the drives for your colleagues. Most users in a network don't understand the concept of shared folders at first. Perhaps with continued training, you can resolve this. Typically, they know they have a G: drive and how to use it but if they meet in the hallway and try to discuss it with other colleagues, things can get confusing for them if they aren't all using the same letters.

I tend to use the same letters to designate resources for my users so they are all speaking the same language. If someone finds a cool graphic to use for their desktop, they save it to the G: drive, which is a mapped drive to a share called GRAPHICS, and then they tell all of their friends they can get to it on the G: drive. If someone else tries to access the cool graphic and their G: maps to somewhere else, I usually get a phone call.

If someone in the organization shouldn't have access to a folder, I skip whatever letter I used for them; I don't use it to map to some other resource. For instance, if all of the secretaries use the letter S: to map to a share for them, I don't also use S: for the administration to map to some completely separate share for them. If they all end up in the hallway and mention they all have access to S:, I also get a phone call. In a smaller LAN, you can get away with that. In a larger LAN, it might not be as easy because you are restricted to a total of 26 letters.

Once you enter the path to the share you wish to map a drive to and click through the Wizard, it doesn't seem like much happens. Give it a second, however, and a window for that folder should pop open. You should now have a new drive letter in My Computer. Open My Computer to check. The icon for the new drive letter should look different than your other drives to signify it is a network drive.

You can now save files in this new folder by dragging and dropping or by using Save As while in an application.

Open Notepad and click on File > Save. In the drop down list for Save In, you should see your mapped drive listed.

Mapping a drive simply makes it easier for users to access resources in a network. You can map a drive in both a workgroup environment and a domain environment. First, let's join a domain and then test that theory.

JOINING A DOMAIN

If you have a domain account, you need to configure the computer to join the domain before you can log into the domain. To do so in Windows 2000 Professional, right click on My Computer > Properties > Network Identification > Properties. In Windows XP Professional, right click on My Computer > Properties > Computer Name > Change. Click the radio button next to Member of Domain and enter the name of the domain you wish to join.

Figure 10.9

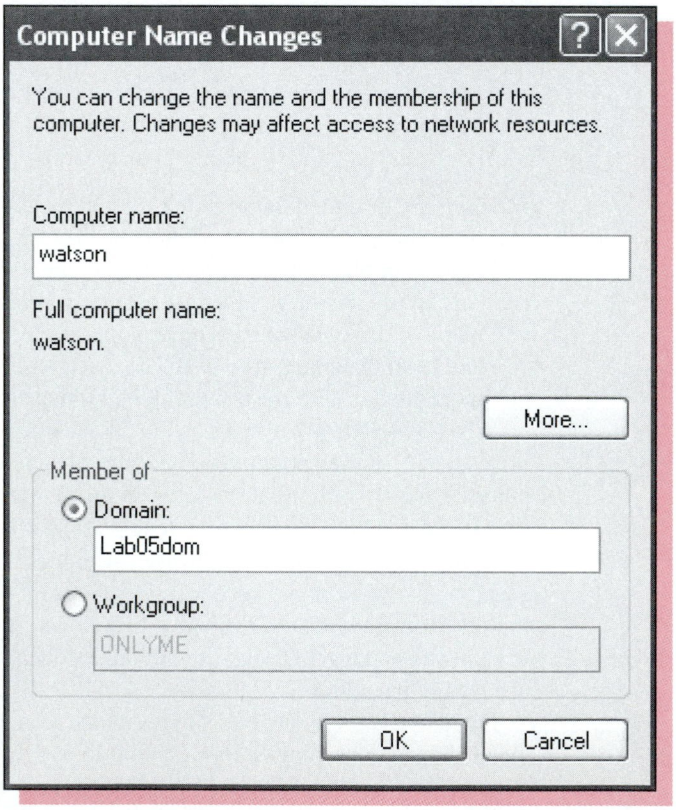

You should be prompted for a username and password. This is different than joining a workgroup. When you joined a workgroup, it didn't ask for authentication. The domain shouldn't let just anyone in, though; it should only allow valid members who have accounts.

After entering a username and password, your computer contacts the domain, authentication takes place, and you are welcomed to the domain and told to reboot.

When you do, you should see three lines when you log in, one for a username, a second for a password, and a third for the domain name, which should automatically be listed. Log in and we'll map drives.

Accessing a Share in a Domain

There is more than one way to map a drive in a domain and you'll see that one makes more sense than another. You can map a drive locally on a workstation to a share on the server or anywhere else in the network using the same steps previously discussed for mapping a drive in a workgroup. One minor difference is that you no longer have Computers Near Me when you have joined a domain and you have to browse for the resources a little differently. Of course, you can always enter the path yourself rather than browse. The syntax is the server name (not the domain name) and then the share name. Why do you enter the server name and not the domain name? Remember, a domain can have more than one server.

Another way to map drives in a network makes more sense but will only be introduced here. You could write logon scripts or use Group Policy Objects. One bonus to a domain environment is that a user can log into the domain no matter which computer in the domain they use. If you map the drives from one local computer, they don't have access to their resources unless they use that computer.

Figure 10.10

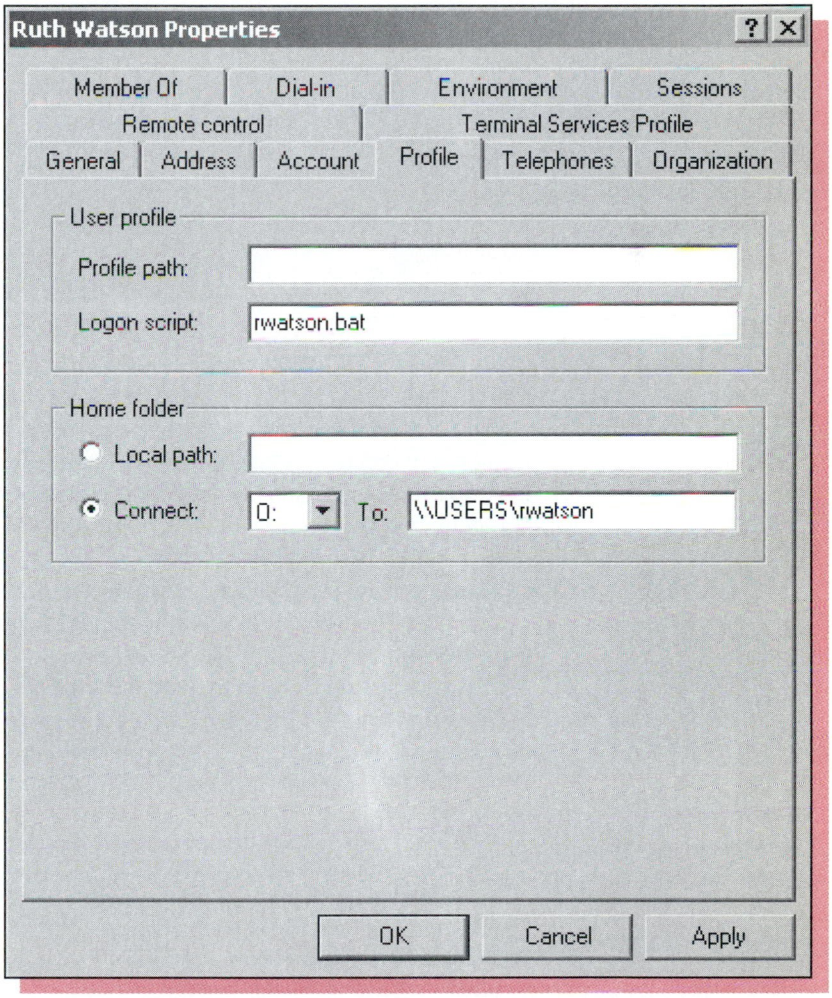

What makes more sense is to have a script, similar to a batch file, centrally located on the server. No matter which computer is used to log into the domain, the user's script is run and the drives are mapped. On a domain controller, you specify the name of the script that should run for each user in the Profile tab. This will only work on a domain controller. However, you can set a home directory on either a domain controller or on a member server. You do that by clicking the Connect radio button, selecting a drive letter, and giving a path to where you want the home directory to be created. A home directory is a folder that a particular user has access to but usually no one else. The drive will be mapped each time the user logs in.

Disconnecting a Mapped Drive

Disconnecting a mapped drive is much easier than mapping one. Simply right click on the drive letter in My Computer and choose Disconnect. You can also choose Disconnect Network Drive from the Tools menu in My Computer.

Figure 10.11

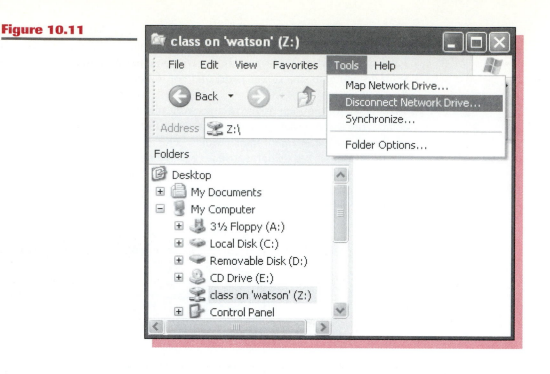

MOVING A SHARE

Earlier, you created a share on your desktop called CLASS. Let's assume that the operating system you are currently booted into is on the F: drive (because you have more than one operating system on the computer). If you are logged in as the Administrator, the exact path to the share is F:\documents and settings\administrator\desktop\class.

When you practiced mapping drives to each other's shares, however, did you include any of that information? No, the syntax was \\computer name\share name. If your computer name is LAB05, the path to map it is \\LAB05\CLASS. What does that tell you about the share called class? Can you ever have two shares on a computer with the same share name?

The answer is "no," but don't take my word for it; test the theory. In fact, you should do that as often as possible with computers to help you learn more. Don't just read about something; do it.

NOTES   You know you can't create another folder on your desktop called CLASS because you can't have two folders with the same name in the same subdirectory. So create another folder called CLASS somewhere else on your computer, like in My Documents. Then right click and choose Sharing. Click the radio button to share it. Remember when you did it before it automatically put in the name of the share for you? It is blank now, right? What happens if you type in CLASS for the share name and click apply?

Figure 10.12

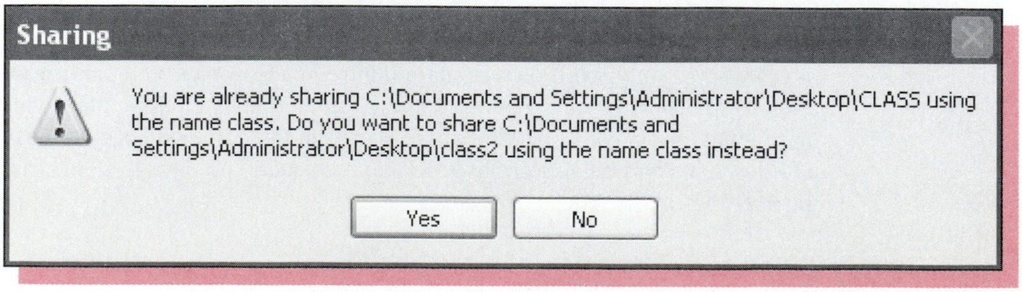

Sharing

⚠ You are already sharing C:\Documents and Settings\Administrator\Desktop\CLASS using the name class. Do you want to share C:\Documents and Settings\Administrator\Desktop\class2 using the name class instead?

[Yes]   [No]

If you try to create a second share with the same name, you should get an error message saying that you already have a share with that name. It is asking if you want to unshare the folder CLASS on your desktop and share this one as CLASS instead.

What happens if you answer is "yes"? On your end, the CLASS folder on the desktop is no longer shared and the CLASS folder in My Documents now is. If someone else in the lab had mapped a drive to a CLASS share on your computer, do they need to do anything different now? Will their mapped drive still work?

Let's ask the same question a little differently. Say you have a share called GRAPHICS on your F: drive and the partition is nearly full. You decide to move the folder to another partition even though several people in the company map to it as a resource. If you move your share, will the others who map to it even need to be told?

The answer is "no." All of the work is done on your end and since the share name and computer name will remain the same, nothing needs to be reconfigured on their computer. When you move the share on your end, the operating system will stop sharing it, however. You will simply need to reshare it with the same name when you get it to its new partition or folder.

Figure 10.13

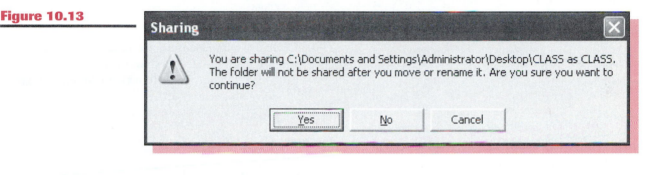

Sharing

You are sharing C:\Documents and Settings\Administrator\Desktop\CLASS as CLASS. The folder will not be shared after you move or rename it. Are you sure you want to continue?

[Yes]   [No]   [Cancel]

Summary

One of the main resources in a networked environment is shared folders with files in them. Printers, of course, are another good reason to connect computers together. In the early days of computing, sharing files was known as "sneakernet." You copied files to a floppy and ran down the hall with it. While it was great exercise, it wasn't the most economical way to run a business.

To give access to files in a LAN, you create a folder, share it, and apply the appropriate permissions to the appropriate group. Sometimes group members may need to be able to modify the files; often they just need to view or copy the files. To determine what is needed, a network administrator may need to do a little investigating and a lot of talking with the users and administra-

tion within the organization. Who has access to what and how much access they have is very important.

Some shares may be hidden by appending a $ to the end of the name. This means that network users won't see it in My Network Places. To access any share, hidden or otherwise, the user must have permission to access it. In addition, you can make it easier for them to access it by mapping a drive to it. That means that the user will get an additional drive letter in My Computer.

You can access shares in either a peer-to-peer or client/server network. To be a member of a client/server network, you must join the computer to the domain. Your computer is then another resource in the domain.

ACTIVITIES

Review Questions

1. In your own words, explain what a shared folder is. How do you create one?

2. In your own words, explain what a mapped drive is. How do you create one?

3. In your own words, explain what permissions are. How do you configure them?

4. With a hidden share, does the $ go before the share name or after? If the computer name is LAB07, the share name is TECHNO and you made it a hidden share, what is the path you would enter to map to it? Be sure to use the correct syntax.

5. Compare working in a workgroup environment to working in a domain environment.

Hands-on

1. If one is available, join a domain using information provided by the instructor such as a username and password. Explain the steps you needed to take.

2. When you are logged into a domain, do you still see Computers Near Me? Reconfigure your computer when you are done to return it to its original configuration.

3. In Chapter 9, you created two groups, Faculty and Tech, and placed Lawrence Jones and Kenneth Vince in the Faculty group and Robert Smith and Deborah Sue Murphy in the Tech group. Create two new shares and also call them Faculty and Tech. Give the appropriate groups Modify permissions to the appropriate shared folders.

4. Create a new share called USERS. Give the account Kenneth Vince a home directory. Use the Profile tab for his account, select a drive letter where it says Connect As, and then enter the correct path to the USERS folder. For instance, if your computer name is LAB03, the correct path is \\LAB03\USERS\%username% where %username% is a variable you can use in place of the real username. You can either enter %username% or the real username. Using the word username with the percent signs before and after make it similar to a wildcard except in this case it is going to replace the variable with the correct username. This is especially helpful when you are working with multiple accounts at once. List your steps and the exact path you used.

5. Test Kenneth Vince's account by logging into it. You should have a T: drive in My Computer. Next, map a drive to the Faculty share. Does it work? List your steps.

Important Terms

Using www.webopedia.com or another online technical dictionary, define:

domain   map   share

Multiple Choice Questions

1. **Which icon designates that the folder is shared?**

   a.

   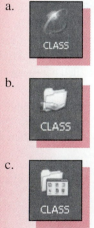

   b.

   c.

   d.

2. **The _____ button applies any changes you have made but leaves the Properties window open.**

   a. Apply

   b. OK

   c. Change

   d. Modify

3. **The _____ button applies any changes you have made but closes the Properties window.**

   a. Apply

   b. OK

   c. Change

   d. Modify

4. **If you are using a computer named LAB04 and you are trying to access shares on computers called LAB08 and LAB10, which computer must you have an account on?**

   a. LAB04

   b. LAB04, LAB08

   c. LAB08, LAB10

   d. LAB04, LAB08, LAB10

5. **You can find other computers in the same workgroup by first clicking on My Network Places and then clicking on _____.**

   a. Add network place

   b. Entire network

   c. Computers

   d. Computers near me

6. **You hide a folder when you share it by appending a _____ to the _____ of the share name.**

   a. % beginning

   b. % end

   c. $ beginning

   d. $ end

7. **The WINNT folder, which houses all of the system files, is a hidden share called _____.**

   a. WINNT

   b. C$

   c. ADMIN$

   d. IPC$

Figure 10.14

Home folder
○ Local path: [   ]
● Connect: [T: ▼] To: [\\lab03\users\%username%]

8. _____ is/are how we control how much access a user has to the network resources.
   a. Modify
   b. Explicit
   c. Implicit
   d. Permissions

9. The highest level of permissions you would typically give a regular end user is _____.
   a. List
   b. Read only
   c. Modify
   d. Full Control

10. We map drives to resources on other computers for our users to _____.
    a. give them permissions to it
    b. share it for them
    c. hide the share
    d. make it easier for them to find the resources

11. The correct syntax to map a drive using the Wizard is _____.
    a. /share//server
    b. \share\\ server
    c. \\domain\\share
    d. \\server\share

12. If you have a hidden share called **CLASS** and it is on a computer named **LAB09**, the correct syntax to map a drive to it using the Wizard is _____.
    a. /%CLASS//LAB09
    b. \CLASS$\\LAB09
    c. \\LAB09\CLASS$
    d. \\LAB09\%CLASS

13. When you map a drive to a resource, you can use _____.
    a. any letter
    b. any letter available on the client computer
    c. any letter available on the server
    d. F–Z

14. When you move a share on your computer and reshare it with the same name, the people mapped to it _____.
    a. will need to remap the drive
    b. won't need to do anything
    c. will no longer have access
    d. will need to know what partition or folder you move it to

15. You can have _____ share(s) with the same name on a computer.
    a. one
    b. two
    c. ten
    d. as many as you want

CHAPTER 11

Network Maintenance

OBJECTIVES

After reading this chapter, you will be able to:

- Explain the importance of a Disaster Recovery Plan
- Describe a backup rotation scheme
- Demonstrate how to boot a computer into safe mode
- Explain the role of services
- Explain the role of service packs
- Explain the difference between a static and a dynamic IP address
- Explain what the DHCP service does
- Demonstrate how to use TCP/IP troubleshooting tools including PING and TRACERT
- Explain what the DNS service does

INTRODUCTION

O nce the network is in place, the real work begins. Maintaining a network is a primary role of a network administrator. It involves not only fixing things when they break but also monitoring resources to prevent them from breaking in the first place. Remember, when the equipment isn't working, neither are the users. Staying connected to the network is critical for the users to have access to the resources.

TRICKS OF THE TRADE

Server Backups

Although you worked with the Backup utility in Chapter 4, the topic of backups is so important it warrants a second look. The most common reason I've ever known for network administrators to be fired was that after a system failure they didn't have a current backup. It wasn't the system failure that got them fired. It was the fact that they hadn't followed the company's Disaster Recovery Plan and maintained current backups of the data.

All companies have some sort of a Disaster Recovery Plan. Some may be simply understood informally but most are formal documents with procedures outlined in the event of certain catastrophic failures. This would include some timeframe wherein the network must be fully functional again following the failure. In a very small environment, the network administrator may have a day or two. In a mission critical environment, especially where lives are at stake, most companies have redundant systems in place so there is no real downtime. If the network went down on your campus, what would you say is a reasonable timeframe to have it up and running again? How long can you go without access to the application software you use for your classes, e-mail, or student services including registration and financial aid?

What if you were responsible for devising the backup schedule? How many tapes would you need? The answer depends on the rotation schedule you use for your backups. Do you have to do a full backup every day? Or should you only back up what has changed since yesterday? When is it safe to reuse a tape and overwrite its contents with new data in the process? It can be difficult to figure out these answers on your own but fortunately there are some guidelines to get you started. Two of the best known examples are the Tower of Hanoi rotation scheme and the grandfather-father-son backup schedule and we'll leave learning more about them as a hands-on assignment.

Briefly, you may need up to a dozen tapes or more. Your backup schedule may include a full backup once a week with incremental backups during the week. When would you schedule your backups to run? The software that handles the backing up usually skips any files that are open when the backup is running. So it makes more sense to schedule the backup when there are few or no people around.

Services

You already know that your computer or server is running several services. Examples of services that might be running on a server are DNS and DHCP, and these services perform specific functions in the local area network. There are several others, however, that just deal with making the operating system function.

Figure 11.1

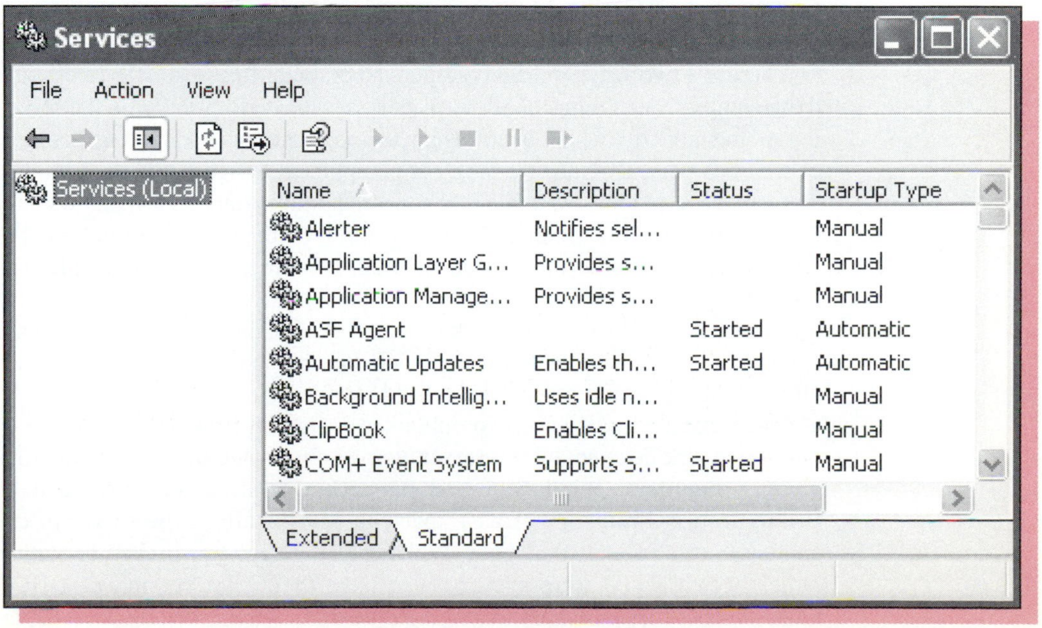

As you can see, the Startup Type column determines when the service is started. Services can be configured to be disabled, manually started, or automatically started when the system boots. If you aren't sure what the service does, you should leave it alone until you've learned more about it. However, some services, such as the FTP service (file transfer protocol) can be disabled here if you know for sure no one should be transferring files to and from your computer using FTP.

Again, you should monitor which services are running and try to learn more about them over time. You can get some clues by looking at the properties of each. Many of the services list what they are dependent upon and what is dependent upon them to run. Using a search engine like Google is also a great way to get started.

Service Packs

Because new flaws are found and enhancements are developed in operating system and application software every day, you should regularly check for updates at the Microsoft site. To check for operating system updates, go to http://windowsupdate.microsoft.com. There is also a link on that page to check for Microsoft application updates.

Keeping current with the updates for both the operating system and the applications you use will help to keep your software running at its best and help to secure your computer.

Miscellaneous

There are many other routine maintenance tasks that you should perform and tricks that you should know. Some have been mentioned in other chapters. For example, in addition to monitoring which processes are running on your computer, Task Manager is a way to close an application that is hanging without having to reboot your computer. Installing and constantly updating your antivirus software, using Performance Monitor to establish a baseline or check for bottlenecks, and installing firewalls are a few other examples.

You can also purchase utilities from companies such as Norton or Symantec to help maintain a system. Norton has a whole suite of software to help you keep your system running at peak performance. Whichever path you take, keeping a system or a network well maintained will help to avoid system downtime and the ensuing panicked attempts to repair something while your phone rings off the hook.

CONFIGURING AND TESTING IP ADDRESSES

Most computers in a LAN are also configured to access the Internet. Every device on the Internet must have a unique IP address. It is up to the network administrator to configure the computers to use the IP addresses and install, configure, and maintain the correct protocols.

There are two ways we can configure a computer to use an IP address: the easy way, assigning them dynamically from a range of allowed addresses located centrally on the server; and the hard way, assigning them statically, which means entering them one-by-one into each computer and then keeping track of who has what IP. Once we have our computers configured, we need to be able to maintain them and there are several tools available to a network administrator in a Windows environment to do so.

The first step in assigning IP addresses to a computer is to install the TCP/IP protocol stack on the client computer. You do that by going to Start > Settings > Network and Dial-up Connections in Windows 2000 Professional. In Windows XP Professional, Start > Control Panel > Network Connections then right click and choose Properties. Click on Local Area Connection > Properties and Install. You have three choices: client, service, or protocol. Which one do you choose? You need to install TCP/IP, which is actually a whole suite of protocols and related services, so choose Protocols.

Once installed, you have two options to assign an IP address: static or dynamic. If your Windows-based network does not have a server, you've eliminated the easiest way to assign IP addresses to your client computers. Windows-based network operating systems have a service, Dynamic Host Configuration Protocol (DHCP), that you can install on the server to dynamically allocate the IP addresses to clients as they boot. Without DHCP, you are limited to statically addressing the clients. Other network operating systems also have their own version of DHCP to dynamically allocate addresses but they call them something different.

Static IP Addresses

To statically assign IP addresses to your computer, click the radio button that says "Use the following IP address" and then key the information in for the IP address, the subnet mask, the default gateway, and the DNS. Because client computers must have unique addresses, you'll need to remember which numbers you've assigned so you don't try to reassign a duplicate number to another computer in the LAN.

Subnet masks and gateways are beyond the scope of this book. In essence, the subnet mask is used to help determine if the network can broadcast data because the sender and recipient are on the same network segment, or if it must route data to another segment. The gateway is the address of the device that will do the routing of the data if needed. The DNS handles the interpretation from name to IP address and vice versa.

Dynamic IP Addresses

DHCP stands for Dynamic Host Configuration Protocol and in addition to the range of available IP addresses you can also configure your DNS and Default Gateway information into the DHCP service. This involves no additional work on the client side because, by default, when you install an operating system on the client computer the operating system is set to obtain an IP address from a DHCP server. So if you opt to use a DHCP server to dynamically allocate addresses, you should not have to do any configuration on the client side. The exception to that, of course, is if the computers were already statically assigned numbers and you need to reconfigure them to obtain DHCP-assigned numbers because you just installed the DHCP service on the server. You install the service from the network operating system CD; you don't have to buy it separately.

The DHCP service allows you to enter a range of IP addresses that you want your clients to use. This range is typically based on the set of IP addresses that has been assigned to your organization. For example, if you have been assigned the range 205.163.1.1 to 205.163.1.255, you would reserve some of the numbers to use statically and you might list 205.163.1.20 to 205.163.1.255 as available numbers in the pool. As computers boot, they grab the next available number. When the computer is turned off, the number goes back into the pool of available addresses for another computer to use.

The DHCP service also allows you to enter the other required information such as the gateway and DNS so that you only have to do it one time on the server rather than on each client computer. As the client computers boot, they pull this information from the DHCP server.

NOTES   **Is your computer configured statically or dynamically? How can you find out? Go to Start > Settings > Network and Dial-up connections in Windows 2000 Professional. In Windows XP Professional, Start > Control Panel > Network Connections then right click and choose Properties. Right click on Local Area Connection > Properties. Double click TCP/IP or click it once to select it and then click Properties.**

If you are configured to dynamically obtain an IP address, the radio button to obtain automatically will be checked. If you are statically configured, the information will all be keyed in.

Built-in Tools to Troubleshoot IP Problems

Static or dynamic, once you have your clients configured with IP addresses you will need to maintain them and that's where some command-line utilities come in. There are times when you will have problems with clients connecting to the local area network or to the Internet and you'll need to troubleshoot the problem. Sometimes, the problem is that the DHCP service is unavailable to assign the correct IP addresses to your clients.

IPCONFIG   If you ever want to know what your IP address is, type IPCONFIG or IPCONFIG/ALL at the Command prompt. IPCONFIG does need to be done at the Command prompt. If you try to use Start > Run > IPCONFIG the IP information flies by too quickly and then closes the Command window before you can see anything. If you enter it at the Command prompt, IPCONFIG will tell you all about your address, the MAC address of your network interface card, and other information.

Remember, in the same way the client computer must have a unique IP address, the network interface card must have a unique MAC (hardware) address. This address is burned in at the factory and each factory is assigned a range of addresses they can use so there are no two MAC addresses the same in the world.

Figure 11.2

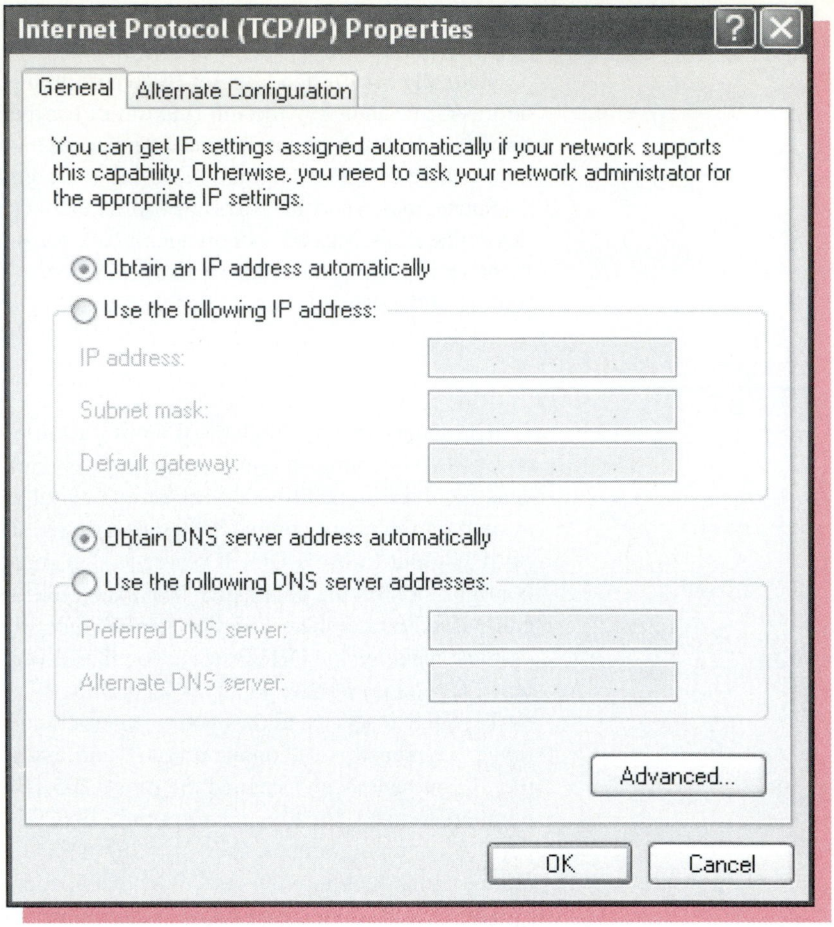

Internet Protocol (TCP/IP) Properties

General | Alternate Configuration

You can get IP settings assigned automatically if your network supports this capability. Otherwise, you need to ask your network administrator for the appropriate IP settings.

○ Obtain an IP address automatically
○ Use the following IP address:

IP address:
Subnet mask:
Default gateway:

◉ Obtain DNS server address automatically
○ Use the following DNS server addresses:

Preferred DNS server:
Alternate DNS server:

Advanced...

OK | Cancel

NOTES **What IP address is your computer using now?**

APIPA In a Windows environment, Microsoft resolves the problem of an unavailable DHCP server with APIPA (Automatic Private IP Addressing. Note the word "private." APIPA is only a temporary solution that allows your clients to continue to communicate on the LAN but does not give them Internet access. That's because the address range that APIPA uses is from 169.254.0.1 through 169.254.255.254 and those are not valid IP addresses for the Internet. They have been reserved by IANA (Internet Assigned Numbers Authority) for APIPA. That only makes sense—APIPA is available to every Windows-based LAN and if more than one LAN is using the numbers to access the Internet, the numbers would not be unique. Every IP address on the Internet must be unique.

If a computer is configured to obtain an IP address from a DHCP server and the DHCP server is unavailable for whatever reason, the operating system assigns an APIPA number to the computer temporarily. If the DHCP server becomes available again, the operating system automatically obtains a valid IP address from it.

Ping If your problem isn't your DHCP service but you still can't access anything, there are a few things you should try. First, determine if it is a problem local to the client. You can do that by "pinging" your LOCALHOST. The IP address 127.0.0.1 is reserved just for the task. At the Command prompt, type PING 127.0.0.1

This is you. The computer you are currently sitting at is your LOCALHOST and is also known as 127.0.0.1. You can use these alternate names to refer to a computer to help troubleshoot any problems it may be having.

When you PING something, it's like sending an echo to that address. The echo travels to the destination and bounces back to you to let you know it found its target and how long it took to get there. If it doesn't find the target, it gives an error message. Sending one PING doesn't cause a problem. The device you PING can generally handle the request and respond to it. However, there are programs that have been written to flood a device by pinging them repeatedly. The device is unable to keep up with the requests and also handle all of its other tasks, such as providing Web content. This is known as a Denial of Service (DoS) attack. Many companies use firewalls to help avoid this. If you PING a site with a firewall, you may get a message that it timed out and it appears as though the site doesn't exist.

When you PING 127.0.0.1, you should get a reply back (see Figure 11.3). If you don't, there is either something wrong with the network interface card or the TCP/IP stack. First remove the stack, reboot, install the stack, reboot, and try again. Still not working?

Figure 11.3

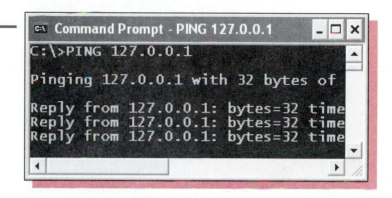

Check the network interface card first by reseating it or using another available slot on the motherboard and then by trying it in another machine. You may need to delete it in Device Manager because when you reboot your computer the operating system will think it has found yet another network interface card. To delete it in Device Manager, right click on My Computer > Properties > Hardware and then choose Device Manager. Expand the listing for your network adapter, right click on the entry for your network interface card and choose Uninstall (see Figure 11.4). Shut the computer down, reseat the card, and then reboot the computer.

Figure 11.4

If you do get the reply back when you PING 127.0.0.1, then the problem isn't your network interface card and you need to check further into your network. The next step is to PING the default gateway. Execute the IPCONFIG/ALL command to learn the IP address of your default gateway and then PING that IP address.

If that works, the problem is probably not inside your network; it is most likely somewhere on the Internet. So try Pinging somewhere in the world. If you don't get a reply, it could be a problem with your gateway or just beyond it or it could be a problem with the DNS.

DNS Problems Sometimes the problem is the DNS, domain name service, which resolves IP address to URL (Uniform Resource Locator) and back again. When we visit someplace on the Internet, we enter an easy-to-remember address such as www.microsoft.com but that particular server also has an IP address assigned to it and it is the same thing as using the URL (name). When you visit a Web site with a browser, you can also enter the IP address to get there.

To find out what the IP address of a Web server is, PING it. If you can PING somewhere in the world, including your own server, by IP address but not by name, the problem is always your DNS. You should always try to remember the IP address of some site so you can use it to test for a potential DNS problem.

TRACERT Another option to track down why your client can't get somewhere in the world is to run TRACERT (Trace Route Utility), which bounces an echo to the destination you enter and shows every router that it must pass through along the way. It isn't uncommon to have a portion of the Internet unavailable because of line problems. If this is the case, depending on how close the problem is to you, you should be able to get to some places but not all. You can also download and install some freeware or shareware applications that do a visual TRACERT using a map. NeoTrace and VisualRoute are two examples.

TRACERT sounds an echo similar to a PING. Because of issues with Denial of Service attacks, the results of a TRACERT may time out as it nears the destination device.

Figure 11.5

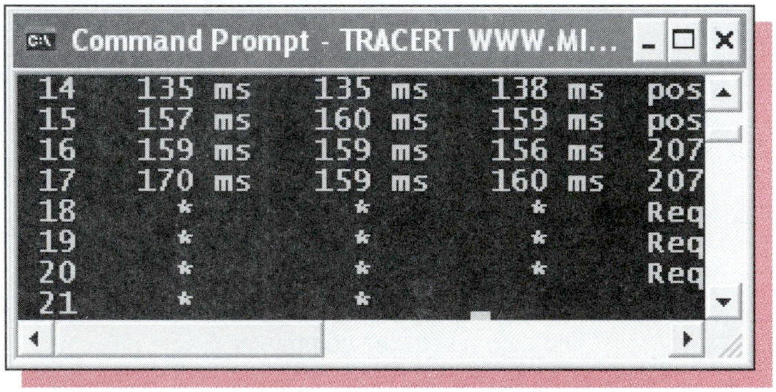

Hostname Another command that gives you information about yourself is Hostname. It simply does what the name implies; it tells you the host name of the computer you're currently sitting at.

NETSTAT NETSTAT lets you know what communication ports on your computer are in use and who is using them. It is common for applications to use ports so you shouldn't be surprised to see them in use. However, there are some applications, such as some Trojans, that also connect to your ports to gain access to your computer so you should be aware that such things exist.

The common ports range from 0–1024 and if you are in a Windows-based environment you will see ports such as 135 and 139 in use. These ports are what allow you to be listed in My Network Places. Any additional applications you use on your computer will start with 1025 and continue. Trojans typically use high numbers, such as 31785. That isn't always the case, however, and Trojans have been found to use the common port numbers as well.

Summary

Maintaining a LAN and keeping things running smoothly takes up a lot of time. It includes things like scheduling backups of your users' data, repairing things when they break, keeping network services running, downloading and installing patches for operating systems and application software, and troubleshooting connection problems.

Sometimes, repairing a problem is a lot like being a detective. In addition to "Is it plugged in?" one of the first questions you should ask is "What happened?" Seems simple enough, but it really is a time saver. If it was working before and it isn't

working now, what event happened in between to cause something to stop working?

Connectivity problems are fairly common and there are some tools you can use to troubleshoot them. These tools, such as PING and TRACERT, are installed on the computer when TCP/IP is installed. If you suspect a connectivity problem associated with TCP/IP, you should first PING yourself at 127.0.0.1, also known as LOCALHOST. If the reply is positive, both your TCP/IP stack and your NIC are fine. You might next PING your default gateway to see if you can get to your router. If that works,

PING somewhere in the world by IP address versus URL. If it works by IP and not by name, there is a problem with your DNS.

You might also use IPCONFIG to check for your current IP address and other settings. If your IP address starts with a 169.254 number, you might have a problem getting an IP number from your DHCP server. APIPA is designed to give you a 169.254 number so you can continue to work locally until the DHCP server is available again.

ACTIVITIES

Review Questions

1. What is the difference between static and dynamic IP addresses?

2. How can you tell if your IP address is static or dynamically obtained?

3. How would you know if your computer was using an APIPA number?

4. What is a Denial of Service attack?

5. What is LOCALHOST? How does it compare to 127.0.0.1?

Hands-on

1. What happens when you type PING 127.0.0.1 at the Command prompt and why might you do this?

2. What happens when you type NETSTAT -AN at the Command prompt? What information are you given?

3. Visit a Web site and then do a NETSTAT -AN again. Do you see the site you visited in the foreign address list? How can you tell for sure?

4. Using the Internet, look up the Tower of Hanoi rotation scheme and the grandfather-father-son backup schedule and compare them in your own words.

5. Reboot your computer and go into Safe mode. List the steps you took and explain any differences you may have found while in safe mode.

Important Terms

Using Windows Help, www.webopedia.com or another online technical dictionary, define:

APIPA	IANA	PING
DoS attack	IPCONFIG	TCP/IP
DHCP	NETSTAT	TRACERT

Multiple Choice Questions

1. A(n) _____ includes some timeframe wherein the network must be fully functional again following the failure.

   a. Emergency Plan

   b. Emergency Recovery Plan

   c. Disaster Plan

   d. Disaster Recovery Plan

2. In a _____ environment, especially where lives are at stake, most companies have redundant systems in place so there is no real downtime.

   a. mission critical

   b. recovery mode

   c. disaster recovery

   d. operation crucial

3. You should try booting into _____ if the system becomes unstable after installing a new device driver.

   a. Disaster recovery mode

   b. Safe mode

   c. POST

   d. Recovery mode

4. When a computer boots, it performs the _____. You may see a message about the version of the BIOS that is loaded and then the computer usually checks its drives.

   a. System setup

   b. Power up test

   c. Power on check

   d. Power on self test

5. Services can be configured to be _____ when the system boots.

   a. disabled

   b. manually started

   c. automatically started

   d. all of the above

6. A computer configured with a _____ IP address always has the same IP address every time it boots.

   a. stationary

   b. static

   c. dynamic

   d. delegated

7. A computer configured with a _____ IP address may have a different IP address every time it boots.

   a. stationary

   b. static

   c. dynamic

   d. delegated

8. The _____ is used to help determine if the network can broadcast data because the sender and recipient are on the same network segment, or if it must route data to another segment.

    a. DNS

    b. DHCP

    c. subnet mask

    d. gateway

9. The _____ is the address of the device that will do the routing of the data if needed.

    a. DNS

    b. DHCP

    c. subnet mask

    d. gateway

10. The _____ handles the interpretation from name to IP address and vice versa.

    a. DNS

    b. DHCP

    c. subnet mask

    d. gateway

11. The _____ service can be installed on a server to allocate IP addresses and other information.

    a. DNS

    b. DHCP

    c. subnet mask

    d. gateway

12. In addition to other information, the _____ command will tell you what your IP and MAC addresses are.

    a. IPCONFIG/ALL

    b. NETSTAT -AN

    c. Hostname

    d. PING

13. The _____ command will return the name of your computer.

    a. IPCONFIG/ALL

    b. NETSTAT -AN

    c. Hostname

    d. PING

14. The _____ command will show you all of the communication ports that are being used on your computer.

    a. IPCONFIG/ALL

    b. NETSTAT -AN

    c. Hostname

    d. PING

15. A(n) _____ number is used on a client computer if the DHCP server is unavailable for some reason.

    a. static

    b. dynamic

    c. APIPA

    d. IANA

Introduction to the Internet

OBJECTIVES

After reading this chapter, you will be able to:

- Differentiate between the Internet and the World Wide Web
- List at least three application protocols from the TCP/IP suite
- Explain the directory structure of a given URL
- Explain what IIS is
- Demonstrate how to install IIS
- Explain what Internet Services Manager is for
- Demonstrate how to create a simple Web page
- Explain the difference between a search engine and a subject guide
- Describe how Web content is indexed
- Explain the role of a Meta tag
- Demonstrate how double quotes can help narrow a search
- Explain what Boolean operators are and list three
- List at least two clues that can be used to determine the validity of a Web site
- Define portal

INTRODUCTION

Most students would consider themselves to be fairly knowledgeable about the Internet because they use it on a regular basis. But what exactly is the Internet? Is the Internet the World Wide Web (WWW)? Are they one and the same? Although people tend to refer to them as if they were the same, the technically correct answer is "no." The World Wide Web can be considered the multimedia portion of the Internet. By some accounts, in September of 1993 WWW traffic accounted for only 1 percent of the traffic on the NSF (National Science Foundation) backbone[1] and by the end of 1994 it accounted for 70% of the traffic.[2]

It seems like a long time ago but in evolutionary terms it hasn't even been the blink of an eye yet. And where are we now with the Internet? According to State of the Internet 2000,[3] there are more than 300 million people worldwide using the Internet on a regular basis.

THE INTERNET

Legend has it the Internet was created in response to the launching of Sputnik in 1957. Sputnik wasn't launched by the USA, of course; it was launched by its enemy at that time, the USSR. The legend says that those in power in the US were frightened that if the enemy could launch a missile into space, surely they could send a rocket across the ocean and bomb the middle of the US. If that happened, would the US be able to communicate? In essence, could the president direct the armed services and government agencies to protect us all?

The answer was "no." As a result, one of America's foremost "think tanks" at the time was charged with the task of figuring out how we could communicate in the event of such a catastrophe. They came up with the concept of the Internet. It was, however, almost called the Intergalactic Network.

Although the Internet has been around since the 1960s, it was considered difficult to use because you could only enter rather cryptic commands at a command line (think DOS) and you had to remember the exact commands in order to do anything. In terms of what you could do, you were pretty much limited to e-mail and FTP-ing files. The Internet was developed primarily to facilitate communication and sharing of information and was intended for the military and eventually the higher education community. It was not developed for the majority of the public to use.

That was actually OK with the majority of the public since they had no real inclination to learn cryptic commands in order to use it. It wasn't until the early 1990s that the World Wide Web (WWW) came about. So the WWW isn't the Internet. Rather, it is the multimedia portion of the Internet. The Internet existed for decades before but didn't become truly popular until it became easier to use.

That's why you get to point and click instead of keying in lengthy commands. While Vint Cerf is considered the father of the Internet, Tim Berners-Lee is considered the father of the World Wide Web because of his vision of how hypertext could include the rest of the public in what he believed the world of communication and information access should be like. Of course, the development of standards, such as TCP/IP, were also extremely important.

Internet Protocols

As you already know, TCP/IP is a suite of protocols that include some core protocols and a lot of related services with it. You're already familiar with some of those protocols and related services and may not have made the connection.

Ever notice that every Web address (URL) seems to start with HTTP? What is HTTP and is that the only thing that can go in front of a URL? HTTP stands for Hypertext Transfer Protocol and it comes from TCP/IP. Actually, although HTTP is the most common protocol used on the Internet it is not the only protocol that can begin a Web address. Telnet and FTP are also valid protocols that could go in a Web address before the colon. In "the olden days," we used to have to key in HTTP as a required part of the address because it wasn't the most common option but now it is considered the default. The precursor to using HTTP was something called Gopher and before the appearance of HTTP://most addresses started with gopher://. Gopher is a directory-driven way to navigate the Internet. Rather than keying in complex commands, you finally had something to click on! Gopher was created at the University of Minnesota and the creators named it after the university mascot. It is a technology that made navigating the Internet a little easier and allowed you to access directories and files on other servers around the world. It is completely text based, but you can download documents and images from other sites. Some Gopher sites, such as the Library of Congress site shown in Figure 12.1, still exist; however, due to security issues, IE no longer supports the Gopher protocol.

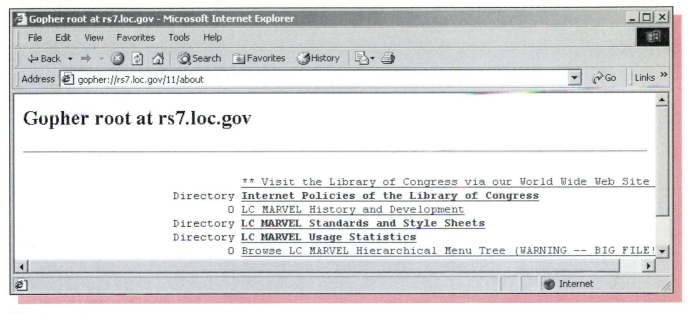

Figure 12.1

Several other technologies came and went in the interim but the development of Web browsers allowing graphics, motion, and sound with hypertext links is what got the rest of the world hooked. HTTP is the protocol that allows us to do that and it is now the standard.

So you only have to enter the first part of a Web address before the colon if it is not HTTP (e.g., gopher:\\rs7.loc.gov or ftp:\\sunsite.unc.edu). HTTP, FTP, and Telnet stem from TCP/IP. Telnet allows you to remotely log into another computer. Because HTTP allows you to view and download content on other computers with the click of a mouse, FTP and Telnet are no longer as common as they once were.

How Do You Get There From Here?

When you enter a URL or IP address, how do you really get to the right place? If you dial a number on a telephone, a technology called circuit switching makes sure that you speak to the party you dialed. With the Internet, it's a technology called packet switching that gets you to the correct destination. How does this have anything to do with Sputnik and communicating after some catastrophic event?

Remember from Chapter 7–Introduction to Networks how routers work? They keep track of all the networks in a table and they send data (packets) along the next best path, depending on what that path might be at any given moment. The Internet is made up of those routers and if one fails, the packets can usually be rerouted through one that is functional. So communication takes place along the next best path. When you enter a URL, the DNS takes care of translating it from the name that you use to numerical IP address the routers understand and all of that is what gets you to the proper destination. But, in addition to the name of the site, what does the rest of an address mean?

What Does a URL Mean?

What information does the URL (Uniform Resource Locator) provide? If you want to learn more about packet switching, you can go to http://www.webopedia.com/TERM/p/packet_switching.html and read Webopedia's definition. Clearly, Webopedia's main address is http://www.webopedia.com and you know that the HTTP in the front of the address means it is using the hypertext transfer protocol. So what does the rest of the address tell you? What is/TERM/p/packet_switching.html?

Directory Structures on a Web Server You create directories or folders on your disks to organize your data. You wouldn't want to put all of your files in one directory because it would be too hard to find things. Web servers are the same way. Assume that the root of the directory structure is www.webopedia.com.

Based on the graphic, what would you suggest the rest of the URL http://www.webopedia.com/TERM/p/packet_switching.html is telling you? There is a folder on the Web server called TERM. To better organize the definitions, the Webmasters at Webopedia then created one folder for each letter of the alphabet and placed the pages for the terms in there.

The actual directory structure of a Web server doesn't have a folder called [root], however. On a Microsoft Web server, there is a folder called InetPub with other folders inside of it including one called wwwroot. Any file placed in the wwwroot folder becomes Web content. The wwwroot folder is equivalent to the [root] folder shown in Figure 12.2.

Figure 12.2

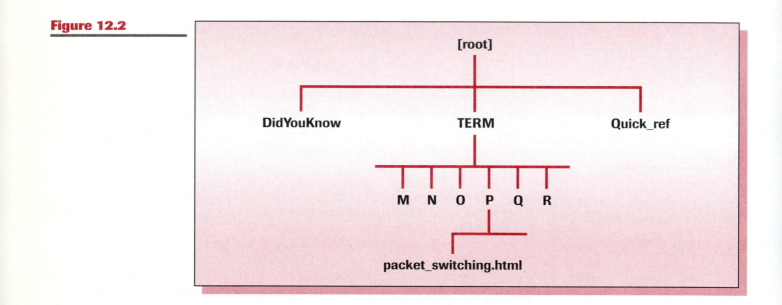

Figure 12.3

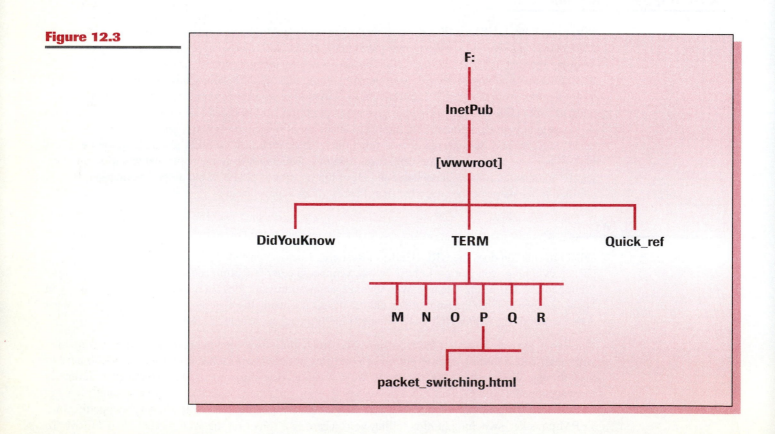

What Makes a Web Server a Web Server?

The initial directory structure on a Web server is created when you install the Web services (e.g., IIS). Just as you can install the DHCP or DNS services on a server, you can also install Web services to make your server a Web server. It doesn't matter if the server is a member server or a domain controller. It is recommended, however, that any server simply providing resources, such as a Web server, be a member server rather than a domain controller for security reasons. Actually, IIS used to be a separate install but is now installed automatically when you install the network operating system. Microsoft Windows 2000 Professional and Windows XP Professional also allow you to install it from the CD as a separate install, however, so you can play with it even if you don't have a server.

You install it from the installation CD by clicking Start > Programs > Control Panel, Add/Remove Programs in Windows 2000 Professional. In Windows XP Professional, use Start > Control Panel > Add/Remove Programs. Choose Add/Remove Windows Components on the left side of the window.

Figure 12.4

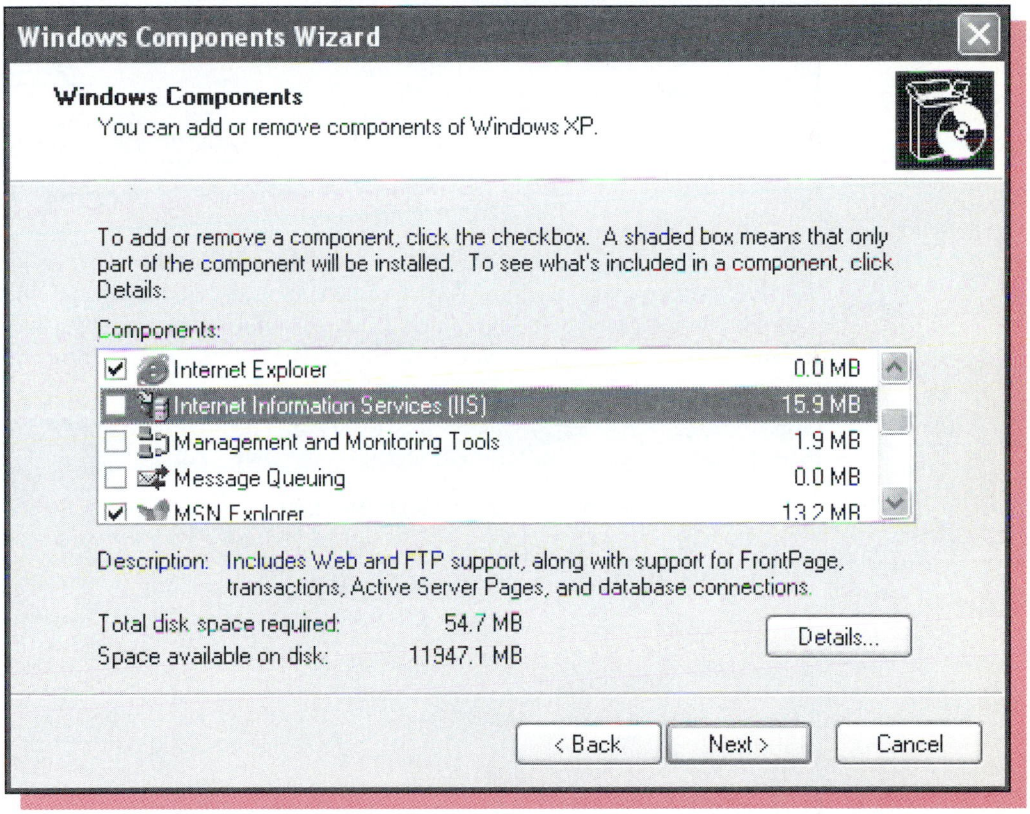

Click one time on Internet Information Services. You don't want to click the check box next to it; you only want to select it so you can click on the Details button. There are several services listed under Internet Information Services and if you check the box you are telling the operating system to install them all. We want to be more selective. So click one time on Internet Information Services and then click Details. Choose the World Wide Web server and the Internet Information Services snap-in will automatically be selected as well.

It will probably ask you for the installation CD and the Wizard should walk you through the rest. When you are done, you should have a new tool listed in Administrative Tools.

When you install the Web services, you get another administrative tool to manage it called Internet Services Manager (ISM). Internet Services Manager allows you to manage not only your WWW service but other services as well, including the FTP (File Transfer Protocol) and SMTP (Simple Mail Transport Protocol) services. The default settings for the Web service typically suffice and you shouldn't have to make any changes to them once the service is installed.

Figure 12.5

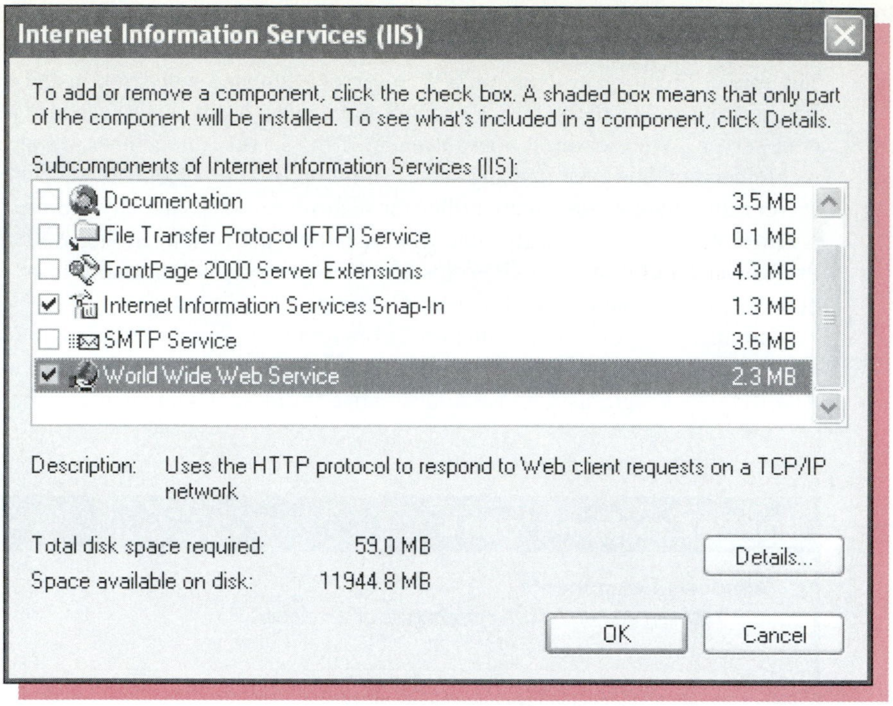

One of those settings is where the directory structure for the Web service will be stored. Of course, you can put it on any partition you choose. You choose the partition when you install the services. Internet Services Manager then knows what partition you chose and it is automatically configured in Internet Services Manager for you.

Figure 12.6

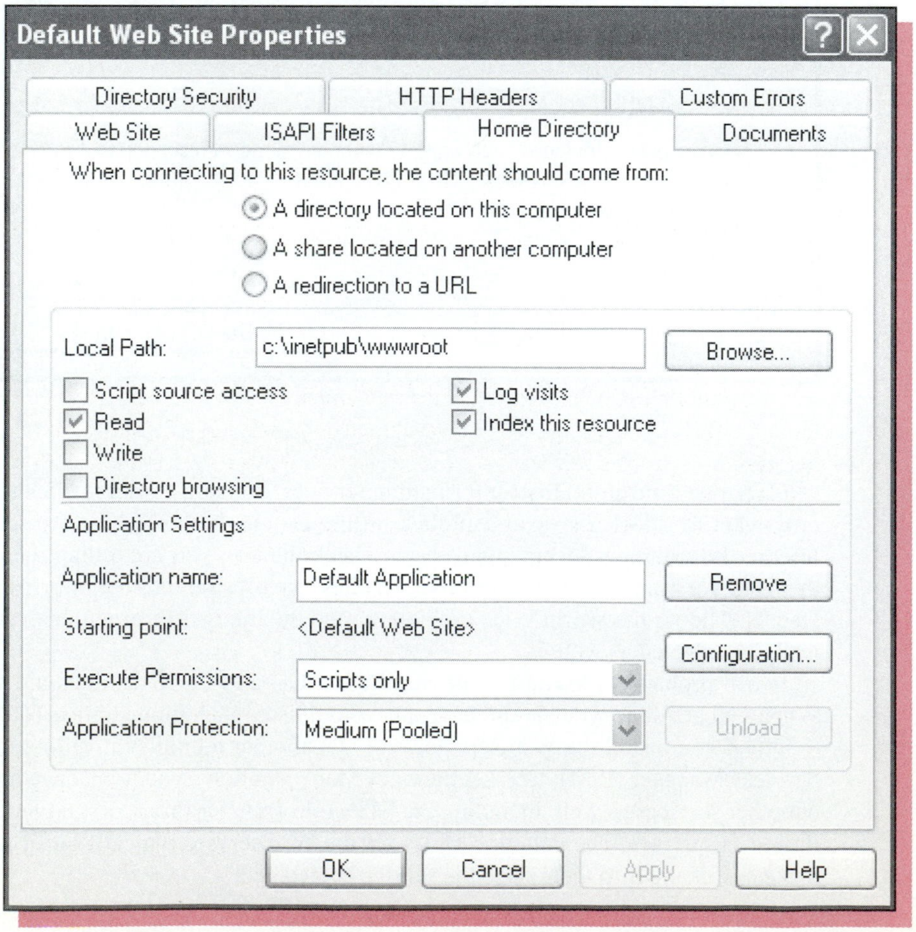

Although you shouldn't need to reconfigure many settings in Internet Services Manager, you should understand what a default Web page is. When you enter an address such as http://www.linux.org, how does the site's Web server know which Web page to display? There could be many pages in each directory. How does the Web server know exactly which one to display for you if you don't specify a name? You know from the previous discussion that this is the root of their Web server directory structure and there must be a Web page to display by default when you visit their site. How does it know which one?

Figure 12.7

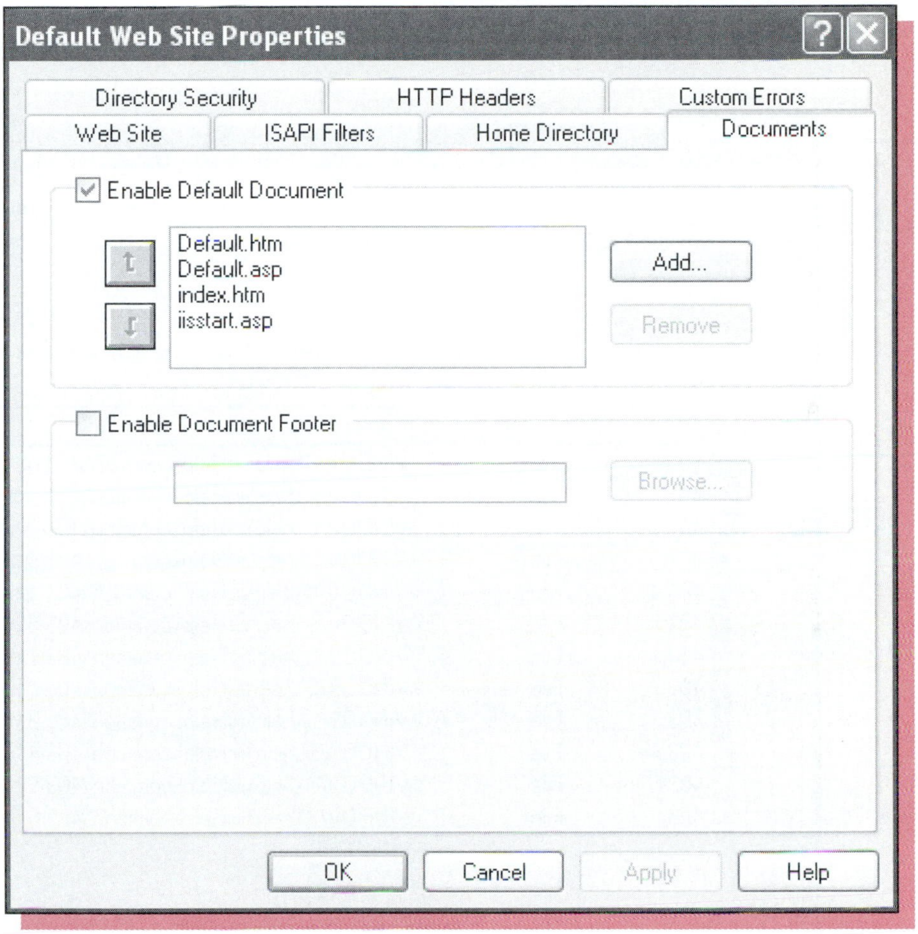

That is one of the things you configure in Internet Services Manager on a server using IIS (Internet Information Services). IIS is Microsoft's Web server software. Chances are very good the Linux organization is not using IIS so they use some other tool to configure their Web services. The Apache Web server is another well-known Web server software. On a Microsoft Web server, the standard file name they use for the Web page to be automatically displayed is default.htm. So if there are any files in the directories with the name DEFAULT.HTM and you enter the path to the directory, the Web services software displays the default page for you.

On a UNIX or Linux server, the standard filename they use for the Web page to automatically be displayed is INDEX.HTML. You can change the standard name to anything you'd like. It doesn't have to be default or index. You do it by clicking Add and then entering the default file name you wish to use on your server. Any time you create new directories, you'll want to make sure they have a file with this name in them so your visitors never get an error message.

NOTES

Using your Web browser, key in the address http://www.linux.org. Next, add default.htm to the address so it looks like http://www.linux.org/default.htm. You should get a message that the page doesn't exist. Finally, try http://www.linux.org/index.html and you should see the same page that you see when you enter http://www.linux.org because the index.html page is the one that is automatically displayed when you go to the Linux Web site.

Whenever you visit a Web site, it must display a Web page for you or give you an error message that a Web page you requested doesn't exist. Since remembering the main address is bad enough, Webmasters don't want to push the limits and require you to remember the name of the file they use for their main page or homepage to display as well. They configure the Web services software to display a specific file by default when you visit their main site.

The errors that you see when you enter an incorrect address are also just Web pages stored on the Web server. They are displayed in response to specific events (e.g., the file you requested doesn't exist). Since those error messages are also just Web pages, they can be edited to display additional information, such as a company logo or a search field to help you more easily find the content you want.

Figure 12.8

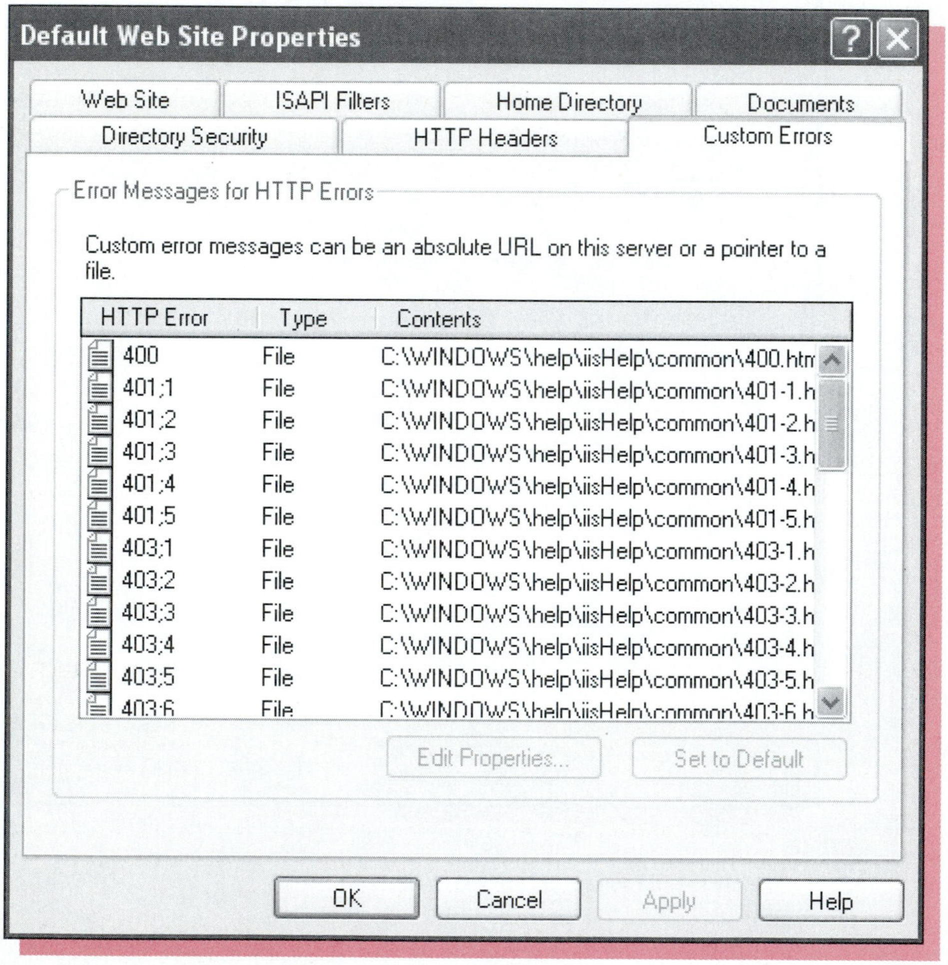

Become a Webmaster

Now that you have a better idea of what a Web server is, what is a Webmaster? That can be someone who manages the Web server and develops the content for it. In some places, the Webmaster just develops the content and the network administrator manages the Web server. Some companies need to develop so much content they have more than one Web server or more than one Webmaster. Some Webmasters even work from home.

Developing Web content can be a great job. Typically, you should have an eye for design but producing quality Web sites requires more than just pretty graphics. Internet users have the entire world to play in and they have very little patience for poorly developed Web sites. Content should be easy to find and quick to load. How often have you clicked off a site after a millisecond has passed because it was "taking too long?" In addition, knowledge of databases and writing the code to access data in the databases is extremely important. When you visit Amazon.com to purchase a book, all of that data is housed in databases. E-commerce relies quite heavily on them.

HTML, hypertext markup language, is the code used to develop simple Web pages. It is easy to learn and this would be the first step to becoming a Webmaster. Of course, there are code generators such as

Microsoft's FrontPage and Macromedia's Dreamweaver to automatically generate the HTML code for you. Knowing how to use tools such as these may get you a job, but understanding the code behind the pages will allow you to keep the job. Surface knowledge of any topic is rarely sufficient in a competitive job market.

Using HTML   To begin, open Notepad. The code to develop a simple Web page is below. You do not have to have a Web server to try this. You can write the code in Notepad and then use a Web browser to open it the same way you would open any document.

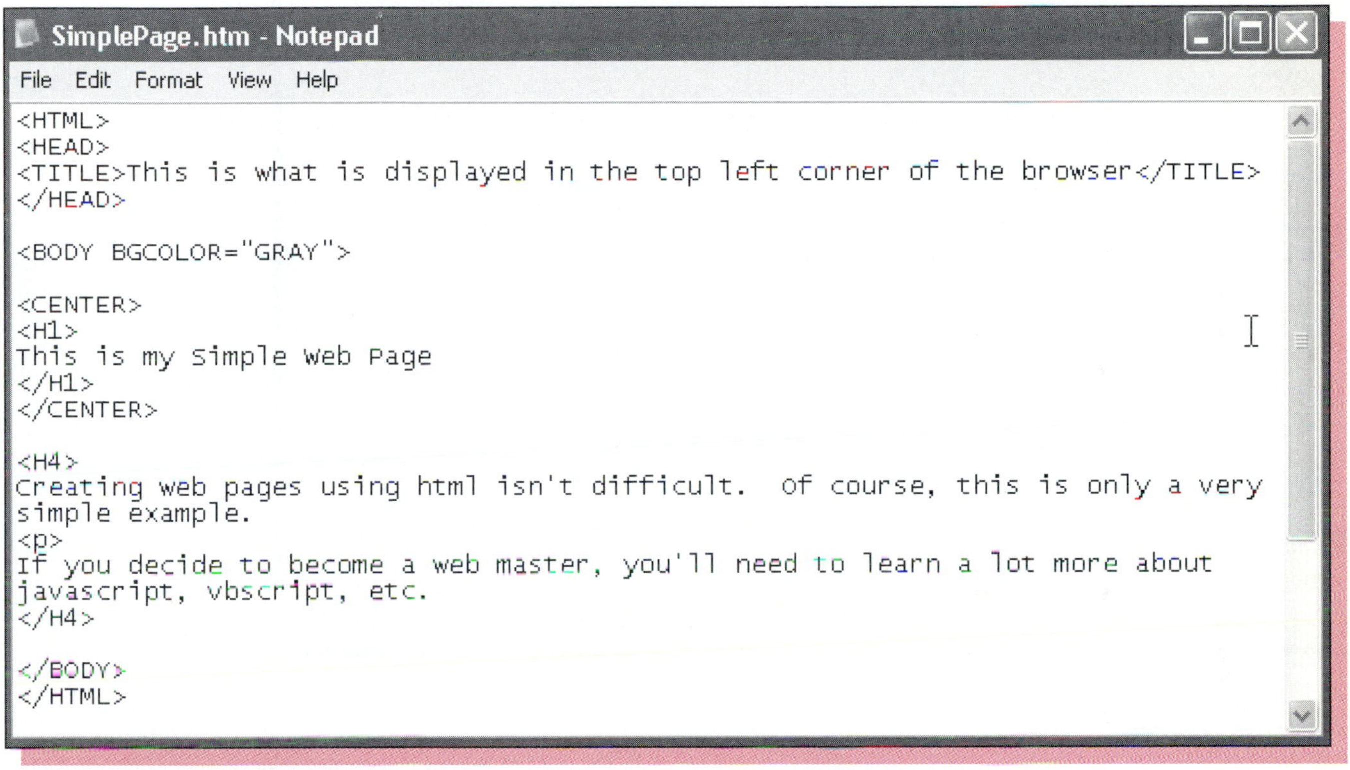

```
SimplePage.htm - Notepad

File   Edit   Format   View   Help

<HTML>
<HEAD>
<TITLE>This is what is displayed in the top left corner of the browser</TITLE>
</HEAD>

<BODY BGCOLOR="GRAY">

<CENTER>
<H1>
This is my Simple web Page
</H1>
</CENTER>

<H4>
Creating web pages using html isn't difficult.  Of course, this is only a very
simple example.
<p>
If you decide to become a web master, you'll need to learn a lot more about
javascript, vbscript, etc.
</H4>

</BODY>
</HTML>
```

Figure 12.9

After entering the code, save the file as SimplePage.htm. You must remember to append the .htm part of the filename because the default extension for Notepad is .txt. The icon for the file should then look like a Web page, not a text file. Open the file in your browser to view it.

Now let's look at the code section by section. The first and last line of the code is simply telling the browser to expect HTML code. Notice that each command, called a tag, is in brackets and has an opening and corresponding closing tag. The closing tag is the same as the opening tag but it also has a forward slash. The tags are not case sensitive but all CAPS were used in the example for readability.

<HTML>

<HEAD>

<TITLE>This is what is displayed in the top left corner of the browser.</TITLE>

</HEAD>

The text enclosed in the TITLE section is what determines what your users will see in the top left corner of the browser. It is also the text that will be bookmarked, so you want it to make sense.

<HTML>

<HEAD>

<TITLE>This is what is displayed in the top left corner of the browser</TITLE>

</HEAD>

<BODY BGCOLOR = "GRAY">

<CENTER>

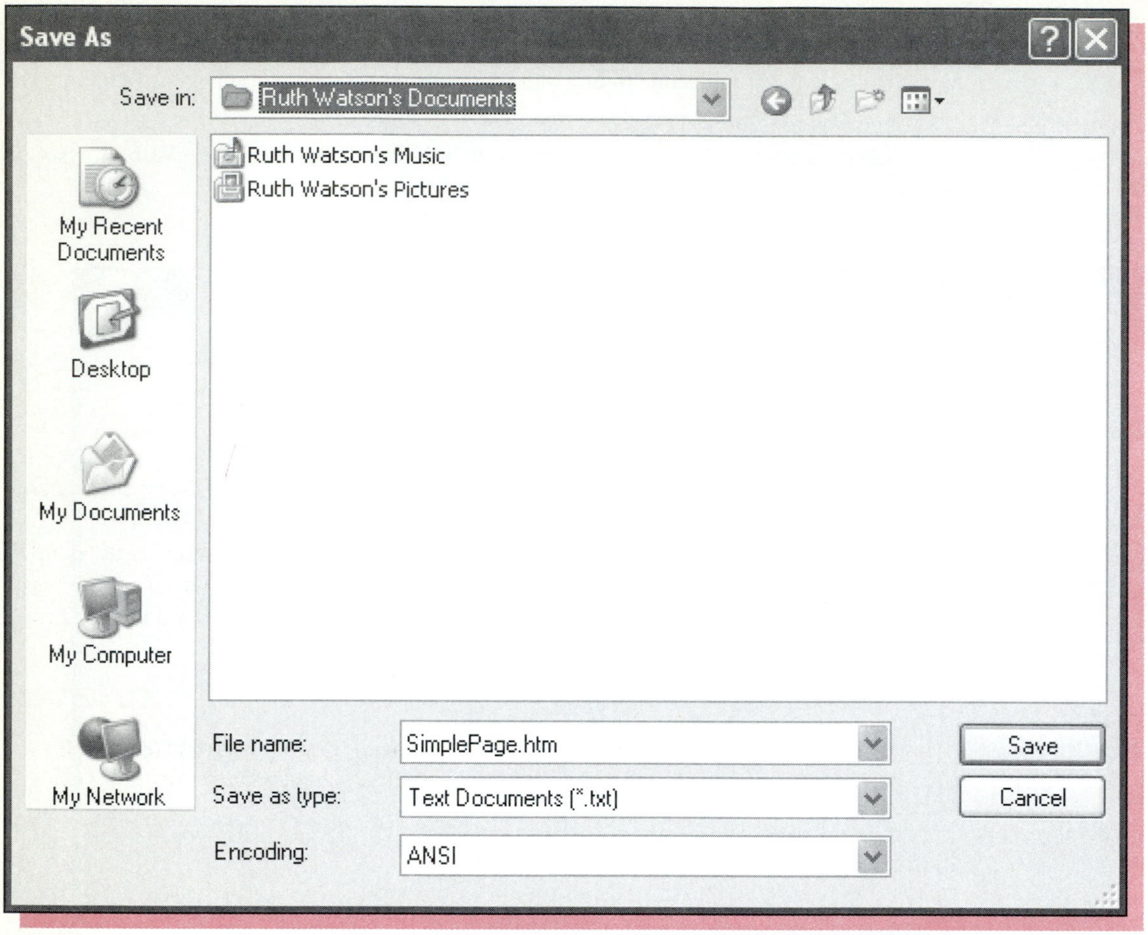

Save As

Save in: Ruth Watson's Documents

Ruth Watson's Music
Ruth Watson's Pictures

My Recent Documents

Desktop

My Documents

My Computer

My Network

File name: SimplePage.htm

Save as type: Text Documents (*.txt)

Encoding: ANSI

Save

Cancel

Figure 12.10

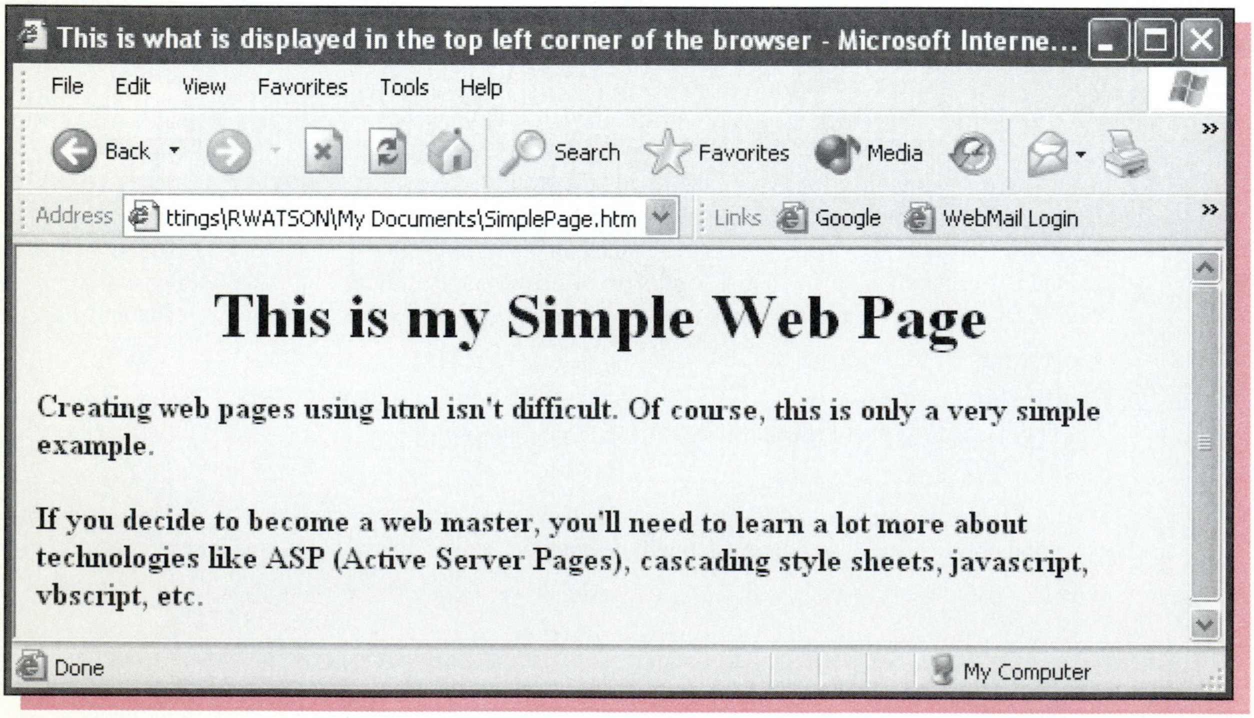

This is what is displayed in the top left corner of the browser - Microsoft Interne...

File   Edit   View   Favorites   Tools   Help

Back   ×   Search   Favorites   Media

Address: ttings\RWATSON\My Documents\SimplePage.htm   Links   Google   WebMail Login

This is my Simple Web Page

Creating web pages using html isn't difficult. Of course, this is only a very simple example.

If you decide to become a web master, you'll need to learn a lot more about technologies like ASP (Active Server Pages), cascading style sheets, javascript, vbscript, etc.

Done   My Computer

Figure 12.11

<H1>

This is my Simple Web Page

</H1>

</CENTER>

<H4>

Creating Web pages using HTML isn't difficult. Of course, this is only a very simple example.

<P>

If you decide to become a Webmaster, you'll need to learn a lot more about technologies like ASP (active server pages), cascading style sheets, javascript, vbscript, etc.

</H4>

</BODY>

</HTML>

The main portion of the document is what falls between the BODY tags. This is where your content is keyed in. The body command in the example includes a reference to the color of the background. You can use the name of the color or the hexadecimal equivalent of the color. The hexadecimal equivalent of gray is #808080. You can convert colors to the hexadecimal format using tools on the Internet. These tools convert from the RGB (red/green/blue) color codes that most applications understand to the hexadecimal format that Web browsers understand.

NOTES

Open Microsoft Word or some other word processor and enter some text. Highlight the text to select it and then change the color of it. In addition to the color palette, you should have an option for more colors or custom colors. You can see the RGB equivalent of any color here.

Figure 12.12

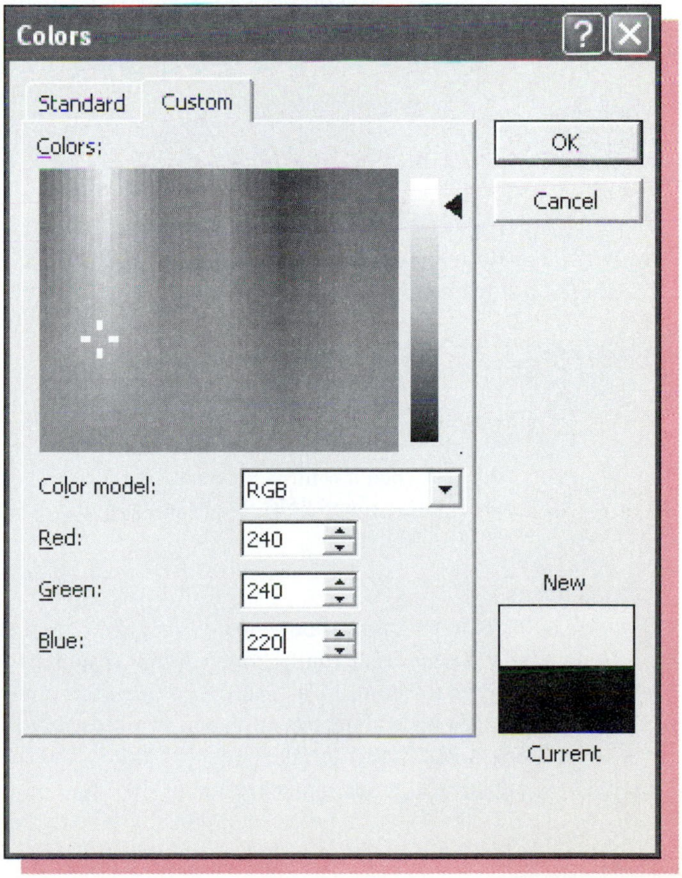

The code to use the hexadecimal equivalent of a color is <BODY BGCOLOR = "#808080">. You can also use a graphic for the background and the code is <BODY BACKGROUND="FILENAME.GIF">. You can use gif or jpg files on the Internet. It also comprehends a few others but they aren't as commonly used. If you use a code generator to make a Web page, you can use any type of graphic file but it ultimately converts the graphic to either a gif or jpg.

You can also have additional tags to format that content of your Web page. The H1 and H4 tags refer to the size of the text. The P tag is a paragraph break and the CENTER tag centers the text. The default alignment is left-aligned. Getting content to display in exact positions on a Web page is the tricky part but if you decide to be a Webmaster, you'll be learning more about that in future courses.

If you wanted this page to be displayed on a Web server, you would save it to a directory in the wwwroot directory structure on the Web server. If you installed the IIS services on your computer, you can view each other's pages by using the IP address. Chances are your computer doesn't have a registered domain name but the IP address is still a valid address. Remember that any folder you place the file in and the name of the file become part of the path.

Now that you know a little about the history of the Internet and how Web servers and Web pages work, let's talk about how you can use the Internet more effectively.

FINDING RESOURCES EFFECTIVELY

You no doubt have a favorite search engine that seems to find what you want most of the time. Do you really know how to use all of its features, though? Why is it that one search engine seems better than another?

There are many tools that you can use to search for things of interest on the Internet and knowing how to use them effectively will save a lot of time. Before the explosion of the World Wide Web, when you were assigned to write a paper for a class you physically went to the library and found anything they had that even came close to your topic. You were limited to whatever the library had on the shelves and you certainly didn't want to go out of your way so you made do with whatever you could find and crossed your fingers.

Now when you do research you have the entire world at your fingertips. So access to resources that really pertain to your topic is no longer a problem. Filtering through the millions of search results you get is the problem. Who has time to read that many documents and how do you know which are valid sources? There are a few tricks that might help to make finding useful resources a little easier.

Search Engines

We've all used them but can we use them more effectively? Say you're looking for information on the history of the Internet. What would you ask for? Should you even bother using the words *of* and *the*? Some search engines automatically discard common words. What if you want to force the use of a word?

> **NOTES**   Go to your favorite search engine. How many results do you get for the phrase *history of the Internet*? Using Google, I get 3,200,00 results. Do you think all of them are about the history of the Internet? Does your search engine use all of the words you entered or does it discard the common ones? It will tell you when it returns the results if it discarded any of the terms. How many results do you get if you put quotes around *"history of the Internet"*? Google gets 38,900. Does your search engine use all of the words this time?

First, let's talk about what exactly the search engine was searching and then discuss why the quotes help. There are actually two different resources you can use, search engines and directories. We tend to refer to them all as search engines but compare Google (http://www.google.com/) with Yahoo (http://www.yahoo.com/). Yahoo is a directory that is organized by category and is considered a subject guide. Typically, the sites that Yahoo and other subject guides keep indexed were submitted by a human who wrote a description of the site.

Search engines index their sites by sending "agents" out on the Internet to devour whole Web sites. These little agents, also known as Bots or Spiders, crawl through the Internet at offpeak times and index the contents of Web servers.

If you launch a new Web site today, when will you be indexed? The answer depends on the search engine or subject guide. Sometimes you can manually list yourself with such a resource. If you go to Yahoo's site, for instance, you'll notice a link at the bottom that explains how you can include your site. Some search engines or subject guides allow you to do that, others don't. Some rely strictly on their agents to find new sites but the frequency with which they index sites varies. While Inktomi's Slurp agent might search nightly, for example, some other agent may only search once a week or even less frequently.

You can tell that your Web server has been visited because most Web server software tracks visitors and logs information about them. Do not assume you are anonymous when you visit Web sites. Usually, information such as your IP address, the browser you're using, what pages you visited, how long you looked at them, and sometimes even what site you were on before in terms of what page linked you to the site. Webmasters can read the text file that is created each day on the server or take that raw data and use applications to produce reports showing how many people in each country and/or state visited their Web server and a lot of other stats that will help a company decide which pages are popular and which are not.

How often a search engine sends its agents forth into the world of the Internet to index Web content also has a lot to do with how good your search results are when you use the search engine. But what exactly are those Bots and Spiders indexing? The answer varies but here are some examples.

META Tags What is a META tag and why would you want one? You know what tags are; they are the commands you use to write a Web page. Have you ever viewed the code of a Web page you were looking at? It's a great way to learn how to write HTML code.

NOTES Your browser should have a menu option to view the source. In Internet Explorer, you click on View > Source. Notepad launches and you can see the code of the Web page. At the top of the page in the <HEAD></HEAD> section, you should see some META tags. An example would be <meta name="keywords" content="LAN, network operating systems, network, administrator, permissions">.

This META tag is listing several keywords that would be indexed in some search engines. As you can see, this site has to do with networks. If you enter any of these key words in a search, this sample site might be listed as a result. Other META tags give information about the tool used to create the page and the character set used.

Search Tips Other bots or spiders might be indexing all of the text that is on the Web page. Google is an example. You can test that theory by visiting a Web site, copying a paragraph from it, and pasting it into Google's search field. You will have better luck if you enter quotes around it.

Why is that? The double quote notation indicates to the search engine that it should look for the exact phrase. When you searched for history of the Internet without using the quotes, the search engine was looking for every instance of the words history and Internet no matter where they appeared on the page. Chances are it discarded the words *of* and *the* because they were too common. When you put the quotes around the phrase, it then searched for the exact phrase. This resulted in a much more useful listing of Web sites.

Keep in mind that it is terribly easy to find resources and then copy and paste them into your assignments. Remember that is called plagiarism if you do not cite your sources. The reverse is also true. Teachers can copy your words and paste them into a search engine to see if you borrowed someone else's work. There are also sites dedicated to finding plagiarism that teachers can use.

Another way to force the search engine to use words even if they are common is to put a plus sign (+) in front of the word (e.g., +history +of +the +Internet). Doing so will force to search engine to look for all of those words but, again, it does not pay attention to what order they are in when it finds them. If you want to look for an exact phrase, you must use the double quotes.

What if you don't want the search engine to find something. Can you filter it out? What if you want HISTORY and INTERNET but not ISOC? Can you do that? Just as you can use the + symbol to force a search engine to include a word, you can usually use the − symbol to force a search engine to exclude a word (e.g., +history +Internet −ISOC).

What if you only want the results in English? Many search engines now allow you to choose the language for your results so you can filter out any sites that are written in a foreign language that you may not understand. Another feature in regard to foreign languages is the ability to translate from one language to another. Some search engines will translate a Web page on the fly from one language to another when you click on the link. Other search engines have text fields to allow you to enter a phrase and it will convert from one language to another. As many students have learned, this can come in handy when you're doing your homework in a foreign language class. Keep in mind, however, that it isn't always 100 percent accurate.

Does your search engine support "stemming" (e.g., a search on "singing" would also return "sing")? In some cases this might be a handy feature; in others it may result in returning too many pages that don't apply to your topic.

Some content simply cannot be found by using a search engine. That is because the content is actually stored in a database. While many Web pages are static, meaning the content was written and saved as a Web page, others are dynamically created from databases. Think of Amazon.com as an example. Information about all of their books and everything else they have available for sale is stored in the database. They do not write one Web page for each thing they want to sell. Rather, it is stored in the database and when you request information about a particular book from their Web site a Web page is created on-the-fly from the database.

Often, these pages end with an .asp extension rather than an .htm extension. ASP stands for "active server pages." The code of the Web page pulls the data dynamically from the database so the skeleton of the page remains the same but the content will be different depending on what data you requested at the time. If you end up being a Webmaster, you will really need to learn ASP code.

Boolean Operators Every computer geek should know about Boolean operators. They are used not only in search engines but also in programming. George Boole was a famous mathematician who can help make your searches more effective. Boolean operators are used to help narrow the search and include words like AND, NOT, and OR. Various search engines also support NEAR which means the words must appear in close physical proximity in searched text.

A number of search engines allow you to key in the Boolean operators in your key word search. Others have a link for an advanced search form and have drop-down lists allowing you to choose the Boolean operators to better customize your search.

Validity of Results

Another key factor in using online resources is determining the validity of the results. Often, the site hosting the content can be a good clue. If the site is controlled by a reputable organization you can be fairly certain the content is valid. For example, *Scientific American* is considered to have a good reputation. If you find an article on their site, you can be reasonably certain that you can use it as a resource safely. Other sites you might assume have valid content are government or military agencies and educational institutions. The URL of these sites would end with gov, mil, or edu. K-12 school sites would end with their state information and .us (e.g., k12.xx.us, where xx is the state abbreviation).

You should evaluate the Web sites that you use for resources by asking a few questions. Is the content updated often? Do they clearly list the author's information? Is it easy to find the content? Are there a lot of misspellings? Be wary of sites that have a lot of broken links. Often, this indicates the site is not maintained.

Portals

A portal is a Web site that is considered an entry point to some resource. From the portal, you should be able to find everything you need in one place. Some search engines are also portals. Yahoo, Infoseek, and some news sites such as FOXNews.com are examples. In addition to the news, for instance, a news site may also have links for stock quotes, weather, schedule guides, and subscriptions to get up-to-the-minute news flashes via e-mail.

Colleges and universities often have portals for their students that include easy access to their e-mail, registration and course information, financial aid, and anything else a college student might need.

All fifty American states also have a portal. You can visit any one of them by using a common URL, www.state.xx.us, where xx is the two letter abbreviation for the state. While some of these portals are better designed than others, most include links to all of the government agencies for the state and additional information including travel and tourist information.

Libraries

Many states also have online libraries for universities and colleges and most public libraries are online also. There should be no excuse for most library patrons to return books overdue because they can now renew them online.

In addition to renewing them online, you can also search for them by author, title, ISBN number, or keywords. In some states, many of the university and college libraries are connected together and you can request books from any of the participating libraries in the state and it will be delivered to your campus for pickup.

Online Magazines and Journals

Many magazines and journals are also online and are a great resource for writing research papers. While some include only the abstracts, many are full text and are often in PDF format. PDF stands for "portable document format" and it was designed by Adobe to make it easier and faster to publish documents on the Web while retaining all of their formatting. PDF files are generally small in size even when a lot of graphics are used and are supported on most operating systems. You can download the Adobe PDF Reader free from their site but you have to pay for their software if you want to make your own PDF files. If you can think of any magazine or journal in print, you should do search for it on the Internet. The chances are very good they have an online version.

> **NOTES** Think of a magazine that you enjoy or that might be useful to you for an upcoming assignment. For an example, say you have to write a paper on some scientific topic. What magazines or journals can you think of? *Scientific American* comes to mind. Try finding it using your favorite search engine. What other magazine or journal can you think of? There's *Popular Science*, *Discover Magazine*, and so on. If you can think of it, there's probably a Web site for it.

Miscellaneous Resources

There are a million other resources on the Internet but I think you're getting the idea so I'll just list a few others briefly. Any popular TV news station, sites that list famous quotations, maps, dictionaries, encyclopedias, newspapers, and writing guides to help write that research paper are all online. Now all you have to do is get busy.

References

1. Cailliau, R. (1995). A Little History of the World Wide Web from 1945 to 1995.
Online: *[HTTP://www.w3.org/History.html]*.
2. Schulzrinne, H. (2002). Long-Term Traffic Statistics.
Online: *[HTTP://www.cs.columbia.edu/~hgs/internet/traffic.html]*.
3. Retrevied on United States Internet Council & ITTA, Inc. (2000). State of the Internet 2000.
Online: *[HTTP://www.usic.org/papers/stateoftheinternet2000/intro.html]*.

Summary

The Internet and the World Wide Web are not the same thing. While the Internet has been around since the early 1960s, the World Wide Web has only been around since about the early 1990s. The World Wide Web might be considered the multimedia portion of the Internet. It allows the transfer of HTML, graphics, sound, video, and other media. Prior to that, the Internet was strictly text-based and you needed to know some special commands if you wanted to navigate around.

Now, of course, everyone knows about the Internet and Web addresses are common in advertisements. HTTP and other protocols used stem from TCP/IP. Most URLs (uniform resource locator) begin with HTTP which stands for "hypertext transfer protocol." The actual URL, or Web address, is dependent upon the directory structure of the Web server. If you have a tendency to create a lot of folders, your addresses might end up being very long. Since most people can't remember really long addresses, you might want to seriously consider keeping your directory structure simple.

A Web server becomes a Web server when you install Web service software on it. Microsoft has IIS, Internet Information Services, and it is installed by default when you install the server operating system. Another well-known Web service software is Apache. It is a freeware Web service software and there are versions for UNIX and Windows-based operating systems.

Using the Internet is common in education. Using it effectively, however, takes a bit of work and a lot of knowledge. There are a lot of tools available to help you find what you want but knowing the characteristics of each will help you determine which tools are best for the job. Some tools are subject guides whereas others are search engines. Another important factor is how often they index Internet content.

You can drastically narrow a search by enclosing a phrase in quotes. Knowing what content is valid is important and this can partly be determined by a site's address. You can now access resources online from places that typically offered information only in person in the past. Libraries, newspapers, magazines and journals now often have at least some of their content online.

ACTIVITIES

Review Questions

1. What is the difference between the Internet and the World Wide Web?

2. What is IIS?

3. What is a META tag and where do they come from?

4. What is a Boolean operator? List three examples. What is "stemming"?

5. Explain the difference between a search engine and a subject guide and cite at least two examples of the differences.

Hands-on

1. Using the Internet as a resource, explain what Vint Cerf's contribution to the growth of the Internet was.

2. Using the Internet as a resource, explain what Tim Berners-Lee's contribution to the growth of the World Wide Web was.

3. The RGB color code for red is 255 0 0, for green it's 0 255 0, and for blue it is 0 0 255. Using an online converter, what is the hexadecimal equivalent for each?

4. Using the Internet as a resource, explain what ARPANET is.

5. Using the Internet as a resource, explain who Marc Andreesen is.

Important Terms

Using www.webopedia.com or another online technical dictionary, define:

Apache Web Server	Gopher	packet switching
browser	HTML	portal
CERN	HTTP	robot
circuit switching	Internet	search engine
FTP	Meta tag	site map
	Mosaic	spider

Telnet	Web Server	Yahoo
URL	World Wide Web	

Multiple Choice Questions

1. The _____ has been around since the 1960s.
   a. ARPANET
   b. World Wide Web
   c. Internet
   d. both a and c

2. The _____ has only been around since the early 1990s.
   a. ARPANET
   b. World Wide Web
   c. Internet
   d. a and c
   e. a, b, and c

3. The father of (the) _____ is considered to be Vint Cerf.
   a. CISCO
   b. World Wide Web
   c. Internet
   d. both a and d

4. The father of the _____ is considered to be Tim Berners-Lee.
   a. CISCO
   b. World Wide Web
   c. Internet
   d. both a and d

5. _____ allows you to remotely log into other computers.
   a. WAIS
   b. Gopher

c. Telnet

d. FTP

6. _____ allows you to transfer files to and from other computers.

a. WAIS

b. Gopher

c. Telnet

d. FTP

7. _____ is a directory-driven way to navigate the Internet.

a. WAIS

b. Gopher

c. Telnet

d. FTP

8. A telephone uses a technology called _____ to make sure that you speak to the party you dialed.

a. packet switching

b. circuit switching

c. protocol switching

d. none of the above

9. The Internet uses a technology called _____ to make sure your data gets to the intended destination.

a. packet switching

b. circuit switching

c. protocol switching

d. none of the above

The next three questions are based on the graphic in Figure 12.13.

If you had a Web server whose address is www.prenhall.com and the directory structure, which is installed on the F: partition, in www-root looks like the graphic in Figure 12.13:

10. What is the correct URL to the page called h2.htm?

a. F:\\inetpub\wwwroot\homework\h2

b. F:\inetpub\wwwroot\homework\h2.htm

c. http://www.prenhall.com/wwwroot/homework

d. http://www.prenhall.com/homework/h2.htm

11. What is the correct URL to the page called study.htm?

a. F:\\inetpub\wwwroot\study.htm

b. F:\inetpub\wwwroot\studyguides\study.htm

c. http://www.prenhall.com/studyguides/study.htm

d. http://www.prenhall.com/wwwroot/study.htm

12. What if a link in the code for the study.htm file referenced this: ..\graphic.gif. Which folder houses the graphic?

a. wwwroot

b. Homework

c. studyguides

d. assignments

13. Typically, you make a Microsoft server into a Web server by installing (the) _____ Services.

a. DHCP

b. DNS

c. Internet Information

d. Active Directory

Figure 12.13

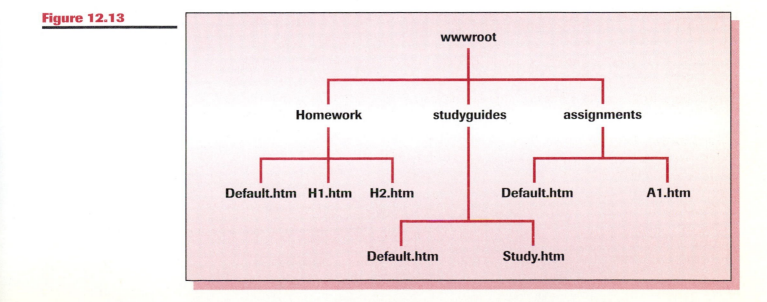

14. For security reasons, it is recommended that a Web server be a _____.
    a. member server
    b. domain controller
    c. DHCP server
    d. DNS server

15. _____ is the code used to develop simple Web pages.
    a. HTTP
    b. SMTP
    c. HTML
    d. HGML

16. One of the biggest problems with research now is _____ all of the results to find the most relevant.
    a. using
    b. filtering through
    c. saving to disk
    d. plagiarizing

17. Yahoo is a directory that is organized by category and is considered a _____.
    a. subject guide
    b. theme guide
    c. subject channel
    d. theme channel

18. Yahoo stands for _____.
    a. Your Absolute Handiest Online Object
    b. Your Absolute Handiest Overbearing Objective
    c. Yet Another Hierarchical Officious Object
    d. Yet Another Hierarchical Officious Oracle

19. Search engines _____ other sites by sending agents out on the Internet to devour whole Web sites.
    a. index
    b. guide
    c. direct
    d. steer

20. You can force a search engine to find an exact phrase by using _____.
    a. a plus sign
    b. a minus sign
    c. Boolean operators
    d. double quotes

21. You can force a search engine to include words by using _____.
    a. a plus sign
    b. a minus sign
    c. Boolean operators
    d. double quotes

22. _____ are used to help narrow the search and include words like AND, NOT, and OR.
    a. A plus sign
    b. A minus sign
    c. Boolean operators
    d. double quotes

23. A(n) _____ is a Web site that is considered an entry point to some resource.
    a. portal
    b. gateway
    c. entry
    d. home page

24. PDF stands for _____ and it was designed by Adobe to make it easier and faster to publish documents on the Web while retaining all of their formatting.
    a. public domain format
    b. portable domain format
    c. portable document file
    d. portable document format

Appendix

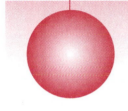

I f you are working on a home improvement project, such as building new stairs, you would not only need to purchase the supplies to build the stairs. You might also need some special tools, such as a carpenter's square, to help you accurately calculate the angles of the stringer. You could try to complete the project using just any tools that you happen to have lying around but that often results in poor craftsmanship and can sometimes even make a job harder. For instance, if I can't find a screwdriver, sometimes a butter knife works in a pinch. It's not built to be a screwdriver, however, and it just doesn't give the same torque, resulting in more work on my part and a lesser quality end product. To do a job correctly, you need the proper tool for the job. In a lot of ways, buying a new computer is like buying a new tool. If you were planning to purchase a new computer, what kinds of decisions would you need to make to ensure that you buy the right tool for you?

CHOOSING THE RIGHT OPERATING SYSTEM

First, what do you plan to use the computer for? A lot of us need to do office-type work on the computer, producing documents, spreadsheets, and databases. Others are interested in computers for gaming, creating and editing graphics or video, or for running educational applications for school children. If you want to make sure that your new computer meets your needs and will be worth what you pay for it, ask yourself first what you plan to do with it. This will, of course, help you determine what your hardware needs are as well. Anyone interested in editing video will need to purchase a computer with a acres of storage space, for instance. Also, some additional time investigating current technology for the video card should be done.

But what about the operating system? What determines which operating system you should purchase? Although the vast majority of desktop computers are running some version of a Microsoft operating system, there are other choices available. What are some other options for operating systems? Or, if you do decide to purchase a computer with a Microsoft operating system on it, which one should it be?

Macintosh

History There is a great story on the Internet called the History of the Microcomputer Revolution. It's actually the transcript from a radio broadcast and can usually be found here: http://exo.com/~wts/mits0013.HTM. It is a must read for anyone wanting to know the history of both Windows-based and Apple computers and it has the scoop on where two of the better known operating systems got their start. If nothing else, you can amaze and astound your friends and family with the inside story. My favorite part is segment 13 where it explains where both Bill Gates and the Apple people took a walk in the PARC (Palo Alto Research Parc) and borrowed a lot of really cool ideas from Xerox about what a computer should look like. But in another segment it interested me to learn that Bill Gates owes a big "Thanks" to a group of moms selling cookies.

Segment 9 discusses when the first Apple computer was born, and the Apple II that most educators are familiar with came soon after. Apple was selling computers before Bill Gates had an operating system, so they have been around since the 1970s. In addition to being the first real microcomputer option, most educational software was written for the Apple computers in the beginning and that explains why many in education purchased them.

Ease of Use   Although not on a regular basis, I do use a Macintosh computer. Whenever I develop new Web content, for instance, it is a good idea to check it out on different platforms (operating systems) using different browsers or different versions of browsers. It is usually a slow, cumbersome event for me. The mouse only has one button, for instance, and that doesn't feel right to me. For some reason, it seems harder to find and launch applications and find the utilities to maintain the Mac.

That's not the Mac's fault, of course; it's mine. I am more accustomed to working on a PC-based machine running some version of Windows. A Macintosh user would say that it is much easier to use a Mac. I can attest to the fact that it is easier to network them. Plug them in and they see the other devices on the network without much additional configuring. The newest version of the Macintosh operating system is called Mac OS X and it is said to be very user friendly.

One feature that I find appealing on a Mac is the ability to configure how much memory you want a specific application to use. And, whenever you want to eject a disk you simply drag its icon to the trash can and it pops the disk out for you. But why is there a small proportion of people in the world convinced that a Mac is the way to go? If choosing an operating system is like choosing the correct tool, what tool or tools does a Mac have to offer?

In the past, most educational software was written for a Mac but that isn't the case anymore. There are just as many titles available for PC-based computers. So for educational purposes, deciding which operating system you purchase shouldn't be based on this factor. However, if you wish to network the computers to share printers or have Internet access and do not have adequate tech support, you may find that an Apple network is the way to go, especially if a teacher who "speaks Mac" volunteers to set it up and keep it running.

The Mac has always been known for its graphics and video capturing abilities and that is probably the main reason people choose it now. Most graphic artists I know prefer to use a Mac and at most copy stores you will typically find Mac enthusiasts there as well.

The third reason people might choose a Mac may be ease of use, particularly with networking, and the fourth main reason might be habit—they have simply always used a Mac. As a network administrator, I don't care for Macs because they nearly always work. Simply plug them in and they rarely have any problems. I prefer job security where people have problems with computers all day.

A Mac is designed to capture video easily. In fact, you can plug a VCR directly to it and port portions of a video tape to it for editing. There is some easy-to-use, free application software, called iMovie, which comes bundled with a Mac and allows you to create and edit video. When you visit the Web site for the newest version of the operating system, it's easy to see that they emphasize the fun part of using the Mac. That's not to say that you cannot run office applications on a Mac. In fact, you can run the Mac version of Microsoft Office and share files with a PC user without worrying about compatibility.

Security   All operating systems have issues with security. As a result, all operating systems have Web sites that allow you to download security patches. One such Mac site is http://www.securemac.com/.

I haven't had any security problems with the Macs that I work with, however. Over the years, they have been infested with viruses but even that didn't bother me. They tend to be "cute" viruses with names like the Xmas tree virus. Typically, they are designed to amuse and not destroy. As with any operating system, keeping current with antivirus software should deter any serious infestations.

Stability   Why might a Macintosh be more stable than a Windows-based or Linux-based machine? You don't buy the operating system and the hardware separately. When you buy a Mac, it comes with the operating system installed. That means that the operating system programmers have complete knowledge of and/or control over what hardware components their operating system has to work with. Needless to say, that allows them to write a much more stable operating system.

Of course, you can purchase upgrade versions of the operating system as newer versions come out but you are still installing it on hardware with which the operating system programmers were fully familiar. You can install a Mac-emulated operating system on a PC-based machine but every such installation I have ever seen appears to inherit the instability of most other operating systems that are also installed on a PC-based machine.

A couple of years ago, some K-12 teachers I know told me they were going to attend a workshop on how to repair Macs and they would be in the same building I was planning to be in that day working on a LAN project. I was intrigued and said I would pop in and out if they didn't mind. During the course of the day, I did stop by to listen and watch periodically and I saw them do things like repair the extensions so the operating system would know what applications to relate things back to.

At the end of the day they asked if I had any questions. I did have one: "How could they have a workshop on repairing Macs and never once take the case off?" They all turned and looked at me like I was an idiot and finally one of them sighed and attempted to patiently explain to me that Macs rarely have hardware issues. No doubt that is another reason why some people prefer a Mac. A lot of us, however, enjoy taking things apart just because we can and will probably stick with our PC-based machines. In fact, there are some days when locking yourself in a room and just working with the hardware is rather like therapy.

Cost Although it hasn't always been true, the cost of a Macintosh computer with the operating system installed is currently comparable to purchasing a PC-based desktop computer with a Windows operating system installed. Purchasing an upgrade of the operating system tends to be less expensive on a Mac than purchasing an upgrade for a Windows operating system. As with any purchase, it is best to shop around for the best price.

Server vs. Client In addition to the client operating system, you can also have a Macintosh server. Like a Windows 2000 Server, the Mac has its own services to run a Web server and is fairly easy to configure and maintain. In fact, I believe that is what most Mac users would say is the best feature of a Mac—it is easy to use. When you visit a Web site hosted on a Mac, Windows, Linux/UNIX or Novell operating system you cannot tell the difference. They are platform independent. Just as a Mac client can visit a Windows-based Web server, a Windows client can visit a Mac or Linux/UNIX Web site.

Unix/Linux

History UNIX had its start on mainframe computers and has been around for several decades. Linux is a freeware version of an operating system that is similar to UNIX. Linux was first developed by Linus Torvalds while he was a college student. Since then, many people all over the Internet have made contributions to the code. Both UNIX and Linux have a history of being the preferred operating system for heavy-duty programmers.

One reason for this is the customizability of the shell, or user interface. Unlike a Windows operating system where you have little choice over the user interface, UNIX and Linux have several different options for use and you choose the one that has the tools to make your job easier. Since programmers are accustomed to working with code, the interface they often choose to use doesn't have a lot of flash to it. Rather, they work at a command line entering the cryptic codes they love.

Ease of Use I have been playing with Linux off and on for about a decade. In the beginning, it was strictly command line driven but has come a long way to being more user friendly in an attempt to gain a wider audience. In addition to the command line shells, you can also choose GUI shells to run on Linux that look very much like Windows.

There is also an office suite, called Star Office, which you can run on Linux. It looks very much like Microsoft Office and the files you create in one are compatible with the other. Star Office costs around $50 − $75 for the suite.

So why would you use Linux? Well, it's free—that's always a good reason. But it also isn't Microsoft. Some people looking for alternate operating systems do so because of anti-Microsoft sentiment. With the new user interfaces available, such as Gnome or KDE, Linux can be just as easy to use as Microsoft Windows. Perhaps the main group of users opting for UNIX or Linux is programmers, and some flavors of Linux are also designed specifically for serious gamers. Many CAD developers swear by UNIX.

Security As mentioned, all operating systems have issues with security. Patches are available and these patches should be applied on a regular basis. However, Linux has the additional issue of its code being "open source". Think of it: if you are hacker it's going to be easier to crack the code if you can sit and read the code versus another operating system that doesn't allow such ready access to code.

Stability Because UNIX has been around for so long, the code is time-tested and it is considered to be a very stable operating system. Linux, on the other hand, has given me some problems over the years.

Although most Linux users would say that Linux is a more stable operating system than Windows, the problems that I have had have always stemmed from the hardware components inside the machine.

When you install Linux, you'll notice that it is more interested in the hardware components than a typical installation of Microsoft Windows. Each installation of Linux is slightly different because Linux actually compiles the operating system based on your specific hardware components. This can make it a more stable operating system if it is compatible with the hardware. On occasion, however, I have had problems with some video cards depending on the model of the computer.

That is not to say that Microsoft never has similar issues with hardware compatibility but most of the big-name computer manufacturers assume that you'll be installing a Microsoft operating system and they usually make sure that the hardware components are on Microsoft's hardware compatibility list.

Whenever I have had my students install Linux and Windows operating systems in my classes, they usually get more excited during the Linux installs. Perhaps it is just because it's different but the little things usually elicit exclamations of surprise and impromptu comparisons. For instance, the Linux install doesn't just tell you to insert another CD, it opens the CD-ROM drive's door for you. The graphics tend to be more colorful on a Linux installation as well and most students prefer the Red Hat Linux map over the Microsoft map when choosing a time zone.

Cost Linux has several different distribution versions of it. Red Hat, Caldera, Mandrake, and Debian are some examples. They come from the same original code but have additional features added to each of the different flavors of Linux that makes one more suited for gaming whereas another might be a better choice for an office environment. Linux is free. You can buy books for them that have a CD of the operating system included but you are technically purchasing the book and getting the operating system for free.

UNIX is not free and must be purchased. It is not typically purchased by your regular home user but can be found in businesses that require a stable operating system.

Server vs. Client In addition to the client operating system, you can also install a Linux or UNIX server. Like a Windows 2000 Server, the server version has its own services to run a Web server. Perhaps the most common Web service application for Linux/UNIX is Apache.

Novell Netware

History The first local area network operating system I was exposed to was Novell NetWare Version 2.2 in the very early 1990s, when my campus first started migrating from a VAX minicomputer that used dumb terminals. A dumb terminal is the monitor and keyboard but no CPU, and the monitor was monochrome. With a dumb terminal, all of the processing is performed on the main computer. You had a black background with either yellow or green text and worked completely at a command prompt. Back then, our VAX was about four and a half feet tall and about 12 feet long and required its own wall-sized air conditioner to keep it cool. Our VAX had its own operating system called VMS and also had programming languages such as COBOL, Pascal and FORTRAN in addition to text editors to create documents. You can still purchase a VAX running VMS for a server but the server is now the size of a regular server and new editions of the operating system are available.

At that point in time, local area networks were replacing mainframe and minicomputers everywhere. Novell had been developing its network operating system for a few years and was one of the most popular local area network operating systems on market. It wasn't until Microsoft developed its own network operating system, Windows NT, in the early 1990s that Novell had competition. Since that time, Microsoft has taken over the lead in installed units.

Ease of Use Novell NetWare seemed easy to use to me in the early 1990s because it was command line based just like DOS. It has come a long way since then and is currently up to Version 6 which does have a GUI interface for easier use.

It does not, however, look anything like Microsoft Windows and that seems to be the biggest hurdle for my students. You're always more comfortable with things that look familiar and over the years my students have become more accustomed to using Windows. Although the concepts in Novell NetWare are similar – you create accounts and groups and apply permissions – finding the utilities to accomplish these tasks seems to take a little longer for my students. This is due to the fact that they have had more exposure to one operating system over another and does not imply that one is better than another.

Security Novell NetWare has the honor of being hacked just as often as most other operating systems with the exception of the Macintosh operating system which doesn't appear to warrant as much effort from the hacking community. As with any operating system, you must keep current with all security patches.

Stability Novell NetWare is considered a stable operating system and as you might guess Novell argues that they are the best option whereas Microsoft would beg to differ. If you are truly in the market for a network operating system and you've narrowed it down to these two, you'll want to check out Web sites that offer a comparison. Be sure to check out sites in addition to Microsoft or Novell. The comparisons you find will be based on administrative needs and the services that each operating system provides. While Netware appears to take the lead in some areas, Microsoft is said to be better in others. Your choice between the two will be based on what you need the operating system to excel at but it does appear that Microsoft is currently chosen more often than Netware.

Cost It's difficult to compare pricing between Novell NetWare and Microsoft operating systems because they use different pricing schemes. With Novell NetWare, you purchase a specific number of licenses bundled with the operating system. For instance, you can buy the operating system with the license for five users, ten users, 25, 50, 100, 250, etc.

With the Microsoft server operating system, you pay for the network operating system separately from the client access licenses (CALs). This makes it more difficult to do comparison of apples to apples, especially because there are different prices available for education versus business and even for K-12 versus higher ed. In addition, you may receive discounts depending on the number of CALs purchased at one time. Each company will argue that they have the lowest total cost of ownership (TCO) when you factor in several other variables as described on their Web sites.

Server versus Client Novell NetWare does not have a client version of its operating system. Instead, you would use some other client operating system, such as Microsoft, and install some additional files on the client workstation that will allow you to attach to your Novell NetWare LAN. The current versions of Novell NetWare also have services that enable it to be a Web server.

The Windows Family

History Microsoft has a whole family of operating systems and has been around since the early 1980s beginning with DOS. There are now two sides of the family, one that is based on DOS and the other which is based on NT. Microsoft Windows 95, 98, and ME are based on the DOS side of the family. Microsoft Windows NT, 2000, and XP are based on the newer side, and development began in the early 1990s.

Ease of Use Without a doubt, Microsoft has a huge share of the operating system market. This means that most people learned to use a computer with a Windows operating system on it. As with anything, the first thing you learn seems to be the easiest. While beginning users may find the Windows interface confusing, continued exposure increases their comfort level. Today, most Windows users would say it is an easy operating system to use. Most Macintosh users would argue that point and newer interfaces for Linux are very comparable to the Windows interface, making the transition much easier.

Many businesses prefer the Microsoft operating systems for word processing and other office-type functions. Having more than one operating system allows Microsoft to customize them for different reasons and they may build in different features for gaming or graphics for the home users than they would for the office users.

Security Microsoft operating systems are probably targeted the most for hacking. There are two main reasons for this, in my opinion: one is the anti-Microsoft sentiment and the other is simply because it is used most often. In addition to the operating system being targeted for hacking, the Microsoft application software is also a target. You must regularly upgrade the security patches for both, you should use a current antivirus application, and you should seriously consider a firewall. Those cautions are true for all operating systems.

Stability Because Microsoft kept one side of the operating system family backward compatible with DOS, it is less stable than the NT side of the family. Microsoft has moved away from the DOS side, however, and future versions of Windows operating systems will come from NT technology. The NT side of the Microsoft family is considered a stable operating system by most.

In contrast to a Macintosh computer, we try to integrate a Windows operating system with any components we can find. In fact, if you are somewhere with a group of computer geeks, you probably all have enough individual computer parts lying around to build a whole computer. Someone has an old video card because they just upgraded, someone has a hard drive or two, and everyone has some older memory sticks lying around. Microsoft has drivers for the most common hardware components included with their operating systems to make it easier but you can add drivers for those not included in the list.

In contrast to a Linux installation, which compiles the operating system specifically to the components inside each box, Microsoft tries instead to just skim across the top of any component to make the Windows 2000 operating system more consistent in each installation.

Cost The pricing structure for the Microsoft operating systems is varied and can often be confusing. This is not as true for the typical home user who purchases the operating system bundled with a new computer. But it can be confusing for network administrators in various environments to keep up with the many options for pricing that are available.

In a typical network environment you are expected to purchase the network operating system, the client operating system, and also client access licenses (CALs) to access your network for each machine that will use the network. The pricing for each is generally different if you are in business versus education.

Server vs. Client Previously, the DOS side of the family was marketed to home users and the NT side was marketed the business. Now, however, the NT side of the family has a version for home users, a professional version for business users, and server versions as well that include built-in services for a Web server.

References

"Raw Bytes Computer News." History of the Microcomputer Revolution. Spokane Public Radio, National Public Radio Network. KPBX, Spokane. 7 May, 1997. Online: [*http://exo.com/~wts/mits0013.HTM*].

Summary

I should point out that your choice of an operating system isn't absolute. You can have all of these operating systems running in one LAN. It would be a complicated LAN to be sure but it is technically possible. Your decision for which operating systems are needed should be based on what you plan to use the computer for. The computer is not a magical thing. Rather, it is another tool to facilitate your work—or play!

The operating systems mentioned here are not the only choices you have. There are many others that you can purchase or download freely. Some are also "open source", allowing you to see and edit the code, and are available primarily for educational purposes. Minix is one such example. Why would you ever want to do that? Because you can.

Index